Allied Internment Camps in Occupied Germany

Between 1945 and 1950, approximately 130,000 Germans were interned in the Soviet zone of occupied Germany, including in former Nazi concentration camps. One-third of detainees died, prompting comparisons with Nazi terror. But what about the western zones, where the Americans, British, and French also detained hundreds of thousands of Germans without trial? This first in-depth study compares internment by all four occupying powers, asking who was interned, how they were treated, and when and why they were arrested and released. It confirms the incomparably appalling conditions and death rates in the Soviet camps but identifies similarities in other respects. Andrew H. Beattie argues that internment everywhere was an inherently extrajudicial measure with punitive and preventative dimensions that aimed to eradicate Nazism and create a new Germany. By recognizing its true nature and extent, he suggests that denazification was more severe and coercive but also more differentiated and complex than previously thought.

ANDREW H. BEATTIE is Senior Lecturer in German and European Studies at the University of New South Wales, Sydney. An authority on the politics of history and memory in Germany, he is the author of *Playing Politics with History: The Bundestag Inquiries into East Germany* (2008).

Allied Internment Camps in Occupied Germany

Extrajudicial Detention in the Name of Denazification, 1945–1950

Andrew H. Beattie

University of New South Wales

CAMBRIDGE
UNIVERSITY PRESS

CAMBRIDGE
UNIVERSITY PRESS

University Printing House, Cambridge CB2 8BS, United Kingdom

One Liberty Plaza, 20th Floor, New York, NY 10006, USA

477 Williamstown Road, Port Melbourne, VIC 3207, Australia

314–321, 3rd Floor, Plot 3, Splendor Forum, Jasola District Centre,
New Delhi – 110025, India

79 Anson Road, #06–04/06, Singapore 079906

Cambridge University Press is part of the University of Cambridge.

It furthers the University's mission by disseminating knowledge in the pursuit of
education, learning, and research at the highest international levels of excellence.

www.cambridge.org
Information on this title: www.cambridge.org/9781108487634
DOI: 10.1017/9781108767538

© Andrew H. Beattie 2020

First published 2020

Printed in the United Kingdom by TJ International Ltd. Padstow Cornwall

A catalogue record for this publication is available from the British Library.

ISBN 978-1-108-48763-4 Hardback

To Melanie

Contents

Illustrations

Acknowledgements

It is a pleasure to acknowledge the many people who have contributed in diverse ways to this book, which has been a long time coming but also came about quite quickly, as I only decided to write it in 2016.

The book emerged from an evolving (and continuing) project on the reception first of Soviet internment and then of internment across occupied Germany, which has been funded variously by internal research grants and sabbaticals from the University of Technology, Sydney, and the University of New South Wales, Sydney, by a Discovery Project from the Australian Research Council (DP110100300), and by four fellowships: a Max Weber postdoctoral fellowship at the European University Institute in Florence, a Leibniz summer fellowship from the Centre for Contemporary History in Potsdam, a junior fellowship with the History and Memory research group at the University of Constance funded by Aleida Assmann's Max Planck Research Award, and a Humboldt Research Fellowship for experienced researchers from the Alexander von Humboldt Foundation hosted by Habbo Knoch at the University of Cologne. I would like to thank all of those organizations, institutions, and individuals, as well as Robert Buch, Gerard Goggin, Martin Sabrow, Stefan-Ludwig Hoffmann, Birgit Schwelling, and Nina Fischer, for their roles in facilitating those grants and fellowships and thus supporting my research, as well as the late Axel Schildt, Christoph Strupp, and Dorothee Wierling for a brief stay at the Research Centre for Contemporary History in Hamburg.

In early 2016, I was still committed to writing only a comparative history of internment's reception, not its 'actual' history. But as I struggled with word count and continued to encounter scholarship and journal peer reviewers wedded to (in my view) inaccurate understandings of Soviet and/or western internment, I realized there were things I wanted to say about internment and that I could and must write separate books. I would like to thank Robert Buch and Ronan McDonald for a crucial conversation in that realization process and to humbly acknowledge an ARC assessor's rectitude in suggesting several years earlier that internment's history was insufficiently settled to write the history of its reception.

I have benefitted greatly from the supportive research environment within Arts & Social Sciences at UNSW Sydney, especially within the School of Humanities and Languages and in particular the History and Area Studies group and the Imperial, Colonial, and Transnational Histories research cluster. In particular, I would like to thank Lisa Ford, Martyn Lyons, Mina Roces, and especially Louise Edwards for advice, encouragement, and assistance particularly with the book proposal.

Beyond UNSW, I gratefully acknowledge the assistance of the staff of the more than forty archives and memorials whose collections I have consulted for the larger project, only twenty of which are cited in this book. My understanding of internment and its context has profited from many discussions, including at conferences and seminars whose participants are too numerous to acknowledge individually. I particularly thank Andreas Ehresmann, Andrea Genest, Enrico Heitzer, Julia Landau, Günter Morsch, Wolfram von Scheliha, and Bernd Weisbrod for their interest and encouragement; Richard Bessel and Norman Naimark for insisting I include the French zone; two anonymous peer reviewers, especially for suggesting I include comparisons with Austria; Michael Watson and Liz Friend-Smith at Cambridge University Press for their immediate interest in the topic and Atifa Jiwa and Lisa Carter for their professionalism during production; my parents James and Margaret for careful editing and everything else besides that has helped get me to this point; and Alexander, Claudia, and Melanie for accompanying me on shorter and longer trips, putting up with my frequent physical and mental absences, and not taking me too seriously, and Melanie again for the initial inspired suggestion, a long time ago, to look into this topic. For that and much more besides, this book is dedicated to her.

Abbreviations

ACA	Allied Control Authority
ACA (BE)	Allied Commission for Austria (British Element)
ACC	Allied Control Council
ACICR	Archives du Comité international de la Croix-Rouge, Geneva
AEKR	Archiv der Evangelischen Kirche im Rheinland, Düsseldorf
AEM	Archiv des Erzbistums München und Freising Munich
BAB	Bundesarchiv Berlin
BDM	Bund Deutscher Mädel
BHStA	Bayerisches Hauptstaatsarchiv, Munich
CCS	Combined Chiefs of Staff
CDU	Christian Democratic Union
CIC	Counter Intelligence Corps
CIE	Civilian Internment Enclosure
DIAC	Directorate of Internal Affairs and Communications
DP	displaced person
DzD	*Dokumente zur Deutschlandpolitik*
EAC	European Advisory Committee
EKD	Evangelical Church in Germany
ELAB	Evangelisches Landeskirchliches Archiv in Berlin
EZA	Evangelisches Zentralarchiv, Berlin
FO	Foreign Office
FORD	Foreign Office Research Department
FRG	Federal Republic of Germany
FRUS	*Foreign Relations of the United States*
GDR	German Democratic Republic
Gestapo	Secret State Police
GPU	State Political Directorate
GULAG	Main Administration of Corrective Labour Camps and Labour Settlements

GUPVI	Main Administration for POW and Internee Affairs
HHStA	Hessisches Hauptstaatsarchiv, Wiesbaden
HStAS	Hauptstaatsarchiv Stuttgart
ICRC	International Committee of the Red Cross
IMT	International Military Tribunal
JCS	Joint Chiefs of Staff
KPD	Communist Party of Germany
LAELKB	Landeskirchliches Archiv der Evangelisch-Lutherischen Kirche in Bayern, Nuremberg
LDPD	Liberal Democratic Party of Germany
LKAB	Landeskirchliches Archiv Bielefeld
LKAD	Landeskirchenarchiv Dresden
LKAE	Landeskirchenarchiv Eisenach
LKAK	Landeskirchliches Archiv Kiel
LKAS	Landeskirchliches Archiv Stuttgart
MVD	Ministry for Internal Affairs
NADSC	Nazi Arrest and Denazification Subcommittee
NCO	non-commissioned officer
NDPD	National Democratic Party of Germany
NKVD	People's Commissariat for Internal Affairs
NL	Nachlass
NLAH	Niedersächsisches Landesarchiv Hanover
NSDAP	National Socialist German Workers' Party
OMGUS	Office of Military Government, United States
POW	prisoner of war
PSC	Public Safety Committee
RSHA	Reichssicherheitshauptamt
SA	Sturmabteilung
SD	Sicherheitsdienst
SED	Socialist Unity Party of Germany
SHAEF	Supreme Headquarters, Allied Expeditionary Forces
SMAD	Soviet Military Administration in Germany
SMERSH	Special Methods of Spy Detection
SMT	Soviet Military Tribunal
SPD	Social Democratic Party of Germany
SS	Schutzstaffel
StAH	Staatsarchiv Hamburg
StAL	Staatsarchiv Ludwigsburg
TNA	The National Archives of the United Kingdom, London
ZAEKHN	Zentralarchiv der Evangelischen Kirche in Hessen und Nassau, Darmstadt

Introduction

If asked when 7,080 prisoners were detained without trial in a camp at Neuengamme or 2,841 at Dachau or 9,783 at Buchenwald, most people would probably answer some time in the 1930s or early 1940s. These are, after all, the names of some of the most notorious Nazi concentration camps. But these figures in fact come from May 1946, January 1948, and January 1950, months and years after the defeat and collapse of Nazi Germany. At these points in time, the camps were operating under the aegis of the United Kingdom, the United States, and the USSR, respectively.[1] The detainees were thus not prisoners of Nazi Germany but were among the large number of Germans (and some foreigners) arrested by the victorious Allied powers that occupied Germany at the end of the Second World War. In total, more than 400,000 Germans were interned without trial: as many as 170,000 by the Americans; approximately 130,000 by the Soviets; at least 91,000 by the British; and around 21,500 by the French.[2]

A tiny minority of internees were suspected of war crimes, but most were detained because the occupiers deemed them 'dangerous' enough to be taken into what the western powers called 'automatic arrest'. The

---

[1] Heiner Wember, *Umerziehung im Lager: Internierung und Bestrafung von Nationalsozialisten in der britischen Besatzungszone Deutschlands* (Essen: Klartext 1991), 370; Gabriele Hammermann, 'Das Internierungslager Dachau 1945–1948', *Dachauer Hefte* 19 (2003), 58; Bodo Ritscher, *Spezlager Nr. 2 Buchenwald: Zur Geschichte des Lagers Buchenwald 1945 bis 1950* (Weimar: Gedenkstätte Buchenwald, 1995), 234.

[2] Kathrin Meyer, *Entnazifizierung von Frauen: Die Internierungslager der US-Zone Deutschlands 1945–1952* (Berlin: Metropol, 2004), 98; Klaus-Dieter Müller, 'Verbrechensahndung und Besatzungspolitik: Zur Rolle und Bedeutung der Todesurteile durch Sowjetische Militärtribunale', in Andreas Weigelt, Klaus-Dieter Müller, Thomas Schaarschmidt, and Mike Schmeitzner (eds.), *Todesurteile sowjetischer Militärtribunale gegen Deutsche (1944–1947): Eine historisch-biographische Studie* (Göttingen: Vandenhoeck & Ruprecht, 2015), 36; Wember, *Umerziehung im Lager*, 7; Rainer Möhler, 'Internierung im Rahmen der Entnazifizierungspolitik in der französischen Besatzungszone', in Renate Knigge-Tesche, Peter Reif-Spirek, and Bodo Ritscher (eds.), *Internierungspraxis in Ost- und Westdeutschland nach 1945* (Erfurt: Gedenkstätte Buchenwald, 1993), 64. For discussion of the numbers, see Chapter 3.

primary targets were members and officials of Nazi organizations, who were interned precisely on the grounds of their membership, rank, or position therein. Senior Nazi leaders were among the internees, but so were many public servants, teachers, farmers, and tradespeople who had held various positions in Nazi Germany, as well as some people rather arbitrarily detained by Allied forces. Internees were held in scores of camps, many of which were established on the sites of former German prisoner-of-war (POW) or concentration camps or former military barracks or prisons, while others were located at more improvised sites. Not surprisingly given the general chaos across the country at the end of the war, detention conditions were tough everywhere in 1945, but over time they became adequate, even generous, in the occupation zones run by the three western powers. In contrast, they remained totally inadequate in the Soviet 'Special Camps', leading to the death of approximately one-third of the inmates. The last internment camps in each zone closed in 1949–50.

How should one make sense of this transnational chapter of German history, which is neither completely unknown nor well understood? Internment raises a host of questions about 'regime change', occupation, and transitional justice in the wake of the 'Third Reich'. Was internment a logical step towards the Allied goal of eradicating Nazism? Or was it an irreconcilable contradiction to use mass extrajudicial detention to that end? Were the occupying powers more concerned with exacting punishment and revenge than with promoting justice and democracy? If numerous Nazi concentration camps were 'liberated' only to be reused after a change of personnel, were the Allied camps also 'concentration camps'? Were the Allies perhaps not so different from the Nazis after all? Does internment indicate that the occupation was more coercive, and that denazification was more rigorous than is commonly believed? Why did all four occupying powers make use of internment but to such varying extents? Why did it take a more lethal path in the Soviet zone than in the western zones? What does internment ultimately reveal about Germany's postwar transition? And what does it say about the history of camps more broadly? This book – the first detailed, systematic, comparative study of the subject – aims to answer such questions and thus to contribute to a number of recent and long-standing scholarly and public debates.

The History of Camps

In recent years, there has been much discussion of the camp as the 'nomos of the modern' and of the twentieth century as the 'century of camps'.[3] While Nazi concentration camps and the Soviet GULAG (Main Administration of Corrective Labour Camps and Labour Settlements) still dominate the discussion, the global history of camps has been recognized and other instances of encampment in diverse contexts have received increasing attention. Cases of nineteenth-century encampment, especially in colonial settings, have helped shift the focus away from an exclusive preoccupation with totalitarian regimes.[4] Considerable attention has been paid to the internment during the two world wars of 'enemy aliens', that is, civilians who were citizens of, or ethnically related to, enemy states, whether by Australia, Britain, Canada, Germany, Japan, or the United States, among others.[5] POW camps are also well researched but are far from central to the broader discussion.[6] Diverse camps in post–Second World War Germany and Austria are the focus of recent and ongoing research: those for 'displaced persons' (DPs), including both Jews who had survived German occupation, slave

---

[3] Giorgio Agamben, 'The Camp as the *Nomos* of the Modern', in Hent de Vries and Samuel Weber (eds.), *Violence, Identity, and Self-Determination* (Stanford, CA: Stanford University Press, 1997), 106–18; Joël Kotek and Pierre Rigoulot, *Das Jahrhundert der Lager: Gefangenschaft, Zwangsarbeit, Vernichtung* (Berlin: Propyläen, 2000).

[4] See Andrea Pitzer, *One Long Night: A Global History of Concentration Camps* (New York: Little, Brown, 2017); Dan Stone, *Concentration Camps: A Short History* (Oxford: Oxford University Press, 2017).

[5] For overviews of the phenomenon in the First World War, see Matthew Stibbe (ed.), 'Civilian Internment and Civilian Internees in Europe, 1914–1920', in *Captivity, Forced Labour and Forced Migration in Europe during the First World War* (London: Routledge, 2009), 49–81; Matthew Stibbe, 'Ein globales Phänomen: Zivilinternierung im Ersten Weltkrieg in transnationaler und internationaler Dimension', in Christoph Jahr and Jens Thiel (eds.), *Lager vor Auschwitz: Gewalt und Integration im 20. Jahrhundert* (Berlin: Metropol, 2013), 158–76. On specific cases, especially from the Second World War, see, among others, Richard Dove (ed.), *'Totally Un-English'? Britain's Internment of 'Enemy Aliens' in Two World Wars* (Amsterdam: Rodopi, 2005); Klaus Neumann, *In the Interest of National Security: Civilian Internment in Australia during World War II* (Canberra: National Archives of Australia, 2006); Christina Twomey, *Australia's Forgotten Prisoners: Civilians Interned by the Japanese in World War II* (Melbourne: Cambridge University Press, 2007); John Christgau, *Enemies: World War II Alien Internment* (Lincoln: University of Nebraska Press, 2009 [1st ed. 1985]). 'Enemy aliens' were of course not the only captive civilians during the wars. See Annette Becker, 'Captive Civilians', in Jay Winter (ed.), *The Cambridge History of the First World War*, vol. 3: *Civil Society* (Cambridge: Cambridge University Press, 2014), 257–81.

[6] The literature on POWs and POW camps is so extensive that reference is made here only to encyclopaedic accounts: Jonathan F. Vance (ed.), *Encyclopedia of Prisoners of War and Internment*, 2nd ed. (Millerton, NY: Grey House Publishing, 2006); Heather Jones, 'Prisoners of War', in Jay Winter (ed.), *The Cambridge History of the First World War*, vol. 2: *The State* (Cambridge: Cambridge University Press, 2014), 266–90; Bob Moore, 'Prisoners of War', in John Ferris and Evan Mawdsley (eds.), *The Cambridge History of the Second World War*, vol. 1: *Fighting the War* (Cambridge: Cambridge University Press, 2015), 664–89.

labour, and genocide and non-Jewish Eastern Europeans who had fled to Germany to evade the advancing Red Army; those for ethnic German refugees and expellees from Central and Eastern Europe; and those for refugees from the communist German Democratic Republic (GDR) founded in East Germany in 1949.[7] Twenty-first-century camps associated with the 'war on terror' and with western states' efforts to contain and deter unwanted migrants and refugees have also prompted debate and consternation. In light of this diversity of camps, it is increasingly recognized, as Dan Stone put it recently, that 'Concentration camps are not only products of "mad" dictators but have a global history that belongs to the liberal West as well.'[8] This is an important point, even if it begs the question of whether every camp that holds civilians against their will constitutes a 'concentration camp'. Considerable care and precise criteria are needed to distinguish different types of camps.

Allied internment camps in occupied Germany, especially those of the western powers, are largely missing from this discussion but can add productively to the field, where there is room for more even-handedness, rigour, and nuance. Even recent works that self-consciously address camps run by dictatorships *and* democracies either gloss over or entirely fail to mention the western powers' internment camps in Germany, while paying the Soviet camps some attention.[9] Remarkably, too, in his excellent study of the internment of Germans in the United Kingdom during the First World War, Panikos Panayi claims that 'In the British case mass internment comes to a close with the Second World War.' He notes the detention of people suspected of links with Irish Republican Army terrorism in the 1970s or with Islamicist terrorism more recently but is

---

[7] See Tara Zahra, '"Prisoners of the Postwar": Expellees, Displaced Persons, and Jews in Austria after World War II', *Austrian History Yearbook* 41 (2010), 191–215; Avinoam J. Patt and Michael Berkowitz (eds.), *'We Are Here': New Approaches to Jewish Displaced Persons in Postwar Germany* (Detroit, MI: Wayne State University Press, 2010); Anna Holian, 'The Ambivalent Exception: American Occupation Policy in Postwar Germany and the Formation of Jewish Refugee Spaces', *Journal of Refugee Studies* 25, no. 3 (2012), 452–73; Jan-Hinnerk Antons, 'Displaced Persons in Postwar Germany: Parallel Societies in a Hostile Environment', *Journal of Contemporary History* 49, no. 1 (2014), 92–114; Henrik Bispinck and Katharina Hochmuth (eds.), *Flüchtlingslager im Nachkriegsdeutschland: Migration, Politik, Erinnerung* (Berlin: Ch. Links, 2014); Sascha Schießl, *'Das Tor zur Freiheit': Kriegsfolgen, Erinnerungspolitik und humanitärer Anspruch im Lager Friedland (1945–1970)* (Göttingen: Wallstein, 2016).

[8] Stone, *Concentration Camps*, 10.

[9] Kotek and Rigoulot, *Jahrhundert der Lager*, 473–85; Vance (ed.), *Encyclopedia of Prisoners of War*, 377–8; Bettina Greiner and Alan Kramer (eds.), *Welt der Lager: Zur 'Erfolgsgeschichte' einer Institution* (Hamburg: Hamburger Edition, 2013), which reprints a photo of the American camp at Darmstadt but does not mention western internment camps in the text; Stone, *Concentration Camps*, 81, 96–8; Pitzer, *One Long Night*, 155–6.

completely oblivious to Britain's mass internment of civilians in occupied Germany.[10]

The present book aims to include Allied internment in the global history of encampment and to promote a more comprehensive and critical comparative discussion of various camp forms. The book demonstrates that Britain and other major democratic powers have resorted to the use of camps more extensively and recently than is widely understood, that they have done so beyond the geographical confines of overseas empires and outside wartime, that they have defined groups to be targeted not just in ethnic and military but also in political-ideological categories, and that they have not always treated their prisoners in accordance with international norms. Guantanamo Bay and even Abu Ghraib are thus perhaps historically less exceptional than is sometimes assumed. Recognizing this, however, should not obscure important distinctions between different types and experiences of incarceration and encampment in different contexts or even within the same context, such as postwar Germany.

The History of Occupied and Postwar Germany

The book also aims to promote internment's integration into the history of Germany's occupation at the end of the Second World War. Internment was a major component of the occupation experience that warrants greater attention than it often receives. To be sure, civilian internees were less numerous than other prototypical characters of postwar German history such as DPs, POWs, returned soldiers, expellees and refugees, and the 'rubble women', who cleared away debris in many German cities. Yet being interned was one of several 'collective fates' in occupied Germany.[11] Historians neglected it for a long time. Until the 2000s,

---

[10] Panikos Panayi, *Prisoners of Britain: German Civilian and Combatant Internees during the First World War* (Manchester: Manchester University Press, 2012), 306–7.

[11] If the first groups all numbered in the millions, the number of 'rubble women' was smaller than their iconic status would suggest. See Leonie Treber, *Mythos Trümmerfrauen: Von der Trümmerbeseitigung in der Kriegs- und Nachkriegszeit und der Entstehung eines deutschen Erinnerungsortes* (Essen: Klartext Verlag, 2014). On the other groups, see Patt and Berkowitz (eds.), *'We Are Here'*; Anna Holian, *Between National Socialism and Soviet Communism: Displaced Persons in Postwar Germany* (Ann Arbor: University of Michigan Press, 2011); Gerhard Daniel Cohen, *In War's Wake: Europe's Displaced Persons in the Postwar Order* (Oxford: Oxford University Press, 2012); David Rock and Stefan Wolff (eds.), *Coming Home to Germany? The Integration of Ethnic Germans from Central and Eastern Europe in the Federal Republic* (New York: Berghahn Books, 2002); Frank Biess, *Homecomings: Returning POWs and the Legacies of Defeat in Postwar Germany* (Princeton, NJ: Princeton University Press, 2006); Birgit Schwelling, *Heimkehr – Erinnerung – Integration: Der Verband der Heimkehrer, die ehemaligen*

historical surveys often did not go beyond citing Lutz Niethammer's characterization of the results of early American denazification measures as being 'full internment camps and empty offices' and failed to ask what happened to internees.[12] Internment has become more prominent in the new millennium, but general histories still often mention it only briefly and sometimes not at all. Meaningful recognition as a significant element of the history of the occupation and the transition from the Nazi to the postwar eras is rare. Yet internment played an important role in facilitating an exchange of elites and establishing a new political order. It also contributed to a widespread sense of uncertainty, helplessness, and existential insecurity for significant sections of the population as well as to broader social phenomena such as the absence of men, especially husbands and fathers, to a perceived crisis of the family, and to the politicization of the food question.[13] In short, histories of occupied Germany and of the transition from the Nazi to the postwar era are incomplete without internment.

Moreover, as is the case in the literature on camps, there is scope for greater balance and for more, and more precise, comparisons between the eastern and western parts of the story. Three decades after the end of the Cold War, the dichotomous western master narrative – according to which the Soviets raped, pillaged, murdered, arrested, and deported Germans en masse, while the western occupying forces, especially the Americans, behaved as 'friendly enemies' – still needs to be overcome.[14] On both sides, the reality was more complicated. Recent work demonstrates that the reality of the American occupation does not match the

---

Kriegsgefangenen und die westdeutsche Nachkriegsgesellschaft (Paderborn: Ferdinand Schöningh, 2010); Christiane Wienand, *Returning Memories: Former Prisoners of War in Divided and Reunited Germany* (Rochester, NY: Camden House, 2015).

[12] Lutz Niethammer, *Die Mitläuferfabrik: Die Entnazifizierung am Beispiel Bayerns* (Berlin: J. W. H. Dietz, 1982 [1st ed. 1972]), 12. Cf. Lutz Niethammer, 'Alliierte Internierungslager in Deutschland nach 1945: Vergleich und offene Fragen', in Christian Jansen, Lutz Niethammer, and Bernd Weisbrod (eds.), *Von der Aufgabe der Freiheit: Politische Verantwortung und bürgerliche Gesellschaft im 19. und 20. Jahrhundert – Festschrift für Hans Mommsen zum 5. November 1995* (Berlin: Oldenbourg Akademieverlag, 1995), hereafter cited as Niethammer, 'Alliierte Internierungslager (1995)', 469.

[13] See Lu Seegers, *'Vati blieb im Krieg': Vaterlosigkeit als generationelle Erfahrung im 20. Jahrhundert – Deutschland und Polen* (Göttingen: Wallstein, 2013), 88–96; Atina Grossmann, 'Grams, Calories, and Food: Languages of Victimization, Entitlement, and Human Rights in Occupied Germany, 1945–1949', *Central European History* 44, no. 1 (2011), 118–48; Alice Weinreb, '"For the Hungry Have No Past nor Do They belong to a Political Party": Debates over German Hunger after World War II', *Central European History* 45, no. 1 (2012), 50–78.

[14] Heinrich Oberreuter and Jürgen Weber (eds.), *Freundliche Feinde? Die Alliierten und die Demokratiegründung in Deutschland* (Munich: Olzog, 1996).

'good occupation' of popular myth and much history writing and that the extent of theft and other forms of criminality and exploitation by American personnel was greater than often assumed.[15] The historian's challenge is to acknowledge the western powers' brutality and illiberality without blowing them out of proportion or suggesting they were the equivalent of the much more severe and lethal Soviet brutality and illiberality. For instance, in the occupation's early phases, distrust, nervousness, hatred, and revenge led soldiers of all Allied armies to kill German captives and civilians, but the number of victims of the western Allies was dwarfed by the more than 120,000 German civilians killed by the Red Army in German territories east of the Oder–Neisse rivers that would become the new German-Polish border. Similarly, Allied soldiers in the West – including American forces to a larger degree than often recognized – raped considerable numbers of German women; yet the scale and violence of rape by Soviet troops were vastly higher.[16] In addition to mass rape, however, there were also cases of genuinely amorous relations between German women and Soviet men.[17]

In this vein, a balanced, comparative history of internment can contribute to a more nuanced and complex understanding of the occupation. Like numerous histories of camps, many accounts of the occupation refer to Soviet but not western internment. A less extreme variant of this tendency is to focus a discussion largely, but not completely, on the Soviet case.[18] Both the asymmetrical attention devoted to western and Soviet internment and their inconsistent evaluation perpetuate black-and-white depictions of wicked Soviets and virtuous westerners. It is time to acknowledge shades of grey. One does not need to exaggerate the virtues of the western occupiers to see the sins of the USSR. Although

---

[15] See Susan L. Carruthers, *The Good Occupation: American Soldiers and the Hazards of Peace* (Cambridge, MA: Harvard University Press, 2016), 72–5, 227–34; Thomas Kehoe, 'Control, Disempowerment, Fear, and Fantasy: Violent Criminality during the Early American Occupation of Germany, March–July 1945', *Australian Journal of Politics and History* 62, no. 4 (2016), 561–75.

[16] See Richard Bessel, *Germany 1945: From War to Peace* (London: Simon & Schuster, 2009), 82, 152–64; Norman M. Naimark, *The Russians in Germany: A History of the Soviet Zone of Occupation, 1945–1949* (Cambridge, MA: Harvard University Press, 1995), 69–140; and, not unproblematically, Miriam Gebhardt, *Als die Soldaten kamen: Die Vergewaltigung deutscher Frauen am Ende des Zweiten Weltkriegs* (Munich: Deutsche Verlags-Anstalt, 2015).

[17] Stefan-Ludwig Hoffmann, 'Besiegte, Besatzer, Beobachter: Das Kriegsende im Tagebuch', in Daniel Fulda, Dagmar Herzog, Stefan-Ludwig Hoffmann, and Till van Rahden (eds.), *Demokratie im Schatten der Gewalt: Geschichten des Privaten im deutschen Nachkrieg* (Göttingen: Wallstein, 2010), 47–9.

[18] See Martin Kitchen, *A History of Modern Germany 1800–2000* (Oxford: Blackwell, 2005), 317; Gregor Dallas, *1945: The War That Never Ended* (New Haven, CT: Yale University Press, 2005), 591.

the western powers intended eventually to reestablish German democracy, they ran what Niethammer called a 'liberal occupation dictatorship' in which civil rights and the rule of law were circumscribed. This is overlooked by scholars of Soviet internment such as Bettina Greiner, who suggests that western internment reflected the western powers' determination to 'counter state-sanctioned injustice with the democratic rule of law – an intention that the Soviet occupying power did not honour'.[19] Such an assessment applies to western and Soviet policy towards Germany over the longer term but misrepresents the early western occupation in general and internment in particular. Liberal western powers have resorted to illiberal methods in other contexts and it is increasingly recognized that democracies are not immune from abusing their prisoners.[20] The coercive and problematic aspects of their occupation of Germany should no longer be overlooked. By the same token, not every coercive measure taken by the Soviets can be characterized exclusively as, or attributed solely to, wicked Stalinization.

The History of Transitional Justice in Germany

The fate of Nazis after 1945 has long sparked interest. This book builds upon, and contributes to, a reassessment of the conventional and still influential view that Allied and German efforts at 'transitional justice' in the early postwar years were an inadequate failure and that all but a handful of Nazis and war criminals avoided serious consequences for their roles and actions. Recent research has demonstrated that more criminals were investigated and prosecuted in Germany and across Europe than previously thought.[21] It has also shown that the massive whitewash described by Niethammer in his pioneering and still influential study of denazification in Bavaria – first published in 1972 and republished in 1982 with the catchier and paradigmatic title 'The

---

[19] Niethammer, *Mitläuferfabrik*, 653; Bettina Greiner, *Suppressed Terror: History and Perception of Soviet Special Camps in Germany* (Lanham, MD: Lexington Books, 2014), 348.

[20] See Dieter Waibel, *Von der wohlwollenden Despotie zur Herrschaft des Rechts: Entwicklungsstufen der amerikanischen Besatzung Deutschlands 1944–1949* (Tübingen: J. C. B. Mohr, 1996); Geoffrey P. R. Wallace, *Life and Death in Captivity: The Abuse of Prisoners during War* (Ithaca, NY: Cornell University Press, 2015).

[21] Norbert Frei (ed.), 'Nach der Tat: Die Ahndung deutscher Kriegs- und NS-Verbrechen in Europa–eine Bilanz', in *Transnationale Vergangenheitspolitik: Der Umgang mit deutschen Kriegsverbrechern in Europa nach dem Zweiten Weltkrieg* (Göttingen: Wallstein, 2006), 32–4; Edith Raim, *Nazi Crimes against Jews and German Post-War Justice: The West German Judicial System during Allied Occupation, 1945–1949* (Berlin: Walter de Gruyter, 2015).

Follower Factory' – cannot simply be extrapolated to other parts of the country. In sum, as Paul Hoser puts it, 'if the older research generally saw denazification ... as a failure, the more recent research emphasizes the palpable sanction that it meant for those affected'.[22]

Internment can and should play an important part in any comprehensive reassessment, but studies and accounts of 'transitional justice', denazification, and the handling of the Nazi past in postwar Germany long paid it surprisingly little attention. The literature was preoccupied instead with criminal trials, dismissals from employment, questionnaires, various categorization procedures, discussion of the 'guilt question', and efforts at 'reeducation'. Numerous early studies did not mention arrests and internment at all, while others did so only in passing.[23] To be sure, some early explorations of denazification referred to internment, but it was far from central. Niethammer, for instance, briefly discussed American arrest policies and internment, but still effectively reduced denazification to 'the experience of the work of the *Spruchkammern*', that is, the denazification panels established in 1946, at internment's expense.[24] This was true of many other works through to the 1990s, which focused on procedures for removing Nazis from the public service, the economy, and the professions, and where internment merited at best brief discussion.[25] Internment has received more attention in recent years. It is perhaps most prominent in studies of the American occupation zone, where the camps were most thoroughly integrated – institutionally and procedurally – into the zonal denazification system in 1946. Yet even here internment is often relegated to an excursus and does not feature in the wider analysis.[26]

---

[22] Niethammer, *Mitläuferfabrik*; Paul Hoser, 'Entnazifizierung in der Stadt Dachau', in Norbert Göttler (ed.), *Nach der 'Stunde Null': Stadt und Landkreis Dachau 1945 bis 1949* (Munich: Herbert Utz Verlag, 2008), 197. See Armin Schuster, *Die Entnazifizierung in Hessen 1945–1954: Vergangenheitspolitik in der Nachkriegszeit* (Wiesbaden: Historische Kommission für Nassau, 1999).

[23] For the first category, see Peter Steinbach, *Nationalsozialistische Gewaltverbrechen: Die Diskussion in der deutschen Öffentlichkeit nach 1945* (Berlin: Colloquium Verlag, 1981). For the second, see Constantine FitzGibbon, *Denazification* (London: Michael Joseph, 1969).

[24] Niethammer, *Mitläuferfabrik*, esp. 12, 27 (quotation), 255–9, 455–67.

[25] For examples in English, see Elmer Plischke, 'Denazification in Germany: A Policy Analysis', in Robert Wolfe (ed.), *Americans as Proconsuls: United States Military Government in Germany and Japan, 1944–52* (Carbondale: Southern Illinois University Press, 1984), 212–17, 223; Ian D. Turner (ed.), 'Denazification in the British Zone', in *Reconstruction in Post-War Germany: British Occupation Policy and the Western Zones* (Oxford: Berg, 1989), 239–67.

[26] See Schuster, *Entnazifizierung in Hessen*, 12, 239–58, 333–8, 348–51; Hans Hesse, *Konstruktionen der Unschuld: Die Entnazifizierung am Beispiel von Bremen und Bremerhaven 1945–1953* (Bremen: Selbstverlag des Staatsarchivs Bremen, 2005),

This relative marginality is partly due to the Allies' failure to develop a dedicated directive on arrest and internment, as discussed in Chapter 1. Yet it is also due to terminological problems. The term 'denazification' is used both expansively and more narrowly. Sometimes it describes all measures taken to destroy Nazism and achieve transitional justice, including the prosecution of Nazi criminals. Henceforth, the 'eradication of Nazism' is generally used for this broad understanding. More commonly, however, criminal prosecutions are regarded as separate from 'denazification', which on this understanding covers a range of non-judicial political, legal, and administrative measures aimed at removing Nazi influence from German public life, including one-off steps such as abrogating Nazi law and removing Nazi names and symbols from public space as well as the more difficult and controversial process of vetting and purging Nazi personnel. Frequently, however, the term is understood more narrowly still as referring only to the purge of Nazis, including both their removal or exclusion from positions of influence and their arrest and internment.[27] In a further narrowing, it is often equated with removal and exclusion from office or with the vetting work of denazification committees, especially the *Spruchkammern* in the American zone, as per Niethammer's approach as already mentioned. The prevalence of this narrowest understanding – the only one that effectively excludes internment – has contributed to internment's neglect in many discussions of 'denazification'. Indeed, as discussed further in subsequent chapters, it has contributed to confusion about whether Soviet internment in particular had anything to do with eradicating Nazism.

In giving internment due consideration within the broader context of post-Nazi transitional justice, this book makes several points. The first is that the effort to eradicate Nazism was more severe than is often suggested. As recognized by almost every author who takes it seriously, internment constituted the toughest official Allied sanction against a

---

194–221; Angela Borgstedt, *Entnazifizierung in Karlsruhe 1946 bis 1951: Politische Säuberung im Spannungsfeld von Besatzungspolitik und lokalpolitischem Neuanfang* (Constance: UVK Verlagsgesellschaft, 2001); Bianka J. Adams, *From Crusade to Hazard: The Denazification of Bremen Germany* (Lanham, MD: Scarecrow Press, 2009); Angelika Königseder, 'Das Ende der NSDAP: Die Entnazifizierung', in Wolfgang Benz (ed.), *Wie wurde man Parteigenosse? Die NSDAP und ihre Mitglieder* (Frankfurt/Main: Fischer, 2009), 151–66. See also Mary Fulbrook, *Reckonings: Legacies of Nazi Persecution and the Quest for Justice* (Oxford: Oxford University Press, 2018), 210–11.

[27] See Plischke, 'Denazification', 212–13; Elmer Plischke, 'Denazifying the Reich', *The Review of Politics* 9, no. 2 (1947), 156–7; Perry Biddiscombe, *The Denazification of Germany: A History 1945–1950* (Stroud: Tempus, 2007), 9–10.

sizable portion of the population of occupied Germany.[28] It is thus unsurprising that its near absence from many earlier and some recent histories corresponded with emphasis on denazification's mildness and inadequacy.[29] And it is only logical that internment's rising prominence coincides with, and supports, a reinterpretation that stresses at least initial and even medium-term severity. The fact that hundreds of thousands of Germans were arrested and spent considerable time in internment camps cannot be left out of the reckoning.

The second point is that Allied policy for eradicating Nazism was more variegated than it often appears. Especially in accounts that ignore internment, Allied approaches to the personnel of Nazi Germany often appear two-dimensional, with the top surviving leadership and relatively few other criminals facing prosecution, on the one hand, and the mass of members of the National Socialist German Workers' Party (NSDAP, the Nazi Party) and fellow-travellers facing temporary professional and political restrictions, on the other hand.[30] Moreover, internment's absence or marginality in many accounts promotes the notion that the 'small fry' were equally or more severely punished than the 'big' Nazis. In particular, the expansive American attempt to vet the entire adult population has been criticized for having 'indiscriminately exposed activists and mere conformists – indeed, even opponents of National Socialism – to political defamation and existential insecurity'.[31] Yet this ignores the fact that mere conformists and followers, let alone opponents, of Nazism

---

[28] Niethammer, *Mitläuferfabrik*, 259; Volker Dotterweich, 'Die "Entnazifizierung"', in Josef Becker, Theo Stammen, and Peter Waldmann (eds.), *Vorgeschichte der Bundesrepublik Deutschland* (Munich: Fink, 1979), 149; Christa Schick, 'Die Internierungslager', in Martin Broszat, Klaus-Dietmar Henke, and Hans Woller (eds.), *Von Stalingrad zur Währungsunion: Zur Sozialgeschichte des Umbruchs in Deutschland* (Munich: R. Oldenbourg, 1988), 301; Clemens Vollnhals, *Evangelische Kirche und Entnazifizierung 1945–1949: Die Last der nationalsozialistischen Vergangenheit* (Munich: Oldenbourg, 1989), 98; Wember, *Umerziehung im Lager*, 8; Niethammer, 'Alliierte Internierungslager (1995)', 473; Meyer, *Entnazifizierung von Frauen*, 13–14; Alfred Wahl, *La seconde histoire du Nazisme dans l'Allemagne fédérale depuis 1945* (Paris: Armand Collin, 2006), 34.

[29] For recent accounts that stress the mildness of denazification in the western zones and fail to come to grips with, or mention, internment, see Donald M. McKale, *Nazis after Hitler: How Perpetrators of the Holocaust Cheated Justice and Truth* (Lanham, MD: Rowman & Littlefield, 2012); Georg Fülberth, *Geschichte der Bundesrepublik Deutschland* (Cologne: PapyRossa, 2015), 18.

[30] See Steinbach, *Nationalsozialistische Gewaltverbrechen*, 27; McKale, *Nazis after Hitler*. On the NSDAP, see Dietrich Orlow, *The Nazi Party, 1919–1945: A Complete History* (New York: Enigma Books, 2008).

[31] Cornelia Rauh-Kühne, 'Life Rewarded the Latecomers: Denazification during the Cold War', in Detlef Junker (ed.), *The United States and Germany in the Era of the Cold War, 1945–1990: A Handbook*, vol. 1: *1945–1968* (Cambridge: Cambridge University Press, 2004), 72.

were generally not targeted for internment (although some were never-theless caught up in it). Including internment as an additional, inter-mediate sanction against a range of party and state functionaries paints a more complex, differentiated picture. The Allies were in some respects more methodical and precise than they are often given credit for.

The third point concerns the notion of 'collective guilt', which perme-ates accounts of the occupation and transitional justice in postwar Germany even though historians disagree about whether the Allies ever accused the Germans of collective guilt for Nazism, its crimes, or the war. Some historians argue that, despite much tough anti-German war-time rhetoric, Allied policy focused on individual guilt. Accusations of collective guilt, they insist, were a mere figment of the defensive German imagination, a 'straw man' used to delegitimize Allied measures.[32] Other historians argue that collective accusations were not just rhetorical but in fact inspired, and were translated into, policy. Some attribute denazifi-cation to the 'collective guilt thesis'. According to one historian: 'At the beginning stood the collective guilt accusation, especially of the Ameri-cans. It viewed every German as a National Socialist and knew no differentiation.'[33]

While certain Allied policies affected or potentially affected all Germans, they were not necessarily predicated on, or accompanied by, undifferentiated accusations of German collective guilt. Some examples suggest the need for more nuanced analysis and language than the divergent claims for and against the existence of accusations of collective guilt provide. Allied insistence on German reparations, for instance, reflected shared liability for the state's waging of war, not an accusation that every German was 'guilty'. The same can be said of the 'tough' approach proclaimed by the famous American occupation directive, Joint Chiefs of Staff (JCS) 1067/6, which is discussed further in Chapter 1. It stated that Germans should accept that responsibility for their country's devastation lay not with the Allies but with themselves:

---

[32] Wulf Kansteiner, 'Losing the War, Winning the Memory Battle: The Legacy of Nazism, World War II, and the Holocaust in the Federal Republic of Germany', in Richard Ned Lebow, Wulf Kansteiner, and Claudio Fogu (eds.), *The Politics of Memory in Postwar Europe* (Durham, NC: Duke University Press, 2006), 108. See also Norbert Frei (ed.), 'Von deutscher Erfindungskraft, Oder: Die Kollektivschuldthese in der Nachkriegszeit', in *1945 und wir: Das Dritte Reich im Bewußtsein der Deutschen* (Munich: C. H. Beck, 2005), 145–55.

[33] Gisela Schwarze, *Eine Region im demokratischen Aufbau: Der Regierungsbezirk Münster 1945/46* (Düsseldorf: Patmos Verlag, 1984), 195. See also Justus Fürstenau, *Entnazifizierung: Ein Kapitel deutscher Nachkriegsgeschichte* (Neuwied: Luchterhand, 1969), 26; FitzGibbon, *Denazification*, 95–9; Biddiscombe, *Denazification of Germany*, 27; Carruthers, *The Good Occupation*, 67, 117, 131.

It should be brought home to the Germans that Germany's ruthless warfare and the fanatical Nazi resistance have destroyed the German economy and made chaos and suffering inevitable and that the Germans cannot escape responsibility for what they have brought upon themselves.[34]

Allied film and poster campaigns publicizing the evidence of atrocities found at the liberated Nazi concentration camps are also often regarded as having levelled accusations of collective guilt. But even they were not undifferentiated. As Ulrike Weckel observes of the films,

certainly, accusations of guilt were raised, but by no means always against all Germans to the same extent.... There can hardly be any question of preaching the collective guilt of all Germans especially in the films produced directly for a German audience.[35]

Similarly, the famous American poster from 1945 with the headline 'These Shameful Deeds: Your Fault' (*Diese Schandtaten: Eure Schuld*) addressed a plural audience but accused it only of being 'co-responsible' for heinous crimes that were actually committed by 'the Nazi criminals' and 'Hitler's brutish henchmen'; other Germans (merely) 'share in the responsibility' because they had 'looked calmly on and put up with it in silence'.[36] Meanwhile, the Anglo-American ban on 'fraternization' with Germans in the occupation's first months was as much a security meas-ure as an attempt to communicate general disregard for the Germans; it implied that in Allied eyes Germans were untrustworthy, not that they were all guilty.[37] Even applying denazification to the entire adult popula-tion, as the Americans did, did not suggest a desire to accuse or punish all Germans. Although certainly based on a belief that any German might have been a Nazi or militarist to some degree, the aim was precisely to distinguish among 'bigger', 'smaller', and, importantly, non-Nazis. It is

[34] 'Directive to Commander in Chief of United States Forces of Occupation Regarding the Military Government of Germany' (JCS 1067/6), 26 Apr. 1945, in *Foreign Relations of the United States: Diplomatic Papers 1945*, vol. III: *European Advisory Commission; Austria; Germany* (Washington, DC: United States Government Printing Office, 1968), hereafter *FRUS 1945 III*, 487. On JCS 1067/6, see Chapter 1.

[35] Ulrike Weckel, *Beschämende Bilder: Deutsche Reaktionen auf alliierte Dokumentarfilme über befreite Konzentrationslager* (Stuttgart: Franz Steiner Verlag, 2012), 179–80.

[36] Office of Military Government, United States, 'Diese Schandtaten: Eure Schuld!' (poster), 1945, available online at: Lebendiges Museum Online, www.hdg.de/lemo/bestand/objekt/plakat-schande-schuld.html (accessed 6 Feb. 2019). Translations by the website of the UK Imperial War Museum, available online at: www.iwm.org.uk/collections/item/object/29110 (accessed 6 Feb. 2019). The poster was thus more differentiated than a British communications directive of 12 May 1945 that instructed staff to emphasize 'The common responsibility of all Germans for Nazi crimes'. Cited by Christopher Knowles, *Winning the Peace: The British in Occupied Germany, 1945–1948* (London: Bloomsbury, 2017), 20. There was thus no consistent line.

[37] On (non-)fraternization, see Carruthers, *The Good Occupation*, 55–6, 111–31.

thus more appropriate to speak of collective suspicion rather than collective guilt. To suggest that denazification knew no differentiation is to miss the point entirely.

Considering internment sheds further light on this disputed question. Internment belonged to a raft of measures, the very existence of which belies claims of an undifferentiated approach either to the Germans or to questions of guilt and responsibility. Nevertheless, internment was not based on completely individualized incrimination either. The concept of suspicion also better captures internment's preventative rather than purely punitive nature. Internees were detained as much for the potential danger they posed to the Allies' postwar agenda as for any real or imputed 'guilt'. Indeed, as Dominik Rigoll has argued, historians have tended to play down the preventative security motivations for the anti-Nazi purge, focusing instead on punitive and moral considerations.[38] The common focus on 'guilt' is thus misleading. Transitional justice is never entirely juridical or retrospective but inherently political and prospective, and all of the occupying powers viewed denazification and internment as instruments to restructure German society, not just to achieve 'justice'.[39] One of the main aims of this book is to highlight the multiple, often mutually antagonistic dimensions and aims of transitional justice in general and of particular measures such as internment.

The History of Internment

As well as advancing our understanding of the history of camps, of the occupation, and of the attempted eradication of Nazism, the book engages with a number of debates about its specific subject. Specialized research on internment in occupied Germany emerged only in the late 1980s and early 1990s. Since then it has progressed unevenly, but Harold Marcuse's 2010 assertion that 'very little has been written about the Allied internment camps' overlooked a growing body of work, which has expanded further in the meantime.[40] Of the three western zones, the American has attracted most interest, with two monographs, a recent

---

[38] Dominik Rigoll, *Staatsschutz in Westdeutschland: Von der Entnazifizierung zur Extremistenabwehr* (Göttingen: Wallstein, 2013), 34.

[39] Cf. David Cohen, 'Transitional Justice in Divided Germany after 1945', in John Elster (ed.), *Retribution and Reparation in the Transition to Democracy* (Cambridge: Cambridge University Press, 2006), 80; Kim Christian Priemel, *The Betrayal: The Nuremberg Trials and German Divergence* (Oxford: Oxford University Press, 2016), 8.

[40] Harold Marcuse, 'The Afterlife of the Camps', in Jane Caplan and Nikolaus Wachsmann (eds.), *Concentration Camps in Nazi Germany: The New Histories* (New York: Routledge, 2010), 207 (n. 44).

doctoral dissertation, and a number of smaller studies.[41] A first monograph on British internment appeared in 1991 and smaller studies of individual British camps followed.[42] Research is least developed for the often 'forgotten' French zone. It has even been claimed, incorrectly, that 'at no time did the French have any arrangement for the "automatic arrest" of Nazis'.[43]

[41] Schick, 'Internierungslager'; Ulrich Müller, 'Die Internierungslager in und um Ludwigsburg 1945–1949', *Ludwigsburger Geschichtsblätter* 45 (1991), 171–95; Christa Horn, *Die Internierungs- und Arbeitslager in Bayern 1945–1952* (Frankfurt/Main: Peter Lang, 1992); Peter Zeitler, 'Lageralltag in amerikanischen Internierungscamps (1945–1948): Dargestellt am Schicksal eines oberfränkischen SA-Führers', *Archiv für Geschichte von Oberfranken* 76 (1996), 371–92; Christof Strauß, *Kriegsgefangenschaft und Internierung: Die Lager in Heilbronn-Böckingen 1945–1947* (Heilbronn: Stadtarchiv Heilbronn, 1998); Christof Strauß, 'Zwischen Apathie und Selbstrechtfertigung: Die Internierung NS-belasteter Personen in Württemberg-Baden', in Paul Hoser (ed.), *Kriegsende und Neubeginn: Die Besatzungszeit im schwäbisch-alemannischen Raum* (Constance: UVK Verlagsgesellschaft, 2003), 287–313; Hammermann, 'Internierungslager Dachau'; Kathrin Meyer, 'Die Internierung von NS-Funktionären in der US-Zone Deutschlands', *Dachauer Hefte* 19 (2003), 24–47; Meyer, *Entnazifizierung von Frauen*; Albrecht Klose, 'Das Internierungs- und Arbeitslager Regensburg 1945–1948', *Verhandlungen des Historischen Vereins für Oberpfalz und Regensburg* 144 (2004), 7–84; Falko Heinl, '"Das schlimme Lager, in dem man gut leben konnte": Das Internierungslager in Darmstadt von 1946 bis 1949' (unpub. MA thesis, Technische Universität Darmstadt, 2005); Kristen J. Dolan, 'Isolating Nazism: Civilian Internment in American Occupied Germany, 1944–1950' (unpub. PhD thesis, University of North Carolina, Chapel Hill, 2013).

[42] Wember, *Umerziehung im Lager*; Karl Hüser, *'Unschuldig' in britischer Lagerhaft? Das Internierungslager No. 5 Staumühle 1945–1948* (Cologne: SH-Verlag, 1999); Jörn Lindner, 'Das ehemalige KZ Neuengamme als Internierungslager 1945–1948', in Geerd Dahms (ed.), *Die Stunde Null: Nachkriegsjahre in Bergedorf und Umgebung* (Hamburg: Kultur- & Geschichtskontor, 2005), 68–89; Alyn Beßmann, '"Der sozusagen für Euch alle im KZ sitzt": Britische Internierungspraxis im ehemaligen KZ Neuengamme und deutsche Deutungsmuster', and Andreas Ehresmann, 'Die frühe Nachkriegsnutzung des Kriegsgefangenen- und KZ-Auffanglagers Sandbostel unter besonderer Betrachtung des britischen No. 2 Civil Internment Camp Sandbostel', both in KZ-Gedenkstätte Neuengamme (ed.), *Beiträge zur Geschichte der nationalsozialistischen Verfolgung in Norddeutschland*, vol. 12: *Zwischenräume: Displaced Persons, Internierte und Flüchtlinge in ehemaligen Konzentrationslagern* (Bremen: Edition Temmen, 2010), 35–54 and 22–34; Sebastian Weitkamp, 'Internierungslager und Spruchgerichtsgefängnis Esterwegen 1945–1951', in Bernd Faulenbach and Andrea Kaltofen (eds.), *Hölle im Moor: Die Emslandlager 1933–1945* (Göttingen: Wallstein, 2017), 249–54.

[43] FitzGibbon, *Denazification*, 139. In the 1980s and early 1990s regional studies of French-zone denazification devoted increasing attention to internment, with Rainer Möhler emerging as the leading expert, but dedicated research failed to ensue. See Klaus-Dietmar Henke, *Politische Säuberung unter französischer Besatzung: Die Entnazifizierung in Württemberg-Hohenzollern* (Stuttgart: Deutsche Verlags-Anstalt, 1981); Reinhard Grohnert, *Die Entnazifizierung in Baden 1945–1949: Konzeptionen und Praxis der 'Epuration' am Beispiel eines Landes der französischen Besatzungszone* (Stuttgart: W. Kohlhammer, 1991); Rainer Möhler, *Entnazifizierung in Rheinland-Pfalz und im Saarland unter französischer Besatzung von 1945 bis 1952* (Mainz: v. Hase & Koehler,

Internment in the Soviet zone has received much more attention than the three western zones combined. After the fall of the Berlin Wall in 1989 and amid the collapse of the East German dictatorship in early 1990, the discovery of mass graves of Germans who had died in Soviet captivity prompted considerable public and scholarly interest. Many former inmates' reports of their experiences (or compilations thereof) were published, one of which was translated into English: Adrian Preissinger's *From Sachsenhausen to Buchenwald: Death Camps of the Soviets*.[44] In 1998, a large Russo-German research project that examined Soviet archival records produced a weighty collection of essays and an invaluable compendium of Soviet documents in German translation.[45] Scholarly studies have been published on almost every Soviet camp, and exhibition catalogues and 'books of the dead' have been compiled for several. Numerous further studies have explored topics such as camp conditions, interned women, adolescents, and children, and the history of Soviet Military Tribunals (SMTs) in occupied Germany, which is connected to the history of some Soviet camps.[46] In 2010, Bettina Greiner published a survey that sought to synthesize Soviet detention policies, detainees' experiences, and subsequent representations thereof.

1992); Rainer Möhler, 'Internierung im Rahmen der Entnazifizierungspolitik'; Rainer Möhler, 'Die Internierungslager in der französischen Besatzungszone', in Gedenkstätte Berlin-Hohenschönhausen (ed.), *Speziallager – Internierungslager: Internierungspolitik im besetzten Nachkriegsdeutschland* (Berlin: Gedenkstätte Berlin-Hohenschönhausen, 1996), 50–60.

[44] Adrian Preissinger, *From Sachsenhausen to Buchenwald: Death Camps of the Soviets, 1945–1950*, trans. Heather Clary-Smith (Ocean City, MD: Landpost Press, 1994). See Bodo Ritscher, Rosmarie Hofmann, Gabriele Hammermann, Wolfgang Röll, and Christian Schölzel (eds.), *Die sowjetischen Speziallager in Deutschland 1945–1950: Eine Bibliographie* (Göttingen: Wallstein, 1996); Rosmarie Hofmann and Bodo Ritscher, 'Auswahlbiografie zur Geschichte der sowjetischen Speziallager in der SBZ/DDR', in Petra Haustein, Annette Kaminsky, Volkhard Knigge, and Bodo Ritscher (eds.), *Instrumentalisierung, Verdrängung, Aufarbeitung: Die sowjetischen Speziallager in der gesellschaftlichen Wahrnehmung, 1945 bis heute* (Göttingen: Wallstein, 2006), 271–97.

[45] Sergej Mironenko, Lutz Niethammer, and Alexander von Plato (eds.), in collaboration with Volkhard Knigge und Günter Morsch, *Sowjetische Speziallager in Deutschland 1945 bis 1950*, 2 vols. (Berlin: Akademie Verlag, 1998): vol. 1: Alexander von Plato (ed.), *Studien und Berichte*; vol. 2: Ralf Possekel (ed.), *Sowjetische Dokumente zur Lagerpolitik*.

[46] See Bodo Ritscher, 'Die wissenschaftliche Aufarbeitung der Geschichte der sowjetischen Speziallager in der SBZ/DDR seit Beginn der 1990er Jahre – Zwischenbilanz und Ausblick', in Haustein et al. (eds.), *Instrumentalisierung, Verdrängung, Aufarbeitung*, 170–92; Enrico Heitzer, 'Speziallagerforschung und Gedenkstättenarbeit seit 1990', in Detlef Brunner and Elke Scherstjanoi (eds.), *Moskaus Spuren in Ostdeutschland 1945 bis 1949: Aktenerschließung und Forschungspläne* (Berlin: De Gruyter Oldenbourg, 2015), 109–13. On the SMTs, see Andreas Hilger, Mike Schmeitzner, and Ute Schmidt (eds.), *Sowjetische Militärtribunale*, vol. 2: *Die Verurteilung deutscher Zivilisten 1945–1955* (Cologne: Böhlau, 2003); Weigelt et al. (eds.), *Todesurteile sowjetischer Militärtribunale*.

Its English translation, *Suppressed Terror: History and Perception of Soviet Special Camps in Germany*, appeared in 2014. Most recently, Ulrich Merten published *The Gulag in East Germany*, which fails to engage with key literature and debates and makes numerous problematic and inaccurate claims.[47] Until now, Preissinger's, Greiner's, and Merten's works were the only books in English devoted to internment in any zone of occupied Germany.

Soviet internment has sparked not just the most interest but the greatest controversy. In the early 1990s, a heated scholarly and public debate emerged about its purpose and function. The conflict reflected wider discussions about whether the Soviet zone had been more effectively purged of Nazism than the western zones and whether East Germany's roots were genuinely 'antifascist', as the GDR had claimed and not a few westerners believed.[48] Influential and assertive anticommunists suggested the Soviet camps were primarily instruments of Stalinist terror, while a marginal left-wing minority argued that they largely served denazification, broadly understood. An embattled intermediary position insisted that they were a mixture of both. In 1998, the leaders of the already-mentioned Russo-German research project insisted, on the one hand, that there was no historical basis for straightforward justifications of the Soviet camps or for seeing their inmates as 'the' people responsible for Nazi Germany and its crimes. On the other hand, the Russo-German experts also declared:

Whoever outright denies these camps' original connection with Allied denazification, political co-responsibility for the Third Reich, the security of the occupying power, and its needs for reparations, and sees in them only an instrument of communist terror, will in future not be able to invoke any historical basis.[49]

The controversy dissipated somewhat thereafter. Yet no consensus emerged, as demonstrated by Greiner's book, which effectively ignores the just-quoted position. Greiner acknowledges that 'one-dimensional

---

[47] Bettina Greiner, *Verdrängter Terror: Geschichte und Wahrnehmung sowjetischer Speziallager in Deutschland* (Hamburg: Hamburger Edition, 2010); Greiner, *Suppressed Terror*; Ulrich Merten, *The Gulag in East Germany: Soviet Special Camps, 1945–1950* (Amherst, NY: Teneo Press, 2018).

[48] It also fed into debates about the comparability of communism and Nazism. See Andrew H. Beattie, *Playing Politics with History: The Bundestag Inquiries into East Germany* (New York: Berghahn Books, 2008), 108–13, 165–87, 213–19; Corey Ross, *The East German Dictatorship: Problems and Perspectives in the Interpretation of the GDR* (London: Bloomsbury, 2002).

[49] Sergej Mironenko, Lutz Niethammer, Alexander von Plato, Volkhard Knigge, and Günter Morsch, 'Vorwort der Herausgeber', in von Plato (ed.), *Studien und Berichte*, 16.

answers fail to do justice to the issues: there is no either-or', but the unambiguous nature of her position is clear, not least from the use of 'terror' in her book's title. She insists that the 'origins' and 'function' of Soviet internment 'were in no way linked to denazification'. While Merten ignores these debates, he also casts the Soviet camps as instruments of Stalinist terror and dismisses any denazificatory function.[50]

Far from settling the debate, Greiner's and Merten's books highlight the need both for clear and consistent use of key terms and for informed comparisons across the zones. Greiner does not define 'denazification' but slips across its multiple meanings: most of her specific arguments reflect a very narrow definition, while the overall impression she creates speaks to a broad understanding.[51] After all, the debate about the Soviet camps revolves around the extent to which they were part of the attempted eradication of Nazism from German society, not whether they were integrated into specific formalized procedures for removing and excluding compromised personnel from office and imposing other civil and professional sanctions, that is, denazification most narrowly understood. Soviet internment may have had little to do with the latter but pointing this out amounts to a truism under the narrowest conceptualization of denazification, which more or less excludes internment by definition. Greiner also overlooks that several of her arguments about internment's institutional and procedural separation from denazification (narrowly understood) in the Soviet zone also apply to some extent to the western zones; but no one claims that internment there had nothing to do with eradicating Nazism. This is but one example of a common tendency to view Soviet internment overwhelmingly negatively and western internment uncritically.

A systematic, balanced comparison of internment in all four zones is thus overdue. In the 1990s, two edited volumes collected the rather rudimentary state of research on the individual zones and Niethammer published multiple versions of a comparative essay that, for all its strengths, said nothing meaningful about British or French internment.[52] More recent studies of particular zones have offered some comparative remarks, but these have frequently been superficial and ill informed.[53]

---

[50] Greiner, *Suppressed Terror*, 7, 17; Merten, *Gulag in East Germany*, 2, 6–8.
[51] Greiner, *Suppressed Terror*, 15–16, 36, 349.
[52] Knigge-Tesche et al. (eds.), *Internierungspraxis*; Gedenkstätte Berlin-Hohenschönhausen (ed.), *Speziallager – Internierungslager*; Niethammer, 'Alliierte Internierungslager (1995)'; Lutz Niethammer, 'Alliierte Internierungslager in Deutschland nach 1945: Ein Vergleich und offene Fragen', in von Plato (ed.), *Studien und Berichte*, 97–116, hereafter Niethammer, 'Alliierte Internierungslager (1998)'.
[53] This is not least because their authors overlook key publications on the other zones and rely exclusively on Niethammer's comparative essay. See Greiner, *Suppressed Terror*, 348–52; Alexander von Plato, 'Sowjetische Speziallager', in Martin Sabrow (ed.),

This extends to assessments of the existing literature. For instance, like many claims made by those who write about the Soviet case, Greiner's assertion that Allied internment camps are the only camp system of the twentieth century with a 'positive image' ignores the literature on western internment, much of which is highly critical. Indeed, Kathrin Meyer finds 'almost uniformly negative judgements'.[54] In particular, the schematic nature of 'automatic arrest' and its maintenance beyond 1945 have been heavily criticized; for Edward N. Peterson, for instance, 'Arresting people without a hearing, simply because they held some office, was one of the least defensible aspects of denazification.'[55] Numerous authors repeat Niethammer's assessment of American internment as a 'mistake' and 'injustice' or describe western internment camps as 'one of the most displeasing chapters' of the Allies' wider purge. Even when such critical views are acknowledged, western internment is generally depicted as 'myopic' while Soviet internment is generally seen as 'malicious', to borrow Andrea Pitzer's terms.[56]

Interzonal comparisons are not only rare, but controversial. Some authors argue that the differences between the western and Soviet cases were so great that they are categorically different and mutually incomparable.[57] I reject suggestions that western and Soviet policies and practices cannot and should not be compared. As has often been stated with regard to Nazism and communism, for instance, comparison does not entail equation, but can identify differences and similarities.[58] It is not

---

Erinnerungsorte der DDR (Munich: C. H. Beck, 2009), 90–7; Merten, *Gulag in East Germany*, 74–6.

[54] Greiner, *Suppressed Terror*, 348; Meyer, *Entnazifizierung von Frauen*, 19. Cf. Dolan, 'Isolating Nazism', 20–2.

[55] Edward N. Peterson, *The American Occupation of Germany: Retreat to Victory* (Detroit, MI: Wayne State University Press, 1977), 145.

[56] Niethammer, *Mitläuferfabrik*, 259; Paul Sauer, *Demokratischer Neubeginn in Not und Elend: Das Land Württemberg-Baden von 1945 bis 1952* (Ulm: Vaas, 1989), 168; Pitzer, *One Long Night*, 14.

[57] Gregor Streim, 'Germans in the *Lager*: Reports and Narratives about Imprisonment in Post-war Allied Internment Camps', in Helmut Schmitz (ed.), *A Nation of Victims? Representations of German Wartime Suffering from 1945 to the Present* (Amsterdam: Rodopi, 2007), 45 (n. 5); Greiner, *Suppressed Terror*, 348–52, 257. Questions of comparability and terminology are discussed further in the Conclusion.

[58] See Michael Geyer and Sheila Fitzpatrick (eds.), *Beyond Totalitarianism: Stalinism and Nazism Compared* (Cambridge: Cambridge University Press, 2009). Whether comparisons actually do so in a balanced fashion is another question. For instance, Merten discusses the western camps only 'in order to show how they differed from the Soviet special camps'. Merten, *Gulag in East Germany*, 43. It is therefore unsurprising that he downplays similarities and does not systematically discuss western internment. The issue of comparability is also highly politicized. See Andrew H. Beattie, 'Ein neuer Historikerstreit? Kommunismus und Nationalsozialismus in der deutschen Erinnerungs- und Geschichtspolitik seit 1990', in Wolfgang Benz (ed.), *Ein Kampf um*

intended, and is also unlikely, to 'relativize' communist injustice or to excuse the Soviet record as is sometimes feared. Instead, it helps clarify precisely how Soviet policies and practices differed from those of the western powers and failed basic humanitarian and legal standards much more comprehensively. After all, although internees in all zones went hungry in 1945, it was only in the Soviet camps that tens of thousands of detainees died. As Jens Gieseke notes, it is not necessary to play down the similarities in order to recognize that 'striking differences' existed from the beginning and grew over time.[59] Moreover, Soviet inhumanity is not diminished, let alone excused, by recognizing the problematic aspects of western internment.

For all the dichotomous thinking about Soviet and western internment, historians have approached the topic in similar ways, despite the fact that on virtually every question – including internment's aims, necessity, execution, justness, consequences, and overall character – there are divergent assessments. For all zones, a strong desire is evident for historically and morally unambiguous and even simplistic assessments and categorizations. Three major approaches can be identified, whose strengths and weaknesses warrant brief discussion.

The first approach claims that the Allies' main or sole aim was to ensure their own security. For example, Greiner argues that Soviet-zone detainees 'were put into the camps and kept there because of Soviet security concerns and what was considered politically expedient. Arrests, internments, convictions and releases all followed the logic of security requirements and the exigencies of day-to-day politics.' Greiner suggests that the preoccupation with security was peculiar to the Soviet occupier and amounted to the 'export' to Germany of Stalinism's 'excessive security principles'.[60] Yet some historians of western internment also emphasize security concerns. Heiner Wember argues that, for the British, 'The goal was the security of the occupation troops. Those affected were taken into a kind of preventive custody'. Similarly, Christa Horn asserts that the 'security of their own facilities in occupied Germany was the Americans' motive for establishing internment camps'; the 'most important goal' was 'the security of Allied troops and the establishment of military government in Germany'.[61] Greiner's argument about Soviet aims is thus merely a variant of a common tendency to focus on security.

---

die Deutungshoheit: Politik, Opferinteressen und historische Forschung – Die Auseinandersetzungen um die Gedenk- und Begegnungsstätte Leistikowstraße Potsdam (Berlin: Metropol-Verlag, 2013), 16–36; Beattie, *Playing Politics with History*, 194–213.

[59] Jens Gieseke, *Die Stasi 1945–1990* (Munich: Pantheon, 2011), 31.

[60] Greiner, *Suppressed Terror*, 14, 349. See also Merten, *Gulag in East Germany*, 43.

[61] Wember, *Umerziehung im Lager*, 25; Horn, *Internierungs- und Arbeitslager*, 241, 19.

Security was undoubtedly a key concern, yet over-emphasizing it is problematic in several ways. First, although most authors acknowledge – in principle – the legitimacy of Allied measures to ensure their security, suggesting that security was the only or major issue can trivialize the motivation behind internment. This is especially true of Horn's emphasis on the protection of 'facilities', which makes the detention of hundreds of thousands of people seem disproportionate.[62] Second, even if the security of Allied personnel is included, mass arrests appear unnecessary if there was no real threat to Allied safety, as numerous authors claim. They point to the lack of attacks by the 'Werewolf' movement that, it was feared, would wage guerrilla war on Allied forces. Horn speaks of American 'hysteria' and an 'incorrectly assessed situation'; Karl Hüser calls British internment 'objectively unnecessary'; and others suggest that security fears were justified at most for a couple of months after the war.[63] They overlook the fact that, although limited, 'Werewolf' and other resistance was no figment of Nazi propaganda minister Joseph Goebbels's or the Allies' imaginations. It lasted in various forms as long as the occupation, albeit on a small scale.[64] Moreover, suggesting that the lack of resistance made internment superfluous overlooks the possibility that internment may in fact have prevented further resistance. Third, Allied terms such as 'security' and 'danger' should not be interpreted too narrowly, that is, merely physically. As Kristen J. Dolan argues, the Allies were concerned about 'potential sabotage – whether directed toward facilities, personnel, or reform efforts'.[65] The aim was not just to prevent guerrilla-style attacks but also to isolate and neutralize key representatives of the Nazi regime who would likely oppose the Allies' overall agenda for Germany. Fourth and most important, motivations and goals other than security should not be overlooked.

---

[62] Schick, 'Internierungslager', 301–3; Horn, *Internierungs- und Arbeitslager*, 16, 241.

[63] Horn, *Internierungs- und Arbeitslager*, 241, 24, 23; Hüser, *'Unschuldig' in britischer Lagerhaft?*, 99; Wember, *Umerziehung im Lager*, 47, 101, 118; Strauß, *Kriegsgefangenschaft und Internierung*, 357; Strauß, 'Zwischen Apathie und Selbstrechtfertigung', 313; Merten, *Gulag in East Germany*, 13.

[64] Contra Merten, *Gulag in East Germany*, 8. For less dismissive discussions of Allied concerns and the (limited) reality of 'Werewolf' and other resistance, see Perry Biddiscombe, 'Operation Selection Board: The Growth and Suppression of the Neo-Nazi "Deutsche Revolution" 1945–47', *Intelligence and National Security* 11, no. 1 (1996), 59–77; Perry Biddiscombe, *The Last Nazis: Werewolf Guerrilla Resistance in Europe 1944–1947* (Stroud: Tempus, 2006); Bessel, *Germany 1945*, 175–6; Naimark, *Russians in Germany*, 382–5.

[65] Dolan, 'Isolating Nazism', 74–5. In contrast, Merten talks only of (dissipating western fears of) 'armed' resistance. Merten, *Gulag in East Germany*, 40.

The second common approach suggests that the sole or paramount purpose was not security but the prosecution of Nazi criminals. Far from making internment appear unnecessary and disproportionate, this approach generally tends to justify it. After all, if it served the prosecution of the Nazis' horrendous crimes, who would object? Many historians argue that all or most western-zone internees were detained because they were suspected of crimes. For example, in relation to the French zone, Bertram Resmini asserts that internees were detained 'because of real or supposed crimes in connection with the events of the war', and Reinhard Grohnert claims, 'All internees stood under suspicion ... of having participated in war crimes and crimes against humanity.'[66] An uncritical, even positive view of western internment often emerges from its depiction as pre-trial detention. In contrast, negative assessments of Soviet internment arise when it appears to deviate from such expectations. Suggestions that western-zone internees were suspected criminals are frequently juxtaposed with claims that Soviet-zone internees were never suspected of, let alone prosecuted for, Nazi crimes. For instance, Greiner argues that the western powers 'treated internment as a kind of pre-trial detention' and implies that it only applied to suspected Nazi and war criminals. In contrast, she claims, it is 'doubtful' that the 'punishment of Nazi crimes' was ever a Soviet intention.[67] Western internment is thus juridified and sanctified, while its Soviet counterpart is dejuridified and delegitimized.

Such an approach is problematic in several ways. First, it overlooks that – like security, which it ignores or minimizes – punishment was only one of several purposes. Second, it fails to recognize that internment was a measure distinct from criminal prosecution, despite some overlap and ambiguity in the relationship between the two. The most common basis for detention is thus misrepresented. Even in the western zones only a tiny minority of internees were suspected of, let alone charged with, individual crimes. Most were taken into 'automatic arrest'. Finally, a double standard is evident when the detention of non-criminal suspects by the Soviets is criticized but its counterpart in the western zones is not, if it is acknowledged at all. Hans-Ulrich Wehler, for instance, raises no concerns about the western powers' detention of hundreds of thousands

---

[66] Bertram Resmini, 'Lager der Besatzungsmächte in Rheinland-Pfalz: Kriegsgefangene, Internierte und Verschleppte im Rheinland nach dem Zweiten Weltkrieg', *Jahrbuch für westdeutsche Landesgeschichte* 19 (1993), 602; Grohnert, *Entnazifizierung in Baden*, 163–4.

[67] Greiner, *Suppressed Terror*, 47, 348. Merten's approach is a somewhat diluted version of this. Merten, *Gulag in East Germany*, 2, 5–6. He invariably refers to western internees 'awaiting trial'.

of people, despite recognizing they were not criminal suspects, but he calls the Soviet equivalent an 'act of revenge'.[68]

A third approach is generally applied only to the Soviet case. It suggests that the aim was neither security nor prosecution but the realization of a particular political-ideological agenda. Numerous authors claim that eradicating Nazism merely offered the Soviets a pretext and justification for arrests and that their actual goal was the repression of real or imagined obstacles to communist rule, as well as the removal of economic elites. For instance, Martin Kitchen says the Soviets used denazification 'to get rid of all manner of opposition elements' and Dolan asserts that their internment policy 'primarily' pursued political and economic aims. Hubertus Knabe sees mass Soviet arrests as 'preparing the ground for the gradual revolution from above'. Perhaps Merten offers the fullest version of this approach, arguing that the 'overriding purpose of the camps was to neutralize all opposition to the Soviet system and, in the process, destroy traditional German *bourgeois* society'.[69] This interpretation, too, is one-dimensional and tends to over-emphasize unrepresentative groups of detainees in the Soviet zone. It also overlooks the political aspects of western internment.

While all three approaches contain a kernel of truth, they all oversimplify a complex, multifaceted phenomenon. In contrast, this book offers a systematic, detailed, and differentiated comparative analysis. It argues that internment was a central element of the Allies' efforts to secure their presence in Germany, to destroy Nazism and punish those deemed responsible for it, and to allow the construction of a new Germany. The book argues further that, despite the vast differences in death rates, internment in the various occupation zones shared more commonalities than is often assumed. Differences between the Soviet and the western zones lay less in the scale or basis of arrests than in the nature of internees' subsequent processing, the duration of their detention, and the conditions under which they were held. There were also differences in the degree of internees' Nazi incrimination, but these should not be exaggerated. Second-order differences existed among the western zones in many of these respects. For all the dissimilarities, however, internment in each zone shared key characteristics. Above all,

---

[68] Hans-Ulrich Wehler, *Deutsche Gesellschaftsgeschichte*, vol. 4: *Vom Beginn des Ersten Weltkriegs bis zur Gründung der beiden deutschen Staaten 1914–1949* (Munich: C. H. Beck, 2003), 957.

[69] Kitchen, *History of Modern Germany*, 317; Dolan, 'Isolating Nazism', 14–15; Hubertus Knabe, *Tag der Befreiung? Das Kriegsende in Ostdeutschland* (Berlin: Ullstein, 2005), 201; Merten, *Gulag in East Germany*, 6 (emphasis in the original). Cf. Ritscher, 'Die wissenschaftliche Aufarbeitung', 183–4.

it was conceptualized in non-judicial terms and was both preventative and retrospective.

Sources, Scope, and Structure

The book builds on the existing literature and diverse published sources, many of which were not available to, or used by, previous authors. These include several collections of Soviet documents that have been published in German or English translation. The book also draws on archival research on key questions and under-examined areas. In particular, it utilizes archival sources that have not featured to any considerable extent or at all in previous studies. These include the records of the Allied Control Authority (ACA) through which the occupying powers sought to coordinate their policies, of the International Committee of the Red Cross (ICRC) in Geneva, and of numerous German churches, which often reveal more about the practice of internment than the files of the interning powers.

The focus is on the four zones of occupied Germany, that is, the territories on which the GDR and the West German Federal Republic of Germany (FRG) were founded in 1949. However, the book also considers Germany's eastern territories that were occupied by the Soviets and transferred to Poland after the war and includes occasional glances to occupied Austria by way of comparison.

The book is divided into four chapters. Chapter 1 examines the development of internment policy from the first discussions in late 1943 through to key western and Soviet arrest directives issued in April 1945, as well as the Allies' failed attempt to develop a common internment policy in late 1945–6. Chapter 2 examines the practice of internment, from initial arrests via various steps to categorize, process, and release internees, through to the winding down of the internment programs in 1949–50. Chapter 3 discusses the questions on which views are perhaps most polarized: who was interned and how internees should be characterized. Chapter 4 explores the camps where internees were held and the conditions under which they were detained. The Conclusion considers the controversial question of how to interpret the camps and assesses internment's broader significance and impact.

1   'It Will Be Desirable on Political Grounds'
The Development of Internment Policy, 1943–1946

In the second half of July and the first days of August 1945, the leaders of the United Kingdom, United States, and USSR met at Potsdam outside Berlin to discuss how to end the war with Japan, how to treat the defeated Germany and its European allies, and how to establish a new postwar order. Among other things, the 'Big Three' agreed that the Oder–Neisse rivers would form the new provisional border between Germany and Poland and that German populations in Poland, Czechoslovakia, and Hungary would be transferred to Germany's remaining territory in an 'orderly and humane' manner.[1] The Allies also established a number of principles for the occupation of the remaining German territory, including that its population should be treated as uniformly as practicable across the four occupation zones that had just been established. They agreed further on a number of occupation goals that are generally encapsulated by numerous terms beginning with 'd'. Historical accounts identify varying sets of three, four, or even five 'ds'. They include disarmament, demilitarization, decentralization, deindustrialization, decartelization, dismantling, denazification, and democratization, although only the first three of these terms actually featured in the Potsdam Agreement.[2]

---

[1] See Michael Neiberg, *Potsdam: The End of World War II* (New York: Basic Books, 2015); R. M. Douglas, *Orderly and Humane: The Expulsions of the Germans after the Second World War* (New Haven, CT: Yale University Press, 2012); Hugo Service, *Germans to Poles: Communism, Nazism and Ethnic Cleansing after the Second World War* (Cambridge: Cambridge University Press, 2013), 49–52.

[2] The first goal listed was 'The complete disarmament and demilitarization of Germany and the elimination or control of all German industry that could be used for military production'. Further references to placing 'primary emphasis' in organizing the German economy on 'the development of agriculture and peaceful domestic industries' indicate that demilitarization of German industry rather than the country's complete deindustrialization was the goal. Decentralization appeared twice in the agreement, in both political and economic contexts. In relation to the latter, the Allies concurred that 'the present excessive concentration of economic powers as exemplified in particular by cartels, syndicates, trusts and other monopolistic arrangements' would be eliminated, for which decartelization became the byword. Dismantling refers to what the agreement

Even though the agreement did not use the term, 'denazification' is perhaps the most consistently cited Potsdam 'd' and was certainly high on the Allied agenda. It was regarded as an essential prerequisite for, and contributor to, democratization. Broadly, the agreement outlined these interconnected goals as follows:

To destroy the National Socialist Party and its affiliated and supervised organizations, to dissolve all Nazi institutions, to ensure that they are not revived in any form, and to prevent all Nazi and militarist activity or propaganda.

To prepare for the eventual reconstruction of German political life on a democratic basis and for eventual peaceful cooperation in international life by Germany.

Numerous further measures were to be taken to remove Nazi influence and allow democracy to flourish. For instance, the Allies resolved that 'German education shall be so controlled as completely to eliminate Nazi and militarist doctrine and to make possible the successful development of democratic ideas.' Similarly, 'more than nominal participants' in the activities of the NSDAP were to be removed from positions of influence in order to allow their replacement by persons 'deemed capable of assisting in developing genuine democratic institutions'.[3]

Somewhat hidden in a clause that began with the punishment of war criminals, the Potsdam Agreement also announced the Allies' intention to intern various Germans. The clause opened with the statement that 'War criminals and those who have participated in planning or carrying out Nazi enterprises involving or resulting in atrocities or war crimes shall be arrested and brought to judgement.' It continued: 'Nazi leaders, influential Nazi supporters and high officials of Nazi organizations and institutions and any other persons dangerous to the occupation or its objectives shall be arrested and interned.'[4]

---

called the 'removal' of industrial equipment for the purpose of reparations. 'Extracts from the Report on the Tripartite Conference of Berlin (Potsdam)', 2 Aug. 1945, in Beate Ruhm von Oppen (ed.), *Documents on Germany under Occupation, 1945–1954* (London: Oxford University Press, 1955), 42–7. Another 'd', 'dismemberment', that is, breaking Germany up into a number of smaller states, had been discussed during the war and seemed to find support at the Yalta Conference of the 'Big Three' in early February 1945, but featured in neither word nor spirit in the Potsdam Agreement. See Philip E. Mosely, 'Dismemberment of Germany: The Allied Negotiations from Yalta to Potsdam', *Foreign Affairs* 28, no. 3 (1950), 487–98.

[3] 'Extracts from the Report on the Tripartite Conference of Berlin (Potsdam)', 2 Aug. 1945, in Ruhm von Oppen (ed.), *Documents on Germany*, 43–4.

[4] Ibid., 43, at III, A, 5. Remarkably, some historians overlook that the formulation 'any other persons dangerous to the occupation or its objectives' was the agreed Allied formulation and attribute it to a Soviet decree. Neiberg, *Potsdam*, 141.

This statement's location helps explain internment's relative neglect, as it was overshadowed somewhat by the preceding statement. The positioning also reflects internment's ambiguous relationship with criminal prosecution and has contributed to its association therewith. The internment of Nazi leaders et cetera was sufficiently closely related to the arrest and judgement of people deemed guilty of atrocities and war crimes to be placed in the same, and not in a separate, clause. Internment was nevertheless a distinct measure, whose targets, it seems, were not to be 'brought to judgement' as the war criminals were but to be detained because they were 'dangerous'. The Potsdam Agreement thus offered a differentiated approach to the Germans and demonstrated the Allies' shared resolve to intern certain groups of them.

If the agreement was the first public announcement of internment as an element" of Allied policy, Potsdam's significance can be overstated. Some authors claim that arrests were made 'on the basis' of Potsdam.[5] Noting that tens of thousands of Germans had already been detained, however, other authors suggest that it merely legitimized what the Allies were already doing.[6] Apparently premature pre-Potsdam arrests by the Soviets are sometimes taken to indicate the illegitimacy of Soviet practices, while those by the Americans are seen as evidence of particular American enthusiasm.[7] Such positions overlook that all four occupying powers – the 'Big Three' as well as France, which did not participate in the conference – made arrests before Potsdam and that they had agreed to do so. The western powers had previously issued joint arrest orders, while there was already tacit agreement with the Soviets that internment would occur and that it would begin as soon as Allied forces entered German territory. Internment was thus never intended to be a purely postwar measure, as emphasis on Potsdam implies. Indeed, for all the differences in their wartime experiences and their diverging interests with regard to Germany's future, the Allies had agreed by 1943 not only to defeat Germany militarily but also to destroy Nazism. Doing so became a

---

[5] Günter Agde, *Sachsenhausen bei Berlin: Speziallager Nr. 7 1945–1950: Kassiber, Dokumente und Studien* (Berlin: Aufbau Taschenbuch, 1994), 9; Volker Dotterweich, '"Arrest" und "Removal": Die amerikanische Besatzungsdirektive JCS 1067 und die Entnazifizierungskonzeption der Westmächte', in Walther L. Bernecker and Volker Dotterweich (eds.), *Deutschland in den internationalen Beziehungen des 19. und 20. Jahrhunderts: Festschrift für Josef Becker zum 65. Geburtstag* (Munich: Vögel, 1996), 287.

[6] Wember, *Umerziehung im Lager*, 13–14.

[7] Hubertus Knabe, 'Einführung', in Stiftung Gedenkstätte Berlin-Hohenschönhausen (ed.), *Totenbuch: Sowjetisches Speziallager Nr. 3 und Haftarbeitslager Berlin-Hohenschönhausen 1945–1949* (Berlin: Jaron Verlag, 2014), 11; Meyer, *Entnazifizierung von Frauen*, 15.

major war aim and a key goal of the occupation, and internment emerged during the war as an important step towards that end.[8]

This chapter examines the wartime formulation of internment policy within the context of the development of broader Allied approaches to Germany. It also compares the key arrest directives issued in 1944 and early 1945, that is, before Potsdam, and discusses the Allies' attempts to flesh out a common internment policy thereafter.[9] The chapter argues that internment was on the Allied agenda earlier and had broader support than many accounts suggest. In particular, it shows that, far from meekly following the Americans' lead, the British were initially ahead of the Americans in contemplating large-scale extrajudicial detention and that they were not fundamentally opposed to the Americans' subsequent expansion of arrest categories. Additionally, the chapter demonstrates that mass arrests were planned *before* the infamous intervention, in late August/early September 1944, into US policy towards Germany by Secretary of the Treasury Henry Morgenthau Jr., to whom they are often incorrectly attributed. The chapter shows further that assertions about the apparently unique approaches of individual occupying powers over-look considerable common ground. In particular, certain features of Soviet policy, which are often regarded as deviant, were in fact covered to some extent by Allied agreements or were not completely alien to western thinking. If differences among the Allies were thus less stark than is often assumed, there were nevertheless significant dissimilarities. The Allies never agreed on precisely who should be interned, and Soviet arrest categories were always broader than those of the western powers. There was also no agreement and indeed little discussion about what would happen to internees after their arrest.

Denazification, it has long been understood, was bedevilled by a failure to distinguish between its political, legal, and moral dimensions. Similarly, internment had diverse motives and objectives that were and are often insufficiently disentangled. The following account of wartime and early postwar policy development shows that, like the broader Allied reckoning with Nazism, internment had both preventative and punitive

---

[8] See Toby Thacker, *The End of the Third Reich: Defeat, Denazification and Nuremberg, January 1944–November 1946* (Stroud: Tempus, 2006). For a brief recent account of the failed attempt to develop a unified policy towards Germany, see Andrew Szanajda, *The Allies and the German Problem, 1941–1949: From Cooperation to Alternative Settlement* (Basingstoke: Palgrave, 2015).

[9] The need for a thorough account is highlighted by Merten's book, which mentions key moments and agents of the development of broad Allied policy towards Germany but barely refers to internment within that context, overlooks key statements of internment policy, and makes some crucial errors, which are discussed later. See Merten, *Gulag in East Germany*, 15–21.

dimensions.[10] Moreover, neither aspect should be interpreted too narrowly. Internment was connected in various ways to Allied discussions about the prosecution of German war criminals, but it was also always a measure in its own right. Its punitive side was primarily extrajudicial and only potentially judicial. Prevention, meanwhile, aimed at more than just ensuring the Allies' physical security. In light of extensive popular support for the Nazi regime, Germany's determined military resistance, the ruthlessness of hard-core groups such as the Gestapo (the Secret State Police) and the Schutzstaffel (SS, 'Protective Squadron', the Nazi Party's elite guard), and the apparent indoctrination and fanaticism of German youth, the Allies anticipated not just sabotage once they entered Germany but more general resistance, and they hoped to prevent both.[11] Internment was intended both to remove expected obstacles to Allied rule and to limit the postwar influence of people who were compromised in a variety of ways by their former roles. Thus, not only the Soviet Union but all the occupying powers conceived of internment not just in terms of security or punishment but also as a political measure.

Policy Development, 1943–1945

Internment is sometimes described as an American idea that the other powers adopted (with reluctance in the British case), but in fact the British and Soviets were ahead of the Americans in late 1943 and early 1944.[12] A Soviet draft surrender document from early October 1943 proposed to intern the SS and 'similar organizations' as well as 'leaders and further members' of the NSDAP.[13] The internment of 'Nazi personnel' also featured in a British 'Draft German Armistice' presented in mid-January 1944 to the new tripartite European Advisory Committee (EAC), which was established in London to prepare the terms of

---

[10] See Dotterweich, 'Die "Entnazifizierung"', 152–3; Dotterweich, '"Arrest" und "Removal"', 289; Klaus-Dietmar Henke, 'Die Trennung vom Nationalsozialismus: Selbstzerstörung, politische Säuberung, "Entnazifizierung", Strafverfolgung', in Klaus-Dietmar Henke and Hans Woller (eds.), *Politische Säuberung in Europa: Die Abrechnung mit Faschismus und Kollaboration nach dem Zweiten Weltkrieg* (Munich: Deutscher Taschenbuch Verlag, 1991), 21; Meyer, *Entnazifizierung von Frauen*, 14, 252–3.

[11] On the Gestapo, see Carsten Dams and Michael Stolle, *The Gestapo: Power and Terror in the Third Reich*, trans. Charlotte Ryland (Oxford: Oxford University Press, 2014). On the SS, see Adrian Weale, *The SS: A New History* (London: Little, Brown, 2010).

[12] Meyer, *Entnazifizierung von Frauen*, 14, 18; Niethammer, 'Alliierte Internierungslager (1998)', 99.

[13] Vorošilov to Molotov, 6 Oct. 1943, in Jochen Laufer and Georgij Kynin (eds.), *Die UdSSR und die deutsche Frage 1941–1948: Dokumente aus dem Archiv für Außenpolitik der Russischen Föderation*, vol. 1: *22. Juni 1941 bis 8. Mai 1945* (Berlin: Duncker & Humblot, 2004), 181.

Germany's capitulation and occupation.[14] Indeed, contrary to depictions of a lack of an independent British policy, internment was a key element of proposals that emerged from the British Foreign Office Research Department (FORD) from early March 1944.[15] In contrast, a plan presented by United States (US) Secretary of State Cordell Hull to the Moscow conference of foreign ministers in October 1943 spoke of 'eliminating' (i.e., dismissing), but not interning, 'All Nazi government officials, in whatever capacity'; American draft 'Provisions for Imposition upon Germany at Time of Surrender' circulated to the EAC in late January 1944 similarly spoke of disbanding Nazi organizations but not of interning their members; and concrete American discussion of targets for detention did not begin until May 1944.[16] Early British support for internment is also indicated by the fact that British officials thought it should be carried out in Austria as well as Germany. In April 1944, the Foreign Office's senior advisor on Germany and Austria, John Troutbeck, noted some 'omissions' from a draft directive for Austria's occupation that had been prepared by the combined Anglo-American military leadership at Supreme Headquarters, Allied Expeditionary Forces (SHAEF): 'There is no provision for interning persons on security grounds, war criminals being the only persons whose arrest is provided for.' He clearly thought that this oversight should be corrected.[17] It is worth noting here that planning for Austria's occupation ran in (partially belated) parallel with, but was rather subordinated to, that for Germany and was marked by ambivalence over whether to treat Austria

---

[14] 'Terms of Surrender for Germany – Memorandum by the United Kingdom Representative', 15 Jan. 1944, Annex 2: 'Draft German Armistice', in Herbert Elzer (ed.), *Dokumente zur Deutschlandpolitik: Europäische Beratende Kommission, 15. Dezember 1943 bis 31. August 1945* (= Series I, vol. 5) (Munich: R. Oldenbourg, 2003), hereafter *DzD* I, vol. 5, 741. On the EAC, see Herbert Elzer, 'Einführung', in ibid., xii–xxxiv; Hans-Günter Kowalski, 'Die "European Advisory Commission" als Instrument alliierter Deutschlandplanung 1943–1945', *Vierteljahreshefte für Zeitgeschichte* 19 (1971), 261–93.

[15] Cf. Jill Jones, 'Eradicating Nazism from the British Zone of Germany: Early Policy and Practice', *German History* 8, no. 2 (1990), 154–62. For an example of claims that only the Americans had their own denazification policy, see Rauh-Kühne, 'Life Rewarded the Latecomers', 65. On the German section in FORD, see Adolf M. Birke, 'Geschichtsauffassung und Deutschlandbild im Foreign Office Research Department', in Bernd Jürgen Wendt (ed.), *Das britische Deutschlandbild im Wandel des 19. und 20. Jahrhundert* (Bochum: Studienverlag Brockmeyer, 1984), 171–97.

[16] 'U.S. Proposal with Regard to the Treatment of Germany', in *Foreign Relations of the United States: Diplomatic Papers 1943*, vol. I: *General* (Washington, DC: United States Government Printing Office, 1963), 721–2; 'Provisions for Imposition upon Germany at Time of Surrender', 25 Jan. 1944, in *DzD* I, vol. 5, 764; Dolan, 'Isolating Nazism', 42.

[17] Minute by J. M. Troutbeck on a draft SHAEF interim directive about civil affairs in Austria, 18 Apr. 1944, the National Archives of the United Kingdom, London (TNA), FO 371/40386.

harshly as a constituent part of the 'Third Reich' or more leniently as the 'first victim' of Nazi aggression, as the tripartite Moscow Declaration had formulated in 1943, and one whose independence from Germany needed to be supported.[18]

Although internment featured in numerous policy proposals, it was not the subject of much inter- or intra-Allied debate during the war. One reason for this was reluctance in Allied capitals to engage in concrete planning for Germany's occupation. While some authors identify this as a Soviet peculiarity, it was shared to a large, if not the same, extent in Washington and London.[19] Another reason was that internment was uncontroversial. For instance, although it featured in several documents presented to the EAC in 1944 and 1945, it was never considered worthy of deliberation, presumably because no one objected. In addition to other proposals discussed here, securing German authorities' assistance with the 'dismissal and internment of Nazi personnel' was mentioned in various versions of a 'General Order' for the assumption of Allied control over Germany that were submitted to the EAC from November 1944 to June 1945, but the matter was never discussed.[20] In turn, the Potsdam Agreement's reference to internment was approved without debate. Christopher Knowles' observation that 'Disarmament and de-nazification ... appeared self-evident and did not need to be explained' applies also to internment specifically.[21]

A further reason for the lack of debate was that internment was largely a means to other ends rather than an end in itself. Internment was conceived as serving a multiplicity of larger goals, but its specific aims were poorly or inconsistently formulated in many policy statements, if they were stated at all. This reticence and inconsistency, along with the

---

[18] See Günter Bischof, 'Allied Plans and Policies for the Occupation of Austria, 1938–1955', in Rolf Steininger, Günter Bischof, and Michael Gehler (eds.), *Austria in the Twentieth Century* (New Brunswick, NJ: Transaction, 2002), 166–72.

[19] See Greiner, *Suppressed Terror*, 14; Hermann Graml, 'Strukturen und Motive alliierter Besatzungspolitik in Deutschland', and Hermann-J. Rupieper, 'Amerikanische Besatzungspolitik', both in Wolfgang Benz (ed.), *Deutschland unter alliierter Besatzung 1945–1949/55: Ein Handbuch* (Berlin: Akademie Verlag, 1999), 24, 34; Jeffrey K. Olick, *In the House of the Hangman: The Agonies of German Defeat, 1943–1949* (Chicago: University of Chicago Press, 2005), 40, 71–2.

[20] See 'Draft General Order', Nov. 1944; 'Minutes by the United States Delegation of Informal Meeting', 30 May 1945; 'Revised Draft Additional Requirements', Jun. 1945, all in *DzD* I, vol. 5, 967, 553, 602.

[21] 'Minutes of the Second Plenary Meeting', 18 Jul. 1945, in *Foreign Relations of the United States: The Conference of Berlin (The Potsdam Conference) 1945*, vol. II (Washington, DC: United States Government Printing Office, 1960), 90–1; Knowles, *Winning the Peace*, 32.

basic difficulty of reconstructing policy makers' intentions, especially in the USSR, make it difficult to pin down internment's precise purpose.[22] In various Allied proposals and directives in 1943–5, internment was variously conceived as a means of promoting the prosecution of war criminals, the disarmament of Nazi paramilitary organizations, the dissolution of the NSDAP and its affiliated organizations, the removal of Nazi and other German elites from positions of influence in German society, the broader destruction of Nazism and militarism, the elimination of threats to Allied security, the removal of obstacles to the achievement of the occupation's overall objectives, and the recruitment of labour for reparations. These goals partially overlapped. Some applied to all targets for detention, while others related only to particular groups. For instance, the already quoted draft Soviet surrender document of October 1943 treated the internment of SS personnel in the context of disarmament but that of NSDAP personnel as a measure accompanying the party's dissolution. Nevertheless, that proposal – like a Soviet capitulation document of early February 1944 that referred to internment under the heading 'Dissolution of the Nazi Party, Disarmament of Germany's Paramilitary Organizations and Extirpation of the Nazi Ideology' – contradicts claims that for the Soviets it had nothing to do with denazification, in the narrower or broader senses.[23] Moreover, none of the goals mentioned reflected an undifferentiated approach to questions of German responsibility or guilt.

The significance of some goals genuinely varied, while others were omitted from certain documents even though they had not disappeared from Allied thinking. The development of British proposals provides a good example. FORD's discussion paper on 'The Dissolution of Nazi Organizations and the Dismissal or Internment of Nazi Personnel' of early March 1944, written by the sociologist Thomas Humphrey Marshall, suggested at least three purposes:

Security will doubtless demand the internment of a considerable proportion of the officers of the para-military formations and of the Security Police (especially the Gestapo) and perhaps of many of the rank and file as well.... *In addition*, as many as possible of those engaged in the administration of occupied territories and all the men employed in guarding concentration camps should be interned in order that *individual charges* against them may be investigated. It will be desirable *on*

---

[22] Cf. Ralf Possekel (ed.), 'Sowjetische Lagerpolitik in Deutschland', in *Sowjetische Dokumente zur Lagerpolitik*, 19; Greiner, *Suppressed Terror*, 6–7.

[23] Vorošilov to Molotov, 6 Oct. 1943, and 'Dokument über die bedingungslose Kapitulation Deutschlands', 3 Feb. 1944, both in Laufer and Kynin (eds.), *UdSSR und die deutsche Frage*, 181, 296–7.

political grounds to intern ... the pillars of the Nazi regime [i.e., senior NSDAP personnel].[24]

Such explicit references to 'political' reasons contradict suggestions that western policy was aimed solely at security or criminal prosecution and that only Soviet internment was political. Marshall's paper also foreshadowed a fourth purpose that appeared more explicitly in a draft directive two weeks later:

It is possible that the internees, or a large part of them, will be sent out of Germany as a labour force on account of reparations.... Should this plan materialise, it may be desirable to intern whole categories of persons, such a[s] members of the SS, SA [Sturmabteilung, 'Storm Division', the Nazi stormtroopers], Gestapo etc.[25]

Subsequent versions of this document, which eventually became British Directive No. 7 on the 'Dissolution and Disbandment of Nazi Organizations', reduced the reasons to two: 'You will be required to detain and place under guard *for security and political reasons* a considerable number of persons who have held or are holding official positions' in Nazi organizations.[26] As will be shown, however, labour recruitment and criminal prosecution remained elements of British thinking beyond this point.

Proposals from other European governments confirm both that internment could serve numerous goals and that it was not an idea solely or primarily of the Americans or the 'Big Three'. A memorandum by the Netherlands government in exile in London from August 1944 stated that 'elements in the National Socialist Party, the German armed forces, the administration, financial and industrial circles or elsewhere in Germany who seem inclined to retard, hamper or obstruct the political

---

[24] Marshall, The Dissolution of Nazi Organizations and the Dismissal or Internment of Nazi Personnel, 4 Mar. 1944, 18 (emphasis added), TNA, FO 371/39141. Cf. Jones, 'Eradicating Nazism', 150; Dotterweich, '"Arrest" und "Removal"', 307. On the Security Police, see George C. Browder, *Foundations of the Nazi Police State: The Formation of Sipo and SD* (Lexington: University Press of Kentucky, 2004); Alexander V. Prusin, 'A Community of Violence: The SiPo/SD and Its Role in the Nazi Terror System in Generalbezirk Kiew', *Holocaust and Genocide Studies* 21, no. 1 (2007), 1–30.

[25] The Dissolution of Nazi Organizations and the Dismissal and Internment of Nazi Personnel, 17 Mar. 1944, 17, TNA, FO 371/39141. On the SA, see Daniel Siemens, *Stormtroopers: A New History of Hitler's Brownshirts* (New Haven, CT: Yale University Press, 2017).

[26] Draft of Directive under Article 54 of the Draft Terms of Surrender, circulated to the War Cabinet's Official Committee on Armistice Terms and Civil Administration on 15 May 1944, 6 (emphasis added), TNA, FO 371/39141. This wording was unchanged in the final version, circulated to the EAC on 27 Oct. 1944. See 'Directive No. 7: Dissolution and Disbandment of Nazi Organisations, etc.', in *DzD* I, vol. 5, 877.

regeneration of Germany should be prevented from pursuing their harmful activities. They should be interned or otherwise restrained.' It recommended specifically that 'principal leaders' of the NSDAP and its subordinate organizations 'be arrested and handed over to the Allies in order to be interned in an Allied country for an indefinite period'.[27] There was no mention of their prosecution. In contrast, in early September 1944 the Norwegian government in exile advocated that German authorities be required to assist 'in interning forthwith and keeping in custody until such time as the authorities of the United Nations may otherwise direct, any or all members and former members' of the Gestapo and the SS, with a view to their prosecution for war crimes. This position reflected discussions dating back to spring 1944 within the United Nations War Crimes Commission.[28]

Beyond political and prosecutorial considerations, internment was more closely related to the disarmament and demobilization of Germany's armed forces than is often recognized. Indeed, there was some fluidity over which personnel would be detained as civilians and which as POWs. The Soviets and various European governments in exile stressed that Allied disarmament policy had to look beyond the Wehrmacht (Nazi Germany's armed forces) to consider other armed groups; otherwise they might avoid being disarmed and contained and remain a threat.[29] The Allies therefore repeatedly specified that disarmament measures also applied to paramilitary and other armed organizations, sometimes including the police. For instance, the British 'Draft German Armistice' of January 1944 stated that 'all references to the German armed forces or forces under German command shall be deemed to include the Nazi Militia, SS, SA, police and such other military, semi-military, pre- or

---

[27] 'Memorandum by the Netherlands Government in Exile, Terms of Surrender for Germany and Machinery for their Enforcement', 26 Aug. 1944, in *DzD* I, vol. 5, 832, 840. The Netherlands government in exile had already developed plans for the internment of Dutch collaborators. See Helen Grevers and Lawrence Van Haecke, 'The Use of Administrative Internment after WWII: The Different Policies of the Belgian and Dutch Governments', in Margo de Koster, Hervé Leuwer, Dirk Luyten, and Xavier Rousseaux (eds.), *Justice in Wartime and Revolutions: Europe, 1795–1950* (Brussels: Algemeen Rijskarchief, 2012), 285–7.

[28] 'Memorandum of the Royal Norwegian Government in Exile, Proposed Terms of Surrender to Be Imposed upon Germany', Annex B: 'War Criminals', 2 Sep. 1944, in *DzD* I, vol. 5, 859; Arieh J. Kochavi, *Prelude to Nuremberg: Allied War Crimes Policy and the Question of Punishment* (Chapel Hill: University of North Carolina Press, 1998), 102–3.

[29] See, for instance, 'Minutes of the Fourth Formal Meeting of the EAC', 3 Mar. 1944, in *DzD* I, vol. 5, 22. On the Wehrmacht, see Rolf-Dieter Müller, *Hitler's Wehrmacht, 1935–1945*, trans. Janet W. Ancker (Lexington: University Press of Kentucky, 2016).

para-military or armed units, formations or associations as the United Nations may specify.'[30]

In July 1944, the EAC agreed that each Allied power had the right, but not the obligation, to declare as POWs 'the SS, SA, and Gestapo, and all other forces or auxiliary organisations equipped with weapons'.[31] This position was reaffirmed by the EAC in May 1945 and announced in the four powers' 'Declaration Regarding the Defeat of Germany and the Assumption of Supreme Authority with Respect to Germany' of 5 June 1945, known as the Berlin Declaration.[32] This policy helps contextualize the Soviet practice, discussed later, of treating members of the SA, the SS, and the People's Militia (*Volkssturm*) as POWs. It also explains Anglo-American vacillation between handling members of the Waffen-SS (Armed SS) under disarmament measures and including them along with members of the regular SS in civilian internment. It is, furthermore, a useful reminder of the wartime context of the conceptualization and early implementation of internment, which is sometimes incorrectly seen as a purely postwar measure.[33] In many respects, internment was the civilian variant of the detention of POWs. Indeed, Bodo Ritscher regards it as 'a specific form of war captivity rather than of "penal custody"', while Dieter Stiefel, going too far, calls it 'a military measure, perhaps comparable with war captivity'.[34] It was comparable with war captivity but was not purely a military measure.

Although the Allies agreed that internment should take place, they envisaged it on rather different scales. In February 1944, the Soviets proposed detaining all members of the SA and the Security Police and NSDAP functionaries down to the lowest levels, including Local Group Leaders (Ortsgruppenleiter, leaders of local party groups), Cell Leaders (Zellenleiter), and Block Leaders (Blockleiter).[35] In contrast, British

---

[30] 'Draft German Armistice', 15 Jan. 1944, in *DzD* I, vol. 5, 744.

[31] 'Minutes of the Seventh Formal Meeting', 25 Jul. 1944, 'Unconditional Surrender of Germany', Article 2, paragraphs a and b, in *DzD* I, vol. 5, 163.

[32] 'Minutes of the Third Formal Meeting', 12 May 1945, in *DzD* I, vol. 5, 487; 'Declaration Regarding the Defeat of Germany and the Assumption of Supreme Authority with Respect to Germany', 5 Jun. 1945, in Ruhm von Oppen (ed.), *Documents on Germany*, 30.

[33] See Horn, *Internierungs- und Arbeitslager*, 19. On the People's Militia, see David K. Yelton, *Hitler's Volkssturm: The Nazi Militia and the Fall of Germany, 1944–1945* (Lawrence: University Press of Kansas, 2002); Sven Keller, *Volksgemeinschaft am Ende: Gesellschaft und Gewalt 1944/45* (Munich: Oldenbourg Verlag, 2013), 131–45.

[34] Ritscher, *Spezlager Nr. 2 Buchenwald*, 22; Dieter Stiefel, *Entnazifizierung in Österreich* (Vienna: Europaverlag, 1981), 263.

[35] 'Protokoll zu den Kapitulationsbedingungen (Entwurf)', 3 Feb. 1944, in Laufer and Kynin (eds.), *UdSSR und die deutsche Frage*, 309. On the local party functionaries, see Carl-Wilhelm Reibel, *Das Fundament der Diktatur: Die NSDAP-Ortsgruppen 1932–1945*

proposals such as the FORD paper of early March and Directive No. 7 spoke of interning NSDAP officials only down to the position of District Leader (Kreisleiter) and the rank of Area Leader (Bereichsleiter, the rank held by Deputy District Leaders), respectively.[36] For their part, the French, who had not been party to the EAC's earlier deliberations, assumed in early 1945 that most people wanted for punishment would be found among POWs (or groups declared as such) and seemed to want to keep the number of civilian internees as small as possible. A suggestion in September 1945 by the French member of the ACA's Nazi Arrest and Denazification Subcommittee (on which more later) to arrest all NSDAP *members* seems to have been mere verbal radicalism and was rejected outright by the other powers' representatives, who recognized that it was impossible and unnecessary to intern several million party members.[37]

Among the western powers, the Americans developed the most extensive plans, but this should not be attributed solely to Secretary of the Treasury Henry Morgenthau Jr., as it often is. Morgenthau has gone down in history as embodying the desire for a 'tough', even vengeful, approach to Germany due to his criticism (not least to President Franklin D. Roosevelt) of the American military's plans for Germany's treatment as too soft and his development of the notorious 'Morgenthau Plan', which called among other things for Germany's dismemberment and for the deindustrialization of the Ruhr and Rhineland.[38] American plans for extensive denazification and internment are often attributed to

---

(Paderborn: Ferdinand Schöningh, 2002); Phillip Wegehaupt, 'Funktionäre und Funktionseliten der NSDAP: Vom Blockleiter zum Gauleiter', in Benz (ed.), *Wie wurde man Parteigenosse?*, 39–59.

[36] Marshall, The Dissolution of Nazi Organizations and the Dismissal or Internment of Nazi Personnel, 4 Mar. 1944, 18, TNA, FO 371/39141; 'Directive No. 7: Dissolution and Disbandment of Nazi Organisations, etc.', in *DzD* I, vol. 5, 877. On the District Leaders, see Armin Nolzen, 'Funktionäre in einer faschistischen Partei: Die Kreisleiter der NSDAP, 1932/33 bis 1944/45', in Till Kössler and Helke Stadtland (eds.), *Vom Funktionieren der Funktionäre: Politische Interessenvertretung und gesellschaftliche Integration in Deutschland nach 1933* (Essen: Klartext, 2004), 37–75; Michael Rademacher, *Die Kreisleiter der NSDAP im Gau Weser-Ems* (Marburg: Tectum Verlag, 2005).

[37] 'War Criminals – Memorandum by the French Delegation', 21 Feb. 1945, in *DzD* I, vol. 5, 1041; Möhler, *Entnazifizierung in Rheinland-Pfalz und im Saarland*, 239; Allied Control Authority, Directorate of Internal Affairs and Communications, Public Safety Committee, Nazi Arrest and Denazification Subcommittee (NADSC), Minutes of the 7th Meeting, 24 Sep. 1945, 1, TNA, FO 1005/635; NADSC, Draft Directive on the Arrest of Nazis and Other Dangerous Persons, 5, TNA, FO 1005/638, DIAC/APSC/NADSC/P (45) 2.

[38] For an account of the events, see Michael Beschloss, *The Conquerors: Roosevelt, Truman and the Destruction of Hitler's Germany, 1941–1945* (New York: Simon & Schuster, 2002). For a critical reading of Morgenthau's mythologization, see Olick, *In the House of the Hangman*, 29–40.

Morgenthau.[39] Yet even before his intervention in late August/early September 1944, SHAEF had adopted proposals for extensive arrests. They were developed largely by German émigré social theorist Herbert Marcuse, who was serving in the US Army's Office of Strategic Services.[40] The fourth draft of SHAEF's *Handbook of Military Government for Germany Prior to Defeat or Surrender*, dated 15 August 1944, included most of Marcuse's categories, with an estimated total of well over 150,000 people to be interned. They included NSDAP Local Group Leaders, non-commissioned officers (NCOs) in the SA and the SS from the rank of Scharführer (staff sergeant) upward, as well as ca. 5,000 civil servants, numerous judicial officials, and more than 300 'business leaders' in particular positions. An indeterminate additional number of 'businessmen who willingly accepted Nazi honors' was also to be detained.[41]

In fact, far from American arrest categories expanding dramatically due to Morgenthau's intervention, there was little difference between the fourth draft that preceded it in August and the final version that was published in December 1944 as SHAEF's *Handbook for Military Government in Germany Prior to Defeat or Surrender*.[42] Indeed, in three respects the final version was less severe: it made the detention of NSDAP Local Group Leaders discretionary rather than mandatory, excluded NCOs in the SA, and did not include business leaders. The only sizable addition was Waffen-SS officers. The earlier version had stated that the Waffen-SS was to be handled under disarmament provisions and its personnel interned as POWs. Morgenthau's intervention thus hardly radicalized western internment policy. To be sure, his plans for the German economy and his proposal to execute Nazi 'arch criminals' without trial met with opposition in Washington, especially from US Secretary of War

---

[39] E.g., Dotterweich, 'Die "Entnazifizierung"', 136; Dotterweich, '"Arrest" und "Removal"', 301; Wember, *Umerziehung im Lager*, 16–17; Frederick Taylor, *Exorcising Hitler: The Occupation and Denazification of Germany* (London: Bloomsbury, 2011), 253.

[40] Herbert Marcuse, 'Dissolution of the Nazi Party and Its Affiliated Organizations', 22 Jul. 1944, in Franz Neumann, Herbert Marcuse, and Otto Kirchheimer, *Secret Reports on Nazi Germany: The Frankfurt School Contribution to the War Effort*, ed. Raffaele Laudani (Princeton, NJ: Princeton University Press, 2013), 256–9. Cf. Priemel, *Betrayal*, 42–5.

[41] Handbook of Military Government for Germany, 15 Aug. 1944, TNA, FO 371/39166. See tables D, E, and F, as well as chapter II, paragraphs 22 and 23, for the judicial and police positions subject to detention. Business and industrial elites were also key targets of wartime proposals for prosecution. See Priemel, *Betrayal*, 56, 63.

[42] Compare the August version just quoted with SHAEF Office of the Chief of Staff, *Handbook for Military Government in Germany Prior to Defeat or Surrender*, Dec. 1944, available at: cgsc.cdmhost.com/cdm/ref/collection/p4013coll9/id/11 (accessed 6 Feb. 2019). See part III, chapter II, paragraphs 277, 283–6, and 'Table "C"': Nazi Party, Police, Para-military and Governmental Officers to Be Interned'.

Henry Stimson, and beyond, although numerous officials in London – including Prime Minister Winston Churchill – also advocated summary executions at various points. Despite disagreements on these aspects of Morgenthau's proposal, the detention of 'large groups of particularly objectionable elements, such as the SS and the Gestapo', was a 'point of agreement' across the US state, war, and treasury departments in early September, at the height of the inter-departmental dispute Morgenthau had unleashed.[43] The development of Allied internment policy thus confirms Jeffrey Olick's contention that 'Morgenthau's proposals were not as extreme and outside of the discourse' as both his rivals and the subsequent mythologization of the 'Morgenthau Plan' have suggested.[44]

In London, the Foreign Office had some concerns about the expanded categories of the August draft of the *Handbook* but no fundamental objections to mass arrests. Marshall thought that the new 'proposals for dismissal and detention are very sweeping'. He was 'very doubtful whether we want to imprison a lot of girls', referring to the proposed arrest of functionaries in the female wing of the Hitler Youth, the Bund Deutscher Mädel (BDM, League of German Girls). But he did not object to other categories. His colleague Con O'Neill questioned whether the envisaged 'detention of a total of some 150,000 people ... would be administratively feasible', but not whether it was desirable or necessary; he believed the proposals 'go rather too far, but that is a mistake in the right direction'. Troutbeck echoed these sentiments, arguing that 'it is better to aim pretty high and fall short of the aim if circumstances make this necessary, rather than to err on the side of leniency'. He suggested excluding female BDM leaders and NCOs of the SA but wanted to be able to detain even lower police ranks than was proposed.[45] The British were reluctant to intern NSDAP Local Group Leaders and especially civil servants, but the latter comprised only a tiny portion of the proposed

[43] Riddleberger to Secretary of State, 4 Sep. 1944; Stimson to Roosevelt, 5 Sep. 1944; 'Memorandum by Secretary of War', 9 Sep. 1944, all in *Foreign Relations of the United States: The Conference at Quebec 1944* (Washington, DC: United States Government Printing Office, 1972), hereafter *FRUS Quebec 1944*, 93–4, 98, 124–5, 127; Michael R. Marrus, *The Nuremberg War Crimes Trial 1945–46: A Documentary History* (Boston, MA: Bedford Books, 1997), 23, 33. Cf. Dolan, 'Isolating Nazism', 47; Priemel, *Betrayal*, 68.

[44] Olick, *In the House of the Hangman*, 33.

[45] Minute by T. H. Marshall, 24 Aug. 1944; O'Neill, Preliminary Minute on SHAEF Handbook, 18 Aug. 1944; J. M. Troutbeck to Charles Peak, SHAEF, with Detailed Criticisms of 'Handbook of Military Government for Germany', 29 Aug. 1944, all in TNA, FO 371/39166. Cf. Biddiscombe, *Denazification of Germany*, 27. On the BDM, see Michael Kater, *Hitler Youth* (Cambridge, MA: Harvard University Press, 2004), 70–112.

targets.[46] Such groups aside, there was a large core of Nazi personnel whose detention was uncontroversial among the major and lesser Allies and among the advocates of a 'hard' and 'soft' peace on both sides of the Atlantic.

For a long time, there was negligible consideration – especially but not only in Moscow – of what would be done with internees.[47] Yet punishment was clearly on the agenda. There was talk in the Soviet People's Commissariat for Foreign Affairs in January 1944 of severely punishing broadly defined 'war criminals', including 'the apparatus of the NSDAP on all levels', SA and SS members, and leadership circles in the military and administration.[48] Soviet authorities gave little attention to how this desire related to internment. According to one leading official in March 1944, 'it is necessary to isolate and remove the Nazis, to wherever'.[49] That same month British planners considered the question more thoroughly. Marshall's initial discussion paper recognized that internment

cannot be used as a means of permanently eliminating Nazis from German life ... The aim, therefore, should be, once order has been established, to reduce internment until it covers primarily those against whom specific charges are being made.... Those detained after these charges have been dealt with would then be convicted criminals, and not political prisoners.[50]

Such proposals – which acknowledged *sotto voce* the political status of internees prior to any such conviction – focused on finding individual war criminals among the mass of detainees.

Plans for more systematic prosecutions emerged in the United States in August and September 1944. It is here, rather than in the arrest provisions themselves, that one finds Morgenthau's indirect influence.

---

[46] Troutbeck to Major General Anderson, War Office, 19 Sep. 1944, TNA, FO 371/39166.

[47] Cf. Niethammer, *Mitläuferfabrik*, 57; Horn, *Internierungs- und Arbeitslager*, 19; Jones, 'Eradicating Nazism', 151; Wember, *Umerziehung im Lager*, 14, 20; Biddiscombe, *Denazification of Germany*, 25–7; Paul Y. Hammond, 'Directives for the Occupation of Germany: The Washington Controversy', in Harold Stein (ed.), *American Civil-Military Decisions: A Book of Case Studies* (Birmingham: University of Alabama Press, 1963), 391.

[48] Majskij to Molotov, 11 Jan. 1944, in Laufer and Kynin (eds.), *UdSSR und die deutsche Frage*, 248. On Soviet war crimes prosecution in the lead-up to the International Military Tribunal, see George Ginsburgs, *Moscow's Road to Nuremberg: The Soviet Background to the Trial* (The Hague: Nijhoff, 1996); Francine Hirsch, 'The Soviets at Nuremberg: International Law, Propaganda, and the Making of the Postwar Order', *The American Historical Review* 113, no. 3 (2008), 701–30.

[49] Gen. Manuil'skij at 92nd meeting of Litvinov commission, 14 Mar. 1944, in Laufer and Kynin (eds.), *UdSSR und die deutsche Frage*, 369.

[50] Marshall, 'The Dissolution of Nazi Organizations and the Dismissal or Internment of Nazi Personnel', 4 Mar. 1944, 18, TNA, FO 371/39141. Cf. Jones, 'Eradicating Nazism', 150.

As already mentioned, in early September, the state, war, and treasury departments agreed on interning 'large groups of particularly objectionable elements' but did not go further than suggesting that they be 'possibly tried'.[51] In response to Roosevelt's criticism – prompted by Morgenthau – of American military planning for Germany's treatment as too 'soft', in late August Stimson proposed punishing 'the Nazi leaders' and then going 'down by steps into the subordinates' responsible for war crimes, particularly the Gestapo and the SA, all of whom would be interned.[52] First drafts of the 'Morgenthau Plan' in early September proposed detaining all members of various Nazi organizations, senior government and police officials, and 'all leading public figures closely identified with Nazism', 'until the extent of the guilt of each individual is determined'.[53] Seeking to wrest the initiative back from Morgenthau and appalled by his proposal for summary executions of 'arch criminals', Stimson sought and found a tough but feasible and defensible alternative. On 15 September, War Department lawyer Lieutenant Colonel Murray C. Bernays proposed a method for dealing with the mass, systemic nature of Nazi criminality. It focused not on 'the commission of specific criminal acts' but on the individual guilt 'that follows inevitably from the mere fact of voluntary membership in organizations devised solely to commit such acts'. In a first step, key individuals 'considered to be representative of the defendant organizations' would be tried for conspiracy to commit war and other crimes. Following their conviction, in a second step, all other members of the organizations could be charged with participating in the conspiracy merely on the basis of their membership.[54] The notion of prosecuting criminal organizations was born.

This novel plan had three main effects on internment's conceptualization. First, it further justified mass detention based on organizational membership. According to one postwar estimate, one million individuals who had survived the war could potentially be charged with membership

---

[51] Riddleberger to Secretary of State, 4 Sep. 1944, in *FRUS Quebec 1944*, 94.

[52] John McCloy, 'Telephone Conversation with Secretary Stimson', 28 Aug. 1944, in *FRUS Quebec 1944*, 76–7. Cf. Hammond, 'Directives for the Occupation', 361.

[53] 'Suggested Post-Surrender Program for Germany', 1 Sep. 1944; and 'Suggested Post-Surrender Program for Germany', appendix B: 'Punishment of Certain War Crimes and Treatment of Special Groups', 5 Sep. 1944, both in *FRUS Quebec 1944*, 88, 106–7. Cf. Bradley F. Smith, *The Road to Nuremberg* (London: André Deutsch, 1981), 28–9.

[54] Murray C. Bernays, 'Trial of European War Criminals', 15 Sep. 1944, in Bradley F. Smith (ed.), *The American Road to Nuremberg: The Documentary Record 1944–1945* (Standford, CA: Hoover Institution Press, 1982), 35–6. Cf. Smith, *Road to Nuremberg*, 50–2; Stanislaw Pomorski, 'Conspiracy and Criminal Organization', in George Ginsburgs and V. N. Kudriavtsev (eds.), *The Nuremberg Trial and International Law* (Dordrecht: Martinus Nijhoff, 1990), 213–17; Priemel, *Betrayal*, 69–70.

of at least one of the organizations that were eventually arraigned by the International Military Tribunal (IMT) at Nuremberg.[55] Second, it strengthened internment's juridical-prosecutorial purpose. Third, it bifurcated that prosecutorial dimension: not only would individual criminal suspects be identified among detainees and prosecuted, but large numbers of members of the targeted organizations would remain in detention pending the outcome of the initial trial and, so it was intended, their subsequent summary proceedings. It should be emphasized, however, that internment long predated the notion of organizational criminality, its targets went well beyond the groups facing indictment, and prosecution was never the sole aim. The last point is confirmed by references to security in a key memorandum on prosecution submitted to Roosevelt by the Secretaries of State and War and the Attorney General in January 1945. It stated that

the Nazi leaders created and utilized a numerous organization for carrying out the acts of oppression and terrorism which their program involved. Chief among the instrumentalities used by them are the SS, from the personnel of which the Gestapo is constituted, and the SA. These organizations consist of exactingly screened volunteers who are pledged to absolute obedience. The members of these organizations are also the personnel primarily relied upon to carry on postwar guerilla and underground operations.[56]

Punishment and security thus reinforced each other as central concerns.

A further aim or at least consideration was recruitment of labour for reparatory purposes. It is sometimes suggested that only the Soviets ever saw internees as a potential workforce or that the western powers entertained this possibility only briefly in response to Soviet interest at the Yalta Conference of the 'Big Three' in early February 1945. Yet, as Ralf Possekel argues, 'the western Allies had no principled objections to the forced employment of German labour' as reparation in kind.[57] Moreover, they entertained the option of using internment to this end for at least a year. As already mentioned, British proposals from early 1944 saw internment as a possible step towards recruiting reparatory labour. In spring and summer 1944, American discussions also viewed SS, Gestapo, and NSDAP personnel that were among the primary targets for internment as potential members of labour battalions, alongside, or in

---

[55] Plischke, 'Denazifying the Reich', 157. Cf. David A. Messenger, 'Beyond War Crimes: Denazification, "Obnoxious" Germans and US Policy in Franco's Spain after the Second World War', *Contemporary European History* 20, no. 4 (2011), 460.

[56] 'Memorandum for the President, Trial and Punishment of Nazi War Criminals', 22 Jan. 1945, in Smith (ed.), *American Road to Nuremberg*, 118–19.

[57] Possekel, 'Sowjetische Lagerpolitik', 32. See Niethammer, 'Alliierte Internierungslager (1998)', 101.

preference to, Wehrmacht soldiers.[58] In September, Morgenthau proposed that 'Apart from the question of established guilt for special crimes, mere membership in the S.S., the Gestapo and similar groups will constitute the basis for inclusion into compulsory labor battalion to serve outside Germany for reconstruction purposes.'[59] The generally more moderate Department of State entertained similar ideas and its reasoning highlights the continuing intersection of various objectives. Its 'Yalta Conference Briefing Book' of January 1945 endorsed the possibility of

the selection of personnel for labor reparation, in case certain of our Allies insist on that form of reparation, from the ranks of active Nazis and of Nazi organizations such as the SS rather than by an indiscriminate draft.

This recommended procedure would place the burden where it most justly belongs and would remove from Germany some of the most dangerous political influences during the period when an effort must be made to establish an acceptable government.[60]

This suggestion shows, again, that a range of motives reinforced one another, but also that tripartite agreement to the use of German labour as reparation in kind at Yalta was neither anomalous nor merely a superficial reaction to Soviet proposals. Indeed, according to opinion polls, in March 1945, 62% of Americans supported the idea, up from 46% in January 1944.[61] The suggestion also indicates that, even if demands for reparations derived from a sense of collective German responsibility or liability, the western Allies at least were considering which groups of Germans were most responsible.

Two weeks after Yalta, the Americans and British were still weighing the advantages and disadvantages of deploying civilian or POW labour in Germany and abroad. For a number of reasons, they decided it was

---

[58] See, for instance, 'Memorandum by the Committee on Post-War Programs: The Treatment of Germany: Policy Recommendations', 31 May 1944; 'Memorandum by the Executive Committee on Foreign Economic Policy: Report on Reparation, Restitution, and Property Rights–Germany', 12 Aug. 1944, both in *Foreign Relations of the United States: Diplomatic Papers 1944*, vol. I: *General* (Washington, DC: United States Government Printing Office, 1966), hereafter *FRUS 1944 I*, 305, 295–6.

[59] See both versions of the 'Suggested Post-Surrender Program for Germany', 1 and 5 Sep. 1944, in *FRUS Quebec 1944*, 88, 107.

[60] State Department, 'Briefing Book Paper: The Treatment of Germany', 12 Jan. 1945, in *Foreign Relations of the United States: The Conferences at Malta and Yalta 1945* (Washington, DC: United States Government Printing Office, 1955), hereafter *FRUS Yalta 1945*, 182. The Secretary of State repeated this proposal in March. 'Draft Directive for the Treatment of Germany', 10 Mar. 1945, in *FRUS 1945 III*, 435.

[61] 'Protocol on German Reparation', 11 Feb. 1945, in *FRUS Yalta 1945*, 983; Steven Casey, *Cautious Crusade: Franklin D. Roosevelt, American Public Opinion, and the War against Nazi Germany* (New York: Oxford University Press, 2001), 143, 209.

feasible to use only POW labour outside Germany, while civilian labour was preferred inside Germany.[62] The question remained which groups might be accorded POW status and thus used abroad. At the end of February, Sir William Strang of the Foreign Office apparently 'felt that it would be desirable' to give 'first place in the employment of prisoners of war outside Germany to Nazi groups such as the SS, SA and Gestapo', a position that Philip Edward Mosely, the political advisor of the US delegation in London, elicited and with which he seemed to agree.[63] Yet the Americans and British wanted to reduce the number of POWs and certainly not to extend POW rights and privileges to such highly compromised Nazi personnel. They therefore abandoned plans to use the key groups targeted for civilian internment as sources of reparatory labour, at least for deployment outside Germany.[64]

In contrast, and unencumbered by legal or moral qualms or by obligations regarding POWs' treatment under the 1929 Geneva 'Convention Relative to the Treatment of Prisoners of War' to which it was not a signatory, the Soviet Union at least initially pursued its ardent desire for civilian and POW labour. As soon as Soviet forces entered territories with ethnic German populations in South Eastern Europe in late 1944, they began interning and deporting ethnic German men and then women to the USSR in large numbers, reaching ca. 110,000 by February 1945.[65] In early 1945 when the Red Army advanced into the eastern parts of the German Reich that would soon be transferred to the USSR and Poland, all fit German men aged between seventeen and fifty were to be 'mobilized'; by the time this practice was halted in mid-April, almost 100,000 had been deported.[66] Additionally, of a further ca. 138,000 Germans

---

[62] 'Use of German Labour by the Allies after the Surrender of Germany – Memorandum by the UK Representative', 27 Feb. 1945, in *DzD* I, vol. 5, 1043–5. Dolan identifies continuing uncertainty in mid-March. Dolan, 'Isolating Nazism', 84.

[63] 'Memorandum by the Political Adviser of the US Delegation', 28 Feb. 1945, in *DzD* I, vol. 5, 1389.

[64] See the discussion of work in Chapter 4. On extensive French use of POW labour in France and the controversial question of transferring POWs to civilian status, see Arthur L. Smith Jr., 'Die deutschen Kriegsgefangenen und Frankreich', *Vierteljahreshefte für Zeitgeschichte* 32, no. 1 (1984), 109–11; Resmini, 'Lager der Besatzungsmächte', 611; Fabien Théofilakis, *Les prisonniers de guerre allemands, France, 1944–1949: Une captivité de guerre en temps de paix* (Paris: Fayard, 2014). See also Richard D. Wiggers, 'The United States and the Denial of Prisoner of War (POW) Status at the End of the Second World War', *Militärgeschichtliche Zeitschrift* 52, no. 1 (1993), 91–104.

[65] Possekel, 'Sowjetische Lagerpolitik', 35. Cf. Filip Slaveski, *The Soviet Occupation of Germany: Hunger, Mass Violence, and the Struggle for Peace, 1945–1947* (Cambridge: Cambridge University Press, 2013), 74.

[66] 'Beschluß des Staatlichen Verteidigungskomitees Nr. 7467ss zur Unterbindung terroristischer Anschläge und zur Ausweitung der Mobilisierung von Deutschen', 3 Feb. 1945; and 'Schreiben des Volkskommissars für Inneres Berija an Stalin', 16

arrested according to the People's Commissariat for Internal Affairs (NKVD) Order No. 0016 of 11 January 1945, on which more shortly, ca. 66,000 civilians were deported, irrespective of their physical fitness, to work in internment camps in the USSR, while members of paramilitary organizations were transferred to POW camps, where they also laboured.[67] All of this would seem to suggest, as Alexander von Plato argues, the (initial) 'precedence for the Soviet Union of the question of workers above punishment of Nazis and denazification', yet it also helped the territorial and population changes to Germany's east.[68] The indiscriminate deportation of civilians stopped in April with NKVD Order No. 00315, the key directive governing internment in the Soviet zone of Germany, which is discussed shortly. Yet subsequent attempts to mobilize labour from the camps established there indicate that Soviet leader Joseph Stalin had not abandoned his interest in internees as a source of labour but merely put it on hold. They remained a 'labor reserve on call'.[69]

Allied Directives for Arrest and Internment, 1944–1945

If the Soviet pursuit of civilian labour marked a key difference from the policy (if not the deliberations) of the western powers and the end (or suspension) of deportations therefore constituted a significant convergence, additional policy developments in April 1945 brought about further, if incomplete, convergence. This resulted from a degree of moderation of initially more expansive Soviet arrest categories and a simultaneous extension of originally more limited western plans. Let us begin with the western side.

Until April 1945, western policy was contained in two documents, both of which dealt with the period of occupation prior to Germany's capitulation. The first was a 'Directive for Military Government in Germany Prior to Defeat or Surrender', which SHAEF had prepared and which the Anglo-American Combined Chiefs of Staff (CCS) issued

Apr. 1945, both in Possekel (ed.), *Sowjetische Dokumente*, 147, 174. Cf. Service, *Germans to Poles*, 74–5; Holm Kirsten, *Das sowjetische Speziallager Nr. 4 Landsberg/Warthe* (Göttingen: Wallstein, 2005), 21–6.

[67] 'Beschluss des Staatlichen Verteidigungskomitees Nr. 7161ss zur Mobilisierung und Internierung von arbeitsfähigen Deutschen für den Einsatz in der UdSSR', 16 Dec. 1944, in Possekel (ed.), *Sowjetische Dokumente*, 133–5; Possekel, 'Sowjetische Lagerpolitik', 46, 47.

[68] Alexander von Plato, 'Zur Geschichte des sowjetischen Speziallagersystems in Deutschland: Einführung', in von Plato (ed.), *Studien und Berichte*, 25. See Service, *Germans to Poles*.

[69] This is Greiner's rendering of Niethammer. Greiner, *Suppressed Terror*, 38.

to General Dwight Eisenhower as Supreme Commander, Allied Expeditionary Forces, on 28 April 1944. Known as CCS 551, it called – under different headings – for the arrest of:

- 'Adolf Hitler, his chief Nazi associates and all persons suspected of having committed war crimes'
- 'the heads of all ministries and other high political functionaries of the German Reich and those Germans who have held high positions in occupied allied countries found within occupied territory'
- 'high Party officials' and
- members of the Security Police, including the entire personnel of the Gestapo and the Security Service [Sicherheitsdienst, SD], but not the Criminal Police.

The aim of arresting the first two groups was investigation and punishment, while arresting NSDAP officials was supposed to aid the party's dissolution. The vagueness of the reference to party officials confirms the point made earlier that American discussion of specific internment targets did not start until May 1944.[70]

The second, more detailed document was the SHAEF *Handbook for Military Government in Germany Prior to Defeat or Surrender*, which, as already mentioned, went through multiple iterations before Eisenhower issued the final version in December 1944. Under the heading 'Nazi Officials, War Criminals and Other Criminals', it called, like CCS 551, for the arrest of Hitler, his associates, war criminals, and German officials from the European territories Germany had occupied. They were to be held for investigation and further unspecified instructions, presumably prosecution by the Allies or transfer to the formerly occupied countries. In contrast, the detention of other, larger categories, was presented and explained under the heading 'Eradication of Nazism':

An essential step, complementary to the removal of Nazis from governmental positions and positions of influence, will be the internment of certain government and Party officials and members of police and para-military formations, whose presence at large might be a threat to the security of the Allied Forces or an impediment to the attainment of the objectives of Military Government in Germany.

---

[70] 'Directive for Military Government in Germany Prior to Defeat or Surrender' (CCS 551), 28 Apr. 1944, in *FRUS 1944 I*, 219–20. Cf. Niethammer, *Mitläuferfabrik*, 57; Meyer, *Entnazifizierung von Frauen*, 38. On the SD, see Browder, *Foundations of the Nazi Police State*; Michael Wildt (ed.), *Nachrichtendienst, politische Elite und Mordeinheit: Der Sicherheitsdienst des Reichsführers SS* (Hamburg: Hamburger Edition, 2003).

In addition to an estimated 15,000 members each of the Gestapo and the SD, several hundred senior police officials were to be interned. More significantly, the *Handbook* defined CCS 551's 'high Party officials' as anyone in the NSDAP holding the rank of Area Leader or higher (estimated at 30,000 people), while Local Group Leaders were to be subject to surveillance and discretionary internment. Additionally, all SS and Waffen-SS officers were to be arrested, as were officials at certain ranks in the SA, the Hitler Youth, and other Nazi organizations, giving a total of over 133,000 members of paramilitary groups. Finally, more than 4,400 public officials – including an estimated 3,000 who had served in occupied territories, 700 district administrators (*Landräte*), and 95 lord mayors of cities with more than 100,000 inhabitants – were also to be apprehended. In total, 198,000 people were estimated to belong to these automatic-arrest categories, excluding the Local Group Leaders.[71] These were the instructions under which American, British, and French forces under SHAEF command operated until April 1945.[72]

That month, plans for the immediate post-surrender period were introduced in recognition of the fact that, even though Germany was yet to capitulate, 'post-surrender' conditions already prevailed in some areas.[73] Again, there were multiple policy documents that were not entirely mutually consonant but that all expanded on the pre-surrender policies to some extent. The situation was complicated by the fact that the already quoted (in)famous overall American directive for the immediate post-surrender period, JCS 1067/6 of 26 April 1945, was official policy only of the United States, whereas a SHAEF arrest and detention directive of 13 April (and a SHAEF *Arrest Categories Handbook* issued later that month) also applied to British and French forces in Germany and, with minor variations, in Austria.[74] Some differences between the JCS and SHAEF instructions derived merely from the greater precision

---

[71] SHAEF Office of the Chief of Staff, *Handbook for Military Government in Germany Prior to Defeat or Surrender*, Dec. 1944, available at: cgsc.cdmhost.com/cdm/ref/collection/p4013coll9/id/11 (accessed 6 Feb. 2019), paragraphs 89, 90, 277, 286, and 'Table "C"'. The increase from the ca. 150,000 from the fourth version was largely due to the inclusion of Waffen-SS officers. On the Waffen-SS, see Bernd Wegner, *The Waffen-SS: Organization, Ideology, and Function* (Oxford: Blackwell, 1990); Jan-Erik Schulte, Peter Liebe, and Bernd Wegner (eds.), *Die Waffen-SS: Neue Forschungen* (Paderborn: Ferdinand Schöningh, 2014). On the Hitler Youth, see Kater, *Hitler Youth*.

[72] Horn, *Internierungs- und Arbeitslager*, 20; Wember, *Umerziehung im Lager*, 35; Grohnert, *Entnazifizierung in Baden*, 13. Cf. Meyer, *Entnazifizierung von Frauen*, 38–40. Merten overlooks these directives entirely. Merten, *Gulag in East Germany*.

[73] Kenneth O. McCreedy, 'Planning the Peace: Operation Eclipse and the Occupation of Germany', *The Journal of Military History* 65, no. 3 (2001), 729–30.

[74] Horn, *Internierungs- und Arbeitslager*, 20–3; Meyer, *Entnazifizierung von Frauen*, 39; Grohnert, *Entnazifizierung in Baden*, 20. In contrast, Möhler claims the December

of the latter. In some respects, the SHAEF directive was less severe than JCS 1067/6. For instance, the former called for the arrest of police officers in a range of units down to the rank of colonel, in contrast to the lower rank of lieutenant in JCS 1067/6; and whereas the latter called for the arrest of all officers of the Waffen-SS and all other SS personnel, the SHAEF directive excluded the lowest NCOs (Unterscharführer, sergeant) of the Waffen-SS, and included only officers and NCOs in the regular SS as well as female SS and Waffen-SS auxiliaries (SS-Helferinnen and SS-Kriegshelferinnen) but not other SS personnel. Similarly, according to JCS 1067/6, Nazis and Nazi 'sympathisers' in key positions in agriculture, commerce, finance, and industry were to be interned, but the SHAEF instructions made no mention of this.[75]

In other respects, however, the SHAEF instructions were more radical than JCS 1067/6. While the latter called for the mandatory internment of NSDAP officials down to and including Local Group Leaders, the SHAEF directive extended this to the lower rank of Community Leaders (Gemeinschaftsleiter, the rank held by Cell Leaders) and to Local Group Department Leaders (Ortsgruppenamtsleiter). Moreover, the SHAEF directive was, remarkably, the first western directive that specified the arrest of most personnel of Reichsführer of the SS Heinrich Himmler's Reich Security Main Office (Reichssicherheitshauptamt, RSHA) in which key intelligence and security agencies (including the SD and Gestapo) had been gathered since 1939. Significantly, in all these instances, the milder of the April directives was equally if not more severe than the pre-surrender *Handbook*, as is most readily apparent in the move from discretionary to mandatory arrest of Local Group Leaders.[76]

1944 *Handbook* continued to be used. Möhler, *Entnazifizierung in Rheinland-Pfalz und im Saarland*, 358–9. On JCS 1067, see Dotterweich, '"Arrest" und "Removal"'; Hammond, 'Directives for the Occupation'. On Austria, where the Headquarters of US Forces released their own slightly modified arrest categories on 4 August 1945, see Oskar Dohle and Peter Eigelsberger, *Camp Marcus W. Orr: 'Glasenbach' als Internierungslager nach 1945* (Linz: Oberösterreichisches Landesarchiv/Salzburger Landesarchiv, 2011), 106–7; Florentine Kastner, '373 Camp Wolfsberg: Britische Besatzungslager in Österreich von 1945 bis 1948' (unpub. MPhil thesis, Universität Wien, 2011), 61, 67.

[75] On the female SS auxiliaries, see Jutta Mühlenberg, *Das SS-Helferinnenkorps: Ausbildung, Einsatz und Entnazifizierung der weiblichen Angehörigen der Waffen-SS* (Hamburg: Hamburger Edition, 2011).

[76] The only evident exception was that the SHAEF directive made no mention of interning lord mayors, although many would be caught through party and other affiliations. Compare 'Directive to Commander in Chief of United States Forces of Occupation Regarding the Military Government of Germany' (JCS 1067/6), 26 Apr. 1945, in *FRUS 1945 III*, 490; SHAEF directive, 'Arrest and Detention – Germany', 13 Apr. 1945, in Meyer, *Entnazifizierung von Frauen*, 262–4; and the reconstruction of the *Arrest Categories Handbook*, in Wember, *Umerziehung im Lager*, 35–7. On the RSHA, see

This toughening is often attributed to Morgenthau's influence or to the horror emerging from the liberated Nazi concentration camps, but it rather reflected a common view that pre-surrender measures were to be limited in order not to jeopardize the immediate goal of military victory, whereas the post-surrender purge would inevitably be more extensive. As Hajo Holborn noted in 1947, denazification had been 'given from the outset the strongest impetus, and it was always understood that it was to gain even greater momentum once the Allies achieved full control of German affairs'.[77]

While western policy thus became more severe in the transition from the pre- to the post-surrender period, the opposite was the case with Soviet policy. The already mentioned NKVD Order No. 0016 of January 1945 ('On Measures to Cleanse the Rear of the Red Army of Hostile Elements') had mandated 'Chekist measures' that were directed as much against potential Eastern European as German resistance and also targeted Soviet citizens who had fought against the USSR in former Red Army Lieutenant General Andrey Vlasov's German-allied 'Russian Liberation Army'. These measures included the arrest and deportation 'of spies and subversives of the German secret services, of terrorists, of members of various enemy organizations and groups of bandits and rebels' as well as of the leaders of prisons and concentration camps, various police, military, and legal personnel, mayors and other civil and economic administrative personnel, editors of newspapers and magazines, the authors of anti-Soviet publications, and 'members of fascist organizations', among others.[78] The instructions applied not just to

---

Michael Wildt, *An Uncompromising Generation: The Nazi Leadership of the Reich Security Main Office*, trans. Tom Lampert (Madison: University of Wisconsin Press, 2010).

[77] Hajo Holborn, *American Military Government: Its Organization and Policies* (Buffalo, NY: William S. Hein, 1975 [1st ed. 1947]), 37. It should be noted that, while American public opinion against Germany had been hardening slowly in 1944 and early 1945, a real stiffening emerged following the revelations from the concentration camps the Americans liberated, which were the subject of a concerted public relations campaign initiated only *after* Generals Eisenhower, Patton, and Bradley visited the Ohrdruf camp on 12 April 1945. The campaign thus cannot have influenced the development of the SHAEF arrest directive issued on 13 April, which had already been in preparation. See Casey, *Cautious Crusade*, 212–13.

[78] 'Befehl des Volkskommissars für Inneres Nr. 0016 "Über Maßnahmen zur Säuberung des Hinterlandes der Roten Armee von feindlichen Elementen"', 11 Jan. 1945, in Possekel (ed.), *Sowjetische Dokumente*, 144. Cf. Greiner, *Suppressed Terror*, 34–5. 'Chekist' refers to the first Soviet state security organization, the Cheka, which established the framework and tradition for subsequent Soviet security agencies. See Aaron Bateman, 'The KGB and Its Enduring Legacy', *The Journal of Slavic Military Studies* 29, no. 1 (2016), 23–47. On the Vlasov army, see Peter J. Lyth, 'Traitor or Patriot? Andrey Vlasov and the Russian Liberation Movement 1942–45', *Journal of Strategic Studies* 12, no. 2 (1989), 230–8. More generally on the defection of Soviets to

German territory but throughout the 'rear' of the Soviet forces across Eastern and Central Europe, including in Austria.[79]

In April 1945 People's Commissar for Internal Affairs Lavrentiy Beria reported the results of that order to Stalin. More than 215,000 people had been arrested, including 138,200 Germans, 38,660 Poles, 27,880 Soviet citizens, 3,200 Hungarians, and smaller numbers of Slovaks and Italians. Of these, 123,166 were regarded as 'members of fascist organizations'. Beria reported that, as a result of the order, 'a considerable number of ordinary members of the various fascist organizations (unions, labour organizations, youth organizations)' had been arrested. He suggested that more restrictive categories now be applied. With a view to the final assault on Berlin and thus the Red Army's entry into what would become the Soviet zone of occupied Germany, Beria and Stalin agreed on a policy modification. The resulting NKVD Order No. 00315 of 18 April 1945 ('On the Partial Amendment of the Order of the NKVD of the USSR No. 0016 of 11 January 1945') contained somewhat more restrictive but still poorly defined categories. Rather than 'members' of fascist organizations, now only 'active members' of the NSDAP and 'leaders of the fascist youth organizations' were to be arrested, as were members of the Gestapo, the SD, and other German 'punitive organizations'. Significantly, too, as already mentioned, Order No. 00315 ceased internees' deportation and instructed that they be detained in NKVD camps in situ. This did not apply to all arrestees, however. Anyone who had evidently committed acts of terrorism or sabotage was to be 'liquidated' immediately. Moreover, as had been determined in February, members of the paramilitary organizations, including the SA, the SS, and the People's Militia, as well as the personnel of prisons, concentration camps, and military courts, were not to be detained as civilian internees but deported to POW camps in the USSR.[80]

---

the German side, see Mark Edele, *Stalin's Defectors: How Red Army Soldiers Became Hitler's Collaborators, 1941–1945* (Oxford: Oxford University Press, 2017).

[79] This despite the fact that the Third Ukrainian Front of the Red Army which occupied Hungary and Austria was not explicitly addressed in Order No. 0016. See 'Speech by NKVD Brigadier I. Pavlov Regarding Espionage Activity', Mar. 1945, in Csaba Békés, László Borhi, Peter Ruggenthaler, and Ottmar Traşcă (eds.), *Soviet Occupation of Romania, Hungary, and Austria, 1944/45–1948/49* (Budapest: Central European University Press, 2015), 262–70.

[80] 'Schreiben des Volkskommissars für Inneres Berija an Stalin', 17 Apr. 1945, and 'Befehl des Volkskommissars für Inneres Nr. 00315 "Zur teilweisen Abänderung des Befehls des NKVD der UdSSR Nr. 0016 vom 11. Januar 1945"', 18 Apr. 1945, both in Possekel (ed.), *Sowjetische Dokumente*, 176, 178–9; Possekel, 'Sowjetische Lagerpolitik', 45. For an English translation of the order, see Günter Morsch and Ines Reich (eds.), *Sowjetisches Speziallager Nr. 7/Nr. 1 in Sachsenhausen (1945–1950): Katalog der Ausstellung in der Gedenkstätte und Museum Sachsenhausen* (Berlin: Metropol, 2005),

The reasons for the policy changes in April remain subject to speculation. According to Possekel, possible factors included a practical desire to alleviate stress on the transport system that was needed to transfer dismantled German industrial plants to the USSR; a tactical desire to limit undifferentiated coercion of the German population, which seemed only to be stiffening German resistance against the Red Army's advance; and a strategic desire for a more differentiated and constructive approach to the territory that was about to become the Soviet zone of occupation (and that was therefore not to be subjected to population transfers that were implemented east of the Oder–Neisse rivers in line with the redrawing of Germany's eastern borders). Whatever the reasons, the new order, which would remain in force with only minor alteration until late 1947, represented a partial convergence with western policy.[81] As Niethammer puts it, it was the 'Chekist version of the American internment policy against Nazis, supporters of the system and security risks'.[82] Interestingly, various instructions that followed Order No. 00315 about detaining internees in camps in situ did not include the Third Ukrainian Front that had entered Austria in March and which continued to transfer, rather than to encamp, arrestees. This reflected a different Soviet approach to denazification in Austria where a provisional government was established in April 1945 in the Soviet occupation zone, which was recognized throughout the country in October, and where the Soviets largely left denazification to the Austrian authorities, as discussed further later.[83]

Some authors make much of the fact that Order No. 00315 made no mention of denazifying or prosecuting internees but spoke merely of

---

72–3. Cf. Merten, who claims the categories were expanded, in *Gulag in East Germany*, 96.

[81] Possekel, 'Sowjetische Lagerpolitik', 50–1, 54. See also Ralf Possekel, 'Strukturelle Grausamkeit: Die sowjetische Internierungspolitik in Deutschland als Produkt sowjetischer Herrschaftspraktiken 1945 bis 1950', in Klaus-Dieter Müller, Konstantin Nikischkin, and Günther Wagenlehner (eds.), *Die Tragödie der Gefangenschaft in Deutschland und der Sowjetunion 1941–1956* (Cologne: Böhlau, 1998), 233–6. On German resistance to the Soviet advance, see Ian Kershaw, *The End: Hitler's Germany, 1944–1950* (London: Allen Lane, 2011).

[82] This is Greiner's rendition of Niethammer, 'Alliierte Internierungslager (1998)', 102. Greiner, *Suppressed Terror*, 349.

[83] 'Beschluß des staatlichen Verteidigungskomitees Nr. 8377ss zur Einrichtung der Funktion eines Stellvertreters des Frontoberbefehlshabers für zivile Angelegenheiten', 2 May 1945, and 'Befehl des Volkskommissars für Inneres Nr. 00461 "Zur Organisation von Lagern (Gefängnissen) bei den Frontbevollmächtigten des NKVD der UdSSR"', 10 May, both in Possekel (ed.), *Sowjetische Dokumente*, 185–6, 189–92; Pavlov and Semenenko, 'Operational Plan for Securing Rear of the Third Ukrainian Front by NKVD Troops', 3 May 1945, in Békés et al. (eds.), *Soviet Occupation*, 280–1; Stiefel, *Entnazifizierung in Österreich*, 25, 33, 39–44.

'secur[ing] the rear of front-line troops of the Red Army'.[84] Yet SHAEF's April arrest directive also spoke only of 'safeguarding the security of the Allied Forces and accomplishing the destruction of Nazi organizations' and said nothing about investigating or punishing internees or democratizing German public life.[85] In light of the evidence presented in this chapter, one cannot deny that removing and punishing key Nazi personnel were among the purposes of internment – whether western or Soviet – just because particular directives did not spell out its various aims and motivations in full. That was simply not in the nature of such documents. Indeed, neither the Soviet nor the SHAEF directive said anything about what would be done with internees after their encampment, a question that remained undecided for the moment.

Quadripartite Policy Discussions, 1945–1946

If the tripartite Potsdam Agreement outlined the overall objectives of the occupation, it became the task of the quadripartite Allied Control Council (ACC) to oversee their implementation. To this end, a complex bureaucracy emerged in the form of the ACA, which had numerous divisions, headed by directorates, which in turn established multiple committees and subcommittees.[86] Various directorates were interested in internment policy, including the legal directorate (which was responsible for policy on prosecuting war criminals), and the military, air, and naval directorates (that were concerned with the control of military and paramilitary personnel). However, primary responsibility rested with the Directorate of Internal Affairs and Communications (DIAC).[87] Its Public Safety Committee (PSC) created the already mentioned Nazi Arrest and Denazification Subcommittee (NADSC), whose title indicates at once the importance of arrests as well as their simultaneous close relationship with, and distinctness from, denazification, narrowly

---

[84] E.g., Klaus-Dieter Müller, 'Sowjetische Speziallager in Deutschland und ihre Rolle in der deutsch-sowjetischen Geschichte: Einführende Überlegungen', in Günter Fippel, *Demokratische Gegner und Willküropfer von Besatzungsmacht und SED in Sachsenhausen (1946 bis 1950): Das sowjetische Speziallager Sachsenhausen – Teil des Stalinschen Lagerimperiums* (Leipzig: Leipziger Universitätsverlag, 2008), 23.

[85] Meyer, *Entnazifizierung von Frauen*, 262.

[86] For a recent discussion of the ACC, see Szanajda, *The Allies and the German Problem*, esp. 41–57. For a contemporary account, see Eli E. Noblemann, 'Quadripartite Military Government Organization and Operations in Germany', *The American Journal of International Law* 41, no. 3 (1947), 650–5.

[87] ACA, Coordinating Committee, Arrest, Trial and Internment of Various Categories of Germans – Definition of Responsibility, 8 Dec. 1945, enclosing CORC P (45) 190, including a memorandum of the same name by the British representative, TNA, FO 1005/391.

understood. The PSC decided in early September 1945 that 'it was essential for the subcommittee to produce directives on the question of nazi arrest and removal at the earliest possible date, in order to implement the policy laid down in broad outline at the Potsdam conference'.[88] Drafting a directive on 'removal' proved relatively straightforward, leading to the proclamation of Control Council Directive No. 24 on the 'Removal from Office and from Positions of Responsibility of Nazis and of Persons Hostile to Allied Purposes' on 12 January 1946.[89] Agreeing to a directive on arrests proved more difficult. Indeed, the distinct arrest directive originally envisaged never materialized. This failure no doubt contributed to internment's neglect in much of the literature on occupied Germany, while internment's eventual handling within a later, broader directive has undoubtedly contributed to the common tendency to associate it with the punishment of war criminals.

The fact that arrests did not become the subject of a distinct Control Council directive was due in part to the various powers' differing and changing views about the details of internment policy and in part to internment's complex relationship with other aspects of occupation policy, including the prosecution of Nazi criminals and demilitarization. Initially, disagreement emerged between the British and the three other powers, particularly the Americans. At the NADSC in mid-September 1945, the British proposed to exempt some groups (including NSDAP Deputy Local Group Leaders and Local Group Department Leaders, BDM personnel, female SS and Waffen-SS auxiliaries, and senior civil servants) from automatic arrest and to detain them only if this seemed warranted *after* investigation.[90] The British were beginning to implement such a policy in their zone, as discussed in Chapter 2. This can be understood as part of a broader British reconsideration of policy towards Germany away from a primarily punitive and controlling one towards one that also offered hope for reconstruction. However, the extent of the change should not be exaggerated: the British did not abandon their concerns for security or their commitment to denazification and were modifying rather than discarding automatic arrest and

[88] PSC, Minutes of the 2nd Meeting, 10 Sep. 1945, 2, TNA, FO 1005/623.
[89] 'Control Council Directive No. 24: Removal from Office and from Positions of Responsibility of Nazis and of Persons Hostile to Allied Purposes', 12 Jan. 1946, in Ruhm von Oppen (ed.), *Documents on Germany*, 102–7. Numerous disagreements subsequently arose about the directive's interpretation, implementation, and modification. See Biddiscombe, *Denazification of Germany*, esp. 38–9.
[90] Draft Directive on the Arrest of Nazis and Other Dangerous Persons, n.d. [21 Sep. 1945], TNA, FO 1005/638, DIAC/APSC/NADSC/P (45) 2.

internment.[91] Nevertheless, the other powers opposed the adoption of the British proposal as quadripartite policy. In late September, the American representative on the NADSC objected both to any revision of the mandatory arrest categories and to the release of anyone already arrested thereunder. Indeed, he intimated that the Americans might stop applying SHAEF's April directives and switch to the somewhat more expansive JCS 1067/6. The American, French, and Soviet members also rejected a British suggestion that military government units receive advance warning of the impending arrest of Germans in their employment. The French insisted that one should learn from the experience of the German occupation of France, where the Gestapo had found that advance notice led to the flight of those sought.[92] In mid-November, the subcommittee approved a 'Recommended Directive Concerning the Arrest of Nazis and Other Dangerous Persons', based on a Soviet draft. It excluded advance warning but included the distinction proposed by the British between automatic-arrest categories and 'categories of persons subject to preliminary investigation before arrest'. A compromise had been found: an additional clause permitted the extension of the automatic-arrest categories to groups beyond those listed as such at zone commanders' discretion. The draft thus treated its automatic-arrest stipulations as a minimum and permitted more extensive mandatory arrests.[93] Despite agreement at the subcommittee, at the PSC the Americans voiced their continuing objection to investigations before arrests and the matter was postponed at numerous meetings in the final weeks of 1945 and the first weeks of 1946.[94]

In February, however, the Americans changed their position and put forward their own proposal to reduce the automatic-arrest categories. At the NADSC's first meeting for over two months, in early March 1946, the American representative explained that they had 're-estimated the security situation' in their zone, that they felt that 'only those people whom the Nurnberg [sic] Trials have indicted should be arrested', and that military government lacked 'sufficient resources to administer the

---

[91] Cf. Knowles, *Winning the Peace*, 20, 29, 48.

[92] See NADSC, Minutes of the 5th, 6th, and 7th Meetings on 19, 21, and 24 Sep. 1945, in TNA, FO 1005/635. See also 'Further Statement by Major Nichol (American)', 24 Sep. 1945, attached to Draft Directive on the Arrest of Nazis and Other Dangerous Persons, n.d. [21 Sep. 1945], TNA, FO 1005/638, DIAC/APSC/NADSC/P (45) 2.

[93] Recommended Directive Concerning the Arrest of Nazis and Other Dangerous Persons, n.d. [14 Nov. 1945], TNA, FO 1005/638, DIAC/APSC/NADSC/P (45) 4. See NADSC, Minutes of the 16th and 17th Meetings on 9 and 13 Nov. 1945, TNA, FO 1005/635.

[94] See PSC, Minutes of the 12th–15th Meetings in Nov.–Dec. 1945, TNA, FO 1005/623; and those of the 18th–21st Meetings in Jan.–Feb. 1946, TNA, FO 1005/624.

program of the ultimate disposition of a large number of persons arrested under the original categories'. It was now the turn of the British and the other powers to raise concerns about apparently excessive American moderation. The British representative asked why the Hitler Youth, 'which he considered the greatest security danger on a long-term basis', and other groups were not included. His American counterpart explained: 'We took persons and organizations indicted at Nurnberg [sic]. To that we added War Criminals and then a category of Security Suspects which every Zone Commander will arrest.' The suggestion was that functionaries of the Hitler Youth and other groups now to be exempted from automatic arrest – including those who would have fallen under 'compulsory investigation' according to the subcommittee's earlier proposal – could still be arrested as individual security suspects.[95] In contrast to suggestions that prosecution was or became internment's sole purpose, security suspects thus remained a central, broad category of internees in this American proposal and in the eyes of the other powers. Importantly, too, even members of the organizations indicted at Nuremberg were not described as 'war criminals' in this context.

In the meantime, a deadlock had emerged. It was proving impossible to consider arrests in isolation from demilitarization and the punishment of war criminals and members of the indicted organizations, and the failure to finalize an arrest directive was holding up the deliberation of those related matters. In January, DIAC had charged the PSC with 'coordinating the preventive measures recommended by other directorates and reconciling the gradations of treatment therein proposed with the penal measures resulting from the trial of war criminals'.[96] Yet the PSC and the NADSC felt they could not address the other issues until the arrest directive was finalized.[97] The deadlock was broken in March by a British suggestion to deal with the detention of war criminals, Nazis, militarists, and potentially dangerous Germans in 'a new comprehensive draft directive'. In May, the distinct arrest directive that had been drafted the previous November was declared 'dead'.[98] Following its demise, there was no further discussion of a quadripartite policy on who should be taken into automatic arrest.

---

[95] NADSC, Minutes of the 20th Meeting, 5 Mar. 1946, TNA, FO 1005/636.

[96] DIAC, The Arrest, Trial and Internment of Certain Categories of Germans, 4 Jan. 1946, TNA, FO 1005/595, DIAC/P (46) 7. See also DIAC, Memorandum for the PSC, 12 Jan. 1946, TNA, FO 1005/603, DIAC/Memorandum (45 [sic]) 19.

[97] See, for example, PSC, Minutes of 19th Meeting, 25 Jan. 1946, 1, TNA, FO 1005/624; NADSC, Minutes of the 20th Meeting, 5 Mar. 1946, 3, TNA, FO 1005/636.

[98] NADSC, Minutes of the 21st Meeting, 13 Mar. 1946, 1, and Minutes of the 27th Meeting, 28 May 1946, 4, both in TNA, FO 1005/636.

Instead, internment was henceforth explored as but one of a number of longer-term sanctions that could be imposed on Germans (including those already interned) after, rather than before, their investigation and formal categorization. According to the British representative on the NADSC, 'there were two classes to be considered, the guilty who would have to be punished and the long term security suspects who would have to be interned or placed under surveillance'.[99] The Americans and British regarded the new comprehensive directive as 'urgent' because in their zones 'many thousands of Germans are under detention who cannot be charged with any specific crime and therefore cannot be brought to trial' under Control Council Law No. 10 on the 'Punishment of Persons Guilty of War Crimes, Crimes against Peace and against Humanity' of 20 December 1945, which laid the basis both for the occupiers' individual military tribunals and for German trials.[100] In response to this admission, the Soviet delegate questioned why there were 'many thousands of internees who had not been tried'. Claiming to uphold a position that was in fact utterly inconsistent with Soviet policy, as discussed earlier, and with Soviet practice, as shown in Chapter 2, he 'felt that large numbers of people should not be kept in custody without a charge or without being brought to trial. If the person is not guilty, then he should be released.' The British chairman of the NADSC responded by insisting on 'the distinction between the guilty and the merely dangerous', and the American delegate observed that

the U.S. have been arresting since the Occupation, Germans by categories. Against many of these persons there is no evidence on which to apply C.C. Law No. 10, yet by reason of their former position or training they may be potentially dangerous. We therefore propose to classify such persons under the categories listed in this paper and apply the sanctions for each category after semi-judicial hearing.[101]

It is hard to imagine a clearer refutation of scholarly claims that western-zone internees were all war criminals or were seen or treated as such.

If the Soviets appeared to see only two categories, that is, those who should be incarcerated and those who should not, at least by spring

---

[99] NADSC, Minutes of the 21st Meeting, 13 Mar. 1946, 2, TNA, FO 1005/636.
[100] The Arrest and Punishment of War Criminals, Nazis, Militarists and the Internment, Control and Surveillance of Potentially Dangerous Germans, 29 Jun. 1946, 3, TNA, FO 1005/639, DIAC/APSC/NADSC/P (46) 1 (Revise). See 'Control Council Law No. 10: Punishment of Persons Guilty of War Crimes, Crimes against Peace and against Humanity', 20 Dec. 1945, in Ruhm von Oppen (ed.), *Documents on Germany*, 97–101. On the trials by the individual occupying powers and by German courts, see Frei (ed.), *Transnationale Vergangenheitspolitik*; Raim, *Nazi Crimes against Jews*.
[101] NADSC, Minutes of the 27th Meeting, 28 May 1946, 5–7, TNA, FO 1005/636.

1946 the western powers took a more differentiated approach. Apart from the innocent or exonerated, they conceived of three main groups: the guilty, who were to be prosecuted; the dangerous, who would be interned; and the potentially dangerous, who would be placed under various other forms of control and surveillance. At a meeting of the NADSC in late May, the Soviet delegate questioned the mere surveillance of the last group and declared that 'the Germans who are potentially dangerous to the Allied Cause should be interned and imprisoned' (which contradicted the above-quoted suggestion that only the 'guilty' should be detained and more closely reflected Soviet policy and practice). In response, the British chairman of the NADSC insisted that

We want to do what is practicable, therefore we want to lock up only persons known to be dangerous and exercise control and surveillance over those who might only become dangerous. It is impossible to lock up hundreds of thousands of persons in the British and U.S. Zone, and it would lead to unnecessary irritation and grave discontent.

We are trying to educate Germany to democracy and useful work, not to look upon the world from the inside of a Concentration Camp.[102]

It should be noted that the British themselves had only just arrived at this position. As recently as January, a meeting of key figures in British military government had defined the object of internment precisely as 'neutralis[ing] the activities of *potentially* dangerous persons'.[103] Again, the Soviet and the western positions were closer than is often assumed, even if they continued to envisage detention on different scales. Importantly, in contrast to Marshall's initial paper from March 1944, which had anticipated continuing to detain only those internees who were convicted on criminal charges, even the western powers now viewed internment as a longer-term measure against a hard core of dangerous, non-criminal (or non-prosecutable) Germans.

Indeed, establishing a basis for such longer-term internment was one of the key goals of the new comprehensive directive, although it differentiated insufficiently between punitive imprisonment and preventative internment. In mid-April, the title of what would eventually be proclaimed on 12 October 1946 as Control Council Directive No. 38 was agreed: 'The Arrest and Punishment of War Criminals, Nazis, and Militarists and the Internment, Control, and Surveillance of Potentially

---

[102] Ibid., 4.
[103] Minutes of a Conference held at HQ BAOR, 7 Jan. 1946, 2, TNA, FO 1032/792 (emphasis added). Cf. Wember, *Umerziehung im Lager*, 23.

Dangerous Germans'.[104] Even more than the title, the text distinguished explicitly 'between imprisonment of war criminals and similar offenders for criminal conduct and internment of potentially dangerous persons who may be confined because their freedom would constitute a danger to the Allied Cause'. It spoke further of 'the internment of Germans, who, though not guilty of specific crimes are considered to be dangerous to Allied purposes', as opposed to 'the punishment of war criminals, Nazis, Militarists, and industrialists who encouraged and supported the Nazi Regime'. Note that here the people facing internment are 'dangerous', whereas in the previous quotation they were merely 'potentially dangerous'. Either way, as in the Potsdam Agreement, internment thus appeared primarily preventative rather than punitive. Yet the directive failed to uphold its own distinctions. To be sure, its 'sanctions' included the death penalty or imprisonment for life or for a period of five to fifteen years for 'Major Offenders having committed a specific war crime', as did Control Council Law No. 10. But 'Offenders' and 'Major Offenders' who were not guilty of specific war crimes could be either 'imprisoned or interned' for up to ten years. There were no stipulations about any differences between the two forms of incarceration.[105]

If the distinction between imprisonment and internment was thus muddied, that between 'the guilty', on the one hand, and the 'security suspects' or 'dangerous Germans', on the other, was also far from clear. As the British representative on the NADSC noted when making this very distinction in March, there was 'considerable shading off ... into one another' between these two 'classes'.[106] The directive did not spell out who belonged to which group. Clearly those Major Offenders who had committed individual crimes were 'guilty', but the criteria for being deemed a Major Offender went well beyond individual criminality to encompass 'anyone who gave major political, economic, propagandist or other support to the national socialist tyranny', anyone who had held a 'leading position' in the NSDAP or its affiliates, and any member of the

---

[104] NADSC, Minutes of the 23rd Meeting, 18 Apr. 1946, 2, TNA, FO 1005/636. Bizarrely, Merten claims the directive was drafted in August 1945 and casts it as the major basis and legitimation for internment. Merten, *Gulag in East Germany*, 17, 40, 125. He thus overlooks that it was, among other things, precisely an attempt to determine how to process internees after their (already lengthy) internment, rather than the basis for their initial arrest.

[105] 'Control Council Directive No. 38: The Arrest and Punishment of War Criminals, Nazis, and Militarists and the Internment, Control, and Surveillance of Potentially Dangerous Germans', 12 Oct. 1946, in Ruhm von Oppen (ed.), *Documents on Germany*, 168–79. Cf. Cohen, 'Transitional Justice', 69; Biddiscombe, *Denazification of Germany*, esp. 38–40.

[106] NADSC, Minutes of the 21st Meeting, 13 Mar. 1946, 2, TNA, FO 1005/636.

Wehrmacht's High Command, among others. Offenders, in turn, were by definition not war criminals but were deemed to meet any of numerous criteria for being categorized as 'activists', 'militarists', or 'profiteers' by virtue of their 'position or activity' in Nazi Germany. They were thus defined by their pasts. No direct mention was made of them posing a present danger, but it was assumed that they did. Only two instances of postwar dangerousness constituted explicit grounds for categorization: an 'activist' was

anyone who, after 8 May 1945, has endangered or is likely to endanger the peace of the German people or of the world, through advocating national socialism or militarism or inventing or disseminating malicious rumours

and a 'militarist' was

anyone whose past training ... has in the opinion of Zone Commanders contributed towards the promotion of militarism and who the Zone Commanders consider likely to endanger Allied purposes.

The sanctions to be applied to such Offenders were the same as those categorized as such merely for their Nazi and militaristic pasts.[107] A clause stating that 'this Directive in no way limits the right of Zone Commanders to hold in internment any persons considered by them to be dangerous to the security of their forces' was removed from the penultimate draft directive of late June 1946 but included as a recommendation to the Control Council in the PSC's mid-August memorandum to the DIAC accompanying the final draft.[108] The Allies thus remained committed to preventive arrests merely on security grounds. Yet their codified policies focused on categories of Germans they wanted simultaneously to punish and to neutralize.[109]

Even if Directive No. 38 dealt with post- rather than pre-categorization detention, its elaboration and final form had much in common with the overall picture of the development of internment policy discussed in this

---

[107] 'Control Council Directive No. 38', in Ruhm von Oppen (ed.), *Documents on Germany*, 171–3.

[108] Compare DIAC/APSC/NADSC/P (46) 1 (revise), 29 Jun. 1946, 5, and DIAC/APSC/ Memo (46) 61, 16 Aug. 1946, both in TNA, FO 1005/639.

[109] The Allies' continuing commitment is confirmed by American and British insistence on the right to intern security suspects in the context of the postwar development of new protections in international law for civilians in time of war and occupation. See Mark Lewis, *The Birth of the New Justice: The Internationalization of Crime and Punishment, 1919–1950* (Oxford: Oxford University Press, 2014), 236, 255. In contrast, Merten incorrectly asserts that the western powers strictly separated security and punitive concerns and suggests that their overriding priority was democratic reconstruction, which downplays their punitive desires and their illiberal tendencies. Merten, *Gulag in East Germany*, 39–40, 42.

chapter. First, the various powers favoured different degrees of rigour. In the case of Directive No. 38, the British wanted the extensive list of positions whose occupants were to be charged under the various categories to be treated merely as a guide (which would mean they did not have to be fully implemented), while the Soviets regarded them as mandatory.[110] Yet, second, such differences were not insurmountable, in part because zonal autonomy and discretion were writ large but primarily because there was basic agreement on the need for, and legitimacy of, internment. Third, such agreement was informed by numerous goals and motivations, which included but were not limited to Allied security and the desire to punish not only war criminals but other Nazis and militarists as well. The fact that Offenders could be imprisoned or interned 'in order to perform reparation and construction work' is a reminder of this additional restitutive consideration, which did not otherwise play a significant role in the ACA's internal debates. Indeed, the shared overarching aims of the directive's sanctions were 'the exclusion of national socialism and militarism from the life of the German people and reparation of the damage caused'. Fourth, although internment thus had economic, military, and quasi-legal dimensions, it was ultimately also inherently political. The directive acknowledged this indirectly in stating that '*Political* internment after 8 May 1945' could be taken into account when sentencing Offenders.[111] Finally, this multiplicity of goals and motivations and internment's close connections with other Allied measures created considerable ambiguity in internment policy. As the following chapters show, such ambiguity persisted throughout internment's execution.

---

[110] PSC, Minutes of the 40th Meeting, 6/7 Aug. 1946, TNA, FO 1005/624.
[111] 'Control Council Directive No. 38', in Ruhm von Oppen (ed.), *Documents on Germany*, 176, 175, 168 (emphasis added).

2 'Not Consistent with Civil Liberties'
Internment in Practice, 1945–1950

This chapter examines the practice of internment in occupied Germany from the initial arrests to the ultimate winding down of the camps. Just as the preceding chapter demonstrated considerable common ground among the Allies, despite important differences over internment policy, this chapter reveals both commonalities and dissimilarities in its execution. The most fundamental similarity across the four zones was that, as David Cohen observes, 'Automatic arrest and ensuing internment without trial were practiced by all the Allies.'[1] As they entered German territory, sought to establish their presence amid widespread chaos, and began to implement their various policies, waves of arrests swept over the country. Germans were apprehended in a variety of manners, including through mandatory registrations, large-scale raids, and targeted or more random arrests. Before the conclusion of hostilities, but particularly in the immediate postwar weeks and months, every occupying power erred on the side of detaining too many rather than too few people. Initial inconsistency was evident in every zone, as were an acceleration of arrests in summer 1945 and a subsequent deceleration. By year's end, each power held tens if not hundreds of thousands of internees. Although this is often overlooked, arrests and internments continued into 1946 and 1947 in all four zones.

Despite the convergence of Allied policies during the final stages of the war, the appearance of unity at Potsdam, and the commonality of mass arrests in every zone, substantial differences emerged in 1945 and continued to grow. Those relating to the identity of internees and the conditions under which they were held are discussed in Chapters 3 and 4. The central questions in this chapter concern the Allies' approaches to categorizing, processing, and releasing their internees. It was here – rather than in the basis of arrests – that key differences emerged from late 1945 between the Soviet and western

---

[1] Cohen, 'Transitional Justice', 69.

zones, with second-order differences developing among the latter. If automatic arrest was, as Richard Bessel puts it, a 'blunt instrument', the western powers at least sought to sharpen it.[2] The Soviets, in contrast, wielded it carelessly and recklessly. Yet one should not exaggerate the differences as many historians do, including some who perceive rather than overlook the initial similarities. For instance, Gieseke suggests that 'the paths of Allied internment policy diverged conclusively in 1946–47'.[3] Even in these middle years and thereafter, internment in the various zones shared more commonalities than is often recognized, notwithstanding the fact that implementation of Control Council Directive No. 38 varied considerably among the zones. In particular, the speed and nature of internees' processing differed less between the Soviet and the western zones than is widely assumed, and idealized scholarly understandings of western internment do not stand up to scrutiny. In reality, the western occupation remained coercive longer than is often recognized.

In all zones, internment retained its largely extrajudicial character. From a comparative perspective, it often seems that the more internees in a particular zone appear as criminals awaiting prosecution or serving a sentence, the better the relevant occupying power's internment regime looks; and the opposite applies too. Soviet authorities sometimes claimed or implied that all their internees had been investigated, charged, or convicted by a court prior to their internment, which was untrue and completely misrepresented internment in the Soviet zone and in general.[4] More realistically, but still reflecting the GDR's self-serving official narrative of a more thorough reckoning with fascism in the Soviet zone than the western zones, in 1984 East German historian Günter Benser emphasized that in January 1947, 37% of Soviet-zone detainees had been convicted, compared with just 1% in the American zone, 'although the main culprits were above all to be sought in this group of people'. In contrast, non-communist historians generally argue the opposite. For instance, von Plato claims that, whereas the Soviet camps held 'a very high proportion of people who ... never received a trial', internees in the western zones were handed over to the 'German judiciary after a short

---

[2] Bessel, *Germany 1945*, 189.   [3] Gieseke, *Die Stasi*, 31.
[4] That was the implication of the exchange quoted at the end of Chapter 1 where the Soviet member of the NADSC asked why the western powers still held internees who had not been convicted. See also Report to the Council of Foreign Ministers from the Allied Control Authority in Germany, 24 Feb. 1947, Section II, Part 3, d, 4, TNA, FO 1030/7. Cf. Christian Meyer-Seitz, *Die Verfolgung von NS-Straftaten in der sowjetischen Besatzungszone* (Berlin: Berlin Verlag, 1998), 35.

period of case-by-case review'.[5] This not only exaggerates the speed but also distorts the nature of the procedures applied in the western zones. Other authors claim that the western powers 'implemented internment as a kind of pre-trial detention', that western-zone internees 'awaited their trials before Allied military tribunals', or that the function of western camps 'was limited to the internment of the members of criminal Nazi organizations' convicted by the IMT at Nuremberg.[6] This chapter demonstrates that it is misleading both to suggest that the western powers prosecuted all or most of their internees and to reduce western internment to remand custody for Nuremberg. Automatic arrest remained the basis for mass detention longer than is often recognized.[7]

The apparent belief that internment amounted (or should have amounted) to pre-trial custody for suspected criminals reflects unrealistic expectations that the highest standards of criminal justice should and could have been applied in occupied Germany. As Donald Bloxham notes, 'the vast number of suspects created in the criminal state that was Nazi Germany made a proper accounting with each of them all but impossible'.[8] Rather than expecting rigorous and expeditious individual investigations and trials of any and all suspects or pretending that this is what occurred in the western zones, it should be recognized that all four occupying powers were willing and prepared to detain (and thus punish) significant numbers of Germans even if they had not committed specific crimes or if their crimes had not been, and had no prospect of being, proven in a court of law. Possekel points in this direction by suggesting that Moscow saw internment not as a preliminary measure in advance of

---

[5] Günter Benser, 'Konzeptionen und Praxis der Abrechnung mit dem deutschen Faschismus', *Zeitschrift für Geschichtswissenschaft* 32, no. 10 (1984), 961; Alexander von Plato, 'Internierungen in Ost und West nach 1945: Elemente des Vergleichs der Opferhierarchien und Opferkonkurrenzen', in Haustein et al. (eds.), *Instrumentalisierung, Verdrängung, Aufarbeitung*, 102; von Plato, 'Sowjetische Speziallager', 95. See also Wehler, *Deutsche Gesellschaftsgeschichte*, vol. 4, 957.

[6] Greiner, *Suppressed Terror*, 348; Katharina von Kellenbach, *The Mark of Cain: Guilt and Denial in the Post-war Lives of Nazi Perpetrators* (Oxford: Oxford University Press, 2013), 20; Meyer-Seitz, *Verfolgung von NS-Straftaten*, 35. See also Thacker, *End of the Third Reich*, 153–60; Niethammer, 'Alliierte Internierungslager (1998)', 100; Merten, *Gulag in East Germany*, 2, 6, 17.

[7] Cf. Cohen, 'Transitional Justice', 68–71. Merten fails to come to grips with the significance of automatic arrest, arguing in relation to the western zones that 'At the beginning of the occupation, this often led to abuse such as arresting individuals without hearings, simply because they had held high office in the Nazi regime.' Merten, *Gulag in East Germany*, 24. Arrest for holding high office was not an abuse of the system; it was the system.

[8] Donald Bloxham, 'British War Crimes Trial Policy in Germany, 1945–1957: Implementation and Collapse', *Journal of British Studies* 42, no. 1 (2003), 104.

prosecution but as a punishment in itself.[9] The western powers also regarded it as such, among other things. The British military government detachment in Hamburg informed the city's mayor in September 1945 that 'It is Allied policy to detain certain categories. They are NOT merely detained for investigation.... inmates are interned for punishment.'[10] While one may wish it to have been otherwise, a degree of extrajudicial punishment was unavoidable given the massive numbers of those held responsible in one way or another for Nazism, and not just for its heinous crimes.

Not only was internment's punitive dimension primarily extrajudicial, but internment also retained a preventative element throughout, with political and security considerations continuing to play important roles. Indeed, several of the goals and motivations behind the wartime development of internment policy remained salient throughout its implementation. In particular, security did not disappear, as suggested by some authors who argue that prosecution replaced security as the primary or sole aim.[11] While such sequentialist accounts are preferable to static mono-dimensional versions, they overlook that the various goals were not consecutive but overlapped. Indeed, there was considerable continuity, as demonstrated by a summary of internment policy by the Deputy Military Governor of the British zone, Lieutenant-General Sir Brian Robertson, in July 1946, which identified a range of goals:

The Arrest Policy ... was, and still is, framed to ensure the security of the occupying forces, the liquidation of the German Intelligence Services, the disbandment and dissolution of the Nazi Party, its para-military and affiliated organizations, and the suppression of all Nazis or Militarists who could endanger the growth of a democratic Germany.[12]

As discussed in Chapter 1, in October 1946 Control Council Directive No. 38 confirmed the continuing importance of prevention and sought, if rather unsuccessfully, to distinguish between punitive imprisonment and preventative internment. It is well known that the Soviets used

---

[9] Possekel, 'Sowjetische Lagerpolitik', 88–9.

[10] R. C. Allhusen to Petersen, 29 Sep. 1945, 3, Staatsarchiv Hamburg (StAH), 131–1 II, no. 607 (emphasis in original). Cf. Meyer, *Entnazifizierung von Frauen*, 17. Contra Cohen, 'Transitional Justice', 69.

[11] Wember, *Umerziehung im Lager*, 25; Niethammer, 'Alliierte Internierungslager (1998)', 100; Greiner, *Suppressed Terror*, 348; Merten, *Gulag in East Germany*, 23, 40–1. For other sequentialist accounts, see Möhler, 'Internierungslager in der französischen Besatzungszone', 53, 59; Possekel, 'Sowjetische Lagerpolitik', 71; Meyer, *Entnazifizierung von Frauen*, 249; Ritscher, 'Die wissenschaftliche Aufarbeitung', 181. Cf. Heitzer, 'Speziallagerforschung', 117–18.

[12] Report on Persons Held in Internment Camps, sent by Robertson to Sir Arthur Street, Control Office for Germany and Austria, London, 2 Jul. 1946, 1, TNA, FO 938/345.

internment to neutralize real or imagined 'dangers' and it is often assumed that the western powers did not.[13] Yet this was not the case, as both the first and third sections of this chapter demonstrate. The latter presents two specific indications of the ongoing importance of political and broadly defined security considerations in the western zones. In 1946–7 people suspected of being 'anti-French', particularly internees and their families, were deported from the Saarland. And in 1947, the British created a 'civil internment settlement' for the long-term detention of 'dangerous' militarists, Nazis, and their families.

More broadly, this chapter's comparative analysis of internees' categorization, processing, and release shows that most internees were never handed to the judiciary or came before a criminal court. Only a tiny number were suspected of, let alone tried for, individual crimes. Moreover, large numbers of internees in every zone did not fall under the IMT's 1945 indictment, let alone its 1946 conviction, of Nazi organizations.[14] Only in the British zone were summary courts (*Spruchgerichte*) established to try members of the organizations the IMT deemed 'criminal' in its verdict, and only a minority of British-zone internees were brought before these courts. Meanwhile, the *Spruchkammern* (denazification panels) that eventually processed internees in the American and French zones were not criminal courts but 'a hybrid of political tribunal and court of law'.[15] Moreover, many internees in every zone were released through administrative processes and various amnesties, often for highly political reasons. A range of extrajudicial, semi-judicial, and judicial mechanisms was thus used to process them. This is indeed typical of 'transitional justice', which is rarely, if ever, purely juridical.

Soviet and western processes differed above all in two respects: the former did not afford internees opportunities to plead their case; and Soviet decisions lagged behind those of the western powers. Arrest categories were reduced in all zones in 1945–6, but more quickly and extensively in the west. Soviet authorities were largely unconcerned by mistaken or unwarranted detention and Moscow did not endorse calls from Soviet-zone officials for substantial releases. In contrast, the western powers moved relatively quickly – if more slowly than numerous scholars suggest – to adjust their practice with a view to releasing at least

---

[13] E.g., Jörg Morré, 'Speziallager als Mittel sowjetischer Repression', *Horch und Guck: Zeitschrift der Gedenkstätte Museum in der 'Runden Ecke' in Leipzig* 24, no. 1 (2015), 64–8; Merten, *Gulag in East Germany*, 23, 40, 42–3.

[14] Niethammer, 'Alliierte Internierungslager (1998)', 107; Möhler, *Entnazifizierung in Rheinland-Pfalz und im Saarland*, 370.

[15] Hoser, 'Entnazifizierung in der Stadt Dachau', 195. Contra Merten, *Gulag in East Germany*, 25, 38.

some internees. Whereas some scholars have stressed that policies such as JCS 1067/6 and SHAEF's April 1945 arrest directive remained in place much longer than initially intended, indeed until 1947 and 1948, respectively, in reality western policy demonstrated greater movement than this implies.[16] Moreover, only the western powers at certain times gave some internees opportunities to apply for their release or to defend themselves against various charges. As a result, in the western zones significant releases began in the first postwar autumn and winter; approximately half the internees were discharged by early 1947; and civilian internment all but ended by the end of 1948, with only a few hundred detainees remaining in early 1949. In contrast, the Soviet Union did not grant internees opportunities to plead their case, did not make substantial releases until mid-1948, and continued to hold approximately 13,500 internees until early 1950. Due to that slowness, most Soviet-zone internees did not undergo a formal (narrowly understood) denazification procedure, which wound down before they were released. However, this does not mean that Soviet internment had nothing to do with eradicating Nazism. In every zone, internment was distinct from formalized denazification procedures but still served the destruction of Nazism. This is further confirmed by the Austrian case that is discussed at relevant points in this chapter.

Arrests

The transition from war to peace was a drawn-out and chaotic affair, which was experienced in different ways over an extended period of time, thus relativizing the significance of the nationally important date of Germany's capitulation on 8 May 1945. With Allied armies fighting their way into German territory in late 1944 and early 1945, the occupation and the 'postwar' era were beginning, locally, well before the final surrender. As Kenneth McCreedy puts it, 'the terminal operation of the war overlapped the initial operation of the peace'.[17] As the Allies captured ever more German territory, their first priority was achieving military victory. When the front moved on and Allied forces began to establish their authority locally, the safety of Allied personnel was a key concern. According to American intelligence officer Saul Padover,

---

[16] Hammond, 'Directives for the Occupation', 438; Frank M. Buscher, *The U.S. War Crimes Trial Program in Germany, 1946–1955* (New York: Greenwood Press, 1989), 19; Horn, *Internierungs- und Arbeitslager*, 23; Meyer, *Entnazifizierung von Frauen*, 39; Waibel, *Von der wohlwollenden Despotie*, 84–5.

[17] McCreedy, 'Planning the Peace', 728. On the broader transition, see Bessel, *Germany 1945*.

Everybody was convinced that the Germans, whom we assumed to be fanatical Hitlerites, would snipe at any American back the moment it was turned. Among us there was a curious unanimity of agreement that the SS and the Gestapo had left agents behind them and that no American was safe unless heavily armed.[18]

Such views exemplify the Allies' general suspicion of the Germans, while also indicating that some groups were feared more than others. In these early months, both military effectiveness and Allied security prompted the detention of significant numbers of Germans. For instance, when American forces captured Aachen in the autumn of 1944 many civilians who had remained in the city were interned, transferred to Belgian territory, interrogated, and then released; and in early January 1945 a teenage member of the BDM was arrested in Monschau on suspicion of 'Werewolf' activity but released in early March.[19] As these examples indicate, such detention was often relatively brief.

In this early period, as they began to grapple with myriad other logistical, humanitarian, and economic problems, the Allies were also actively seeking out and arresting Germans who belonged to automatic-arrest categories or who were mentioned on 'Black Lists' of prominent Nazis and war-crimes suspects. Unlike the above examples, these detainees were not released so quickly. Such early efforts yielded some prominent scalps, including Robert Wagner, Gau (regional) Leader and Reich Governor of Baden and head of the occupation administration in Alsace, whom the French arrested and then tried and executed in 1946. Frequently, however, senior personnel had fled or committed suicide, and only less senior – but by no means just lowly – ranks remained. For instance, when Marburg capitulated on 29 March, most leading party and military officials had absconded, but the NSDAP District Leader, who was also the district administrator, and a few other functionaries had stayed put and were promptly arrested by the Americans.[20]

---

[18] Saul K. Padover, *Experiment in Germany: The Story of an American Intelligence Officer* (New York: Duell, Sloan and Pearce, 1946), 11. For similar British expectations, see 'Control Commission for Germany (British Element), Intelligence Bureau, Intelligence Review No. 1', 12 Dec. 1945, in M. E. Pelly and H. H. Yasamee (eds.), *Documents on British Foreign Policy Overseas*, Series I, vol. V: *Germany and Western Europe, 11 August–31 December 1945* (London: Her Majesty's Stationery Office, 1990), 439–40. Cf. Bessel, *Germany 1945*, 172.

[19] Taylor, *Exorcising Hitler*, 14, 34–6. On the interrogations, see Padover, *Experiment in Germany*, 31–48.

[20] Grohnert, *Entnazifizierung in Baden*, 17; John Gimbel, *A German Community under American Occupation: Marburg, 1945–52* (Stanford, CA: Stanford University Press, 1961), 16. Cf. Horn, *Internierungs- und Arbeitslager*, 39; Hans Woller, *Gesellschaft und Politik in der amerikanischen Besatzungszone: Die Region Ansbach und Fürth* (Munich: Oldenbourg, 1986), 67–9; Kershaw, *The End*, 318–19, 324, 343, 355–6.

There were considerable differences across Germany in this period, both among and within the territories occupied by the various Allies. As mentioned in Chapter 1, for all their common goals, until mid-April 1945 the most important difference was that the Soviet Union deported arrestees to the USSR, whereas the western powers detained them in Germany (the Aachen exception notwithstanding). Yet just as other aspects of the occupying forces' conduct and treatment of Germans varied from one region or locality to another, so too did their approach to arrests. Individual military, intelligence, and security units responded to local circumstances – such as the level of German resistance or assistance they encountered – and used their discretion in interpreting and implementing orders. Particularly in the British zone there seems to have been considerable pragmatic flexibility and hence inconsistency. Meanwhile variations in the execution of arrest policy in the French zone also reflected a lack of strong centralized command, a degree of indifference to instructions developed by the Anglo-Americans, and the political diversity of French occupation personnel, who ranged from former Vichyites to communist resistors.[21] In the American zone, too, much depended on the extent to which the 'anti-Nazi spark' was 'ignited' in individual officers.[22]

Germans were arrested in diverse manners in the final weeks before, and the months following, Germany's capitulation on 8 May 1945. Some, perhaps underestimating the extent to which their positions compromised them in Allied eyes, were arrested in their offices or when they sought employment. When Augsburg capitulated on 28 April, the lord mayor, mayor, and a senior legal official – all of whom held additional positions in Nazi organizations – were detained while eating a meal as they waited to meet American officials to whom they had been

---

[21] Bessel, *Germany 1945*, 144; Wember, *Umerziehung im Lager*, 40–1, 116–17; Henke, *Politische Säuberung*, 36, 40; Biddiscombe, *Denazification of Germany*, 158–9, 161; Grohnert, *Entnazifizierung in Baden*, 21; Kurt Jürgensen, 'Towards Occupation: First Encounters in North Germany', in Ulrike Jordan (ed.), *Conditions of Surrender: Britons and Germans Witness the End of the War* (London: I. B. Tauris, 1997), 60–1; Niethammer, *Mitläuferfabrik*, 65; Gabriele Hammermann, 'Verhaftungen und Haftanstalten der sowjetischen Geheimdienstorgane am Beispiel Thüringens', in von Plato (ed.), *Studien und Berichte*, 165–6; Julia Wambach, 'Vichy in Baden-Baden: The Personnel of the French Occupation in Germany after 1945', *Contemporary European History* (pub. online 20 Dec. 2018), doi.org/10.1017/S0960777318000462 (accessed 6 Feb. 2019). On the relationships between Russians and Germans in the final months of the war and the first months thereafter, see Jan Foitzik, *Sowjetische Militäradministration in Deutschland (SMAD) 1945–1949* (Berlin: Akademie Verlag, 1999), 52–70; Naimark, *Russians in Germany*; Slaveski, *Soviet Occupation of Germany*.

[22] Padover, *Experiment in Germany*, 250.

summoned.[23] Many others were apprehended when they registered for ration or identity cards or when members of Nazi organizations, or all men, or members of certain professions, were called on to report to central locations in towns and cities. Allied intelligence agencies – the Counter Intelligence Corps (CIC) and the *Sûreté* in the western zones and the NKVD and Special Methods of Spy Detection (SMERSH) in the Soviet zone – sought out known individuals at home, such as the well-known example of the national-revolutionary author Ernst von Salomon, whom the Americans arrested in early June, or issued instructions for them to report to military government offices, where they were apprehended.[24] Others, including some who had fled their homes and workplaces and sought to disguise their identity, were found at checkpoints, during sweeps of hospitals or of POW and DP camps, or through raids of varying dimensions. In late July, the Americans conducted zone-wide security check-ups under the operational name 'Tally-ho', which saw the arrest of 80,000 Germans over two days, although relatively few were interned.[25] In the first half of August, NKVD and Red Army forces combed through large areas of the Soviet zone, including forests, initially arresting more than 64,000 people and detaining more than 3,000.[26] For all zones there are also reports of completely arbitrary arrests, whether 'off the street' or 'from the field' as an internee transport went past or 'off

[23] Wilhelm Ott, 'Erinnerungen an die Tätigkeit als geschäftsführender Bürgermeister Augsburgs', in Karl-Ulrich Gelberg (ed.), *Kriegsende und Neuanfang in Augsburg 1945: Erinnerungen und Berichte* (Munich: R. Oldenbourg, 1996), 27–8.

[24] Ernst von Salomon, *Der Fragebogen* (Reinbek bei Hamburg: Rowohlt, 2011 [1st ed. 1951]), 540; Karl Wilhelm Fricke, *Politik und Justiz in der DDR: Zur Geschichte der politischen Verfolgung 1945–1968: Bericht und Dokumentation* (Cologne: Verlag Wissenschaft und Politik, 1979), 57–61; Horn, *Internierungs- und Arbeitslager*, 36–40; Meyer, *Entnazifizierung von Frauen*, 52–3; Möhler, *Entnazifizierung in Rheinland-Pfalz und im Saarland*, 359; Greiner, *Suppressed Terror*, 100–1; Wember, *Umerziehung im Lager*, 38–9, 46; Hammermann, 'Verhaftungen und Haftanstalten', 163–6. On von Salomon's arrest and internment, see Gregor Fröhlich, *Soldat ohne Befehl: Ernst von Salomon und der Soldatische Nationalismus* (Paderborn: Ferdinand Schöningh, 2018), 330–8.

[25] Earl F. Ziemke, *The U.S. Army in the Occupation of Germany 1944–1946* (Washington, DC: Center of Military History United States Army, 1975), 318–19; Horn, *Internierungs- und Arbeitslager*, 42–3; Meyer, *Entnazifizierung von Frauen*, 52; Dolan, 'Isolating Nazism', 100–3.

[26] Greiner, *Suppressed Terror*, 101. Another large-scale operation, leading to the arrest of almost 20,000 people, of whom more than 18,000 were released almost immediately, was conducted in April 1948. Jan Foitzik and Nikita W. Petrow, 'Der Apparat des NKWD-MGB der UdSSR in Deutschland: Politische Repression und Herausbildung deutscher Staatssicherheitsorgane in der SBZ/DDR 1945–1953', in Foitzik and Petrow (eds.), *Die sowjetischen Geheimdienste in der SBZ/DDR von 1945 bis 1953* (Berlin: De Gruyter, 2009), 39–40.

the back of a truck' when an unwitting individual hitched a ride on a vehicle headed for an internment camp and ended up in detention.[27]

Germans assisted the occupying forces with arrests in various ways, whether officially or unofficially. Early on, antifascist and leftist groups were a vital source of information and themselves carried out arrests, handing detainees over to the Allies.[28] This even occurred in the district of Schwarzenberg in Saxony, which initially was not occupied by any Allied army.[29] Newly appointed police also conducted arrests, while retained or newly engaged local officials helped by finding information about local Nazi organizations or by running registrations of local residents or party members. Information about individuals was obtained from such officials and from private persons. Internees often viewed such collaboration as denunciation and betrayal and it no doubt involved much personal and political score settling as well as honest mistakes, but local and especially linguistic knowledge was frequently crucial for identifying and detecting compromised individuals and determining who belonged to the arrest categories.[30] The Soviet authorities regarded such assistance not only as a responsibility of newly created local German authorities but as an obligation of the entire population.[31] One should also not overlook the role of many (former) Germans who had left Germany during or even before the Nazi years and who returned in 1945, often in American or British uniform. Their linguistic and other

---

[27] Greiner, *Suppressed Terror*, 102; Merten, *Gulag in East Germany*, 106, 137; Wember, *Umerziehung im Lager*, 42–3, 67; Horn, *Internierungs- und Arbeitslager*, 40; Lutz Niethammer, 'Was wissen wir über die Internierungs- und Arbeitslager in der US-Zone?', in Knigge-Tesche et al. (eds.), *Internierungspraxis*, 53; Kirsten, *Das sowjetische Speziallager Nr. 4*, 41.

[28] Helga A. Welsh, *Revolutionärer Wandel auf Befehl? Entnazifizierungs- und Personalpolitik in Thüringen und Sachsen (1945–1948)* (Munich: R. Oldenbourg, 1989), 25, 27; Müller, 'Internierungslager in und um Ludwigsburg', 172; Thomas Boghardt, 'Dirty Work? The Use of Nazi Informants by U.S. Army Intelligence in Postwar Europe', *The Journal of Military History* 79, no. 2 (2015), 398.

[29] Gareth Pritchard, *Niemandsland: A History of Unoccupied Germany, 1944–1945* (Cambridge: Cambridge University Press, 2012), 141–2; Lenore Lobeck, 'Zum Beispiel Schwarzenberg: Verhaftungen im Landkries Schwarzenberg im Zeitraum 1945–1950', *Zeitschrift des Forschungsverbundes SED-Staat* 34 (2013), 36–8.

[30] Bessel, *Germany 1945*, 167; Gimbel, *A German Community*, 48; Horn, *Internierungs- und Arbeitslager*, 37–8; Meyer, *Entnazifizierung von Frauen*, 54–6; Hammermann, 'Verhaftungen und Haftanstalten', 162–4; Biddiscombe, *Denazification of Germany*, 161; Dolan, 'Isolating Nazism', 100–1; Naimark, *Russians in Germany*, 379–82; Greiner, *Suppressed Terror*, 103–10.

[31] 'Anweisungen des Kriegsrats und der Politischen Verwaltung der 1. Ukrainischen Front an die Militärkommandanten deutscher Städte zur Schaffung örtlicher Verwaltungen und zur Arbeit mit der deutschen Bevölkerung', 13 May 1945, in Jan Foitzik (ed.), *Sowjetische Kommandanturen und deutsche Verwaltung in der SBZ und frühen DDR: Dokumente* (Berlin: De Gruyter, 2015), 431, 433–4.

knowledge was crucial for Allied efforts to identify and interrogate Nazis.[32]

If arrests began as soon as the Allies entered German territory, they accelerated dramatically with the war's end and continued at a high rate until late 1945. The British interned 28,784 people by June 1945 and in November held 53,285 in internment camps. The significance of arrests relative to dismissals – which invariably receive more attention in accounts of the occupation and denazification – in the British zone is indicated by the fact that by October 50,000 people had been arrested, but only 23,000 had been dismissed from their positions.[33] In November, there were 11,120 people in internment camps in the French zone and 1,463 more in prisons; a further 1,666 were arrested in the second half of December alone. What such zonal numbers could mean locally is indicated by the example of the city of Karlsruhe: here the French arrested approximately 1,500 people between April and July, a significant number relative to the population that increased over the same period from a war-induced nadir of 60,000 to just over 100,000.[34]

In the US zone, the number of automatic arrestees jumped from 1,000 in March to 80,000 at the end of July. The Americans arrested 200 people per day in April, a figure that rose to 700 per day by June and almost 1,000 in July, before falling to 600 in August and 400 in September and October.[35] While the rate of arrests slowed further thereafter, they by no means stopped. In early December, Deputy Military Governor of the US zone General Lucius D. Clay reported that more than 90,000 people were being held under automatic-arrest directives, that such arrests were 'continuing at substantial rate', and that ca. 25,000 members of paramilitary organizations who were still held in POW camps also fell under automatic arrest. According to other sources, the Americans had

---

[32] See Helen Fry, *Denazification: Britain's Enemy Aliens, Nazi War Criminals and the Reconstruction of Post-War Europe* (Stroud: History Publishing Group, 2010); Boghardt, 'Dirty Work?', 395–6.

[33] Wember, *Umerziehung im Lager*, 369; 'Minutes of Military Government Conference Held on 12/13 Oct. 1945 at Main Headquarters, Control Commission for Germany (British Element), Lübbecke', in Pelly and Yasamee (eds.), *Documents on British Foreign Policy*, 224–5.

[34] Möhler, *Entnazifizierung in Rheinland-Pfalz und im Saarland*, 359–60; Manfred Koch, 'Karlsruhe: Landeshauptstadt oder Aschenbrödel?', in Karl Moersch and Reinhold Weber (eds.), *Die Zeit nach dem Krieg: Städte im Wiederaufbau* (Stuttgart: W. Kohlhammer, 2008), 184, 186. For slightly different zonal figures, see Grohnert, *Entnazifizierung in Baden*, 162.

[35] Biddiscombe, *Denazification of Germany*, 58. The figures for May vary between 200 and 700. Horn, *Internierungs- und Arbeitslager*, 46–7; Meyer, *Entnazifizierung von Frauen*, 53; Niethammer, *Mitläuferfabrik*, 256.

interned 117,512 people by 6 December and as many as 128,000 by the end of the year, some of whom had already been released.[36] For the Soviet zone, Beria reported to Stalin that under Order No. 00315 the NKVD had arrested 57,657 Germans and ca. 12,000 non-Germans by 1 September, and that 16,000 more were arrested in September and almost 8,000 in October. A total of ca. 94,000 had thus been arrested between May and October 1945. The pace slowed significantly only in December.[37] On 1 November, 55,824 people were in internment camps and prisons in the Soviet zone. This rose to 74,088 by 1 February 1946, of whom 66,720 were Germans. If there were fewer Germans in internment camps in the Soviet than in the American zone at this point, this was mainly because 68,451 German military, paramilitary, and prison and camp personnel had been deported to the USSR as POWs in accordance with the NKWD orders discussed in Chapter 1.[38]

Most detainees were thus interned in 1945 or early 1946, but arrests and internments continued in the following months and years. As indicated by Clay and discussed in subsequent chapters, numerous Germans who were initially detained as POWs were only later converted to civilian-internee status, becoming 'new' internees in 1946 and 1947. They were not the only people interned after the initial waves of arrests had subsided. In the French zone, more than 7,000 people were interned between the beginning of 1946 and June 1947.[39] Moreover, not everyone interned in 1946 or thereafter belonged to automatic-arrest categories due to their positions in the Nazi state or movement; other 'security' arrests continued after 1945 as well. In his July 1946 report to London, Robertson spoke of 'a comparatively small number of persons who have

---

[36] Clay to Hilldring, 8 Dec. 1945, in Jean Edward Smith (ed.), *The Papers of General Lucius D. Clay, Germany 1945–1949*, vol. 1 (Bloomington: Indiana University Press, 1974), 130; Niethammer, *Mitläuferfabrik*, 255; Meyer, *Entnazifizierung von Frauen*, 97. The latter figures are consistent with claims that ca. 12,000 internees were released by January 1946. Horn, *Internierungs- und Arbeitslager*, 66. See the discussion of internee numbers in Chapter 3.

[37] Reports by Beria to Stalin, Molotov, and Malenkov, 10 Sep., 24 Oct., and 23 Nov. 1945, all in Possekel (ed.), *Sowjetische Dokumente*, 205, 209, 216; Greiner, *Suppressed Terror*, 44; Hammermann, 'Verhaftungen und Haftanstalten', 165; Foitzik and Petrow, 'Apparat des NKWD-MGB', 39.

[38] 'Meldung des NKWD-Bevollmächtigten in Deutschland Serov an Berija', 4 Nov. 1945, and 'Meldung des NKWD-Bevollmächtigten in Deutschland Serov an Kruglov', 7 Feb. 1946, both in Possekel (ed.), *Sowjetische Dokumente*, 214, 224. Cf. Merten, *Gulag in East Germany*, 21.

[39] Author's calculation based on figures quoted above for those detained in 1945 and figures quoted below of those released in 1946 and the first half of 1947 and those remaining in June 1947.

been arrested on security grounds as a result of subversive activities committed since the Occupation'. He indicated, further, that such arrests were continuing at varying rates depending on the political situation. The British and the Americans interned numerous members of neo-Nazi networks in 1947.[40] The number of postwar 'subversives' and (non-Nazi) political opponents interned by the Soviets was certainly higher but, as Chapter 3 demonstrates, not as high as often suggested. In mid-1946 the recently renamed Ministry for Internal Affairs (MVD), previously the NKVD, insisted that the 'Werewolf' persisted and needed to be targeted, while anti-Soviet and pro-British propaganda and espionage emerged as new focuses.[41] The point here is that the Soviets were by no means the only occupiers prepared to intern real or potential opponents and obstacles on the basis of their occupation-era rather than Nazi-era activities. After all, as stressed throughout this book, internment – in every zone – was never just about punishing Nazis' past deeds; it was always also preventative and political. It should also be noted that Allied notions of security remained broad throughout internment's implementation. A paper by British military government's Legal Division from March 1946 spoke of making decisions about individuals' internment on the basis of their 'danger to German democratic security'.[42] It was thus not just about preventing physical sabotage or armed resistance.

Nevertheless, basic similarities but also differences across the zones were evident in the detention of Germans, especially adolescents, for offences such as illegal firearms possession and other breaches of military government decrees. Such arrests by the Soviets are often invoked to indicate how unjustified Soviet internment was.[43] This disregards the seriousness of breaches of firearms prohibition and overlooks the fact that the western powers also arrested people who disobeyed such orders. However, in the western zones young people arrested for possessing

---

[40] Report on Persons Held in Internment Camps, sent by Robertson to Sir Arthur Street, Control Office for Germany and Austria, London, 2 Jul. 1946, 3, TNA, FO 938/345; Biddiscombe, 'Operation Selection Board', 74.

[41] See 'Direktive des Chefs der Inneren Truppen des MWD in Deutschland Generalmajor Kusnezow an die Regimentskommandeure "Über die Intensivierung der Suche und Festnahme von feindlichen und verbrecherischen Elementen"', 21 Jun. 1946, in Foitzik and Petrow (eds.), *Die sowjetischen Geheimdienste*, 265–8.

[42] Control Commission for Germany (British Element), Legal Division (Main H.Q.), Disposal of 'Hard Core' Nazis: Memorandum on Imprisonment, Internment, and Machinery for Review Subsequent to Deprivation of Liberty, 25 Mar. 1946, TNA, FO 1032/792.

[43] E.g., Gerhard Finn, 'Die Speziallager der sowjetischen Besatzungsmacht 1945 bis 1950', in Deutscher Bundestag (ed.), *Materialien der Enquete-Kommission 'Aufarbeitung von Geschichte und Folgen der SED-Diktatur in Deutschland'*, vol. IV (Frankfurt/Main: Suhrkamp, 1995), 345.

weapons were generally not interned but either let off with a warning or prosecuted by military courts. Similarly, if 'American authorities repeatedly arrested German youths who had formed gangs, chanted nationalistic songs replete with Nazi propaganda, and occasionally clashed with Displaced Persons', as Thomas Boghardt puts it, they generally did not intern them. In the Soviet zone, in contrast, such youthful indiscretions could lead to prosecution by military tribunals or to internment.[44]

The overall situation in Austria was similar, but there were both minor and major differences. In general, the western Allies' initial approaches to denazification in Austria resembled those they took in Germany. The belief, propounded by the 'Big Three' in the Moscow Declaration of 1943, that Austria had been Hitler's 'first victim', had some moderating influence, but here, too, all the Allies sought to sanction and neutralize core Nazi personnel, including through internment.[45] Here, too, many incriminated personnel fled their posts, but there were still some significant early arrests. For instance, the Gau Leader and Reich Governor of Salzburg, Gustav Adolf Scheel, initially fled but gave himself up to the Americans on 14 May 1945.[46] Here, too, there was a significant exodus out of Soviet-controlled areas. There were also some returns: on 2 June, a local NKVD unit arrested ten suspected active NSDAP members who were returning home after having initially fled in advance of the Soviet invasion. Many others left and did not return so soon, if at all.[47] In

---

[44] Evangelisches Stadtpfarramt Herrenalb to Evangelischer Oberkirchenrat Stuttgart, 20 Feb. 1946, Landeskirchliches Archiv Stuttgart (LKAS), A 126, no. 2273: 57; Boghardt, 'Dirty Work?', 393 (quotation). See also Meyer, *Entnazifizierung von Frauen*, 59; Altmeier to Minister President Boden, 20 Jan. 1947, in Peter Brommer (ed.), *Quellen zur Geschichte von Rheinland-Pfalz während der französischen Besatzung, März 1945 bis August 1949* (Mainz: Kommission des Landtages für die Geschichte des Landes Rheinland-Pfalz, 1985), 352; Möhler, *Entnazifizierung in Rheinland-Pfalz und im Saarland*, 384; Kehoe, 'Control, Disempowerment'; Wolfram von Scheliha, 'Ein Bärendienst an den Stalinismus-Opfern', *Horch und Guck: Zeitschrift der Gedenkstätte Museum in der 'Runden Ecke' Leipzig*, no. 3 (2009), 72–3; Kastner, '373 Camp Wolfsberg', 71–2.

[45] Stiefel, *Entnazifizierung in Österreich*, 21–4. For a more recent brief discussion of Austrian denazification, see Robert Knight, 'Denazification and Integration in the Austrian Province of Carinthia', *The Journal of Modern History* 79, no. 3 (2007), 572–612.

[46] Ernst Hanisch, 'Braune Flecken im Goldenen Westen: Die Entnazifizierung in Salzburg', in Sebastian Meissl, Klaus-Dieter Mulley, and Oliver Rathkolb (eds.), *Verdrängte Schuld, verfehlte Sühne: Entnazifizierung in Österreich 1945–1955* (Munich: R. Oldenbourg Verlag, 1986), 16, 322.

[47] Stiefel, *Entnazifizierung in Österreich*, 33, 90; Klaus-Dieter Mulley, 'Zur Administration der Entnazifizierung in Niederösterreich', in Walter Schuster and Wolfgang Weber (eds.), *Entnazifizierung im regionalen Vergleich* (Linz: Archiv der Stadt Linz, 2004), 275–6; Martynov, Bushkov, 'NKVD Report on the Investigation and Arrest of Austrians', 4 Jun. 1945, in Békés et al. (eds.), *Soviet Occupation*, 293–4.

Austria, too, a number of (often rival) Allied security services were responsible for arrests, above all the military counter-intelligence forces, the British units being called Field Security Sections, not CIC as in Germany. In Austria, too, much depended on the inclinations of individual occupation officials, while the occupying authorities also often sought and received help from the local population. In a radio address in August, a senior British official encouraged the Styrian population: 'You know the Nazis. Show us the Nazis.'[48] The postwar acceleration of arrests seems to have occurred somewhat later in Austria, not least due to the Americans' adoption of Austrian-specific denazification and automatic-arrest guidelines in early August, by which time the rate of American arrests in Germany had already peaked.[49] In Austria, the French were even less well prepared and more improvisational than in Germany, not least because they had been granted an Austrian occupation zone only in April 1945 and because some instructions were available only in English and not in French. In Austria, too, arrests continued into 1946 and sometimes had what can only be termed an outright political purpose. In a two-day action in Voralberg in March 1946 the French arrested hundreds of 'illegal' party members (i.e., those who had been members between the NSDAP's prohibition in Austria in 1933 and the country's annexation by Germany in 1938). The aim was to put the former Nazis in their place and impress them and the broader population with French rigour on the occasion of the annexation's anniversary.[50]

The major exception to the overall similarity to the Allies' approach in Germany was Soviet policy. NKVD Order No. 00315 was not applied in Austria. Instead, as already mentioned, the Soviets largely left denazification to the Austrians, who developed and pursued their own measures (on which more later), at least in the Soviet zone and Vienna, due to the fact – mentioned in Chapter 1 – that initially only the Soviets recognized Austria's new provisional government. The Soviets therefore did not feel a need to undertake extensive internments themselves but repeatedly called on the Austrian government to be more vigorous in its efforts. In summer 1945, the NKVD did arrest some suspected war criminals, SS

---

[48] Kastner, '373 Camp Wolfsberg', 60, 67 (quotation); Klaus Eisterer, *Französische Besatzungspolitik: Tirol und Voralberg 1945/46* (Innsbruck: Haymon Verlag, 1991), 166–9, 187; Mulley, 'Zur Administration der Entnazifizierung', 276–8.

[49] See Kurt Tweraser, 'Von der Militärdiktatur 1945 zur milden Bevormundung des "Bargaining-Systems" der fünfziger Jahre: Verhaltensmuster und Interaktionen von Amerikanern und Österreichern auf der Military-Government-Ebene', in Alfred Ableitinger, Siegfried Beer, and Eduard G. Staudinger (eds.), *Österreich unter alliierter Besatzung 1945–1955* (Vienna: Böhlau, 1998), 326–8.

[50] Eisterer, *Französische Besatzungspolitik*, 15–16, 163–6, 170, 206–8.

members, and NSDAP officials, often only Local Group Leaders and above, but it promptly released many whom it did not suspect of offences against the USSR or other atrocities. Those it did suspect were generally prosecuted by Soviet military tribunals and deported, not interned or imprisoned in Austria.[51] The number of Soviet arrests thus remained limited, relative to both Germany and elsewhere in Austria, where, prior to recognizing the indigenous government, the western powers pursued their own internment policies. By February 1946, the Soviets had arrested fewer than 1,000 people, whereas the Austrian authorities had arrested almost 10,000 (many of whom had already been released), the French had interned between 2,000 and 4,500 people, the British 6,413, and the Americans 9,462.[52] If denazification and particularly internment were less important for the Soviets and to some extent for the French in Austria than in Germany, internment was arguably even more important within American, British, and French policy for Austria's denazification than for Germany's. Walter Schuster calls internment 'the crux of the American denazification' in Upper Austria. Between July 1945 and April 1946, the Americans dismissed between 9,000 and 10,000 people but arrested 12,056.[53]

---

[51] Wolfgang Mueller, *Die sowjetische Besatzung in Österreich 1945–1955 und ihre politische Mission* (Vienna: Böhlau, 2005), 128–9; Klaus-Dieter Mulley, 'Befreiung und Besatzung: Aspekte sowjetischer Besatzung in Niederösterreich 1945–1948', in Ableitinger et al. (eds.), *Österreich unter alliierter Besatzung*, 394–5; Dieter Stiefel, 'Nazifizierung plus Entnazifizierung = Null? Bemerkungen zur besonderen Problematik der Entnazifizierung in Österrreich', in Meissl et al. (eds.), *Verdrängte Schuld*, 30; Walter Schuster, 'Politische Restauration und Entnazifizierungspolitik in Oberösterreich', in Schuster and Weber (eds.), *Entnazifizierung im regionalen Vergleich*, 201; Mulley, 'Zur Administration der Entnazifizierung', 276–7; Stefan Karner, 'Zur Politik der sowjetischen Besatzungs- und Gewahrsamsmacht: Das Fallbeispiel Margarethe Ottilinger', in Ableitinger et al. (eds.), *Österreich unter alliierter Besatzung*, 403–4, 410–11; Oliver Rathkolb, 'Historische Fragmente und die "unendliche Geschichte" von den sowjetischen Absichten in Österreich 1945', in Ableitinger et al. (eds.), *Österreich unter alliierter Besatzung*, 154; Barbara Stelzl-Marx, 'Entnazifizierung in Österreich: Die Rolle der sowjetischen Besatzungsmacht', in Schuster and Weber (eds.), *Entnazifizierung im regionalen Vergleich*, 432, 438.

[52] Dieter Stiefel, 'Der Prozeß der Entnazifizierung in Österreich', in Henke and Woller (eds.), *Politische Säuberung in Europa*, 113; Stiefel, *Entnazifizierung in Österreich*, 33–4; Eisterer, *Französische Besatzungspolitik*, 193. On Austrian detention camps in 1945–6, see Roland Pichler, 'Volksgerichtsbarkeit und Entnazifizierung unter besonderer Berücksichtigung der Verfahren gegen Frauen vor dem Volksgericht Wien' (unpub. Dr. iur. thesis, University of Vienna, 2016), available at: othes.univie.ac.at/41841/1/2016-03-30_0101619.pdf (accessed 6 Feb. 2019), 67–73.

[53] Schuster, 'Politische Restauration', 196; Kurt Tweraser, 'Die amerikanische Säuberungspolitik in Österreich', in Schuster and Weber (eds.), *Entnazifizierung im regionalen Vergleich*, 369. Compare also the tables of arrest and public service dismissal figures up to September 1946 in Eisterer, *Französische Besatzungspolitik*, 214, 230.

Categorization, Processing, and Release

As noted in Chapter 1, wartime planning paid little attention to what would happen to internees after their arrest, and many directives and the Potsdam Agreement said nothing about this. Soviet planners in particular seem barely to have progressed beyond the already cited suggestion from March 1944 'to isolate and remove the Nazis, to wherever'.[54] In contrast, in early 1945 there was at least the outline of an Anglo-American plan for the treatment of at least some arrestees. Those suspected of individual atrocities were to be tried and punished by the Allies or transferred to formerly occupied countries for prosecution. Meanwhile, for the automatic arrestees, JCS 1067/6 (but not the SHAEF directives or handbooks) spoke of 'trial by an appropriate semi-judicial body'.[55] Rather vague plans also existed to arraign the members of the organizations to be prosecuted by the IMT, but its charter was not agreed until 8 August 1945 and its indictment – and thus the determination of the indicted organizations – was not finalized until 6 October, by which time scores of thousands had already been detained.[56] Moreover, these plans by no means clarified the fate of all internees. The automatic-arrest categories went well beyond the organizations indicted at Nuremberg: the Reich cabinet, the NSDAP Leadership Corps, the SA, the SS, the Gestapo, the SD, and the Wehrmacht's General Staff and High Command. There was also the possibility (which subsequently became a reality) that some of these groups would not be convicted, and it remained unclear what would happen to their members, at least until Control Council Directive No. 38, which effectively ignored the IMT verdict, as discussed later. Questions remained too about the treatment – and especially the release – of people who might be arrested by mistake or whose detention might seem unwarranted for other reasons, such as ill-health or age. As the following section shows, considerable differences emerged in the handling of these and related questions between the

---

[54] Gen. Manuil'skij at the 92nd Meeting of the Litvinov Commission, 14 Mar. 1944, in Laufer and Kynin (eds.), *UdSSR und die deutsche Frage*, 369.

[55] 'Directive to Commander in Chief of United States Forces of Occupation Regarding the Military Government of Germany' (JCS 1067/6), 26 Apr. 1945, in *FRUS 1945 III*, 490. See Dolan, 'Isolating Nazism', 84.

[56] See 'Charter of the International Military Tribunal', 8 Aug. 1945, and 'Indictment', 6 Oct. 1945, both in *Trial of the Major War Criminals before the International Military Tribunal, Nuremberg, 14 November 1945–1 October 1946*, vol. I: *Official Documents* (Nuremberg: International Military Tribunal Nuremberg, 1947), 10–16, 27–68. Merten overlooks this when he argues that the western powers 'sent leading Nazis and members of organizations judged criminal by the Nürenberg [*sic*] Military Court [*sic*] to their internment camps'. Merten, *Gulag in East Germany*, 39.

Soviet Union, on the one hand, and the western Allies, on the other, while less acute differences developed among the latter.

Especially in the western zones of Germany, there were also distinctions between various categories of detainees. If almost all targets for arrest were sometimes described as security threats during wartime planning and in the first postwar year, in the western zones three distinct groups of detainees emerged: war-crimes suspects, security suspects, and automatic arrestees. The first were those who either were suspected of individual participation in specific war crimes or other atrocities or were held as hostile witnesses thereto. They were, in general, relatively quickly separated from other internees, and unless insufficient evidence led to their release or transfer to another category, they were tried or heard as witnesses by Allied or German courts or extradited to other European countries. They constituted a small minority of internees, less than 6% (4,044) in the British zone in May 1946, 3% in April 1947, and ca. 7% in February 1948.[57] The French zone was somewhat exceptional here in two respects. First, some Waffen-SS and Wehrmacht divisions that were suspected of war crimes were declared 'blocked units', their members remaining in regular internment camps with a hybrid automatic-arrest/collective war crimes–suspect status. Second, at least in the state of Baden lists of individual war criminals wanted by France were not provided to relevant personnel on the ground until autumn 1947, such that these suspects were not filtered out from the mass of internees as quickly as elsewhere. In the other states in the zone, however, the sorting of suspected war criminals began in October 1945.[58]

The second group – security suspects – were those who were not war-crimes suspects and did not belong to automatic-arrest categories but were nevertheless deemed a threat to the occupation or its objectives. They were the most exposed to arbitrariness. As suggested by Robertson's July 1946 report quoted earlier, these security suspects constituted a small minority of detainees in the western zones, less than 3% (2,100) in the British case, still a significant absolute number.[59] In the American zone, they were the first whose cases were reviewed – upon

[57] Wember, *Umerziehung im Lager*, 38, 28–31; Legal Division Chief to Secretariat, Zonal Executive Offices, 24 Apr. 1947, TNA, FO 1032/795; Hoffmann to Colombo, 8 Mar. 1948, Archives du Comité international de la Croix-Rouge, Geneva (ACICR), B G 44 02-056.03.

[58] Möhler, 'Internierungslager in der französischen Besatzungszone', 55, 57; Grohnert, *Entnazifizierung in Baden*, 167, 169; Möhler, *Entnazifizierung in Rheinland-Pfalz und im Saarland*, 370.

[59] Wember, *Umerziehung im Lager*, 38, 42–3. Cf. Möhler, 'Internierungslager in der französischen Besatzungszone', 59.

application of the internees themselves – by Security Review Boards, which began investigating them and releasing those considered harmless in late autumn 1945. From October 1946 the internment of further security suspects was stopped in the US zone, and applications for release from already interned security suspects could be rejected only if the security threat was proven or if they were now deemed war-crimes suspects.[60]

The vast majority of internees belonged to the third group: those who fell into one (or more) of the automatic-arrest categories by virtue of their rank, office, or professional position.[61] In fact, internees are sometimes equated with the automatic arrestees, while security and war-crimes suspects were and are occasionally omitted from internment statistics and analyses. As mentioned in Chapter 1, in early September 1945, the British were the first to revise their automatic-arrest policy by differentiating within this large, diverse group and releasing the more harmless cases. Arrest remained mandatory for some categories, but others were converted to 'compulsory investigation categories'. Members of these groups who had already been interned were assessed and released, unless they were deemed 'individual dangers to security'. The converted categories included those who had never been key targets of British internment policy or whose inclusion had been questioned at some point during wartime planning: public servants, lower ranks of the regular and criminal police, female auxiliaries of the SS and Waffen-SS, lower ranks of the BDM, and NSDAP functionaries below Local Group Leader. Additionally, medically unfit internees and those aged under seventeen and over sixty-five should now be released even if they belonged to compulsory arrest categories, while detainees for whom petitions were presented and who could show special cause could be released. Most members of the compulsory investigation categories were discharged by March 1946, when further groups were added: female employees of the NSDAP, junior SD staff, and youthful junior officers of the Hitler Youth. By the end of May, more than 25,000 – just over one-third of British-zone internees to that point – had been released.[62]

Although there were competing views within US military government, the Americans were not far behind the British. Some, like Military Governor of Bavaria General George Patton, viewed the mass detention

---

[60] Meyer, *Entnazifizierung von Frauen*, 58–60, 68; Horn, *Internierungs- und Arbeitslager*, 56–69; Schuster, *Entnazifizierung in Hessen*, 247.
[61] Horn, *Internierungs- und Arbeitslager*, 33; Wember, *Umerziehung im Lager*, 38.
[62] Wember, *Umerziehung im Lager*, 47–9.

of apparently harmless automatic arrestees as 'sheer madness'.[63] Most likely he was responsible for the release of NSDAP Local Group Leaders from internment camps in Bavaria in September 1945. However, they were promptly rearrested due to the seeming inconsistency of releasing them while simultaneously extending denazification to private businesses under US Military Government Law No. 8, which banned even ordinary party members from managerial positions. Other American officials were more committed to automatic arrest, even if they acknowledged its problematic nature. Clay blocked initial suggestions to modify it, seeing even lower-ranking internees as 'minor henchmen of the Nazi Party who in fact carried its method to the German people'. Clay opposed their release while ordinary German POWs were still being used for reparatory labour. Yet he was not just concerned with justice and equity. He also feared the political influence of former Nazis on the German electorate ahead of local elections to be held in 1946.[64] This confirms that western internment was far from purely about physical security or justice; it was governed by political considerations.

Nevertheless, from mid-November 1945 Security Review Boards were established in the American zone to receive and assess requests for release from certain categories of internees. These included the security suspects, as already mentioned, and certain automatic-arrest categories but not members of the organizations indicted by the IMT or members of the German intelligence services and the Security Police. Such stipulations, like the inclusion of security suspects in the Americans' February 1946 proposal to the NADSC discussed in Chapter 1, confirm the inaccuracy of claims that western internment was always limited, or at some point was restricted, to members of the indicted organizations. The review boards, which included German boards in advisory capacity, prioritized the cases of public servants and sick, disabled, and elderly internees. The process was selective, bureaucratic, and initially slow, such that only 5,566 people were released by mid-April 1946. By the time the boards wound down in autumn 1946, however, more than 51,000 internees had applied for, and more than 41,000 had obtained, their release.[65] Many other internees did not benefit from such procedures. In early 1946, some groups of internees were removed from automatic-arrest categories (as proposed at the NADSC, as discussed in

[63] Biddiscombe, *Denazification of Germany*, 56; Horn, *Internierungs- und Arbeitslager*, 55.
[64] Ziemke, *U.S. Army*, 387; Horn, *Internierungs- und Arbeitslager*, 51–4 (quotation 51); Dolan, 'Isolating Nazism', 110–11.
[65] Horn, *Internierungs- und Arbeitslager*, 56–69, 73–4; Meyer, *Entnazifizierung von Frauen*, 61–6. Calculation based on figures in the latter, 64–6. They do not include applications and releases in Hessen after July 1946.

Chapter 1), but many that remained in automatic arrest – again especially, but not only, the Nuremberg groups – continued to be 'detained
without benefit of a review of their cases'; this contradicts suggestions
that all US-zone internees enjoyed the right of review.[66] Indeed, in
March 1948 it was still uncertain whether the right of habeas corpus,
which had recently been introduced in the American zone, applied to
internees.[67] One should thus not exaggerate the degree to, and speed
with, which liberal principles about the rule of law were introduced in the
American zone or overlook the continuing contradiction that internment
posed thereto.

The French also took reasonably early steps to modify arrest categories
and assess detainees. In late 1945 there were concerns that many people
liable to arrest remained at large, while many detainees' incarceration
appeared unwarranted. The head of military government in the Saarland,
Gilbert Grandval, argued in January 1946 that 'Even in occupied territory, individual freedom is to be respected and it is unacceptable that
arbitrary and unsubstantiated arrests be carried out.'[68] With their first
independent internment directive, military government *Circulaire 753* of
15 January 1946, the French introduced minor changes. As in the British
zone, NSDAP officials below the rank of Local Group Leader were no
longer to be interned, nor were NCOs of the Waffen-SS, while civil-
servant arrest categories were reduced. Yet in contrast with British steps
in the following months to permit the release of some leaders of Nazi
youth organizations, the French extended automatic arrest to leaders of
the BDM, the *Deutsches Jungvolk*, and the *Jungmädelbund* (the sections of
the Hitler Youth for boys and girls aged ten to fourteen years), perhaps
reflecting particular French concern that such people not endanger the

---

[66] Office of Military Government, U.S. (OMGUS), 'Automatic Arrest', *Weekly Information Bulletin*, no. 29, 16 Feb. 1946, 12, available at: images.library.wisc.edu/History/EFacs/ GerRecon/omg1946n029/reference/history.omg1946n029.i0007.pdf   (accessed   6 Feb. 2019).

[67] See Hessischer Landtag, I. Wahlperiode, *Stenographischer Bericht über die 35. Sitzung*, 11 Mar. 1948 (Wiesbaden: Carl Ritter, 1948), 1173–5, available at: starweb.hessen.de/ cache/PLPR/01/5/00035.pdf; OMGUS Ordinance No. 23, 'Relief from Unlawful Restraints of Personal Liberty', 31 Dec. 1947, in *Military Government Gazette Germany, United States Area of Control*, Issue H, 16 Jan. 1948, 7–14, available at: deposit.d-nb.de/online/vdr/rechtsq.htm (accessed 6 Feb. 2019); Alvin J. Rockwell, Director, Legal Division, OMGUS, 'Habeas Corpus', *Information Bulletin: Magazine of US Military Government in Germany*, no. 127, 27 Jan. 1948, 20–1, available at: images .library.wisc.edu/History/EFacs/GerRecon/omg1948n127/reference/history.omg1948n127 .rockwellhabeas.pdf (all accessed 6 Feb. 2019). Cf. Priemel, *Betrayal*, 77; Waibel, *Von der wohlwollenden Despotie*, 55, 124–5.

[68] Grandval to district officers, 21 Jan. 1946, cited in Möhler, *Entnazifizierung in Rheinland-Pfalz und im Saarland*, 370.

reeducation of German youth. Military government committees (*commissions de triage*) had already begun screening internees in October 1945, leading to first sizable releases in December. In 1946 and the first half of 1947, 13,503 were released, many of whom did not belong to automatic-arrest categories in the first place. Yet as arrests continued, the overall number of internees in the French zone decreased only slowly until early 1947: from 11,120 in November 1945 to 10,923 in January 1947 and then to 8,539 by June.[69]

While the western powers thus took steps in late 1945 and early 1946 to release the more harmless detainees, they were determined to detain members of the organizations on trial since November 1945 before the IMT. In May 1946, Clay acknowledged that keeping 'thousands still in jail without bond awaiting trial until Nuremberg' was 'not consistent with civil liberties'. 'Nevertheless', he argued, 'it is a basic part of our punishment of war criminals and our denazification program.' In December 1945 he estimated that members of the Nuremberg organizations accounted for about three-quarters of automatic arrestees.[70] In tandem with the discussions at the NADSC discussed in Chapter 1, in February 1946 new American arrest directives extended the November changes to allow the release of automatic arrestees who had not been *active* members of the indicted organizations. Under the new stipulations, Block and Cell Leaders of the NSDAP could now apply for discharge, but more senior personnel could not.[71] Yet in addition to the members of the indicted organizations, in mid-1946 American military government was still discussing the continued detention of criminal suspects and witnesses, of security suspects 'whose liberty would be inimical to the occupation forces', and of others who 'were taken into custody on varied charges of having fostered Nazi ideology and otherwise furthered the aims of the National Socialist Party', that is, automatic arrestees who were not members of the indicted organizations.[72]

The delivery of the IMT's judgement on 30 September and 1 October 1946 raised the hopes of many internees that they would soon be

---

[69] Möhler, 'Internierung im Rahmen der Entnazifizierungspolitik', 64; Möhler, *Entnazifizierung in Rheinland-Pfalz und im Saarland*, 359–60, 365; Möhler, 'Internierungslager in der französischen Besatzungszone', 53–4; Henke, *Politische Säuberung*, 40; Biddiscombe, *Denazification of Germany*, 157, 161, 167, 179.

[70] Clay to Echols, 31 May 1946, and Clay to Hilldring, 8 Dec. 1945, both in Smith (ed.), *Papers of General Lucius D. Clay*, 225, 130–1. Cf. Meyer, *Entnazifizierung von Frauen*, 57.

[71] Horn, *Internierungs- und Arbeitslager*, 71–4; Plischke, 'Denazification', 213; Meyer, *Entnazifizierung von Frauen*, 68.

[72] OMGUS, 'Internment Camps', *Weekly Information Bulletin*, no. 52 (Jul. 1946), 16–17, available at: images.library.wisc.edu/History/EFacs/GerRecon/omg1946n052/reference/history.omg1946n052.i0008.pdf (accessed 6 Feb. 2019).

released, but it dashed the hopes of others. The Nuremberg verdict declared the NSDAP Leadership Corps, the SS, the Gestapo, and the SD to be criminal organizations. Yet it exempted various subgroups within each of these organizations, including NSDAP functionaries below Local Group Leader, junior Gestapo office staff, SD informants who were not SS members, members of the *Reiter-SS* (Rider-SS), SS members who had been forcibly recruited, and anyone who had left the convicted organizations before the war. For varying reasons, the IMT also acquitted the SA, the Reich cabinet, and the Wehrmacht's General Staff and High Command. Altogether, the various acquitted or exempted 'non-Nurembergers' were numerous. In October 1946 the French calculated that only 47% of their internees actually fell under the conviction.[73]

The western powers had refused steadfastly to release all but the lowliest members of the indicted organizations before the IMT verdict, but it had little immediate impact on internees. Control Council Directive No. 38 was proclaimed on 12 October 1946, ostensibly to create a common framework for war-crimes and internment policy in the verdict's wake. But the directive did not acknowledge the IMT's distinctions among, or within, the indicted organizations.[74] The IMT charter of August 1945 and Control Council Law No. 10 of December 1945 had already created a shared legal basis for implementing the plan to prosecute members of convicted organizations but had simultaneously granted zonal commanders full discretion over whether and how to do so. As in so many other areas, they made full use of this discretionary power.[75]

The British were most responsive to the verdict. In winter 1946–7 they began releasing internees who did not fall under the IMT conviction.[76] Moreover, somewhat surprisingly, given that prosecuting organizational

[73] See 'Judgment', 1 Oct. 1946, in *Trial of the Major War Criminals*, esp. 257–79; Möhler, 'Internierungslager in der französischen Besatzungszone', 55. On the IMT verdicts on the indicted organizations, see Pomorski, 'Conspiracy and Criminal Organization', 242–6; Priemel, *Betrayal*, 143–4, 147–8.

[74] 'Control Council Directive No. 38: The Arrest and Punishment of War Criminals, Nazis, and Militarists and the Internment, Control, and Surveillance of Potentially Dangerous Germans', 12 Oct. 1946, in Ruhm von Oppen (ed.), *Documents on Germany*, 168–79. Cf. Wember, *Umerziehung im Lager*, 152–4; Möhler, *Entnazifizierung in Rheinland-Pfalz und im Saarland*, 241–2.

[75] 'Charter of the International Military Tribunal', 8 Aug. 1945, Article 10, in *Trial of the Major War Criminals*, 12; 'Control Council Law No. 10: Punishment of Persons Guilty of War Crimes, Crimes against Peace and against Humanity', 20 Dec. 1945, Article II, paragraph I(d), and Article III, in Ruhm von Oppen (ed.), *Documents on Germany*, 98–100.

[76] Wember, *Umerziehung im Lager*, 145, 150–1.

criminality had been an American idea, only the British (and to a lesser extent the Soviets) implemented to any considerable extent the plan to prosecute people merely for being members of the criminal organizations. In early 1947, the British created a system of German-staffed *Spruchgerichte* (summary courts), located near British internment camps, to try approximately 27,000 members, the vast majority of whom were internees.[77] Reflecting the IMT's insistence on individual culpability, the prosecution had to prove that the accused had joined or remained in the organization while knowing of the latter's criminal intent. Of 21,292, proceedings conducted between June 1947 and the end of 1949, 10% were abandoned, while 16% ended with acquittals and 74% with convictions. One-third of sentences consisted of prison terms and two-thirds of fines. Fewer than 3% of convictions entailed prison sentences of more than two years, so most convicts' time in internment was longer than their prison sentence, if they received one. As the courts normally counted internment towards sentences, most internees walked

---

[77] Prosecutions under the other occupying powers should not be underestimated or overlooked, but the British case stands out both quantitatively and qualitatively. Heinz Schneppen's suggestion that only the Americans made systematic use of their ability under ACC Law No. 10 to prosecute German perpetrators including for membership is thus misleading. The Americans charged many defendants at the twelve Nuremberg 'successor trials' with membership of the criminal organizations, among other things. Yet only 75 of the 185 defendants were convicted on that count, mainly in combination with other offences. The extent of French prosecutions for membership of the criminal organizations is unclear but was likely limited. In the Soviet zone, more than 3,000 Germans were prosecuted for membership in criminal organizations. Additionally, to be sure, membership in criminal organizations was an incriminating factor in denazification procedures (narrowly understood) in all zones, but these were not criminal in nature and did not focus exclusively on membership. Thus only the British created a system of courts to deal exclusively with membership. Donald Bloxham's inaccurate claim that the British dealt with members of the criminal organizations, like the Americans, through denazification panels rests on the conflation of the *Spruchgerichte* with US-zone *Spruchkammern* (denazification panels) and reduces the number of Germans who were criminally prosecuted in the British zone from more than 20,000 to more than 1,000. See Heinz Schneppen, 'Das Nürnberger Urteil über die "verbrecherische Organisationen" und seine Folgen', *Zeitschrift für Geschichtswissenschaft* 63, no. 1 (2015), 44, 54, 60, 63–4; Priemel, *Betrayal*, 155, 259, 288; Claudia Moisel, 'Résistance und Repressalien: Die Kriegsverbrecherprozesse in der französischen Zone und in Frankreich', in Frei (ed.), *Transnationale Vergangenheitspolitik*, 275; Clemens Vollnhals, 'Internierung, Entnazifizierung und Strafverfolgung von NS-Verbrechen in der sowjetischen Besatzungszone', in Andreas Hilger, Mike Schmeitzner, and Clemens Vollnhals (eds.), *Sowjetisierung oder Neutralität: Optionen sowjetischer Besatzungspolitik in Deutschland und Österreich 1945–1955* (Göttingen: Vandenhoeck & Ruprecht, 2006), 243; Meyer-Seitz, *Verfolgung von NS-Straftaten*, 31–2; Bloxham, 'British War Crimes Trial Policy', 105, 118; Cohen, 'Transitional Justice', 71–2. On the Nuremberg successor trials, see Kim C. Priemel and Alexa Stiller (eds.), *Reassessing the Nuremberg Military Tribunals: Transitional Justice, Trial Narratives, and Historiography* (New York: Berghahn Books, 2012); Priemel, *Betrayal*.

free after their trial. Only ca. 900 (4% of those charged) served add-itional prison time at the former British internment camp, now German prison, at Esterwegen. For the remainder, apart from fines, the only further consequence was the entry of their conviction into the criminal record (until these entries were erased under West Germany's second law on exemption from punishment of 1954).[78] As a result of the *Spruchgericht* proceedings, the number of internees fell from 23,247 in August 1947 to 13,766 in December, before dropping further to 6,953 in February 1948, 2,172 in April, 715 in June, and 120 in December. Thus, only a minority of British-zone internees faced prosecution, let alone received a conviction, and even the overwhelming majority of those who did regained their liberty by mid-1948. They thus joined the much larger number who had already been released – without convic-tion or even charge – through administrative processes and political decisions. Irrespective of any charge by a *Spruchgericht*, internees still had to undergo denazification proceedings on their release if they sought employment that was subject thereto, which indicates that in the British zone internment was quite distinct from denazification, narrowly understood.[79]

Although awaiting the Nuremberg verdict had become a key justifica-tion for continuing to detain internees, neither its condemnation nor its acquittal of various organizations was of much immediate consequence for internees in the US zone. The Americans took five months to react to the acquittals and their belated response was hardly decisive. They granted discretion over the release of 'non-Nurembergers' to the German state ministers for denazification who, as discussed shortly, had been delegated some responsibility in 1946. In June 1947 the Bavarian minister, Alfred Loritz (head of the *Wirtschaftliche Aufbau-Vereinigung*, Economic Reconstruction Union, a short-lived postwar Bavarian political party), ordered the continued detention of most

---

[78] Sebastian Römer, *Mitglieder verbrecherischer Organisationen nach 1945: Die Ahndung des Organisationsverbrechens in der britischen Zone durch die Spruchgerichte* (Frankfurt/Main: Peter Lang, 1995), 105–6, 110–13, 133; Wember, *Umerziehung im Lager*, 318, 343. Römer's and Wember's numbers differ slightly. For a sense of the sentences, see those of District Leaders and the allowances made for their time in internment, in Rademacher, *Kreisleiter der NSDAP*, 322–34. On the 1954 erasure, see Norbert Frei, *Vergangenheitspolitik: Die Anfänge der Bundesrepublik und die NS-Vergangenheit* (Munich: Deutscher Taschenbuch Verlag, 1999 [1st ed. 1996]), 126.

[79] Wember, *Umerziehung im Lager*, 371–2, 23–4. Merten misconstrues Biddiscombe and suggests that in November 1947 the British held only 500 internees, whereas in fact they still held almost 18,000. Cf. Merten, *Gulag in East Germany*, 32; Biddiscombe, *Denazification of Germany*, 110; Wember *Umerziehung im Lager*, 371.

non-Nurembergers. It took until February 1948 for some, but by no means all, of them to be removed from automatic-arrest categories.[80]

Instead of being prosecuted as members of criminal organizations, internees in the US zone were subjected to the denazification procedures that were developed for the entire adult population in the context of the Americans' 'limited delegation of the praxis of denazification' to the Germans.[81] One aspect of this delegation, discussed further in Chapter 4, was the transfer of responsibility for administering most US-zone internment camps to the zone's German state governments from autumn 1946. Before that, however, the first major step was the state governments' development, in collaboration with US military government, of a Law for the Liberation from Nazism and Militarism (hereafter Liberation Law), which was promulgated on 5 March 1946. Under this law, all German residents of the US zone aged eighteen years or over were screened, and *Spruchkammern* (denazification panels) were established to assign those deemed to fall under the law to one of five categories: Major Offenders, Offenders, Lesser Offenders, Followers, or Persons Exonerated, categories that were subsequently adopted in Control Council Directive No. 38. Unlike the proceedings before the British-zone *Spruchgerichte* with which they are often conflated, those before the *Spruchkammern* were not criminal in nature or focus.[82] Indeed, the Liberation Law largely eschewed the language of criminality and punishment in favour of atonement and reparation. Its stated aims were to exclude 'from influence in public, economic, and cultural life', and to extract 'reparations' from, 'all those who have actively supported the National Socialist tyranny, or are guilty of having violated the principles of justice and humanity, or of having selfishly exploited the conditions thus created'. Panel assessments

---

[80] Horn, *Internierungs- und Arbeitslager*, 114–20; 'Neue Richtlichien für die Internierung: Wer fällt unter den automatischen Arrest?', *Stuttgarter Nachrichten*, 14 Feb. 1948. On Loritz and his party, see Hans Woller, *Die Loritz-Partei: Geschichte, Struktur und Politik der Wirtschaftlichen Aufbau-Vereinigung (WAV) 1945–1955* (Stuttgart: Deutsche Verlags-Anstalt, 1982).

[81] Christoph Kleßmann, *Die doppelte Staatsgründung: Deutsche Geschichte 1945–1955* (Göttingen: Vandenhoeck & Ruprecht, 1982), 89.

[82] One reason for the conflation of the two is that the *Spruchgerichte* were initially called *Spruchkammern*, but the former designation quickly superseded the latter. Compare 'Ordinance 69: Trial of Members of Criminal Organizations/Verordnung Nr. 69: Prozeß gegen Angehörige verbrecherischer Organisationen', 1 Nov. 1946, *Military Government Gazette Germany, British Zone of Control*, no. 16, 1947, 405; and 'Verordnung über die Errichtung der Dienststelle eines Generalinspekteurs in der britischen Zone für die Spruchgerichte zur Aburteilung der Mitglieder der in Nürnberg für verbrecherisch erklärten Organisationen vom 17. Februar 1947', *Verordnungsblatt für die Britische Zone*, no. 2, 30 Apr. 1947, 22. Both available online: deposit.d-nb.de/online/vdr/rechtsq.htm (accessed 6 Feb. 2019).

considered the person's 'individual responsibility and his actual conduct, taken as a whole', and did not focus merely on crimes or membership of criminal organizations. Sentences included confinement to a labour camp (for up to five years for Offenders and up to ten years for Major Offenders) rather than prison, as well as a range of financial, political, and professional sanctions. Convictions were not entered in the criminal record. The Liberation Law did not mention internees but stated – again in a formulation copied in Directive No. 38 – that 'Political internment after 8 May 1945 can be taken into account' when determining labour-camp sentences, a description that not only confirms internment's 'political' nature but also indicates that internees – and former internees – fell under the Liberation Law.[83] The Americans long insisted that internees, with minimal exceptions, be detained until their proceedings were completed. As a result, in the second half of 1946 denazification panels were established at internment camps, becoming known as *Lagerspruchkammern*. The first proceedings before such a panel began in October 1946 shortly after the IMT's verdict, but the decision to create them and not to follow the British path of criminalizing organizational membership had been taken earlier.[84]

The Americans – and indeed all the western powers – took longer to process and release internees than often assumed, which means that internment in the US zone lasted longer than is often believed.[85] The slowness of the Security Review Boards has already been noted. Beyond that, it took months for the limited number of intelligence staff to interrogate the tens of thousands of internees. For example, Kurt Georg Kiesinger, the future chancellor of the FRG (1966–9), was arrested on 30 April 1945 but not interrogated until November, while a former SA Oberführer (colonel) apparently was not interrogated until nineteen months later (and then only cursorily). In addition to the review boards, a youth amnesty in August 1946 and a Christmas amnesty in December that exempted less incriminated young people and socially disadvantaged and physically disabled people from denazification proceedings saw some

---

[83] Law for the Liberation from National Socialism and Militarism, 5 Mar. 1946, quotations from Articles 1, 2, and 15(1) available at: images.library.wisc.edu/History/EFacs/ GerRecon/Denazi/reference/history.denazi.i0013.pdf. The German version referred to 'political custody' (author's translation of *politische Haft*), and not 'internment' as the American version did. See Gesetz Nr. 104 zur Befreiung von Nationalsozialismus und Militarismus, 5 Mar. 1946, available at: www.verfassungen.de/bw/wuerttemberg-baden/ befreiungsgesetz46.htm (both accessed 6 Feb. 2019).

[84] Horn, *Internierungs- und Arbeitslager*, 120–5.

[85] In addition to the example of von Plato already cited, see Müller, 'Sowjetische Speziallager', 30; Merten, *Gulag in East Germany*, 6, 42.

further releases from the camps.[86] Yet all of these and other procedures took a long time to develop and implement, especially those of the *Spruchkammern*. This is indicated by the fact that at the end of March 1947 the German-administered camps in the zone still held 50,485 detainees who were awaiting either their denazification hearing or the result of their appeal against their verdict (which contradicts claims that at the turn of the year 1946–7 only 20,000 were still held in the zone). In contrast, only 262 had a final decision on their case and were serving a labour-camp sentence. In August 1947, there were still 43,737 internees in the US zone, which fell to 32,378 at the end of October. At the end of December, 26,425 internees remained, 77% of whom had not yet had their *Spruchkammer* hearing.[87]

Not least due to this slowness, internment and denazification had become major political problems by early 1948. In February, the Minister for Political Liberation in the state of Hesse, Gottlob Binder (Social Democratic Party of Germany, SPD), publicly defended the Americans' insistence that internees remain in custody until their proceedings:

That National Socialists who belonged to an organization that was declared criminal by the Nuremberg Military Tribunal are held in internment custody on the order of the occupation authorities until the determination of their individual case is a precautionary measure that is necessary if democracy does not want to put itself again at the mercy of the SS and the Political Leaders from the very beginning.[88]

His reasoning confirms that preventative, political considerations continued to feature alongside more punitive and increasingly juridified arguments for internment. Yet the Cold War was now well underway, and during the same month the Soviets announced the end of denazification in their zone (as discussed shortly). A precipitous rush to process

---

[86] Philipp Gassert, *Kurt Georg Kiesinger 1904–1988: Kanzler zwischen den Zeiten* (Munich: Deutsche Verlags-Anstalt, 2006), 161–2; Zeitler, 'Lageralltag', 377. On the amnesties, see OMGUS, Report of the Military Governor, 1 Apr. 1947–30 Apr. 1948, no. 34: *Denazification (Cumulative Review)*, 5, available at: digicoll.library.wisc.edu/cgi-bin/History/History-idx?type=div&did=History.Denazi.i0001&isize=M (accessed 6 Feb. 2019); Meyer, *Entnazifizierung von Frauen*, 206–7; Biddiscombe, *Denazification of Germany*, 65.

[87] OMGUS, Report of the Military Governor, 1 Apr. 1947–30 Apr. 1948, no. 34: *Denazification (Cumulative Review)*, 7. Günther Benser's already cited statistic of just 1% of US-zone internees having been convicted was thus close to the mark. For the inaccurate claim that only 20,000 were still held, see Cornelia Rauh-Kühne, 'Die Entnazifizierung und die deutsche Gesellschaft,' *Archiv für Sozialgeschichte* 35 (1995), 57.

[88] 'Erklärung des Befreiungsministeriums', 3 Feb. 1948, in Clemens Vollnhals (ed.), *Entnazifizierung und Selbstreinigung im Urteil der evangelischen Kirche: Dokumente und Reflexionen 1945–1949* (Munich: Chr. Kaiser, 1989), 206.

the remaining internees in the American zone ensued. Following an agreement between the Americans and the German state governments in March designed to wind up denazification and internment as rapidly as possible, automatic arrest was effectively abolished. Additionally, a previous order from Clay to detain people sentenced to labour camp even before their appeal was settled was repealed. Henceforth people could be detained only if they were serving a labour-camp sentence or if there was an individual risk of flight or of suppression of evidence. As a result, internee numbers dropped rapidly from 18,299 in early April to 7,657 by the end of the month. By September, the camps held just 2,144 people, the majority of whom were serving labour-camp sentences.[89]

Despite the different methods in the American and British zones, the results were rather similar. Just as the British-zone *Spruchgerichte* sentenced only a minority of internees to prison terms, so too the American-zone *Lagerspruchkammern* classified only a minority as Major Offenders or Offenders and sentenced only some of these to labour camp. And because the panels generally took time spent in internment into account in sentencing, many US-zone internees also walked free despite a negative finding (although civil and professional sanctions imposed by the panels continued). This helps explain the fact that, despite 9,600 assignments to labour camp across the US zone by mid-1949, only 300 people were serving such a sentence. In December 1949 just 284 remained.[90]

Procedures and outcomes in the French zone largely echoed those in the American zone, even if the French took longer to abandon plans to bring members of the criminal organizations before military courts. Only in winter 1946–7 was the decision made to subject internees – including members of the criminal organizations but excluding war-crimes suspects – to broader denazification procedures or, more accurately, to make them the main targets of new procedures that were established in spring 1947. Military Governor of the French zone General Marie-Pierre Kœnig informed the French-zone state premiers at a conference on 4 December 1946 that ca. 50% of internees would be handled by German *Spruchkammern* under new uniform zonal denazification

---

[89] Meyer, *Entnazifizierung von Frauen*, 102, 245–6; Alfons Söllner (ed.), *Archäologie der Demokratie in Deutschland: Analysen politischer Emigranten im amerikanischen Geheimdienst*, vol. 1: *1943–1945* (Frankfurt/Main: Europäische Verlagsanstalt, 1982), 218; Dolan, 'Isolating Nazism', 285. On the winding-down of internment and an American push for a rapid end being resisted to some extent by the German state governments, see Dolan, 'Isolating Nazism', 275–89.

[90] Horn, *Internierungs- und Arbeitslager*, 104–5, 120–9; Meyer, *Entnazifizierung von Frauen*, 204–10; Cohen, 'Transitional Justice', 75. Cf. Wember, *Umerziehung im Lager*, 24.

procedures. In the meantime, they were kept in the 'waiting room' of the camps while public administrations and businesses were denazified. Before internees' proceedings got underway, they were subjected to an internal French screening process, which prioritized invalids, as well as older and younger Waffen-SS draftees.[91] This additional layer of screening helps explain why the number of internees fell only slowly from 9,700 in early October 1946 to 7,600 in September 1947, although there were stark differences among the states, largely due to varying levels of personnel and logistical support from regional military governments. As in the American zone, *Lagerspruchkammern* were eventually established in most states in the French zone, although the responsible panel in the Saarland also dealt with non-internees. Panels began work at camps in Balingen in Württemberg-Hohenzollern and Theley in the Saarland in November 1947, more than a year after the first US-zone panel, while in Rhineland-Palatinate they did not begin until May 1948. The speed of the panels' progress also varied significantly. By this time, internment had become a political headache for the French, too. In April 1948, 'for reasons of political expediency' (*pour des raisons d'opportunité politique*), Kœnig allowed the release of those internees not expected to be deemed Offenders or Major Offenders in advance of their *Spruchkammer* hearing. The number of internees fell from 6,403 in January 1948 to 1,075 by October and to 250 by the end of January 1949. In spring and summer 1949, the last internees were released in three states in the zone, but the final twelve internees were not released from the Trier camp in Rhineland-Palatinate until 29 December 1949.[92] It should be noted that, as in the British zone, but unlike the American zone, not all internees underwent 'denazification', narrowly understood, because the French-zone *Spruchkammern* did not deal with the entire population. Whether internees faced a *Spruchkammer* depended on a combination of the level of their incrimination, the time of their release, and the nature of any employment they sought thereafter. Additionally, war-crimes suspects were taken into French pre-trial custody and were removed from the panels' jurisdiction.[93]

---

[91] Grohnert, *Entnazifizierung in Baden*, 164; Möhler, *Entnazifizierung in Rheinland-Pfalz und im Saarland*, 282, 284, 363–7; 'Konferenz der Ministerpräsidenten der französischen Besatzungszone in Baden-Baden', 4 Dec. 1946, in Brommer (ed.), *Quellen zur Geschichte von Rheinland-Pfalz*, 301–2.

[92] Möhler, 'Internierungslager in der französischen Besatzungszone', 55–7; Möhler, *Entnazifizierung in Rheinland-Pfalz und im Saarland*, 369 (quotation), 376, 386–7; Henke, *Politische Säuberung*, 181; Grohnert, *Entnazifizierung in Baden*, 164–5.

[93] Möhler, *Entnazifizierung in Rheinland-Pfalz und im Saarland*, 377–8.

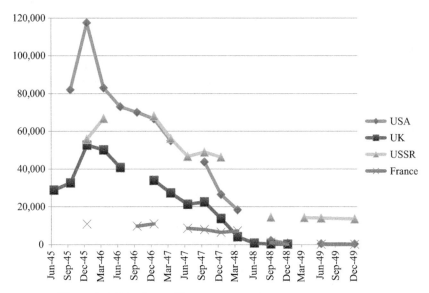

Figure 2.1 Numbers of internees over time.
Note that the British-zone figures and the US-zone figures before
March 1947 include war-crimes suspects and security suspects, while
later figures for the French and US zones include those convicted by
Spruchkammern. Note too that the figures for the western zones include
some foreigners, whereas those for the Soviet zone do not.
Data from: Horn, *Internierungs- und Arbeitslager*, 46; Niethammer,
Mitläuferfabrik, 255; Meyer, *Entnazifizierung von Frauen*, 96–102; Meyer,
'Internierung von NS-Funktionären', 43; Söllner, *Archäologie der Demokratie*,
218; Wember, *Umerziehung im Lager*, 369–72; Möhler, *Entnazifizierung in
Rheinland-Pfalz und im Saarland*, 360, 363, 365–6, 369, 386, 393; Possekel (ed.),
Sowjetische Dokumente, 209, 224, 247–8, 279, 297, 304, 316, 336, 345, 363

In comparison with the efforts of the western powers to categorize and
process internees and to release the more harmless cases, for almost three
years the Soviet Union's practice was marked by inertia. Somewhat
unusually, between September and December 1945, ca. 2,500 detainees
were released from Special Camp No. 4 in Landsberg/Warta (Polish:
Gorzów) in what was now Poland.[94] Yet as Figure 2.1 shows, in stark
contrast to the American and British zones in particular, the number of
internees in the Soviet zone did not fall in 1946; moreover, it remained
high for more than a year after the numbers in the western zones had
dwindled to insignificance by the end of 1948. To be sure, the NKVD
began checking the grounds for internees' detention in early 1946. Yet,

[94] Kirsten, *Das sowjetische Speziallager Nr. 4*, 47–8.

according to a Soviet report, by August 1947 only 1,947 Germans had been released, many of whom were not supposed to be interned in the Soviet zone in the first place (including some military and paramilitary personnel), a figure that clearly overlooks those released from the Landsberg/Warta camp in late 1945.[95] Modifications to Soviet arrest policy were limited to the cessation of new internments of Block and Cell Leaders in early 1946 and the requirement for state-prosecutor approval of all new internments under Order No. 00315 from October 1947, after which they all but ceased. In early 1946, the NKVD and the Soviet Military Administration in Germany (SMAD) made preparations for the release of interned Block and Cell Leaders among others and in December suggested to Moscow the release of up to 35,000 internees. But nothing eventuated except an order to deport 27,500 internees to the USSR for labour, which could only partially be carried out (as discussed in Chapter 4). Further suggestions in 1947, including one to release 13,700 older detainees, produced nothing more than an increase in investigative activity in autumn. It was not until March 1948 that the Ministerial Council of the USSR ordered concerted investigations. On 30 June it authorized the release of 27,749 less incriminated internees, which occurred over the following months. As Possekel argues, the Soviet authorities thus appeared to catch up – two years later – with what the western Allies had accomplished in 1945–6. However, virtually no steps to process the ostensibly more incriminated remaining ca. 14,000 internees ensued until the Soviet Politburo ordered investigations in late October 1949. It resolved on 30 December to release 9,634 people, to hand 3,432 to the authorities of the newly created GDR for prosecution, and to transfer 473 to the Soviet Ministry for State Security for prosecution.[96]

Thus, a small minority of Soviet-zone internees received some form of trial. In addition to the almost 4,000 people who faced prosecution by East German or Soviet authorities in 1950, no doubt some of the almost 11,000 who were deported to the USSR before 1950 were prosecuted there. Additionally, between 4,169 and 6,072 internees were transferred from the camps back to 'operative groups' of the NKVD/MVD or on to

---

[95] 'Bericht des Leiters der SMAD-Verwaltung für Inneres "Über den Zustand der Speziallager und Gefängnisse des MVD in Deutschland zum 1. August 1947"', 15 Aug. 1947, in Possekel (ed.), *Sowjetische Dokumente*, 304. Merten overlooks both groups and claims that the first releases took place in 1948. Merten, *Gulag in East Germany*, 42.

[96] Possekel, 'Sowjetische Lagerpolitik', 87, 95–7; 'Beschluß des Politbüros des SK der VKP(b) zur Liquidierung der Speziallager in Deutschland', 30 Dec. 1949, in Possekel (ed.), *Sowjetische Dokumente*, 365–6. On the SMAD, see Foitzik, *Sowjetische Militäradministration*.

SMTs in the Soviet zone, at least some of whom were prosecuted for Nazi crimes.[97] This contradicts claims by Greiner and others that the Soviet authorities did not investigate internees' pasts and did not prosecute any of them for Nazi crimes. Yet, whether they faced Soviet tribunals or East German courts, they received anything but a fair trial. The trials in April–June 1950 in Waldheim of the internees handed to the GDR were a travesty of justice with show-trial components, such that the failure to count the years spent in internment towards the sentences in all but six cases was the least of the defendants' concerns.[98]

The majority of Soviet-zone internees were thus never afforded a meaningful opportunity to defend themselves in a judicial or a semi-judicial procedure like those of the *Spruchgerichte* and *Spruchkammern* in the western zones or to apply for their release to administrative bodies like the Security Review Boards. Most either died in custody or were released without formal hearing. Greiner is thus correct to argue that Soviet-zone internees 'were permanently denied an investigation of their alleged Nazi past that adhered to due legal process'. But this does not mean that they 'were not screened', that 'detention or case files' were not prepared on them, or that their pasts were never 'investigated', as Greiner also claims. She overlooks the existence of inmate files, while her claim about 'screening' (which she does not define) ignores administrative categorization processes, which were used extensively in every zone.[99] Indeed, the Soviet methods were not inconsistent with Control Council Directive No. 38, according to which 'The classification of all offenders and potentially dangerous persons, assessment of sanctions and the review of cases will be carried out by agencies to be designated by the Zone Commanders.' While the directive spoke of 'tribunals' and

---

[97] 'Bericht des Leiters der SMAD-Verwaltung für Inneres "Über den Zustand der Speziallager und Gefängnisse des MVD in Deutschland zum 1. August 1947"', 15 Aug. 1947, in Possekel (ed.), *Sowjetische Dokumente*, 304; von Plato, 'Zur Geschichte des sowjetischen Speziallagersystems', 44; Achim Kilian, 'Das Speziallager Nr. 1 Mühlberg 1945–1948', in von Plato (ed.), *Studien und Berichte*, 287; Andreas Hilger and Nikita Petrov, '"Erledigung der Schmutzarbeit"? Die sowjetischen Justiz- und Sicherheitsapparate in Deutschland', and Grit Gierth and Bettina Westfeld, 'Zur Tätigkeit sowjetischer Militärtribunale in Sachsen', both in Hilger et al. (eds.), *Sowjetische Militärtribunale*, vol. 2, 97, 559.

[98] Dieter Pohl, *Justiz in Brandenburg 1945–1955: Gleichschaltung und Anpassung* (Munich: Oldenbourg, 2001), 95. On the Waldheim trials, see Wilfriede Otto, 'Die Waldheimer Prozesse', in von Plato (ed.), *Studien und Berichte*, 533–53; Fulbrook, *Reckonings*, 239.'

[99] Greiner, *Suppressed Terror*, 351, 15, 349. Cf. Peter Erler, 'Bettina Greiner, *Verdrängter Terror: Geschichte und Wahrnehmung sowjetischer Speziallager in Deutschland*', *Sehepunkte* 10, nos. 7–8 (2010), www.sehepunkte.de/2010/07/18023.html (accessed 6 Feb. 2019); Wolfram von Scheliha, 'Speziallager-Opfer in den Fallen der Geschichte', *Deutschland Archiv* 43, no. 6 (2010), 1125; Vollnhals, 'Internierung, Entnazifizierung und Strafverfolgung', 226.

allowed zone commanders to use 'German tribunals', these were not requirements and zone commanders were granted 'full discretion' over the application of the directive's principles; the directive did not grant internees or others a right to a hearing.[100] Moreover, while it is correct that releases from the Soviet camps occurred largely on the basis of assessments of whether internees constituted a 'danger' to the 'democratic order in Germany', the previous discussion has highlighted that the western Allies also considered present risk in decisions about releases.[101] Indeed, that was precisely what internment was primarily about. Soviet procedures were certainly less transparent, participatory, and fair than their western equivalents and commenced much later, but this does not mean that Soviet internment was categorically different from western internment.

It is worth pausing here to discuss further aspects of Greiner's argument that Soviet internment had nothing to do with denazification. She argues that internments took place without the involvement of the Soviet Ministry of Foreign Affairs that was responsible for denazification policy, that key Soviet denazification directives did not mention internees, and that decisions to release internees were made for political reasons and 'had nothing to do with denazification as such'. In short, 'There were no structural or institutional links between detention and Soviet denazification procedures.'[102] Her arguments are inconclusive, and some apply to some extent to the western zones. First, it is hardly surprising or consequential that the Ministry of Foreign Affairs was not involved in arresting Germans. In the western zones, too, arrests, interrogations, and internments were not the domain of the foreign ministries, nor even of the military-government branches that were responsible for denazification (narrowly understood), much to the chagrin of the latter. In the British zone, for instance, Intelligence Division was responsible for arrests, interrogations, and releases, whereas Public Safety (Special Branch) was in charge of denazification.[103] Only when American-zone camps came under the authority of the German state ministries for denazification was a direct institutional connection established there. Second, it is doubtful whether a reference to internees, or lack thereof, in particular directives is decisive. For instance, Control Council Directive No. 24 of January 1946, a key statement of Allied denazification

---

[100] 'Control Council Directive No. 38: The Arrest and Punishment of War Criminals, Nazis, and Militarists and the Internment, Control, and Surveillance of Potentially Dangerous Germans', 12 Oct. 1946, in Ruhm von Oppen (ed.), *Documents on Germany*, 169.

[101] Greiner, *Suppressed Terror*, 253.   [102] Ibid., 15–16, 36.

[103] Wember, *Umerziehung im Lager*, 117.

policy mentioned in Chapter 1, did not refer to internees, while British Military Government Ordinance No. 110 on the 'Transfer to the Länder [state] Governments of Responsibility for Denazification' mentioned them only in order to exempt them from the transfer.[104] Third, even if internees were not referred to in SMAD's Order No. 35 of February 1948, which announced the end of the work of denazification commissions in the Soviet zone (but did not mean the end of sanctions or even of investigations for more serious cases, as is sometimes assumed), many less incriminated internees were released from Soviet camps in subsequent months in line with the policy of integrating 'small' Nazis and fellow-travellers that the announcement heralded. As such, internment's continuation after the official 'end' of denazification (narrowly understood) is not necessarily the glaring contradiction that Greiner and others take it for.[105] Fourth, numerous amnesties and decisions to release internees in the western zones similarly had little to do with 'denazification as such' but were taken for pragmatic or political reasons, as indicated by several examples so far in this chapter.[106] In the eyes of many commentators, this turned western practice into a farce and suggested that political priorities had changed with the onset of the Cold War. It does not indicate that the original arrests or internment as such had nothing to do with denazification. Internment and denazification, most narrowly understood, were most clearly separated in the Soviet zone, but this does not mean that Soviet internment was not part of the broad attempt to eradicate Nazism. Indeed, Greiner's acknowledgement that 'the reasons leading to the arrest of those who were *interned* in the majority of cases had to do with their past before 1945' would seem to contradict her own argument, because this was surely no accident.[107]

---

[104] 'Control Council Directive No. 24: Removal from Office and from Positions of Responsibility of Nazis and of Persons Hostile to Allied Purposes', 12 Jan. 1946, and 'British Military Government Ordinance No. 110: Transfer to the Länder Governments of Responsibility for Denazification', 1 Oct. 1947, both in Ruhm von Oppen (ed.), *Documents on Germany*, 102–7, 249.

[105] 'Befehl Nr. 35 des Obersten Chefs der Sowjetischen Militäradministration in Deutschland über die Auflösung der Entnazifizierungskommissionen', 26 Feb. 1948, in Welsh, *Revolutionärer Wandel?*, 189–90. Cf. Timothy R. Vogt, *Denazification in Soviet-Occupied Germany: Brandenburg, 1945–1948* (Cambridge, MA: Harvard University Press, 2000), 111–13; Marcel Boldorf, 'Brüche oder Kontinuitäten? Von der Entnazifizierung zur Stalinisierung in der SBZ/DDR (1945–1952)', *Historische Zeitschrift* 289 (2009), 305–6, 316.

[106] In addition to the already cited example of Kœnig, see another example from the French zone in 1949 in Möhler, *Entnazifizierung in Rheinland-Pfalz und im Saarland*, 391.

[107] Greiner, *Suppressed Terror*, 75 (emphasis in original). Greiner's specific arguments about the SMTs are somewhat more compelling. However, here, too, she overstates the case. Prosecuting Nazi crimes was a major focus early on and remained important, even as the use of prosecutions to drive through societal and political transformations

Another glance at Austria is useful here. The major differences from Germany derive from the early establishment in April 1945 of a provisional Austrian government that was initially recognized only by the Soviets and then the existence from November of an elected national government that all four occupying powers recognized.[108] The provisional government introduced laws on the Prohibition of the NSDAP (Prohibition Law) on 8 May and on War Crimes and Other National Socialist Atrocities (War Criminals Law) on 26 June. The former called for the registration of all members and candidates for membership of the NSDAP and of its paramilitary organizations between July 1933 and April 1945 and imposed various atonement measures, such as dismissal from public office. It also mandated five- to ten-year prison sentences for treason for 'illegal' members of the party between 1933 and 1938, which would be imposed only if the government decided that treason was getting out of hand. Additionally, anyone who continued to work for Nazi goals or organizations after the capitulation faced the death penalty or imprisonment for ten to twenty years. Various groups could also be placed under police supervision, subjected to 'forced labour', or detained in 'forced labour facilities'.[109] The War Criminals Law threatened severe penalties (including death) on war criminals, senior concentration-camp staff, members of the Reich government, and NSDAP leaders at and above the rank of Gau Leader or equivalent.[110] People's Courts (*Volksgerichte*) were established to make rulings under both laws.[111]

increased in the late 1940s. A significant number of SMT convicts were accused and many were indeed guilty of Nazi crimes (which does not mean that they did not become victims of Soviet injustice). See Greiner, *Suppressed Terror*, 16; Andreas Hilger and Mike Schmeitzner, 'Einleitung: Deutschlandpolitik und Strafjustiz: Zur Tätigkeit sowjetischer Militärtribunale in Deutschland 1945–1955', in Hilger et al. (eds.), *Sowjetische Militärtribunale*, 25; Gierth and Westfeld, 'Zur Tätigkeit sowjetischer Militärtribunale', 569–70; Andreas Weigelt, Klaus-Dieter Müller, Thomas Schaarschmidt, and Mike Schmeitzner, 'Vorwort der Herausgeber', in Weigelt et al. (eds.), *Todesurteile sowjetischer Militärtribunale*, 8; Müller, 'Sowjetische Speziallager', 14–15, 21.

[108] Cf. Stiefel, *Entnazifizierung in Österreich*, 22–3.

[109] 'Verfassungsgesetz vom 8. Mai 1945 über das Verbot der NSDAP (Verbotsgesetz)', *Staatsgesetzblatt für die Republik Österreich*, 4. Stück, no. 13, 6 Jun. 1945, 19–22, available at: www.ris.bka.gv.at/Dokumente/BgblPdf/1945_13_0/1945_13_0.pdf (accessed 6 Feb. 2019).

[110] 'Verfassungsgesetz vom 26. Juni 1945 über Kriegsverbrechen und andere nationalsozialistische Untaten (Kriegsverbrechergesetz)', *Staatsgesetzblatt für die Republik Österreich*, 10. Stück, no. 32, 28 Jun. 1945, 55–7, available at: www.ris.bka.gv.at/Dokumente/BgblPdf/1945_32_0/1945_32_0.pdf (accessed 6 Feb. 2019).

[111] Stiefel, *Entnazifizierung in Österreich*, 247–59; Claudia Kuretsidis-Haider, 'Volksgerichtsbarkeit und Entnazifizierung in Österreich', in Schuster and Weber (eds.), *Entnazifizierung im regionalen Vergleich*, 563–601.

The key question thus became how the Allies interacted with the indigenous Austrian authorities and their policies. As already mentioned, having recognized the provisional government, the Soviets largely left denazification to the Austrians and did not practice internment on a significant scale, which further suggests that there was a connection between Soviet denazification and internment policy and practice: in Austria, there was an absence, but in Germany a presence, of both. In contrast, the western powers did not recognize the provisional government and at least initially pursued their own denazification and internment policies. When the British assumed full control of Styria in late July 1945, they ordered the release of significant numbers of prisoners who had been arrested by the Austrians but whose detention was not covered by British categories, including many 'illegal' Nazis.[112] The French also largely followed Allied instructions but also relied somewhat haphazardly on the advice of local Austrian resistance groups, local mayors, and committees about whom to arrest or release, before a more formal system of determining internees' fate by a screening commission (*commission de criblage*) with minimal Austrian input was established in October 1945.[113]

The situation did not change immediately after all four occupiers recognized the new elected Austrian government. To be sure, in February 1946, the Allies stepped back into a supervisory role and gave the government responsibility for denazification. The People's Courts soon began operating in the western zones as well. Yet Allied internment continued, was not well integrated into the Austrian system, and remained distinct from administrative/semi-judicial denazification. In Carinthia in the British zone internees were not subject to the compulsory registration of National Socialists that was at the centre of Austrian denazification and the state authorities for a long time had no access to the British internment camps and no clear idea of who was held there. Meanwhile the French insisted, and sometimes acted, on their right to intern, 'for reasons of public safety', people released by the People's Courts.[114]

For all the various differences, the categorization, processing, and release of the western powers' internees in Austria was similar in many ways to what occurred in Germany. In Austria, too, individual war-

---

[112] Siegfried Beer, 'Die britische Entnazifizierung in Österreich 1945–1948', in Schuster and Weber (eds.), *Entnazifizierung im regionalen Vergleich*, 405.

[113] Eisterer, *Französische Besatzungspolitik*, 176–80, 204.

[114] Wilhelm Wadl, 'Entnazifizierung in Kärnten', in Schuster and Weber (eds.), *Entnazifizierung im regionalen Vergleich*, 253.

crimes suspects were a small minority compared with the mass of automatic arrestees. Together, war-crimes suspects, security suspects, and people arrested for resisting the Allied occupation comprised less than 13% of those the Americans arrested. In the French zone, those suspected of war crimes or presented to a military court comprised 15% of the almost 3,000 internees screened by the Tyrolean screening commission by March 1946. For a long time, it remained unclear how the remaining automatic arrestees would be processed, and interrogations were few and far between.[115] A senior British official in Styria believed the worst interned Nazis should be 'sent to North Africa or some country with a future to develop its communications – but never to return to Austria'. The French also considered deporting the more problematic internees (including more than 1,200 of almost 3,000 who were screened in Tyrol) to Algeria or France but similarly abandoned the idea. The internees thus remained in detention in Austria.[116]

Despite such ideas being abandoned, a basic disconnect between Allied and Austrian approaches needed to be resolved. The problem was that internees had been arrested largely on security-political grounds, but Austrian law at this point allowed only the judicial detention of criminal suspects. In February 1946 a leading British occupation official summarized the situation thus: 'The Austrians' view of denazification is entirely different from our own. Whereas our object is essentially destructive and preventive, theirs is punitive; our method is internment, while theirs is trial – or rather, in practise, prolonged detention pending trial.'[117] This posed problems for resolving internees' fate. According to a British official in May 1946: 'The future of these persons is obscure. There is no immediate prospect either of their being brought to trial or released, and it seems certain that a considerable number must be retained for an indefinite time.'[118] As in Germany, the Allies continued to insist on the need for extrajudicial detention of people deemed dangerous to the new democratic regime. However, in Austria such detention was intended to be an Austrian affair, whereas in Germany it was to remain in Allied hands according to Control Council Directive No. 38. When the Austrian political parties passed a new, more

---

[115] Twerase, 'Die amerikanische Säuberungspolitik', 369; Eisterer, *Französische Besatzungspolitik*, 206; Dohle and Eigelsberger, *Camp Marcus W. Orr*, 32–6, 47.

[116] J. C. Boyd, Memorandum 'Denazification' to Chief of Staff, Allied Commission for Austria (British Element) (ACA [BE]), 2 Mar. 1946, cited by Beer, 'Die britische Entnazifizierung', 422; Eisterer, *Französische Besatzungspolitik*, 203–6.

[117] J. W. Nicholls to Ernest Bevin, 5 Feb. 1946, cited by Beer, 'Die britische Entnazifizierung', 417.

[118] ACA (BE), Labour Division, 1 May 1946, cited by Kastner, '373 Camp Wolfsberg', 91.

moderate, denazification law in July 1946, the Allies insisted on significant toughening, including provisions for detention camps for Offenders.
The resulting National Socialists Law, which amended the 1945 Prohibition and War Criminals Laws and was finally passed in February 1947,
stipulated that Offenders 'must be enlisted for work' and that they 'can
be detained in a camp' if established facts 'make them appear extremely
dangerous for the democratic form of government of the Republic of
Austria'.[119] An additional law to regulate such detention was enacted in
July 1947 but never implemented.[120]

With this impasse unresolved, almost 7,000 internees remained in
British custody and more than 2,500 in French detention in August
1946. By this time, the Allies had released only 8,637 of the 29,186
people they had arrested (30%). The Soviets and French had released
proportionately more, approximately 80% of their arrestees (whereas in
Germany the French and Soviets were slower to release). In autumn
1946, the Allies transferred increasing numbers of internees to Austrian
authorities. In November, the last French camp in Voralberg at Brederis
held just over 400 internees. In contrast, the Americans were slower to
release internees and transfer them to the Austrian authorities. In January
1947, the Americans still held 8,051 people in their last remaining camp,
Camp Marcus W. Orr, which, although technically located on the out-
skirts of Salzburg, is often called 'Glasenbach' due to its proximity to the
train station and post office of the Glasenbach township. Following the
enactment of the National Socialists Law, the Austrian interior ministry
opened a criminal office at the camp and large-scale releases from
American and British camps commenced: 5,758 people were still held
at Marcus W. Orr at the end of May 1947, 3,368 at the end of June, and
1,183 in mid-July. Many were simply released; others were handed to the
Austrian authorities. For a number of reasons, the latter held on to only
some internees. Of 850 internees handed over by the British by September 1946, the Austrians detained only half, not least because they had
been unable to find sufficient remand accommodation for (non-
interned) people who were subject to detention under the Prohibition

---

[119] 'Bundesverfassungsgesetz vom 6. Februar 1947 über die Behandlung der
Nationalsozialisten (Nationalsozialistengesetz)', *Bundesgesetzblatt für die Republik
Österreich*, 8. Stück, No. 25, 17 Feb. 1947, 281–2, available at: www.ris.bka.gv.at/
Dokumente/BgblPdf/1947_25_0/1947_25_0.pdf (accessed 6 Feb. 2019). Cf. Stiefel,
Entnazifizierung in Österreich, 93, 101–8, 268–9.
[120] 'Bundesgesetz vom 3. Juli 1947, betreffend die Anhaltung staatsgefährlicher
Nationalsozialisten in Lagern (Anhaltelagergesetz)', *Bundesgesetzblatt für die Republik
Österreich*, Stück 40, No. 195, 5 Sep. 1947, 842–5, available at: www.ris.bka.gv.at/
Dokumente/BgblPdf/1947_195_0/1947_195_0.pdf (accessed 6 Feb. 2019); Stiefel,
Entnazifizierung in Österreich, 270.

Law.[121] As in the case of the *Spruchkammern* and the *Spruchgerichte* in Germany, the Austrian People's Courts generally counted time spent in internment towards sentences, and as sentences were generally mild most convicts walked free. The automatic arrest was finally rescinded in the US zone at the end of June 1947, and in August the site of Camp Marcus W. Orr was handed to the Austrians, with only the war-crimes enclosure remaining in American hands until January 1948 when the last remaining prisoners were transferred to Austrian custody. That month, the British and French continued to hold a combined total of just over 300 prisoners.[122]

Austrian-specific factors thus influenced not only the basic Soviet approach to internment but also specific details about internees' processing and release in the western zones of the country. Nevertheless, Allied internment in Austria and Germany shared fundamental similarities, including an increasingly but never entirely juridical approach to processing internees who had been arrested on amorphous preventative and punitive grounds, as well as a somewhat half-hearted insistence on the need for purely preventative extrajudicial detention. Moreover, in both countries internment was distinct from, but connected with, broader denazification policies.

Illustrative, if Abortive, Western Cases

If the Soviet case in Germany stands out for its inertia and relative lack of formal proceedings and hearings, two comparatively minor but nonetheless revealing components of western policy and practice warrant brief mention. Both indicate the extent to which western powers remained prepared to consider radical illiberal measures well beyond the cessation of hostilities. First, French plans to bring the Saarland into France's economic, cultural, and political orbit, if not to annex it outright, included the territory's denazification and 'de-Prussianization'. Among other things, this was to take the form of deportations of former Nazis, people not of Saar origin, and people deemed 'anti-French'. While there was talk at various points of deporting anywhere between 15,000 and 150,000 people, the desperate need for labour, individual and collective

---

[121] Stiefel, *Entnazifizierung in Österreich*, 264–5; Eisterer, *Französische Besatzungspolitik*, 212, 216; Beer, 'Die britische Entnazifizierung', 411; Wadl, 'Entnazifizierung in Kärnten', 254; Dohle and Eigelsberger, *Camp Marcus W. Orr*, 9–10, 149, 93.

[122] Dohle and Eigelsberger, *Camp Marcus W. Orr*, 80, 154, 113–14, 92; Florentine Kastner, 'Britische Besatzungslager in Österreich nach dem Zweiten Weltkrieg', *Acta Universitatis Carolinae Studia Territorialia*, nos. 3–4 (2011), 77; Stiefel, *Entnazifizierung in Österreich*, 268.

protests, and doubts about the deportations' wisdom reduced the numbers significantly. In the end, only ca. 1,800 people were deported, mainly in two large-scale actions in July 1946 and June 1947. Internees – particularly SS members and NSDAP functionaries – and their families featured prominently among the proposed and actual targets. The interplay of 'ethnic' and political considerations was evident in the criteria developed in 1947: all NSDAP functionaries above the rank of Local Group Leader would be expelled, as would Local Group Leaders who were not from the Saarland. Even if the total number of deportees was limited and many were able to return in later years, the fear and conformity engendered were considerable.[123]

The second phenomenon reflected British concerns about the influence of Nazi activists and militarists who were not suspected of crimes but were believed to be 'dangerous'. A memorandum from January 1945 by Secretary of State for Foreign Affairs Anthony Eden gives a sense of the strength of these concerns. It expressed the expectation that many Germans – who had been 'brought up to know no ideals and no career save those offered, no facts and no theories save those permitted by National Socialism' – 'will no more be able to live out of the atmosphere of National Socialism than a snail can out of its shell'. They would be so numerous that 'policemen and psychiatrists' alone could not solve the problem and it was 'vain to hope that men such as the worst of these can be "re-educated"'. As a result, 'Only drastic and severe remedies, such as prolonged internment or deportation or long labour service outside Germany in the reconstruction of devastated countries could hold out any hope of working them out of Germany's system.'[124] Such fears had not entirely dissipated by early 1947, when the British began implementing plans to quarantine as many as 15,000 people for up to ten years for security reasons. Plans to use German islands in the North Sea were abandoned in favour of establishing a 'Civil Internment Settlement' at a former airbase at Adelheide near Delmenhorst, southwest of Bremen. The first internees arrived in May 1947, and 537 were held there by December. Most were members of groups that had not been declared criminal by the IMT and that were therefore not indictable by the *Spruchgerichte*: former Wehrmacht officers, members of various Nazi paramilitary organizations including the SA, and Hitler Youth leaders.

---

[123] Bronson Long, *No Easy Occupation: French Control of the German Saar, 1944–1957* (Rochester: Camden House, 2015); Möhler, *Entnazifizierung in Rheinland-Pfalz und im Saarland*, 31–52, esp. 40–1, 45, 47, 50, 240, 374.

[124] 'Memorandum by the Secretary of State for Foreign Affairs', 10 Jan. 1945, in Jordan (ed.), *Conditions of Surrender*, 123.

The plans included bringing internees' families to live with them. As fewer internees were placed in the eligible category than anticipated and in response to German and British protests and concerns from the ICRC, the plan was abandoned in the first half of 1948 and the settlement closed in August.[125]

The Adelheide settlement and especially the Saarland deportations were not representative of overall British and French internment policy. They nevertheless confirm that all the occupying powers were prepared to overlook basic liberal legal-constitutional principles – and indeed the letter of the law of occupied Germany, where the Allies themselves outlawed detention 'without due process of law' in October 1945 – at least temporarily in the western zones and more enduringly in the Soviet zone in dealing with 'dangerous' Germans.[126] This was just one part of what a December 1945 British intelligence review referred to as the 'anomaly of imposing liberalism by authority'.[127] Adelheide and the Saarland deportations also reinforce the non-criminal nature of internees' incrimination in the Allies' eyes. Condemning the Soviets for interning Germans who were not criminal suspects thus misses the point that the western powers also made mass arrests without individual criminal suspicion. Indeed, from the Allied perspective and as surely most historians today would agree, even many internees who were not criminally guilty, or could not be proven to be so, bore significant degrees of responsibility for National Socialism and militarism (and not just for specific crimes). Rather than merely a form of remand custody in advance of criminal prosecution, internment constituted, among other things, an administrative, extrajudicial sanction against people believed to have held such responsibility. However, recognizing this broad punitive aspect should not obscure internment's equally important preventative dimension. The Allies wanted to prevent both physical attacks on their facilities and personnel and broader opposition to their postwar agenda. Here, too, both similarities and differences emerged between the western and the Soviet zones. In all zones, the isolation of purportedly

---

[125] Wember, *Umerziehung im Lager*, 85–6. See the ICRC's file on Adelheide: ACICR, B G 44 02-056.03. On the ICRC's attitudes to civilian internment and the prosecution of war crimes, see Lewis, *Birth of the New Justice*, chapter 8.

[126] 'Control Council Proclamation No. 3: Fundamental Principles of Judicial Reform', 20 Oct. 1945, in Ruhm von Oppen (ed.), *Documents on Germany*, 81. Cf. Möhler, 'Internierungslager in der französischen Besatzungszone', 60.

[127] 'Control Commission for Germany (British Element), Intelligence Bureau, Intelligence Review No. 1', 12 Dec. 1945, in Pelly and Yasamee (eds.), *Documents on British Foreign Policy*, 440.

influential Nazis and militarists through internment helped the formation of new political elites and a new political system.

The key questions, then, are not whether or how many Soviet-zone internees would have faced a *court* in the western zones, as numerous authors suggest, for, as this chapter has shown, most western-zone internees never faced a court either. Similarly, the observation that 'it will never be possible to determine' how many internees 'were culpable in terms of penal law', while possibly true, misses the point that internment was not primarily a criminal-juridical measure but a political-administrative one.[128] Instead, the relevant questions are, first, whether Soviet-zone internees would have been interned in the western zones, and, second, whether, how, and how quickly decisions were made about internees' release or continuing detention. As indicated to some extent in this chapter and shown more fully in the next, the answer to the first question is that many Soviet-zone internees would have been interned in the western zones, while many others would not. As this chapter has demonstrated, the major procedural deviations in the Soviet zone were, first, the failure to grant internees opportunities to argue on their own behalf in proceedings that might lead to their release and, second, the failure to make substantial releases until mid-1948 (by which time almost all western-zones internees had been processed and released) and after that not again until early 1950. These two failings are more relevant grounds for criticizing Soviet internment than misleading complaints that most Soviet-zone internees were never brought to trial.

[128] Greiner, *Suppressed Terror*, 7.

3   Internees

The 'Worst Nazis' or a 'Colourful Assortment'?

The fate of Nazis after 1945 and the issue of who was (or should have been) targeted by post-Nazi transitional justice have long sparked interest. In relation to internment, the question of who internees were is the most vigorously contested issue. All too frequently the question, if not necessarily the answer, has been framed as a binary either/or. For instance, Horn asks whether American-zone internees were 'only followers' or 'criminals' and whether they were 'big' or 'small' Nazis, while Niethammer asks whether they were Nazi leaders or followers.[1] In relation to the Soviet zone, the alternatives appear even starker: were they 'perpetrators' or 'victims'? Such dichotomies reflect the polarization of opinion as well as a desire for simple, unambiguous answers. The debate has been most fierce and explicit in relation to the Soviet zone but is also found in more muted form in relation to the western zones. In general, the Nazi incrimination of western-zone internees, and thus the appropriateness of their incarceration, is held to be much higher than that of their Soviet-zone counterparts. Yet there is a range of views about internees in all zones. Some authors depict them – especially in the western zones – in an undifferentiated fashion as Nazi perpetrators and criminals, thus as Hitler's henchmen and the 'worst Nazis'. Some argue they were mainly 'followers' and hardly more incriminated than the mass of the population.[2] Others, including Horn, suggest they comprised a 'colourful assortment' ranging from serious Nazi criminals to victims of the 'Third Reich'.[3] Still others highlight the presence of various non-Nazis and adolescents in the Soviet camps and suggest that Soviet-zone internees were largely innocent of, or were not interned because of, any Nazi involvement.[4]

---

[1] Horn, *Internierungs- und Arbeitslager*, 155, 148; Niethammer, 'Was wissen wir?', 54.

[2] Wolfgang Benz vacillates between both views. Wolfgang Benz, *Zwischen Hitler und Adenauer: Studien zur deutschen Nachkriegsgesellschaft* (Frankfurt/Main: Fischer Taschenbuch Verlag, 1991), 119, 120.

[3] Horn, *Internierungs- und Arbeitslager*, 156.

[4] Greiner, *Suppressed Terror*, 14, 351, 357; Merten, *Gulag in East Germany*, 1, 2, 5, 7–8, 10, 145–53.

Beyond the disputed degree of their complicity in the 'Third Reich', the status of internees qua internees is also controversial. Some authors cast them as 'political prisoners', especially of the Soviet occupiers.[5] Numerous authors suggest that – irrespective of their Nazi-era roles – many, if not most, internees did not deserve their treatment and thus became victims of Allied injustice. This is most commonly and under-standably the case in the Soviet zone, due to the horrendous conditions, mass death, and lack of any semblance of due process in the Soviet camps. Yet apparently unwarranted or unjustifiably lengthy internment in the western zones also transformed at least some internees there, in the eyes of certain historians, into victims of overblown security fears, accus-ations of collective guilt, or disproportionately long incarceration.[6] Fre-quently, historians assume that only war criminals should have been interned, stress that the purported presumption that internees were criminals was incorrect in most cases, and thus suggest that most intern-ees were falsely impugned and unfairly detained.[7] Such arguments are most common in relation to Soviet-zone internees, who – numerous historians insist – were 'innocent in the legal sense' and at most 'morally' responsible for Nazism.[8] On the other hand, internees are sometimes cast as real, suspected, or convicted criminals. Soviet authorities some-times described their detainees as 'war criminals and active Nazis', while East German historians – to the extent that they referred to internees at all – generally called them 'Nazi- and war criminals'.[9] More recently,

---

[5] J. Jürgen Seidel, *'Neubeginn' in der Kirche? Die evangelischen Landes- und Provinzialkirchen in der SBZ/DDR im gesellschaftspolitischen Kontext der Nachkriegszeit (1945–1953)* (Göttingen: Vandenhoeck & Ruprecht, 1989), 153; Horn, *Internierungs- und Arbeitslager*, 155; Tony Judt, *Postwar: A History of Europe since 1945* (London: Pimlico, 2005), 822; Greiner, *Suppressed Terror*, 357. According to Stone, western camps held 'German suspects including suspected war criminals and camp guards', while the Soviet camps held 'political prisoners'. Stone, *Concentration Camps*, 97, 81. Yet many would be better termed 'prisoners of politics'. On the distinction, see Padraic Kenney, *Dance in Chains: Political Imprisonment in the Modern World* (New York: Oxford University Press, 2017), 27.

[6] E.g., Wember, *Umerziehung im Lager*, 119.

[7] See, for instance, Fürstenau, *Entnazifizierung*, 45; Irmgard Lange, *Entnazifizierung in Nordrhein-Westfalen: Richtlinien, Anweisungen, Organisation* (Siegburg: Respublica Verlag, 1976), 12; Olaf Reichelt, *'Wir müssen doch in die Zukunft sehen …': Die Entnazifizierung in der Stadt Oldenburg unter britischer Besatzungshoheit 1945–1947* (Oldenburg: Isensee Verlag, 1998), 46–7.

[8] Fippel, *Demokratische Gegner*, 40. See also Greiner, *Suppressed Terror*, 7; Merten, *Gulag in East Germany*, 120.

[9] Report to the Council of Foreign Ministers from the Allied Control Authority in Germany, 24 Feb. 1947, Section II, Part 3, d, 4, TNA, FO 1030/7; Wolfgang Meinicke, 'Die Entnazifizierung in der sowjetischen Besatzungszone 1945 bis 1948', *Zeitschrift für Geschichtswissenschaft* 32, no. 10 (1984), 969; Benser, 'Konzeptionen und Praxis', 961.

western-zone internees have been described variously as 'war criminals' (a term that, among other things, overlooks that many Nazi crimes had little to do with warfare), 'purported war criminals', or even 'Nazi convicts'.[10]

Casting internees as arbitrarily selected political prisoners or as suspected or convicted criminals distorts their status and the most common reasons for their arrest. As demonstrated in the previous chapters, many internees in all zones were never suspected of crimes, whether individual or organizational, while even those who belonged to the indicted organizations were detained not only for prosecution but also for security and political reasons. Recognizing the amorphous preventative *and* punitive nature of internment – and particularly of automatic arrest – allows one to see that *most* internees, especially but not only in the western zones, should be seen neither as victims of misplaced security fears nor as (rightly or wrongly) suspected criminals but as administrative detainees who were targeted because they had been apparatchiks of the Nazi state. They were arrested not on the basis of individual criminal suspicion nor due to generic German moral responsibility for Nazism but because the Allies perceived them as members of Nazi Germany's political, administrative, and paramilitary elite at national, regional, district, and local levels.

Beyond that, attempts at answering the question of who internees actually were face numerous difficulties. Generalizations are complicated by the various categories of detainee, by differences among camps, and by changes over time, as well as by the fact that many internees held multiple positions in Nazi organizations that made them liable for arrest.[11] The patchiness and inconsistency of Allied recordkeeping and reporting is a further problem, although research suggests that even

---

[10] For the first term: Angela Borgstedt, 'Die kompromittierte Gesellschaft: Entnazifizierung und Integration', in Peter Reichel, Harald Schmid, and Peter Steinbach (eds.), *Der Nationalsozialismus – Die zweite Geschichte: Überwindung, Deutung, Erinnerung* (Munich: C. H. Beck, 2009), 94; Volker Pieper and Michael Siedenhans, with collaboration from Olaf Eimer, *Die Vergessenen von Stukenbrock: Die Geschichte des Lagers in Stukenbrock-Senne von 1941 bis zur Gegenwart* (Bielefeld: Verlag für Regionalgeschichte, 1988), 14; Michael Siedenhans and Olaf Eimer, 'Das Internierungslager Eselheide und das Sozialwerk Stukenbrock', in ibid., 72. For the second term: Dennis Meyer, 'Entnazifizierung', in Torben Fischer and Matthias N. Lorenz (eds.), *Lexikon der 'Vergangenheitsbewältigung' in Deutschland: Debatten- und Diskursgeschichte des Nationalsozialismus nach 1945* (Bielefeld: transcript, 2007), 18. For the third term: von Kellenbach, *Mark of Cain*, 25. See also Thacker, *End of the Third Reich*, 153–60.

[11] See Natalja Jeske, 'Kritische Bemerkungen zu den sowjetischen Speziallagerstatistiken', in von Plato (ed.), *Studien und Berichte*, 473–80; Niethammer, *Mitläuferfabrik*, 255–9; Ritscher, 'Die wissenschaftliche Aufarbeitung', 181–2.

Soviet internal data about internees' positions and occupations were generally reliable.[12] Meanwhile, there is a danger of over-emphasizing exceptional cases or groups; in the Soviet case in particular, the SMT convicts complicate and often confuse the discussion of internees. There are methodological questions, too, about the significance that should be attributed to internees' 'formal' incrimination based on their ranks and positions, as opposed to the outcomes of their trials or denazification proceedings, especially when the latter often amounted to a whitewash, at least in the western zones. The debate has also been hampered by a lack of consistency regarding the meaning of key terms. As Janosch Steuwer and Hanne Leßau argue, there is still no agreement on the basic question of what defines a 'Nazi', perhaps beyond the view that NSDAP membership constitutes neither a sufficient nor a necessary criterion.[13] The same applies to categories such as Nazi 'elite', 'prominent' Nazi, or 'leading' and 'lower' functionaries. There is thus no consensus about the spectrum of responsibility on which internees are to be placed. Some authors tend to minimize the importance of low- and even mid-level functionaries. Others assume a high level of complicity and use terms such as 'Nazi perpetrator' rather loosely.[14]

This chapter seeks to describe internees in the four zones and identify their commonalities and differences. The discussion concentrates on German internees. It thus largely ignores the sizable number of non-Germans in the Soviet camps, while the SMT convicts held there, like the labour-camp convicts in the American and French zones, are included only where relevant and where it is necessary – or impossible – to distinguish them from the internees. The chapter identifies numerous similarities in the internee populations, particularly relating to their age and sex, and suggests that some of the purported differences between the western and Soviet zones, including in the degree of internees' incrimination, were less stark than is often assumed. Certainly, claims that only 'senior Nazi offenders' were interned in the western zones play down the comprehensiveness of western arrests and ignore the diversity of internees there.[15] On the other hand, Soviet-zone internees were more

---

[12] Vera Neumann, 'Häftlingsstruktur im Speziallager Buchenwald: Quellenbestand und Wertung', in von Plato (ed.), *Studien und Berichte*, 495.

[13] Janosch Steuwer and Hanne Leßau, '"Wer ist ein Nazi? Woran erkennt man ihn?" Zur Unterscheidung von Nationalsozialisten und anderen Deutschen', *Mittelweg 36* 23, no. 1 (2014), 30–51. Cf. Ziemke, *U.S. Army*, 380–3; Niethammer, *Mitläuferfabrik*, 23.

[14] Von Kellenbach, *Mark of Cain*, 30. The term 'perpetrator' is problematic due to its vagueness: sometimes it is used for any active supporter of the Nazi regime, at others as a synonym for criminals.

[15] Müller, 'Sowjetische Speziallager', 30. Merten speaks of 'leading Nazis' and 'high ranking Nazi detainees'. Merten, *Gulag in East Germany*, 2, 21.

compromised by their Nazi pasts than is often assumed. There were not enough non-Nazis among them to justify claims that Soviet internment there was more about repressing the communists' class enemies and (non-Nazi) political opponents than about destroying Nazism. Nevertheless, there were significant differences among the zones. Overall, the chapter shows that more, and more culpable, Germans faced the severe Allied sanction of internment than is commonly believed.

Internee Numbers

There is a dearth of accepted, reliable figures about how many people the Allies interned. Tom Bower makes an exceptional exaggeration, claiming that 'literally millions were under arrest in internment camps' in 1945, which makes sense only if POW camps are included.[16] More commonly, the number of civilian internees is underestimated. Some scholars speak of 'tens of thousands', others of 'more than one hundred thousand'.[17] More realistically, Niethammer speaks of more than 350,000 internees and Perry Biddiscombe of 'more than 400,000'.[18] The numbers interned by the western powers are often underestimated. Their combined subtotal has repeatedly been stated to approximate 180,000, which stems from Wolfgang Friedmann's publication of Allied Control Authority (ACA) statistics of the numbers of Germans interned in 1945–6. This is often assumed to be the total number of internees, but it excludes war-crimes suspects and anyone interned after 1946, while it is questionable whether the numbers are accurate, particularly for the chaotic beginning of the occupation. Nevertheless, the ACA figures have been repeated frequently, sometimes with the British-zone total erroneously reduced by 4,000.[19]

---

[16] Tom Bower, *Blind Eye to Murder: Britain, America, and the Purging of Nazi Germany – A Pledge Betrayed* (London: André Deutsch, 1981), 116.

[17] Schick, 'Internierungslager', 301; Jürgen Weber, *Germany, 1945–1990: A Parallel History*, trans. Nicholas T. Parsons (Budapest: Central European University Press, 2004), 6. Richard Bessel speaks both of 'tens of thousands' and 'hundreds of thousands'. Bessel, *Germany 1945*, 170, 186–7.

[18] Niethammer, 'Alliierte Internierungslager (1995)', 473; Biddiscombe, *Denazification of Germany*, 9.

[19] Wolfgang Friedmann, *The Allied Military Government of Germany* (London: Stevens & Sons, 1947), 332; Report to the Council of Foreign Ministers from the Allied Control Authority in Germany, 24 Feb. 1947, Section II, Part 3, d, TNA, FO 1030/7. See Lange, *Entnazifizierung in Nordrhein-Westfalen*, 12; Clemens Vollnhals (ed.), *Entnazifizierung: Politische Säuberung und Rehabilitierung in den vier Besatzungszonen 1945–1949* (Munich: Deutscher Taschenbuch Verlag, 1991), 251; Cohen, 'Transitional Justice', 69. Fürstenau miscalculates the figures and thus under-reports the British total by 4,000. Fürstenau, *Entnazifizierung*, 44. Fürstenau's figures, including this error, have in turn been cited by others. See Müller, 'Internierungslager in und um Ludwigsburg', 174.

The number of internees was undoubtedly higher than the ACA figures, but how much higher is difficult to say with certainty even for the American and British zones. Diverse figures exist for the former. At the upper end of the spectrum are exaggerations that 200,000 or as many as 260,000–300,000 people were interned in the US zone.[20] At the lower end, some authors – especially those who write about the Soviet zone – claim that the Americans interned only approximately 100,000.[21] Various American sources reported that 117,512 or 128,000 had been interned by December 1945 (the former figure by early that month), some of whom had already been released. An official American history of the occupation states that nearly 150,000 were interned in the first year of occupation (without being clear about its start or end points). Given that arrests (or transfers from POW status) continued even thereafter, reports cited by Meyer that 170,000 were interned by November 1946 are plausible.[22] In the British zone, the ICRC believed that around 100,000 people were interned in January 1946, which seems too high for that point in time or any other. Over time, however, the British interned at least 90,614 people and, according to Wember, possibly close to 100,000.[23] It is widely accepted that the French interned a total of ca. 21,500 people.[24] The subtotal for the western zones can thus be estimated at between 280,000 and 290,000, although more than 9,200 need to be subtracted to avoid double counting internees who were transferred among the western zones in 1947–8.[25]

---

[20] Waibel, *Von der wohlwollenden Despotie*, 202. The latter figure comes from far right-wing publishers. See Erich Schwinge, 'Rückblick auf die Zeit der amerikanischen Besetzung: Morgenthau-Plan und die Mißachtung des Völkerrechts', in Bernard Willms (ed.), *Handbuch zur deutschen Nation: Geistiger Bestand und politische Lage* (Tübingen: Hohenrain-Verlag, 1986), vol. 1, 323. Cf. Müller, 'Internierungslager in und um Ludwigsburg', 174.

[21] Von Plato, 'Sowjetische Speziallager', 95; Ilko-Sascha Kowalczuk and Stefan Wolle, *Roter Stern über Deutschland: Sowjetische Truppen in der DDR* (Berlin: Ch. Links, 2010), 86; Stefan-Ludwig Hoffmann, 'Germany Is No More: Defeat, Occupation, and the Postwar Order', in Helmut Walser Smith (ed.), *The Oxford Handbook of Modern German History* (Oxford: Oxford University Press, 2011), 601; Merten, *Gulag in East Germany*, 21.

[22] Niethammer, *Mitläuferfabrik*, 255; Meyer, *Entnazifizierung von Frauen*, 53, 97, 98; Oliver J. Fredericksen, *The American Military Occupation of Germany 1945–1953* (Darmstadt: Historical Division, U.S. Army Europe, 1953), 98; Waibel, *Von der wohlwollenden Despotie*, 202. See also Dolan, 'Isolating Nazism', iii, 2, 35.

[23] Burckhardt to Division PIC, Geneva, 11 Jan. 1946, ACICR, B G 44 02-056.04; Wember, *Umerziehung im Lager*, 31 (and n. 32).

[24] Niethammer, 'Alliierte Internierungslager (1998)', 100; Möhler, 'Internierung im Rahmen der Entnazifizierungspolitik', 64.

[25] The Americans transferred 7,503 internees to the British and 1,741 to the French zone. Wember, *Umerziehung im Lager*, 243; Möhler, 'Internierungslager in der französischen Besatzungszone', 51.

These western-zone figures include some non-Germans. There were some Alsatians and Lorrainians in French camps in early 1946, but the Americans held the highest numbers of foreigners in the western zones. Numerous US-zone camps held Austrians and ethnic Germans (*Volksdeutsche*) from Eastern Europe, as well as a smattering of other nationalities, many of whom had been drafted into, or volunteered for, the Waffen-SS. In July 1946, of the 18,067 internees in Darmstadt, the largest camp in the American zone, 1,670 (9%) were foreigners; 61% of them were Austrian, while Dutch, Hungarian, and stateless internees each comprised between 4% and 6% of the non-Germans.[26] In late 1946 and early 1947, hundreds of Austrians were transferred from American camps in Germany to the Marcus W. Orr camp in Salzburg, and similar numbers of Germans went in the opposite direction.[27] In contrast, very few non-Germans were held in the British camps, because the British decided in August 1945 to exempt them from automatic arrest. Esterwegen, where war-crimes suspects were concentrated, was therefore highly unusual for having over 20% non-Germans, again mainly Austrians and ethnic German former Waffen-SS members from Hungary, Yugoslavia, and Romania, in spring and summer 1946.[28]

These numbers were dwarfed by the approximately 35,000 non-Germans in the Soviet camps, almost all of whom were Soviet citizens. Some were suspected of collaboration with the Germans during the war, others of various 'counterrevolutionary' activities, but many – especially, but not only, in 1947–8 – were Soviet military personnel stationed in Germany who were accused of various crimes or misdemeanours during the occupation. While initially held in multiple camps (such as several hundred at Landsberg/Warta at the end of July 1945), Soviet citizens were later concentrated in Sachsenhausen and Torgau No. 10, where they generally spent little time before being transported to the USSR.[29]

---

[26] Möhler, *Entnazifizierung in Rheinland-Pfalz und im Saarland*, 372, 384; Horn, *Internierungs- und Arbeitslager*, 117; Karl Vogel, *M-AA 509: Elf Monate Kommandant eines Internierungslagers* (Memmingen: self-published, 1951), 119; Heinl, '"Das schlimme Lager"', 33–5. Cf. Dolan, 'Isolating Nazism', 125. On non-Germans in the Waffen-SS, see Jochen Böhler and Robert Gerwarth (eds.), *The Waffen-SS: A European History* (Oxford: Oxford University Press, 2017). Merten incorrectly calls Dachau the 'main' camp in the US zone, overlooking Darmstadt's significantly greater size. Merten, *Gulag in East Germany*, 22.

[27] Dohle and Eigelsberger, *Camp Marcus W. Orr*, 32–3.

[28] Anthony Glees, 'War Crimes: The Security and Intelligence Dimension', *Intelligence and National Security* 7, no. 3 (1992), 249; Wember, *Umerziehung im Lager*, 35; Weitkamp, 'Internierungslager Esterwegen', 252.

[29] Irina Scherbakova, 'Sowjetische Staatsangehörige und sonstige Ausländer in den Speziallagern', in von Plato (ed.), *Studien und Berichte*, 241–9; Greiner, *Suppressed Terror*, 145–6; Kirsten, *Das sowjetische Speziallager Nr. 4*, 28, 64–7.

The total number of people interned in the Soviet zone is most vigorously contested and is more commonly overestimated than that in the western zones. On the one hand, figures as high as 260,000 are given. On the other hand, the official Soviet figures released in 1990 are widely believed to be too low. According to them, in total 157,837 people were held in the Special Camps: 122,671 Germans, 34,706 Soviet citizens, and 460 other foreigners. Today, the figure of 189,000 total inmates, including approximately 154,000 Germans, is widely if not universally accepted.[30] These figures include SMT convicts, of whom there were probably approximately 23,200 (ca. 15% of the German inmates). A databank prepared for the German Red Cross by the Russian Federal Security Service has entries on 129,629 German internees, a realistic indicator.[31] Added to the likely western zone numbers, this figure gives a total of more than 400,000 German internees in all four zones, as shown in Table 3.1.

Demographics

Many depictions of internees stress their demographic diversity. Some authors mention the range of those interned in order to highlight the comprehensiveness and severity of Allied policy and practice. For instance, referring to the British zone, Michael Siedenhans speaks of 'NSDAP members of both sexes, including BDM girls and men who were highly placed in the hierarchy of the Party, the economy, and the judiciary'. Others depict such diversity as a sign of Allied arbitrariness and injustice. For example, Burkhard Schoebener endorses a critical contemporary assessment of internees in the Darmstadt camp in the American zone as consisting of 'old men and youths ... the guilty and the innocent'. For the Soviet zone, Jan Lipinsky claims that the NKVD

---

[30] Vollnhals (ed.), *Entnazifizierung: Politische Säuberung*, 238; von Plato, 'Zur Geschichte des sowjetischen Speziallagersystems', 53–4; von Plato, 'Sowjetische Speziallager', 92–3; Greiner, *Suppressed Terror*, 1–2. See Jeske, 'Kritische Bemerkungen', 457–80. Heitzer accepts the Soviet figures, speaking of a total of 158,000 prisoners, including foreigners and SMT convicts. Heitzer, 'Speziallagerforschung', 109. Merten uses the figure of 240,000. He claims that 'German official sources estabised these numbers after the collapse of the GDR', but his misattributed references indicate that they actually rely on Social Democratic estimates from 1949. Cf. Merten, *Gulag in East Germany*, 7; Taylor, *Exorcising Hitler*, 323, 324; Naimark, *Russians in Germany*, 378. This overestimation and his underestimation of the western figures lead him to claim, inaccurately, that the Soviet camps held more prisoners than the three western powers' camps combined. Merten, *Gulag in East Germany*, 42.

[31] Natalja Jeske and Jörg Morré, 'Die Inhaftierung von Tribunalverurteilten in der SBZ', in Hilger et al. (eds.), *Sowjetische Militärtribunale*, 653; Müller, 'Verbrechensahndung und Besatzungspolitik', 36.

Table 3.1 *Total numbers of internees*

	American zone	British zone	French zone	*Subtotal western zones*	Soviet zone	Total all zones
ACA detainees	51,006	34,500	10,923	*96,429*	59,965	*156,394*
ACA releases	44,244	34,000	8,040	*86,284*	7,214	*93,498*
ACA totals	95,250	68,500	18,963	*182,713*	67,179	*249,892*
Likely numbers	170,000	≥90,614	21,500	≥282,114	129,629	≥411,743

Note: The table compares figures from a 1947 report of the Allied Control Authority and the best current scholarly estimates. Note that the Soviet-zone figures do not include SMT convicts or non-German internees; that the estimated total and western-zone subtotals include a small number of foreigners (which were largely compensated by Germans interned in Austria); and that approximately 9,000–10,000 need to be subtracted from both these figures to avoid double-counting internees who were transferred between the western zones. Calculations of totals and subtotals by the author, based on Friedmann, *Allied Military Government*, 332; Meyer, *Entnazifizierung von Frauen*, 53, 98; Wember, *Umerziehung im Lager*, 31; Möhler, 'Internierung im Rahmen der Entnazifizierungspolitik', 64; Müller, 'Verbrechensahndung und Besatzungspolitik', 36.

filled its camps 'with men and women, from childhood (alleged 'Werewolf'-suspicion) to old age, … with prisoners of war and even citizens of the USSR'.[32] Many such characterizations depict internees as an arbitrary but representative selection of the entire German population, who suffered on behalf of the nation but were no more culpable than other Germans who were not deprived of their liberty. Internees thus appear the opposite of a hard core of Nazis or those genuinely responsible for the 'Third Reich' and its crimes. A similar impression is created by claims that – far from being demographically representative – Soviet-zone internees were drawn to a large extent from a demographic that bore little to no responsibility for Nazism: adolescents. An extreme example of this tendency is Stefan-Ludwig Hoffmann's claim that half the detainees in the Soviet camps were under twenty years old.[33] Resmini more accurately describes French-zone internees as 'family fathers', but

[32] Michael Siedenhans, 'Das Internierungslager "Eselheide" in Stukenbrock-Senne', *Heimatjahrbuch Kreis Gütersloh* (1986), 140; Burkhard Schoebener, 'Dokumentation einer Kontroverse: Die Bemühungen des Internationalen Roten Kreuzes 1946/47 um den völkerrechtlichen Schutz deutscher Zivilinternierter in der US-Zone', *Die Friedenswarte: Journal of International Peace and Organization* 68 (1990), 151; Jan Lipinsky, 'Sowjetische Speziallager', in Rainer Eppelmann, Horst Möller, Günter Nooke, and Dorothee Wilms (eds.), *Lexikon des DDR-Sozialismus: Das Staats- und Gesellschaftssystem der Deutschen Demokratischen Republik* (Paderborn: Ferdinand Schöningh, 1997), 709.
[33] Hoffmann, 'Germany Is No More', 602. Cf. Heitzer, 'Speziallagerforschung', 116.

this, too, minimizes their culpability and misses the point that the Nazi regime and its crimes relied on the participation of loving fathers.[34]

Both sexes and all ages were present in internment camps in every zone, but internees were less representative of the general population than is sometimes suggested. In particular, claims about huge numbers of adolescents in the Soviet camps are exaggerated. The majority of internees in every zone were middle-aged. In Rhenish Hesse in July 1945, the French apparently found (and promptly released) children as young as eight in camps taken over from the Americans, but in October 41% of internees in the French camp at Idar-Oberstein were over fifty. Of a sample of internees in the Saarland in 1947–8, 40% were in their forties in 1945, with a further 25% each in their thirties and fifties.[35] In the British camp at Paderborn-Staumühle in early 1946, the vast majority of the more than 7,000 internees were in their forties and fifties; only twenty-one were over sixty-five and only fifty-five (less than 1%) were under twenty-five, one of whom was under sixteen. Of the more than 19,000 members of criminal organizations who were prosecuted by British-zone *Spruchgerichte*, 6% were under thirty in 1948, 22% were between thirty and thirty-eight, 49% between thirty-nine and forty-eight, and 33% were over forty-eight, that is, had been born before 1900.[36] In Darmstadt in the American zone, the average age of internees in summer 1946 was forty-three; this was a relatively young camp, with almost 9% aged between seventeen and twenty-seven. In camp No. 74 in Ludwigsburg-Oßweil the age distribution in the first half of 1946 was as follows: 0.6% (nine internees) were twenty or younger; 3% were aged between twenty-one and thirty; 20% were between thirty-one and forty; 43% were aged forty-one to fifty; 29% were fifty-one to sixty, and 6% were between sixty-one and seventy-four. According to a December 1946 report on camps under Bavarian administration, internees were somewhat younger: 16% were aged up to thirty years, 34% from thirty-one to forty, 30% between forty-one and fifty, 16% from fifty-one to sixty, and 4% were over sixty.[37]

In the western zones, the proportion of middle-aged internees increased slightly over time as the oldest and youngest internees were

---

[34] Resmini, 'Lager der Besatzungsmächte', 614.

[35] Möhler, *Entnazifizierung in Rheinland-Pfalz und im Saarland*, 383; Camps d'internés civils, politiques et administratifs, 6 Oct. 1945, ACICR, B G 44 02-058.01; Möhler, 'Internierungslager in der französischen Besatzungszone', 57.

[36] Hüser, *'Unschuldig' in britischer Lagerhaft?*, 64; Wember, *Umerziehung im Lager*, 339.

[37] Dolan, 'Isolating Nazism', 124; Heinl, 'Das schlimme Lager', 35; CIE 74, Age Scale for Camp Total (Jan.–Jun. 1946), Staatsarchiv Ludwigsburg (StAL), EL 904, no. 43; Niethammer, *Mitläuferfabrik*, 456. See also Strauß, *Kriegsgefangenschaft und Internierung*, 391, 513.

prioritized for release or amnesty, although this was counterbalanced somewhat by the addition of Waffen-SS personnel initially held as POWs, who tended to be younger than the party functionaries. In the Dachau Internment and Labour Camp in the first half of 1948, just 4–5% of inmates were in their twenties and 30–1% in their thirties, while those in their forties and fifties together comprised between 63% and 65%. In the last remaining camp in Württemberg-Baden, Camp No. 77 in Ludwigsburg, in February 1949 – by which time labour-camp convicts outnumbered internees awaiting a verdict by nine to one – 2% of inmates were in their twenties, 11% in their thirties, 40% in their forties, 41% their fifties, and 7% were over sixty.[38] Of course, internees also grew older during their detention, which contributed to the aging of the camp populations.

Among those detained by the Soviets, the proportion of younger internees was higher, but not as high as often suggested. Here, too, most internees were middle-aged. In July 1945, 74% of the more than 6,000 internees who arrived in Landsberg/Warta from the short-lived Weesow camp near Werneuchen north-east of Berlin were in their forties or fifties, while only 6% were thirty or younger; over 100 (1–2%) were aged between twelve and seventeen. In Buchenwald in 1945, 61% of all internees were forty-five or older, a further 25% were between thirty-five and forty-four, and 13% were under thirty-five. By late 1949, after two winters in which in most camps mainly older inmates died, the relative size of the younger cohorts had increased somewhat, but those born in or before 1900 still comprised 53%. In October 1946, the total Special Camp population (including a relatively small number of SMT convicts, who tended to be younger than internees) was only slightly younger than the overall Buchenwald figures: 57% were forty-five or older, 24% aged between thirty-five and forty-four, and 18% under thirty-five.[39] Compared with the Bavarian figures from December

---

[38] Based on figures provided by Hammermann, 'Internierungslager Dachau', 59; Lagervorsteher to Vollzugsleiter, 10 Feb. 1949, StAL, EL 904, no. 123.

[39] Kirsten, *Das sowjetische Speziallager Nr. 4*, 58, 61; Neumann, 'Häftlingsstruktur im Speziallager Buchenwald', 489; 'Information des Leiters der Abt. Speziallager "Über das vorhandene Spezkontingent in den MVD-Speziallagern auf dem Territorium Deutschlands"', 30 Oct. 1946, in Possekel (ed.), *Sowjetische Dokumente*, 248. In most Soviet camps, the death rate of internees aged eighteen or younger in 1945 was similar to, or lower than, their proportion among internees overall, but in Ketschendorf, exceptionally, it was two to three times higher. Even there, where 294 internees died who were born between 1927 and 1930 inclusive, the average age of those who died was forty-nine. Andreas Weigelt, 'Sterben und Tod im Speziallager Ketschendorf', in Andreas Weigelt, *Totenbuch: Sowjetisches Speziallager Nr. 5 Ketschendorf 1945–1947*, ed. Initiativgruppe Internierungslager Ketschendorf/Speziallager Nr. 5 e.V. (Berlin: Wichern-Verlag, 2014), 160, 190–1.

1946 cited earlier, the distinctive feature of the Soviet camp inmates in late 1946 was thus not a higher number of under-thirty-year-olds but a lower proportion of people in their thirties and early forties and a higher proportion of older inmates. In May 1948, however, a Soviet report recorded that 588 internees were under sixteen years old, 1,443 were aged between sixteen and eighteen, and 999 were between eighteen and twenty. Those under twenty thus comprised 7% of the total, and 13% of those whose continued detention the report recommended. In late 1949, the younger internees were over-proportionally recommended for release. Of the 3,324 former internees who were convicted in the Waldheim trials in 1950, only 0.6% were under twenty, almost 4% in their twenties, and 8% in their thirties, while 31% were in their forties, 46% in their fifties, and 11% were over sixty.[40] The number of interned adolescents was thus shockingly high, but far from the exaggerated claims that they comprised half the camp inmates. Even Klaus-Dieter Müller's suggestion that almost 14% of all Soviet-zone internees were aged between fifteen and twenty-four seems on the high side. In Buchenwald, 8% had been twenty-six or younger in 1945. Even if one includes the younger SMT convicts, the under-twenty-year-olds in the Soviet camps never comprised anywhere near a majority.[41]

The vast majority of internees in every zone were male. Female detainees were generally housed in separate barracks or zones within the camps. In the western occupation zones women were eventually concentrated in particular camps, in the British zone in Paderborn-Staumühle and in the American zone in Augsburg-Göggingen and eventually only in Camp No. 77 in Ludwigsburg, and their proportion fell over time.[42] In the US zone, women comprised 9% of internees in Garmisch-Partenkirchen in July 1945, ca. 6% of internees across Bavaria in March 1946, between

---

[40] Nikita Petrov, 'Die Apparate des NKVD/MVD und des MGB in Deutschland (1945–1953): Eine historische Skizze', in von Plato (ed.), *Studien und Berichte*, 151; Neumann, 'Häftlingsstruktur im Speziallager Buchenwald', 489; Otto, 'Waldheimer Prozesse', 548.

[41] Müller, 'Verbrechensahndung und Besatzungspolitik', 38; Tina Kwiatkowski, *Nach Buchenwald: Die Beeinflussung Jugendlicher durch ihre Internierung im Speziallager Nr. 2 Buchenwald* (Munich: Rainer Hampp Verlag, 2002), 28. Those born in 1926 or later constituted just under 30% of SMT convicts from 1945 to 1955, many of whom were convicted after 1950. Thanks to the younger SMT convicts, in 1949 46% of Bautzen's inmates were under 35, 25% were between 35 and 45, and 29% were over 45. See table IIIa in the appendix to Hilger et al. (eds.), *Sowjetische Militärtribunale*, 790; von Plato, 'Zur Geschichte des sowjetischen Speziallagersystems', 57.

[42] Wember, *Umerziehung im Lager*, 67; Hüser, *'Unschuldig' in britischer Lagerhaft?*, 50–63; Meyer, *Entnazifizierung von Frauen*, 151–8; Gudrun Lenzer, *Frauen im Speziallager Buchenwald 1945–1950: Internierung und lebensgeschichtliche Einordnung* (Münster: Agenda Verlag, 1996), 72–4.

2% and 3% of internees throughout the zone in late 1946 and early 1947, and 2% of internees in Bavaria in August 1947. The French released a number of women from camps they inherited from the Americans in Rhenish Hesse in July 1945. In October, fewer than 5% of internees in three French camps inspected by the ICRC were women, and in March and April 1946 women comprised 2%, 5%, and 4% of internees in camps at Wörth, Landau, and Theley, respectively.[43] In the British zone, women made up almost 5% of internees in Neumünster-Gadeland in autumn 1945, probably an unusually high figure because female internees from Neuengamme had just been transferred there. After female internees from across the zone were concentrated at Paderborn-Staumühle, they comprised 9% and almost 6% of internees there in May 1946 and May 1947, respectively, but less than 2% of all British-zone internees. By February 1948, there were just forty-three women among 5,681 internees in the British zone (less than 0.8%).[44]

In contrast, the proportion of women increased in the Soviet-zone camps at least until 1948, mainly because they faced slightly less horrendous conditions and survived them better than their male counterparts, which outweighed the fact that they were slightly more likely to be released. Women comprised just under 4% of the ca. 13,000 people interned in Landsberg/Warta during its existence between May 1945 and March 1946, and they were disproportionately represented among those released from there in late 1945; a little over 2% of the remaining internees who were transported to Buchenwald in early 1946 were women. Women comprised over 5% of internees in Mühlberg at the end of 1946, but almost 11% in April 1947 after two lethal winters. In Buchenwald, they accounted for almost 4% of all internees over time, with a lower proportion before 1948 and a higher one thereafter, slightly over 6% in January 1950. In Sachsenhausen, women constituted almost 7% of all inmates in July 1946, but almost 10% if one removes from the total more than 4,000 Wehrmacht officers who were held there at that point but were not regular internees.[45] Müller's claim that women

[43] Meyer, *Entnazifizierung von Frauen*, 99–100, 105; Möhler, *Entnazifizierung in Rheinland-Pfalz und im Saarland*, 383, 372, 384; Camps d'internés civils, politiques et administratifs, 6 Oct. 1945, ACICR, B G 44 02-058.01.

[44] Wember, *Umerziehung im Lager*, 56, 370–1; Beßmann, 'Der sozusagen für Euch alle im KZ sitzt', 38; Hüser, *'Unschuldig' in britischer Lagerhaft?*, 55; Hoffmann to Colombo, 8 Mar. 1948, ACICR, B G 44 02-056.03.

[45] Lenzer, *Frauen im Speziallager Buchewald*, 135–45; Kirsten, *Das sowjetische Speziallager Nr. 4*, 59–61; Kilian, 'Speziallager Nr. 1 Mühlberg', 287–8; Bodo Ritscher, 'Speziallager Nr. 2 Buchenwald', in von Plato (ed.), *Studien und Berichte*, 300; 'Bericht: Bestand und Zustand des Spezkontingents im Speziallager Nr. 7', 13 Jul. 1946, in Morsch and Reich (eds.), *Sowjetisches Speziallager in Sachsenhausen*, 145.

comprised 14% of German internees in the Soviet zone seems too high, but their proportion was likely higher than the 5% of all Special Camp inmates they are sometimes claimed to represent.[46] In October 1946, women constituted almost 6% of all Special Camp inmates, including non-Germans (who were almost exclusively men) and a still relatively small number of SMT convicts. Of 43,853 German internees included in a Soviet report of May 1948, 3,684 were women (8%); of those whose continued detention was recommended, 1,142 were women (7%).[47]

A statistically insignificant but symbolically important demographic cohort in every zone was children, including babies and infants who were interned with their mothers or even born behind barbed wire. In the British camp at Paderborn-Staumühle, where women were concentrated, a five-year-old girl arrived with her mother in May 1946, six children were born in the camp infirmary, and four children arrived in the course of an exchange of internees with the American zone in September 1947. In the two main camps for women in the American zone, Ludwigsburg No. 77 and Augsburg-Göggingen, there were sixteen and seven children, respectively, in July 1947, eleven and seven in November, and two and none in June 1948. The number of babies and children in the Soviet camps was higher. There is evidence of approximately sixty births in the camps. After a mother died shortly after giving birth in Ketschendorf, her new-born son was 'adopted' by a fellow female internee and transferred with her to further camps before being released in summer 1948. In December 1948, there were five mothers with children up to two years old in Buchenwald, six in Bautzen, and twenty-five in Sachsenhausen; one-third of these mothers were internees, the remainder were SMT convicts.[48]

---

[46] Müller, 'Verbrechensahndung und Besatzungspolitik', 36; von Plato, 'Zur Geschichte des sowjetischen Speziallagersystems', 35; Kathrin Mühe, 'Frauen in den sowjetischen Speziallagern', *Deutschland Archiv* 37, no. 4 (2004), 630; Greiner, *Suppressed Terror*, 146. Women comprised almost 10% of all documented SMT convicts in the years 1945–9, with the proportion increasing from under 8% in 1945–7 to over 11% in 1948–9. From 1948, female SMT convicts were concentrated in Sachsenhausen. As a result, the trajectory of the proportion of female inmates in Bautzen, where large numbers of SMT convicts were detained, was somewhat anomalous. It increased from 2% to 3% in 1945 to a peak of 8% in autumn 1946, before falling to 4% in December 1948 and just over 1% in January 1950. Hilger and Schmeitzner, 'Einleitung: Deutschlandpolitik und Strafjustiz', 20; Alexandr Haritonow, 'Zur Geschichte des Speziallagers Nr. 4 (3) in Bautzen', in von Plato (ed.), *Studien und Berichte*, 350.

[47] 'Information des Leiters der Abt. Speziallager "Über das vorhandene Spezkontingent in den MVD-Speziallagern auf dem Territorium Deutschlands"', 30 Oct. 1946, in Possekel (ed.), *Sowjetische Dokumente*, 248; Petrov, 'Apparate des NKVD/MVD', 150.

[48] Hüser, *'Unschuldig' in britischer Lagerhaft?*, 57–8, 84; Meyer, *Entnazifizierung von Frauen*, 104, 106, 156; Alexander Latotzky, *Kindheit hinter Stacheldraht: Mütter mit Kindern in*

Non-Nazis in Internment

Apart from stressing internees' demographic diversity (or skewedness), many accounts highlight the internment of non-Nazis, especially in the Soviet zone. In emphasizing the arbitrariness of Soviet arrests, some authors abandon any attempt at numerical specificity, and 'Nazis' appear no more numerous than non-Nazis. For example, according to Greiner,

Among both internees and SMT prisoners, there were perpetrators, victims, opponents and fellow travelers of the National Socialist regime, as well as thousands who had experienced the Nazi era as children.[49]

In other accounts, people without meaningful Nazi incrimination appear most numerous. For example, Wehler argues that Soviet-zone internees included 'not a few' who would have faced an American 'special court' (whatever that is), but 'even more harmless followers, ideologically suspect "class enemies", arbitrarily apprehended *Jungvolk*-kids, who were accused of "Werewolf" activities'. Hermann Weber provides another example:

Among the internees ... apart from *some* Nazi criminals, Nazi activists, minor offenders, and *many* followers there was a *great number* of denounced and arbitrarily arrested innocent people, from 1946 Social Democrats, Democrats, and even oppositional Communists.[50]

Indeed, some authors mention only various non-Nazis.[51] Merten goes so far as to cast Soviet-zone arrestees in general as 'dissidents'.[52]

---

    sowjetischen Speziallagern und DDR-Haft (Leipzig: Forum Verlag, 2004), 25, 28–30; Weigelt, 'Sterben und Tod', 171.

[49] Greiner, *Suppressed Terror*, 12. See also Rainer Eckert, 'Entnazifizierung', in Eppelmann et al. (eds.), *Lexikon des DDR-Sozialismus*, 248; Lipinsky, 'Sowjetische Speziallager', 709; Klaus Schroeder, *Die DDR: Geschichte und Strukturen* (Stuttgart: Reclam, 2011), 30. Greiner elsewhere acknowledges, 'Evidence available today shows that the majority of internees were civilian functionaries of the Third Reich or of the Nazi Party.' Greiner, *Suppressed Terror*, 7.

[50] Wehler, *Deutsche Gesellschaftsgeschichte*, vol. 4, 957; Hermann Weber, *Die DDR 1945–1990*, 3rd revised and expanded ed. (Munich: R. Oldenbourg, 2000), 11 (emphasis added). See also Berit Olschewski, *'Freunde' im Feindesland: Rote Armee und deutsche Nachkriegsgesellschaft im ehemaligen Großherzogtum Mecklenburg-Strelitz 1945–1953* (Berlin: Berliner Wissenschafts-Verlag, 2009), 178.

[51] Hedwig Richter, *Die DDR* (Paderborn: Ferdinand Schöningh, 2009), 14; Jens Schöne, *Die DDR: Eine Geschichte des 'Arbeiter- und Bauernstaates'* (Berlin: Berlin Story Verlag, 2014), 32. See also Naimark, *Russians in Germany*, 382–90; Pohl, *Justiz in Brandenburg*, 84–7.

[52] Merten, *Gulag in East Germany*, 10. This follows his claims that, despite some 'minor Party workers' (but no 'important Nazis'), 'the majority were individuals denounced as anti-communist' and that the Soviets 'especially targeted' Social Democrats as well as uncooperative Christian and Liberal Democrats and 'any person considered a dissident,

Without wanting to suggest that the internment of the communists' non-Nazi ideological opponents, of adolescents, or of randomly apprehended people does not warrant attention, such cases were less common than these accounts suggest. As Greiner notes, frequently cited reports of random individuals being arrested 'off the street' or 'from a field' often rely on hearsay and are largely apocryphal, even if they should not be dismissed as complete 'fabrications'.[53] Other groups were also smaller than often suggested. According to Soviet records, thirty-six 'factory owners, bank directors, etc.' (0.6%) were transferred from Weesow to Landsberg/Warta in July 1945, while seventy-six (1.3%) were transported from there to Buchenwald in early 1946, undoubtedly unusually high figures given that Weesow and Landsberg held relatively large numbers of 'prominent' internees from Berlin. Again according to Soviet records, estate owners and industrialists comprised 2% of internees in early 1948, and in December 1949 forty-one estate owners and industrialists made up just 0.7% of inmates in Bautzen; in contrast, workers comprised 30% and 39% of these two cohorts, respectively.[54] The number of victims of Nazi persecution (including former concentration-camp inmates) interned by the Soviets was also lower than their prominence in some accounts suggests, if nevertheless disturbingly high. According to Günter Fippel, 222 antifascists were held in the Soviet camps.[55]

It is worth exploring the accuracy of repeated claims that members of postwar political parties, especially Social Democrats, were incarcerated in the Soviet camps in significant numbers. Hoffmann asserts that the Soviet camps 'held more Social Democrats than Nazi leaders', which could be true only if 'Nazi leader' is defined as meaning only those at Reich and Gau levels. Others claim more modestly and specifically that hundreds of Social Democrats were held in both Sachsenhausen and Buchenwald, that about 400 died in Soviet prisons and camps and a

---

class enemy, uncooperative professional, or recalcitrant landowners – even peasants', and young people mistakenly regarded as 'Werewolf'. Merten, *Gulag in East Germany*, 5, 6, 8. At other points he concedes *sotto voce* that the 'majority' of (the thousands of) internees released in 1948 were 'nominal Nazis' and that 'serious cases' remained until 1950, and also that 'officers of the Waffen SS' and 'leaders of the SA, SS, and Hitler Youth' were interned in various camps. Merten, *Gulag in East Germany*, 42, 175, 204.

[53] Greiner, *Suppressed Terror*, 102. Cf. Kirsten, *Das sowjetische Speziallager Nr. 4*, 41.

[54] Kirsten, *Das sowjetische Speziallager Nr. 4*, 57–8, 67–70; Petrov, 'Apparate des NKVD/MVD', 151; Haritonow, 'Zur Geschichte des Speziallagers in Bautzen', 351.

[55] Günter Fippel, *Antifaschisten in 'antifaschistischer' Gewalt: Mittel- und ostdeutsche Schicksale in den Auseinandersetzungen zwischen Demokratie und Diktatur (1945 bis 1961)* (Guben: Verlag Andreas Peter, 2003), 179. See Hermann Weber, *Geschichte der DDR*, updated and expanded ed. (Munich: Deutscher Taschenbuch Verlag, 1999), 63.

further 1,000 after their release, and that at least 5,000 were convicted by SMTs between 1945 and 1955.[56] Social Democrats in the Soviet zone and Berlin undoubtedly suffered diverse forms of repression and intimidation by Soviet and East German communists. Their persecution was particularly severe during, and immediately after, the forced merger in the Soviet zone of the SPD and the Communist Party of Germany (KPD) to form the Socialist Unity Party of Germany (SED) in April 1946 and again in 1948 when 'unreliable' elements were purged during the SED's transformation into a Stalinist 'Party of a New Type'. Yet there is insufficient evidence to support claims that thousands of Social Democrats were interned or imprisoned in the Soviet-zone camps.[57]

The SMTs certainly prosecuted many members of postwar political parties, but not as many as is often assumed. Research by the Hannah Arendt Institute for Totalitarianism Research in Dresden shows that Germans convicted by SMTs between 1945 and 1949 included at least 336 Social Democrats, 212 Communists, and eighty-five members of the SED who had previously belonged to the NSDAP. They also included 238 members of the Liberal Democratic Party of Germany (LDPD), 183 of the Christian Democratic Union (CDU), and two of the National Democratic Party of Germany (NDPD).[58] Most, but not all such convicts were sent to Special Camps; others were held in NKVD/MVD prisons or deported to the USSR. According to a Soviet report, in December 1949, 1,143 SMT convicts (20%) in Bautzen were members

---

[56] Hoffmann, 'Germany Is No More', 602; Wolfgang Buschfort, 'Gefoltert und geschlagen', and Helmut Bärwald, 'Terror als System', both in Günther Scholz (ed.), *Verfolgt – verhaftet – verurteilt: Demokraten im Widerstand gegen die rote Diktatur – Fakten und Beispiele* (Berlin: Westkreuz-Verlag, 1990), 60–1, 18, 21. Merten cites these figures and also asserts, 'Thousands of SPD members were arrested and incarcerated in the special camps.' Merten, *Gulag in East Germany*, 149–50. Cf. Heitzer, 'Speziallagerforschung', 116.

[57] Boldorf, 'Brüche oder Kontinuitäten?', 292; Mike Schmeitzner, 'Genossen vor Gericht: Die sowjetische Strafverfolgung von Mitgliedern der SED und ihrer Vorläuferparteien 1945–1954', in Hilger et al. (eds.), *Sowjetische Militärtribunale*, 283–4. Cf. Greiner, *Suppressed Terror*, 17; Friedhelm Boll, *Sprechen als Last und Befreiung: Holocaust-Überlebende und politisch Verfolgte zweier Diktaturen* (Bonn: Dietz, 2003), 280; Günter Braun and Gunter Ehnert, 'Das Speziallager Buchenwald in einem zeitgenössischen Bericht: Ein seltenes Dokument und ein außergewöhnlicher Fall aus der Internierungspraxis des NKWD', *Deutschland Archiv* 28, no. 2 (1995), 167–8.

[58] Schmeitzner, 'Genossen vor Gericht', 273, 276, 284; Ute Schmidt, '"Vollständige Isolierung erforderlich ...": SMT-Verurteilungen im Kontext der Gleichschaltung der Blockparteien CDU und LDP 1946–1953', in Hilger et al. (eds.), *Sowjetische Militärtribunale*, 389. There is a discrepancy with members of the labour parties. Schmeitzner's figures cited here give a total of 613 from the SPD, KPD, and SED. Yet the database presented by Schmidt gives a total of 2,195 (ibid.). If the proportions of Schmeitzner's lower figures are projected onto the higher figure, possibly 1,165 Social Democrats may have been convicted by SMTs between 1945 and 1949.

of postwar parties: forty-two were members of the SPD and many of the 873 SED members were (former) Social Democrats; additionally, there were 139 members of the LDPD, eighty-eight members of the CDU, and one member of the NDPD. In comparison, there were 827 former members of the Hitler Youth, 1,457 of the NSDAP, and 2,168 people who were not affiliated with any party, past or present.[59] Further SMT convicts were held in Sachsenhausen, where Fippel has identified 101 Social Democrats, ninety-eight Communists, sixty-seven Christian Democrats, forty-four LDPD members, and two NDPD members; together, these 312 prisoners constitute 6% of his database of ca. 5,000 prisoners.[60]

There were fewer members of postwar political parties among the internees than among the SMT convicts, and certainly not enough to justify claims that 800 Social Democrats were detained in Buchenwald alone (where no SMT convicts were held).[61] Fippel claims to have identified almost 500 people who were interned in Sachsenhausen due to real or imagined opposition to the Soviet occupier or the KPD/SED, but makes no claims about their party affiliation. According to a Soviet report from May 1948, of 43,835 German internees, 349 were members of postwar parties, that is, less than 1%: 188 SPD, 112 SED, twenty-eight LDPD, and twenty-one CDU. As none were recommended for release, their proportion increased to 2% of those whose detention continued. These numbers are consistent with the fact that only thirty members of postwar parties (seventeen SPD, six SED, three KPD, four CDU, and three LDPD) were identified through information provided to the Buchenwald Memorial in the 1990s by former internees or relatives. They constituted 2% of the total.[62] The SPD's *Book of Commemoration* for Social Democratic victims of political persecution in the twentieth century includes ten Social Democrats who were interned in a Special Camp, while a documentation of Christian Democrats persecuted in the Soviet zone and early GDR identifies twenty CDU members (six of whom died in internment and five of whom were convicted at

---

[59] Jeske and Morré, 'Inhaftierung von Tribunalverurteilten', 616–53; Haritonow, 'Zur Geschichte des Speziallagers in Bautzen', 351. For the experiences of one such Social Democrat, see Dieter Rieke, *Geliebtes Leben: Erlebtes und Ertragenes zwischen den Mahlsteinen jüngster deutscher Geschichte* (Berlin: Berlin Verlag, 1999).

[60] Fippel, *Demokratische Gegner*, 101–2.   [61] Naimark, *Russians in Germany*, 388.

[62] Fippel, *Demokratische Gegner*, 63; Petrov, 'Apparate des NKVD/MVD', 150–1; Bodo Ritscher, Rikola-Gunnar Lüttgenau, Gabriele Hammermann, Wolfgang Röll, and Christian Schölzel (eds.), *Das sowjetische Speziallager Nr. 2 1945–1950: Katalog zur ständigen historischen Ausstellung* (Göttingen: Wallstein Verlag, 1999), 77.

Waldheim) as well as six CDU sympathizers who were interned.[63] According to Wilfriede Otto, thirty-two postwar political party members constituted ca. 1% of the former internees convicted in the Waldheim trials.[64] Members of postwar parties were thus a tiny minority of Soviet-zone internees, and a significant minority of SMT convicts.

To be sure, highlighting the fate of non- and anti-Nazis – however small their number – is historically justified and morally important. Their cases are illustrative of considerable arbitrariness, of targeted political persecution, and of undeserved suffering. Yet they should not dominate depictions of internees to the extent that they do, often to the neglect of other, larger groups.[65] According to a Soviet commission that reviewed internees in spring 1948, 87% had a Nazi affiliation. Moreover, one should beware a tendency to assume purely 'ideological' motivations behind Soviet arrests. As Mike Schmeitzner argues, one cannot simply assume that members of the postwar parties were prosecuted for postwar political reasons. Some were charged with offences such as theft, others with Nazi and war crimes. According to a report from Saxony-Anhalt from 1949, 16% of SMT convictions of SED members in the previous six months were for wartime crimes against Soviet citizens, and 21% of convicted SED members had been members of the SS, SA, NSDAP, or Hitler Youth. Certainly, there was little to stop the Soviet or East German authorities from manufacturing accusations of Nazi activity against their political opponents, but, equally, many former Nazis joined the postwar parties not least to obscure or compensate for their compromised pasts. Additionally, while the Soviet authorities often condemned any unwanted youthful activity as 'Werewolf' agitation, not every arrested adolescent was wrongly accused of belonging to this supposedly fictitious movement; some faced more specific (and sometimes justified) allegations of possessing weapons or of espionage, sabotage, or agitation against the occupying power, while others were

---

[63] For the Social Democratic internees, see Vorstand der Sozialdemokratischen Partei Deutschlands (ed.), *Der Freiheit verpflichtet: Gedenkbuch der deutschen Sozialdemokratie im 20. Jahrhundert* (Marburg: Schüren, 2000), 89–90, 126, 130, 136, 158, 181, 317, 333, 336, 344–5. For the CDU members, see Günter Buchstab (ed.), *Verfolgt und entrechtet: Die Ausschaltung Christlicher Demokraten unter sowjetischer Besatzung und SED-Herrschaft 1945–1961: Eine biographische Dokumentation* (Düsseldorf: Droste, 1998), 157, 167, 208, 217, 250, 299, 322, 326, 333, 334, 350, 356, 371, 381, 391, 407, 409, 416, 418, 432, and for the CDU sympathizers: 455, 475, 487, 496, 499, 502. Cf. Schmeitzner, 'Genossen vor Gericht', 290.

[64] Otto, 'Waldheimer Prozesse', 550.

[65] Merten spends considerably more time discussing the arrest of Christian Democrats from 1950 onward, that is, after the closure of the Soviet camps, than the arrest of Nazis. Merten, *Gulag in East Germany*, 145–6, 160–1.

accused of having been leaders or members of Nazi youth organizations. In December 1949, 'Werewolf' was listed as the reason for incarcerating 200 people in Bautzen (4% of inmates), while 827 were listed as having belonged to the Hitler Youth (15%).[66] Similarly, one cannot assume that class affiliation alone was decisive for the internment of estate owners and industrialists. As Possekel argues, almost all interned members of the 'exploitative classes' had held positions in Nazi organizations. Their socioeconomic status may also not have been the only reason for the fact that none of them were recommended for release in 1948, in contrast with 77% of interned workers. After all, workers were more likely than industrialists and estate owners to have held the lowliest NSDAP ranks, which were a major focus of the 1948 releases. Finally, it should be noted that industrialists and antifascists were interned in the western zones too, more than often believed.[67]

Accounts of internees in the western zones also give disproportionate attention to unrepresentative cases of apparently undeserved detention. Here, too, they seem to indicate Allied arbitrariness. There are reports, as mentioned in Chapter 2, of people being added randomly to internee transports as well as of denunciations and of antifascists and former inmates of Nazi concentration camps being falsely interned. Approximately 100 antifascists were allegedly interned in Hesse in the US zone, and in early 1947 twenty-five internees in the Regensburg camp (including former Social Democrats and some who had spent time in Nazi concentration camps) were recognized by the denazification prosecutor as having been persecuted by the Nazis. Additionally, numerous people, including war-crimes suspects, were detained due to confusion over

---

[66] Haritonow, 'Zur Geschichte des Speziallagers in Bautzen', 351–2; Schmeitzner, 'Genossen vor Gericht', 270. Cf. Schmidt, 'Vollständige Isolierung erforderlich', 391; Neumann, 'Häftlingsstruktur im Speziallager Buchenwald', 483–4; Michael C. Bienert, *Zwischen Opposition und Blockpolitik: Die 'bürgerlichen' Parteien und die SED in den Landtagen von Brandenburg und Thüringen (1946–1952)* (Düsseldorf: Droste Verlag, 2016), 116, 120–1, 421–6.

[67] Possekel, 'Sowjetische Lagerpolitik', 65; Wegehaupt, 'Funktionäre und Funktionseliten', 45. On industrialists in the western zones, in addition to Hüser quoted earlier, see Ralf Ahrens, 'Von der "Säuberung" zum Generalpardon: Die Entnazifizierung der westdeutschen Wirtschaft', in *Jahrbuch für Wirtschaftsgeschichte* 2010/12: *Europäische Wirtschaftseliten nach dem Zweiten Weltkrieg*, ed. Marcel Boldorf (Berlin: Akademie Verlag, 2010), 30, 43; Paul Hoser, 'Die Entnazifizierung in Bayern', in Schuster and Weber (eds.), *Entnazifizierung im regionalen Vergleich*, 478; and on the British arrest of eighty Ruhr industrial leaders, 'Control Commission for Germany (British Element), Intelligence Bureau, Intelligence Review No. 1', 12 Dec. 1945, in Pelly and Yasamee (eds.), *Documents on British Foreign Policy*, 443–5. See also Priemel, *Betrayal*, 155, 162, 169–85, 196–240.

names or because they had the same name as a wanted person.[68] More frequent for the western zones are claims that Allied zeal and ignorance led to the incorrect internment of numerous people whose titles or job descriptions included morphemes like '*Kreis-*' (district, but also circle), '*-führer*' (leader, but also in some contexts driver), '*-rat*' (councillor), or '*Stab-*' (staff), which were associated with Nazi seniority. Such cases apparently included a district fire-brigade chief (*Kreisfeuerwehrmeister*) in Garmisch-Partenkirchen, a train driver (*Lokomotivführer*) in Recklinghausen, senior grammar school teachers (*Studienräte*) among others in Ludwigsburg, and a circular-saw owner (*Kreissägenbesitzer*).[69] Such cases highlight the problems caused by widespread lack of German-language skills among Allied personnel, which inevitably led to errors in all zones. As Wember notes, 'The description of such mistakes occupies a large space in reports about the internment camps. But that creates a false impression, for these were exceptions and not the norm.' Such exceptional cases may receive considerable attention, but most scholarly accounts of western internment keep them in numerical proportion, unlike the distortions that are common in relation to the Soviet zone.[70] An important difference was that some such mistakes were corrected reasonably quickly, unlike in the Soviet zone, although Niethammer cites an example of a salesman who was denounced by a competitor, where-upon he disappeared for a year into an American internment camp without justification.[71]

It should be noted that what might appear erroneous grounds for arrest were not always the actual reason, and that other or additional grounds often emerged subsequently. An example of the latter was the case of

---

[68] Schuster, *Entnazifizierung in Hessen*, 248; Horn, *Internierungs- und Arbeitslager*, 159–60, 167–8; Liste I und II der Internierten mit antifaschistischer Betätigung oder Widerstandsleistung gegen das NS-System, Hessisches Hauptstaatsarchiv, Wiesbaden (HHStA), 521, no. 216; Klose, 'Internierungs- und Arbeitslager Regensburg', 78; A. H., Bensheim, to Martin Niemöller, 12 Oct. 1947, in Brommer (ed.), *Quellen zur Geschichte von Rheinland-Pfalz*, 495–501.

[69] Schick, 'Internierungslager', 303–4; Horn, *Internierungs- und Arbeitslager*, 54–5; Müller, 'Internierungslager in und um Ludwigsburg', 172–3; Wember, *Umerziehung im Lager*, 39, 66; Möhler, 'Internierungslager in der französischen Besatzungszone', 58; Möhler, *Entnazifizierung in Rheinland-Pfalz und im Saarland*, 359, 370. In Austria, the Americans' Standard Operating Procedure for Denazification of 3 August 1945 explicitly called for the detention of public servants with '*-rat*' in their title, including *Regierungsrat* and *Schulrat*. Tweraser, 'Die amerikanische Säuberungspolitik', 368.

[70] Wember, *Umerziehung im Lager*, 40. See Fürstenau, *Entnazifizierung*, 45; Freda Utley, *The High Cost of Vengeance* (Chicago: Henry Regnery, 1949), 215; Peterson, *American Occupation*, 146; Schick, 'Internierungslager', 304.

[71] Welsh, *Revolutionärer Wandel?*, 36; Möhler, 'Internierungslager in der französischen Besatzungszone', 58; Möhler, *Entnazifizierung in Rheinland-Pfalz und im Saarland*, 403; Niethammer, *Mitläuferfabrik*, 141.

Kiesinger, the future West German chancellor. He was apprehended because American forces that had just arrested a number of SD members in the vicinity suspected he might also be one. It was eventually established that he belonged not to the SD but to the radio propaganda department in the German foreign ministry, which prompted further interest in him.[72] Moreover, one should not mistake the seeming ordinariness, harmlessness, or wide range of internees' vocations and socioeconomic backgrounds for evidence of a lack of Nazi incrimination. After all, members of all professions and classes held political and administrative positions in the 'Third Reich'. For instance, farmers and the self-employed were over-represented among NSDAP Local Group Leaders, while white-collar employees, civil servants, and teachers dominated among the District Leaders. Indeed, teachers were massively over-represented among NSDAP members and mid-ranking party leaders, such that simply being a senior grammar school teacher was likely not the sole reason for the arrest of many of them.[73]

Contested Degrees of Eliteness, Seniority, and Responsibility

Leaving aside the misleading preoccupations with criminal guilt or innocence and with the internment of apparent non-Nazis, the degree of internees' responsibility and seniority and the extent to which they belonged to Nazi Germany's elite are vigorously contested. Reflecting a long-standing left-wing view that the reactionary German social elites that had been crucial in bringing down the Weimar Republic and supporting the 'Third Reich' were not held to account after the war, Niethammer noted critically in 1972/82 that social elites were not generally interned in the American zone and that the few economic and administrative elites who were interned were released by the end of 1946. The remaining internees, he argued, comprised 'more or less leading members of the Nazi-*movement, not* the ruling class of the Third Reich'. Despite the lack of a clear definition of the latter, numerous scholars have endorsed his assessment, particularly in the 1980s and early 1990s, but also more recently.[74] Its echoes can be found in

---

[72] Gassert, *Kiesinger*, 166–75.

[73] Wegehaupt, 'Funktionäre und Funktionseliten', 45, 50; Ingo Haar, 'Zur Sozialstruktur und Mitgliederentwicklung der NSDAP', in Benz (ed.), *Wie wurde man Parteigenosse?*, 72. Cf. Boldorf, 'Brüche oder Kontinuitäten?', 292.

[74] Niethammer, *Mitläuferfabrik*, 457 (emphasis in original). See Horn, *Internierungs- und Arbeitslager*, 153; Vollnhals (ed.), *Entnazifizierung: Politische Säuberung*, 237; Henke, *Politische Säuberung*, 41; Klose, 'Internierungs- und Arbeitslager Regensburg', 68, 82.

Wember's criticism of the British failure to intern judicial and economic elites, while nationalist authors argue more emphatically and misleadingly that there was 'no trace of the elite' in western camps.[75] More recently, historians have tended to place internees somewhat higher on the social hierarchy. For instance, Hüser characterizes British-zone internees as above all 'the middling ruling class in the Nazi state and society'. He highlights, moreover, that numerous leaders of the Ruhr steel industry, including Alfried Krupp, were interned in Paderborn-Staumühle, along with other nationally prominent figures such as the industrialist Hugo Hermann Stinnes and the businessman and politician Alfred Hugenberg, both of whom had played important roles in Hitler's rise to power in 1933.[76]

Assessments of the members of the Nazi movement who were interned in the western zones vary considerably. Some authors more or less uncritically accept Allied claims that internees comprised (a large) part of the Nazi elite, 'top Nazis', or 'major Nazi functionaries'.[77] Others stress the wide spectrum of their seniority. According to Klaus-Dietmar Henke, for instance, internees ranged 'from the Reich Leader to the Block Leader of the NSDAP, from the Reich minister to the mayor, from the Higher SS- and Police Leaders to the junior officer of the Waffen-SS'.[78] At least until the early 1990s, however, there was a strong tendency to minimize their seniority and responsibility. According to Niethammer in 1972/82, after late 1946 American-zone internees were 'largely junior officers of the criminal organizations'.[79] Influenced by Niethammer, but also seemingly wanting to counter a rather nebulous impression of internees' seniority, Christa Schick/Horn argues that they were 'by no means only Reich Leaders, Gau Leaders, or District Leaders of the NSDAP or perfidious Gestapo agents'. Instead, they were largely 'the lower and mid ranks of the Hitler regime', 'middling and lower recipients of orders', 'but not the really influential people', 'almost

---

[75] Wember, *Umerziehung im Lager*, 117, 119; Ekkehard Zimmermann, *Staub soll er fressen: Die Internierungslager in den Westzonen Deutschlands* (Frankfurt/Main: Haag und Herchen, 2008), 30.

[76] Hüser, *'Unschuldig' in britischer Lagerhaft?*, 64–7, 99. See also Hoffmann, 'Germany Is No More', 601.

[77] Fürstenau, *Entnazifizierung*, 28; William E. Griffith, 'Denazification in the United States Zone of Germany', *Annals of the American Academy of Political and Social Science* 267 (Jan. 1950),   69; Friedmann, *Allied Military Government*, 113. See also Müller, 'Internierungslager in und um Ludwigsburg', 171; Konrad H. Jarausch, *After Hitler: Recivilizing Germans, 1945–1995* (New York: Oxford University Press, 2006), 49; Meyer, 'Entnazifizierung', 18; Merten, *Gulag in East Germany*, 2, 21, 23, 31.

[78] Henke, 'Trennung vom Nationalsozialismus', 33.

[79] Niethammer, *Mitläuferfabrik*, 457. See also Vollnhals (ed.), *Entnazifizierung: Politische Säuberung*, 237.

exclusively small office-holders of the Nazi regime', 'for the most part the "small fry"'.[80] Other authors also stress that 'really prominent National Socialists' were absent or exceptional; Kai Cornelius argues that 'there were "only very few of the real Nazi elite"' in western camps.[81] Such tendencies to associate 'eliteness' and 'prominence' only with the national and possibly the regional levels overlook or minimize the significance of district and local elites. In every zone, large numbers of internees in particular camps came from the surrounding district, and district and local elites inevitably outnumbered nationally prominent figures.[82] This was not least because the most important among the latter were detained in separate facilities such as the American's early 'Ashcan' camp, initially in Belgium and then in Luxemburg, and were then often transferred to Nuremberg or elsewhere for interrogation and prosecution.[83]

In addition to emphasizing the non-Nazis, many depictions of Soviet-zone internees mention only the lowliest ranks of Nazis and minimize their involvement and seniority. Indeed, the only interned Nazis often appear to have been mere 'followers'. For instance, Erhard Neubert argues that 'the internees included a large number of small Nazis or nominal members of Nazi organizations'. Greiner also claims that almost half the Soviet-zone internees were 'rank-and-file NSDAP Party members such as Block and Cell Leaders'.[84] Such depictions overlook the fact that even the lowliest apparatchiks were more than just rank-and-file or nominal members.

The discussion is marked by a lack of clear and consistent parameters for assessing the seniority and responsibility of Nazi functionaries. There is no agreement on what constitutes a senior, mid-ranking, or subordinate Nazi leader or official. Some authors, like Horn, view Local Group Leaders as a low rank and District Leaders as a middling rank. Others see

---

[80] Schick, 'Internierungslager', 301; Horn, *Internierungs- und Arbeitslager*, 153, 55, 241.

[81] See Strauß, *Kriegsgefangenschaft und Internierung*, 390, 391; Möhler, 'Internierungslager in der französischen Besatzungszone', 63; Margarete Steinhart, *Balingen 1918–1948: Kleinstadt im Wandel* (Balingen: Stadtverwaltung Balingen, 1991), 258; Kai Cornelius, *Vom spurlosen Verschwindenlassen zur Benachrichtigungspflicht bei Festnahmen* (Berlin: Berliner Wissenschafts-Verlag, 2006), 106.

[82] Siedenhans, 'Internierungslager "Eselheide"', 143

[83] Priemel, *Betrayal*, 81; Steven David Schrag, 'ASHCAN: Nazis, Generals and Bureaucrats as Guests at the Palace Hotel, Mondorf les Bains, Luxembourg, May-August 1945' (unpub. PhD thesis, University of Toledo, 2015).

[84] Erhard Neubert, 'Politische Verbrechen in der DDR', in Stéphane Courtois, Nicolas Werth, Jean-Louis Panné, Andrzej Paczkowski, Karel Bartosek, and Jean-Louis Margolin, *Das Schwarzbuch des Kommunismus: Unterdrückung, Verbrechen und Terror*, trans. Irmela Arnsperger et al. (Munich: Piper, 1998), 863–4; Greiner, *Suppressed Terror*, 7, 15. See also Fippel, *Demokratische Gegner*, 40.

Block and Cell Leaders as a low rank, Local Group Leaders as a middling rank, and District Leaders as a senior rank.[85] Clearly some consistency would be helpful, particularly for comparative purposes. It makes sense to designate the Cell and Block Leaders as the lowest levels, to distinguish them from the low-level Local Group Leaders, and them in turn from the mid-ranking District Leaders, high-ranking Gau Leaders, and highest-ranking Reich Leaders. Irrespective of how they are designated, there is a range of views about the nature, influence, and culpability of specific positions such as Local Group Leader. Whereas many authors trivialize them (sometimes with reference to their unsalaried nature), others are outraged by the apparent belief that their occupants were not 'Nazis' and insist that they 'possessed a certain influence or even power'.[86]

This is not just a semantic or interpretative question but also a methodological one. According to which criteria can internees' culpability be assessed? Are the Allies' expansive summary arrest categories or the tough talk of the Liberation Law or Directive No. 38 appropriate yardsticks? The last included all functionaries down to the lowest rank held by Block Leaders (*Einsatzleiter*) among those presumed to be Major Offenders, and any ordinary NSDAP member who joined prior to 1 May 1937 among those presumed to be Offenders.[87] Or should one be guided by the lenient categorizations of the *Spruchkammern*, which turned even highly incriminated senior figures and criminals into mere followers in what is widely regarded as a whitewash? There is no consensus on this. Some authors accept the denazification panels' effective absolution of many western-zone internees. In contrast to the American expectation that virtually all internees would be classified as Offenders or Major Offenders and sentenced to labour camp under the Liberation Law, Horn stresses that 86% of a sample from the Nuremberg-Langwasser

---

[85] Horn, *Internierungs- und Arbeitslager*, 148–53; Wegehaupt, 'Funktionäre und Funktionseliten', 49; Meyer, *Entnazifizierung von Frauen*, 16; Resmini, 'Lager der Besatzungsmächte', 616; Biddiscombe, *Denazification of Germany*, 24, 196; Detlef Schmiechen-Ackermann, 'Der "Blockwart": Die unteren Parteifunktionäre im nationalsozialistischen Terror- und Überwachungsapparat', *Vierteljahreshefte für Zeitgeschichte* 48, no. 4 (2000), 575–602.

[86] Wolf Stegemann, 'Waren NS-Funktionäre keine Nazis? Die Entnazifizierung in Dorten – Fallbeispiele Ortsgruppenleiter', in Wolf Stegemann (ed.), *Dorsten nach der Stunde Null – Die Jahre danach, 1945 bis 1950* (Dorsten: Dorstener Forschungsgruppe, 1986), 138–45; Meyer, *Entnazifizierung von Frauen*, 241; Hüser, *'Unschuldig' in britischer Lagerhaft?*, 99. District Leaders were the lowest-ranking leaders who received a salary. Wegehaupt, 'Funktionäre und Funktionseliten', 50.

[87] Appendix A to The Arrest and Punishment of War Criminals, Nazis, Militarists and the Internment, Control and Surveillance of Potentially Dangerous Germans, Aug. 1946, TNA, FO 1005/639, DIAC/APSC/NADSC/P (46) Final.

camp were placed in lower categories in the first instance and even more on appeal, with many ending up mere Followers. She concludes, 'From a legal perspective their detention in internment was unjustified.'[88] In contrast, Meyer insists:

Neither the overwhelmingly low ranks of internees in 'criminal' Nazi organizations nor their ultimate categorizations allow one to make sweeping conclusions about the proportionality of internment in general. It should certainly not be deduced therefrom that it was an unjustified measure.

Rather, the almost uniformly low classifications by the *Spruchkammern* and appellate panels need to be seen as a contribution to the rehabilitation of the politically incriminated people, which contradicted the Liberation Law and undermined denazification.[89]

In other words, the panels' judgements are neither a sufficient nor an objective basis for assessing internees' past records or the appropriateness of their internment.[90]

If denazification verdicts are an unreliable and contested guide, historians should consider other parameters for assessing internees' seniority and responsibility. One might consider the assessments of the IMT. It included all ranks, even rank-and-file members, in its conviction of the SS (exempting only the various subgroups mentioned in Chapter 2), and thus also the junior officers whose relative insignificance Niethammer, Horn, and others stress. When it came to the NSDAP Leadership Corps, the IMT indictment included all Political Leaders, while its verdict exempted Block and Cell Leaders from the declaration of the corps' criminality but included Local Group Leaders.[91] One might also consider the view of the NSDAP's own organizational leadership, which described the Local Groups as the party's 'most important territorial unit' (*Hoheitsgebiet*). Moreover, its 1943 organizational handbook described all office holders (*Hoheitsträger*), including Cell and Block Leaders, in the following terms:

Office holders are entrusted with the political sovereignty of their administrative area. They represent the Party both internally and externally and are responsible

---

[88] Horn, *Internierungs- und Arbeitslager*, 92, 156. See also Wember, *Umerziehung im Lager*, 39.

[89] Meyer, *Entnazifizierung von Frauen*, 242. Cf. Niethammer, *Mitläuferfabrik*, 255–9, 579–80.

[90] In particular, Horn's approach overlooks the fact that *Spruchkammern* often made lower classifications not because they genuinely believed that people belonged in lower categories, but because they felt the punishments mandated for the higher categories were too severe. Henke, *Politische Säuberung*, 181–2.

[91] 'Indictment', 6 Oct. 1945, and 'Judgment', 1 Oct. 1946, both in *Trial of the Major War Criminals*, 80–1, 261–2, 273. Cf. Priemel, *Betrayal*, 101.

for the complete political situation within their area. Incumbents exercise control over the duties of those Party offices under their control and are responsible for the maintenance of discipline within their area.[92]

For its part, the NKVD regarded Local Group Leaders as significant, calling them 'regional leaders'.[93]

Above all, historians should surely consider recent scholarly research on the roles performed during the Nazi period by various targets of internment. It indicates that the NSDAP's Local Group Leaders provided the 'foundations' of the dictatorship (whereas the Gau Leaders were its 'cornerstones').[94] According to Detlef Schmiechen-Ackermann, even the lowliest Block Leaders performed a 'constitutive', if not a 'prominent and spectacular' role, as the 'smallest wheels in an extensive machinery of terror'. Together with their assistants in the party and its affiliated organizations, these uniformed, if unsalaried, functionaries were responsible for the surveillance of all residents under their purview (approximately 40–60 households), on whom they maintained a card catalogue, and especially of Jews, slave labourers, and anyone critical of, or reserved towards, the regime.[95] In contrast to the tendencies to minimize the responsibility of many functionaries, Jörg Echternkamp's notion of the NSDAP's 'middle level' (*Mittelbau*) nicely captures the importance of seemingly subordinate personnel. In the German university context, the term refers to non-professorial teaching staff, that is, people who are not in the limelight and enjoy little influence or prominence, but who do much of the work and are essential to an organization's operation.[96]

Varying Levels of Incrimination

Having outlined the key interpretative and terminological issues, it is now time to explore the levels of Nazi incrimination among internees in the four zones. An important – but sometimes exaggerated – difference between the western and the Soviet zones derived from their varying

[92] Wegehaupt, 'Funktionäre und Funktionseliten', 39; 'Organisationsbuch der NSDAP', 1943, in L. Milner (ed.), *Political Leaders of the NSDAP* (London: Almark, 1972), 62.
[93] Klepov to Serov, 21 Dec. 1945, in Possekel (ed.), *Sowjetische Dokumente*, 220.
[94] Reibel, *Fundament der Diktatur*; Wegehaupt, 'Funktionäre und Funktionseliten', 59.
[95] Schmiechen-Ackermann, 'Der "Blockwart"', 591–6, 602 (quotations). Cf. Frank Bajohr, 'The "Folk Community" and the Persecution of the Jews: German Society under National Socialist Dictatorship, 1933–1945', *Holocaust and Genocide Studies* 20, no. 2 (2006), 189.
[96] Jörg Echternkamp, *Die Bundesrepublik Deutschland 1945/1949–1969* (Paderborn: Ferdinand Schöningh, 2013), 66.

policies towards the Nazi paramilitary organizations, especially the SS and the SA. As mentioned in Chapter 1, according to Soviet policy in early 1945 their members were not to be interned in Germany but to be treated as POWs and deported to the USSR. Numerous authors claim on this basis that SS members were totally or virtually absent from the Soviet camps, whereas they constituted the 'hard core' of internees in the western zones.[97] This exaggerates both the lack of SS and other paramilitary members in the Soviet camps and their numerical dominance in the west, and thus exonerates Soviet-zone internees at the expense of their western counterparts. It is often overlooked that an instruction by the NKVD's Department for Special Camps from October 1945 allowed the internment of members of the paramilitary organizations, and the rule had been breached in practice even earlier.[98] In August 1946 there were at least 4,662 rank-and-file members and NCOs of the paramilitary organizations in the Special Camps and in July 1947 at least 2,457 paramilitaries (5% of internees at that point), including 509 SS members (1%). According to research on a sample of inmates in Sachsenhausen at the end of 1949, 2% were registered as SS members.[99] Their actual number was likely higher, because some were not listed as such precisely because they did not 'belong' there according to Order No. 00315. Of the internees transferred to East German authorities in early 1950 and tried at Waldheim, 7% were SS members.[100] Thus, even if they

---

[97] Niethammer, 'Alliierte Internierungslager (1998)', 103; Vollnhals, 'Internierung, Entnazifizierung und Strafverfolgung', 223, 228; Greiner, *Suppressed Terror*, 15, 43, 350; Gieseke, *Die Stasi*, 30–1; Boldorf, 'Brüche oder Kontinuitäten?', 292. Cf. Andrew H. Beattie, 'Verdiente Strafe des harten Kerns oder ungerechte Besatzungsmaßnahme? Die SS und die alliierte Internierung im besetzten Deutschland', in Jan Erik Schulte and Michael Wildt (eds.), *Die SS nach 1945: Entschuldungsnarrative, populäre Mythen, europäische Erinnerungsdiskurse* (Göttingen: Vandenhoeck & Ruprecht, 2018), 61–3.

[98] 'Anordnung des Leiters der Abt. Speziallager zur Aufnahme von Offizieren paramilitärischer Verbände und Einrichtungen in die Speziallager', 24 Oct. 1945, in Possekel (ed.), *Sowjetische Dokumente*, 213; Lutz Prieß, 'Deutsche Kriegsgefangene als Häftlinge in den Speziallagern des NKVD in der SBZ', in von Plato (ed.), *Studien und Berichte*, 253–4; Kirsten, *Das sowjetische Speziallager Nr. 4*, 28, 57–8.

[99] 'Telegramm des MVD-Bevollmächtigten in Deutschland Serov an Innenminister Kruglov zur Entlassung von Militärangehörigen aus den Speziallagern', 11 Aug. 1946, and 'Angaben über das Spezkontingent und die Verurteilten, die sich in MVD-Speziallagern auf dem Territorium Deutschlands befinden', as of 1 Jul. 1947, both in Possekel (ed.), *Sowjetische Dokumente*, 237, 292–4; Heinz Kersebom and Lutz Niethammer, '"Kompromat" 1949: Eine statistische Annäherung an Internierte, SMT-Verurteilte, antisowjetische Kämpfer und die Sowjetischen Militärtribunale', in von Plato (ed.), *Studien und Berichte*, 523. Almost 20% of SMT convicts in Bautzen in late 1949 were former military and paramilitary personnel. Haritonow, 'Geschichte des Speziallagers in Bautzen', 352.

[100] Jeske, 'Kritische Bemerkungen', 474–5; author's calculation based on figures in Otto, 'Waldheimer Prozesse', 547, 549.

comprised a tiny proportion (and certainly much less than the 44% the Soviets claimed in figures supplied to the ACA in February 1947), more SS and other paramilitary organization members were interned in the Soviet zone than is often recognized.[101]

More problematically, numerous authors conclude from the purported absence of SS members that the culpability of internees was 'significantly lower' in the Soviet zone than in the western zones.[102] While this is not implausible, it cannot be deduced merely from the relative lack of SS members in the Soviet camps, which indicates nothing about the culpability of the actual internees. Indeed, some authors over-extend the argument about the paramilitaries, asserting that 'members of the Nazi terror organizations' were not interned in the Soviet zone.[103] This over-looks the internment not only of some SA and SS members but also of larger numbers of other compromised personnel. After the releases in summer 1948 and the arrival of internees from other camps, there were 785 concentration-camp and prison personnel in Buchenwald, comprising almost 8% of its inmates at that point. A further 17% had belonged to the Gestapo, SD, or the Abwehr, the Wehrmacht's intelligence and counterintelligence unit that was largely integrated into the RSHA in 1944; almost 20% more were members of the police and gendarmerie. Moreover, a not insignificant number of Soviet-zone internees held at this point were suspected of mistreating Soviet citizens either in Germany or on Soviet territory during the war.[104] In total, according to Müller, 12% of Soviet-zone internees belonged to the Nazi security and repressive apparatus of Gestapo, SD, police, and judiciary.[105]

In contrast, many accounts exaggerate the western powers' concentration on the 'terrorist core troops' of the Third Reich.[106] As already indicated, the proportion of SS members among western-zone internees

---

[101] In the report, the Soviets claimed that 26,351 of the 59,965 people interned on 1 Jan. 1947 belonged to the SS, a figure that bears no relation whatsoever to the NKVD/MVD's own internal documents. It is noteworthy that in each category (SS, Gestapo, SD, SA, and NSDAP Leadership Corps), except the General Staff Officer Corps, the Soviet figures were slightly higher than the American figures. 'Report to the Council of Foreign Ministers from the Allied Control Authority in Germany', 24 Feb. 1947, Section II, Part 3, d, TNA, FO 1030/7.

[102] Gieseke, Die Stasi, 31. See also Niethammer, 'Alliierte Internierungslager (1998)', 103; Possekel, 'Sowjetische Lagerpolitik', 45–6; Greiner, Suppressed Terror, 43.

[103] Greiner, Suppressed Terror, 43. Cf. Vollnhals, 'Internierung, Entnazifizierung, Strafverfolgung', 228; Possekel, 'Sowjetische Lagerpolitik', 65.

[104] Neumann, 'Häftlingsstruktur im Speziallager Buchenwald', 483–4, 488; Mironenko et al. 'Vorwort der Herausgeber', 14; Kersebom and Niethammer, '"Kompromat" 1949', 525.

[105] Müller, 'Verbrechensahndung und Besatzungspolitik', 39.

[106] Niethammer, 'Alliierte Internierungslager (1995)', 478.

Table 3.2 *Organizational membership of internees at the Darmstadt camp*

	April 1946	April 1947	March 1948
NSDAP Political Leaders	3,834	4,210	955
Waffen-SS	2,573	3,621	783
Regular SS	2,512	2,595	912
SA	265	295	23
Gestapo	451	352	179
SD	208	134	64
Others	19	133	7
Total	9,860	11,340	2,923

Note: Figures in the second and fourth columns are from Heinl, 'Das schlimme Lager', 32–3; those in the third are from a report by Eugen Kogon, reprinted in Vollnhals (ed.), *Entnazifizierung: Politische Säuberung*, 241.

is often overstated. According to one oft-cited statistic that goes back to the Control Authority's report, SS members comprised 52% of US-zone internees in February 1947.[107] Yet at other times their proportion was considerably lower. In July 1945 members of all paramilitary organizations comprised 29%, while NSDAP personnel accounted for 45%, which is largely attributable to many Waffen-SS members still being held as POWs. In April 1948 SS members comprised 33% of American-zone internees.[108] These figures are amalgams of the Waffen-SS and the regular SS (Allgemeine SS). If they are broken down into separate categories, the NSDAP's Political Leaders often emerge as the single largest group, as demonstrated by the figures from the so-called SS camp at Darmstadt shown in Table 3.2. The proportion of SS members was lower still in the French zone. In the Balingen camp in Württemberg-Hohenzollern, only one-quarter of internees belonged to paramilitary organizations. According to the ACA's figures, 18% were SS members on 1 January 1947. In Saarbrücken in June 1947, 58% of internees were party members or functionaries, and only 15% were SS members. In Trier in early 1948, 36% were held as Political Leaders and 25% as SS members, although others held as concentration-camp guards or members of 'blocked units' may have been SS members. In the three camps in Baden in February 1948, regular SS and Waffen-SS together

---

[107] Vollnhals (ed.), *Entnazifizierung: Politische Säuberung*, 251. Cf. Niethammer, 'Alliierte Internierungslager (1998)', 103.
[108] Horn, *Internierungs- und Arbeitslager*, 46; Niethammer, *Mitläuferfabrik*, 256; author's calculation based on Meyer, *Entnazifizierung von Frauen*, 208.

comprised 41% and Political Leaders 32%.[109] In the British zone, SS members accounted for slightly less than one-quarter of the ca. 45,000 internees in April/May 1946, and 33% of those interned at the beginning of 1947. However, by late 1947, they were a clear majority, comprising 58% of defendants before the *Spruchgerichte*, in comparison with 31% Political Leaders and 11% Gestapo and SD personnel.[110]

Meanwhile, SA membership was a relatively negligible basis for internment in the western zones, even before the IMT's acquittal of the organization, as Table 3.2 also demonstrates. In camps under Bavarian administration in January 1947 less than 4% of the ca. 19,000 internees were held as SA members. They constituted a higher proportion in the French zone: 13% of internees across the zone on 1 January 1947, 16% in Saarbrücken in June 1947, almost 10% of a large sample of internees in Theley in late 1947, and 7% in Trier in December 1948.[111]

The purportedly high seniority of western-zone internees is often contrasted with the supposedly subordinate status of Soviet-zone internees. There is considerable truth to such a distinction, but the differences should not be overstated. In all zones, many more internees held ranks and positions at the lower end of the spectrum than at the higher end. This seems surprising and unjust to some commentators, who stress the lowly rank of the bulk of internees and the lack of 'prominent' Nazis among them, even in the western zones. For example, Siedenhans stresses that Otto Georg Thierack, former president (1936–42) of the Nazis' infamous People's Court of Justice (*Volksgerichtshof*) and Reich Minister of Justice (1942–5), was an exceptionally prominent internee in the British camp at Eselheide. Yet as Wember and Meyer point out, the fact that the mass of internees held more subordinate positions primarily reflected the pyramidic structure of the targeted organizations.[112] In the

---

[109] Henke, *Politische Säuberung*, 41; 'Report to the Council of Foreign Ministers from the Allied Control Authority in Germany', 24 Feb. 1947, Section II, Part 3, d, TNA, FO 1030/7; Möhler, *Entnazifizierung in Rheinland-Pfalz und im Saarland*, 373; Möhler, 'Internierungslager in der französischen Besatzungszone', 57; Grohnert, *Entnazifizierung in Baden*, 169.

[110] D. Freeman to F. R. Bears, Whitehall, 15 May 1946, TNA, FO 938/57; 'Report to the Council of Foreign Ministers from the Allied Control Authority in Germany', 24 Feb. 1947, Section II, Part 3, d, TNA, FO 1030/7; Wember, *Umziehung im Lager*, 318.

[111] Niethammer, *Mitläuferfabrik*, 456; 'Report to the Council of Foreign Ministers from the Allied Control Authority in Germany', 24 Feb. 1947, Section II, Part 3, d, TNA, FO 1030/7; Möhler, *Entnazifizierung in Rheinland-Pfalz und im Saarland*, 373, 380. Cf. Grohnert, *Entnazifizierung in Baden*, 163.

[112] Siedenhans, 'Internierungslager "Eselheide"', 143; Wember, *Umziehung im Lager*, 118–19; Meyer, *Entnazifizierung von Frauen*, 250. See also Weitkamp, 'Internierungslager Esterwegen', 250.

NSDAP, for instance, at no time were there more than forty-three Gau Leaders, and only somewhat more than one hundred people ever performed this role. Some did not survive the war and others fled successfully. Some who were captured committed suicide, while the rest were generally separated quickly from 'ordinary' internees in order to be prosecuted or to serve as witnesses at war-crimes trials. It is therefore unrealistic to expect there to have been many of them in any particular internment camp. One former Gau Leader was interned in the entire French zone in October 1946 and one in the Soviet zone in July 1947, while the British camp Eselheide was exceptional for holding three, as was the American camp at Darmstadt for holding two in April 1946.[113] Similarly, it was inevitable that Local Group Leaders would outnumber District Leaders, there having been 28,606 and 831 of each in 1940. Moreover, the Gau, District, and Local Group Leaders were vastly outnumbered by less prominent party officials: in 1940 there were 13,266 Gau officials, 67,972 district officials, and 174,171 Local Group Department Leaders, all of whom were subject to automatic arrest under SHAEF's April 1945 directive.[114]

So how did the interned party personnel compare relative to this hierarchical historical distribution? If Gau and district functionaries comprised less than 5% and 24%, respectively, of the 284,846 party functionaries down to and including Local Group Leaders and Local Group Department Leaders in 1940, they were under-represented by about half among the interned functionaries in Garmisch-Partenkirchen in the US zone in October 1945 (Reich 1.4%, Gau 2%, district 10%). Yet their proportion increased over time as lower ranks were released. In Moosburg in autumn 1946, Reich, Gau, district, and local functionaries

---

[113] Möhler, 'Internierung im Rahmen der Entnazifizierungspolitik', 64; 'Angaben über das Spezkontingent und die Verurteilten, die sich in MVD-Speziallagern auf dem Territorium Deutschlands befinden', as of 1 Jul. 1947, in Possekel (ed.), *Sowjetische Dokumente*, 293; Wember, *Umerziehung im Lager*, 78; Heinl, '"Das schlimme Lager"', 33. Cf. Mike Schmeitzner, 'Konsequente Abrechnung? NS-Eliten im Visier sowjetischer Gerichte 1945–1947', in Weigelt et al. (eds.), *Todesurteile sowjetischer Militärtribunale*, 82. On the Gau Leaders, see Michael D. Miller and Andreas Schulz, *Gauleiter: The Regional Leaders of the Nazi Party and Their Deputies, 1925–1945* (San Jose, CA: R. James Bender, 2012); Walter Ziegler, 'Gaue und Gauleiter im Dritten Reich', in Horst Möller, Andreas Wirsching, and Walter Ziegler (eds.), *Nationalsozialismus in der Region: Beiträge zur regionalen und lokalen Forschung und zum internationalen Vergleich* (Munich: R. Oldenbourg, 1996), 139–58.

[114] Numbers of NSDAP functionaries cited here and below are from Armin Nolzen, 'The NSDAP, the War, and German Society', in Ralf Blank, Jörg Echternkamp, and Karola Fings et al. (eds.), *Germany and the Second World War*, vol. IX: *German Wartime Society 1939–1945: Politicization, Disintegration, and the Struggle for Survival* (Oxford: Oxford University Press, 2008), 118, 121.

accounted for 3.5%, 5.2%, 23%, and 67% of interned Party personnel, respectively, such that the proportions roughly reflected the 1940 organizational distribution.[115] Directly comparable figures for the British zone are not readily available, but a similar picture nevertheless emerges. Of party functionaries convicted by *Spruchgerichte*, 0.13% were Reich Leaders, Reich Main Department Leaders, or Gau Leaders; 6% were Reich Department Leaders, Deputy Gau Leaders, Gau Main Department Leaders, or District Leaders; and 94% were Gau Department Leaders, District Main Department Leaders, District Department Leaders, or Local Group Leaders.[116] Here, as elsewhere, the fact that most internees held less prominent middling or lower ranks or were more anonymous officials does not mean that more prominent or higher-ranked Nazis were not also detained. For instance, several of Hamburg's top Nazis were interned, including Gau Leader and Reich Governor Karl Kaufmann; Governing Mayor Carl Krogmann; State Secretary, SD Leader, and SS Group Leader Georg Ahrens; and Gau Press Department Leader Hermann Okraß. On the other hand, for all the elites at the various levels who were interned, many others of similar rank were not. Of fifty-three party and municipal elites (including police and civil servants) in the district and city of Dachau, thirty spent a lengthy time in internment (57%), meaning that over 40% did not. Lieutenant-General Robertson's estimation, in his July 1946 report cited in Chapter 2, 'that approximately 90% of those persons domiciled in the British zone and who qualify for arrest' had already been apprehended was probably somewhat optimistic, although most former NSDAP District Leaders from the Weser-Ems Gau in what became the British zone were interned for at least two years, and of Berlin city councillors and NSDAP District Leaders who survived the war and whose postwar fate is more or less known 75% were interned by one or other of the occupying powers.[117]

---

[115] Niethammer, *Mitläuferfabrik*, 257, 456. On the internment of District Leaders, see Barbara Fait, 'Die Kreisleiter der NSDAP – nach 1945', in Broszat et al. (eds.), *Von Stalingrad zur Währungsunion*, 225–8.

[116] Based on figures in Wember, *Umerziehung im Lager*, 319.

[117] Werner Skrentny, 'Was aus Hamburgs Nazis wurde', in Maike Bruhns et al. (eds.), *'Hier war doch alles nicht so schlimm': Wie die Nazis in Hamburg den Alltag eroberten* (Hamburg: VSA-Verlag, 1984), 139–42; Hoser, 'Entnazifizierung in der Stadt Dachau', 227; Report on Persons Held in Internment Camps, sent by Robertson to Sir Arthur Street, Control Office for Germany and Austria, London, 2 Jul. 1946, 1, TNA, FO 938/ 345; Rademacher, *Kreisleiter der NSDAP*, 322–34; author's calculation based on Anja Stanciu, *'Alte Kämpfer' der NSDAP: Eine Berliner Funktionselite 1926–1949* (Cologne: Böhlau, 2018), 447.

Turning to the French zone, Henke is right to argue that, even if the 'social profile' of internees was similar to that of the American zone, 'political prominence' was 'even more thinly' represented. At Balingen the former Minister President and Minister for Culture of Württemberg, SA-Obergruppenführer (equivalent to General) Christian Mergenthaler, was 'by far' the most prominent internee and the last to be released.[118] Across the zone, Reich personnel were virtually non-existent and there were relatively few Gau and district functionaries. In October 1946, the proportions of Gau, district, and local functionaries among party leaders from local level upward were 0.05%, 3.2%, and 96.7%, respectively, meaning that the first two groups were significantly under-represented and the local functionaries over-represented. Yet these figures were deceptively good, because they included only those who were covered by the IMT conviction. A considerable number of even lower-ranked NSDAP personnel were also interned. At the end of June 1947, camps in the French zone (excluding the Saarland) still held 816 ordinary NSDAP members and 1,022 who had held the lowest positions up to and including Cell Leader, as well as 703 SA members up to and including Hauptsturmführer (equivalent to captain) and 274 low-ranked members or leaders of other affiliated groups, including the youth organizations. None of these people, who comprised one-third of French-zone internees at that point, fell under the IMT conviction; they were prioritized for release in the following months, as were Local Group Leaders who had held the position only temporarily. In the Saarland, the situation was similar. In Saarbrücken in June 1947, functionaries at Gau, district, and local levels comprised 0.52%, 15%, and 62%, respectively, of interned party personnel, while 19% were ordinary members or Block or Cell Leaders (21, 23, and 28 people, respectively) – a clear divergence from the other western zones. As in the other western zones, however, the 172 Local Group Leaders were the largest single group among all internees (26%). By early 1948, the ordinary members and lowest ranks had been released. Now, of 197 Political Leaders interned in Trier, the District Leaders constituted 6% and officials at Gau and district levels constituted 18%. The 150 Local Group Leaders comprised 76% of interned NSDAP functionaries and were the largest group among all internees at 27% of the total.[119]

---

[118] Henke, *Politische Säuberung*, 41.

[119] Möhler, *Entnazifizierung in Rheinland-Pfalz und im Saarland*, 363, 373, 386; Möhler, 'Internierung im Rahmen der Entnazifizierungspolitik', 64; Grohnert, *Entnazifizierung in Baden*, 163, 167. Percentages calculated by the author.

The accuracy of an assessment by the head of French security forces in Württemberg-Baden in September 1947 that 'the majority of the internees were more or less followers with petty functions' thus depends on one's definition of 'follower' and 'petty'. His view was hardly representative of French military government as a whole, which tried in vain to insist that Local Group Leaders be classified as Offenders. Moreover, the responsibility of the minority that ranked above the local level should not be downplayed, even if many of them were relatively anonymous officials rather than more prominent leaders. In Balingen in early 1948, many local functionaries were joined by fourteen Gau functionaries, twenty-three District Leaders, numerous district officials, as well as one minister president, one minister of state, and one president of a provincial government (*Regierungspräsident*). On the other hand, in February 1948 the French foreign ministry acknowledged that French camps still held some harmless people the Americans had arrested in the first days of the occupation.[120]

A clear pyramidic structure existed in the Soviet zone, too, but here the distribution was even more bottom-heavy than elsewhere. In July 1947, as already mentioned, the Special Camps held just one former Gau Leader. In contrast, NKVD Order No. 0016's instruction to arrest party members and Order No. 00315's instruction to arrest 'active' party members led to the incarceration of more than 30,000 ordinary members and Block and Cell Leaders. The few representatives of these groups who were interned in the American and British zones were released reasonably quickly. In the US zone, there were eighty-seven Block Leaders and forty Cell Leaders (together comprising 6% of interned party functionaries) in Garmisch-Partenkirchen in October 1945, but none in Moosburg a year later.[121] As already mentioned, among the western zones the French camps were exceptional for still holding considerable numbers of these groups in June 1947. Yet even the French numbers are dwarfed by their Soviet equivalents. In July 1945, 3,417 Block and Cell Leaders comprised 56% of the internees transferred from Weesow to Landsberg/Warta, and in January 1946, 3,034 were among the internees transferred from there to Buchenwald (54%). Across all Special Camps in October 1946 there were 2,804 ordinary party members, 20,454 Block Leaders, and 7,971 Cell Leaders; by July 1947 their numbers fell (largely due to death) to 967, 12,510, and 5,371, respectively. The combined proportion of these groups decreased from 81% to 75% of interned NSDAP

---

[120] Henke, *Politische Säuberung*, 41, 181–2; Steinhart, *Balingen*, 259; Möhler, *Entnazifizierung in Rheinland-Pfalz und im Saarland*, 368.
[121] Niethammer, *Mitläuferfabrik*, 257, 456.

Table 3.3 *Distribution of NSDAP functionaries in the French and Soviet zones*

	NSDAP functionaries, Jan. 1940	Interned functionaries in Saarbrücken, French zone, June 1947	Interned functionaries in the Soviet zone, July 1947
Gau functionaries	1.1	0.58	0.004
District functionaries	5.6	16.2	1.6
Local functionaries	45.4	68.2	13.8
Cell Leaders	8.5	8.1	22.2
Block Leaders	39.4	6.6	51.7
Uncertain level			10.7
Total	100	99.68	100.004

Note: In order to draw the comparison with the actual party distribution, the French and Soviet figures exclude interned party members without any rank or function. The local functionaries in columns two and three include Local Group Leaders and Local Group Department Leaders, whereas in column four only Local Group Leaders; and that the functionaries of uncertain level include 5.6% department leaders and 5.1% treasurers and propaganda leaders, likely at local or district levels. Data are from Nolzen, 'The NSDAP, the War, and German Society', 121; Möhler, *Entnazifizierung in Rheinland-Pfalz und im Saarland* 373; 'Angaben über das Spezkontingent und die Verurteilten, die sich in MVD-Speziallagern auf dem Territorium Deutschlands befinden', as of 1 Jul. 1947, in Possekel (ed.), *Sowjetische Dokumente*, 293.

personnel and from 46% to 38% of all internees at each point. They were well represented among the internees released in 1948, their proportion falling from 47% of internees in Buchenwald in March 1948 to under 4% in September, by which time they were finally, if only barely, outnumbered by the Local Group Leaders, who comprised ca. 6% of all internees.[122] Thus, as indicated by Table 3.3, the lowest-ranked functionaries were over-represented in the Soviet camps, while Gau and district functionaries and even Local Group Leaders were significantly under-represented, in comparison both to their actual numbers

[122] Kirsten, *Das sowjetische Speziallager Nr. 4*, 57; 'Information des Leiters der Abt. Speziallager "Über das vorhandene Spezkontingent in den MVD-Speziallagern auf dem Territorium Deutschlands"', 30 Oct. 1946, and 'Angaben über das Spezkontingent und die Verurteilten, die sich in MVD-Speziallagern auf dem Territorium Deutschlands befinden', as of 1 Jul. 1947, both in Possekel (ed.), *Sowjetische Dokumente*, 248, 293; Ritscher et al. (eds.), *Das sowjetische Speziallager Nr. 2*, 73.

and to the French zone, let alone the other western zones. More than the near absence of SS members, this lower level of seniority suggests a significantly lesser degree of Nazi incrimination among Soviet-zone internees than their western counterparts, but by no means its complete absence.

The relative lack of senior Nazi personnel in French and Soviet camps, if not the presence of the lowest ranks, had multiple causes that went beyond differences in internment policy. On the one hand, it reflected the movement of military fronts during the final stages of the war, as more incriminated personnel fled from the eastern and western peripheries of the Reich that the Allies occupied first, into areas in the Reich's interior that were still under German control. Senior Nazis – like German soldiers and civilians in general – were especially desperate to avoid falling into Soviet hands and fled westward in significant numbers. Meanwhile, on the western front there was considerable eastward movement. As a result, the Americans interned numerous people who lived in, but fled from, what became the French zone. In late 1947 when the western powers exchanged internees who were resident in other zones, the Americans transferred many more to the French (and British) than they received in return. The French handed just 110 internees to the Americans but received 1,741, including five District Leaders, forty-five Gau and district officials, and 143 Local Group Leaders, as well as Gestapo, SD, SA, SS, and Waffen-SS personnel. Their absence to this point had contributed to the relatively low level of incrimination of internees in French camps. On the other hand, there was a higher suicide rate in areas occupied by the Soviets, not least of more incriminated people.[123]

The flight of compromised Germans was a relatively small component of the massive population movements in the final stages of the war and the early postwar period. Such mobility had considerable consequences for internment. For instance, German military and paramilitary forces were deployed far from home, and their members were thus often taken into captivity by an occupying power other than that which eventually ran their 'home' zone. This was the main reason that ca. 8,000 British-zone residents ended up in American internment, as the Americans captured them as POWs and then transferred them to civilian-internee status.

---

[123] Kershaw, *The End*, 177, 355–8; Möhler, 'Internierungslager in der französischen Besatzungszone', 51; Henke, *Politische Säuberung*, 40; Thacker, *End of the Third Reich*, 158; Christian Goeschel, 'Suicide at the End of the Third Reich', *Journal of Contemporary History* 41, no. 1 (2006), 153–73; Keller, *Volksgemeinschaft am Ende*, 203–9; Florian Huber, *Kind, versprich mir, dass du dich erschießt: Der Untergang der kleinen Leute 1945* (Berlin: Berlin Verlag, 2015), esp. 121–3.

'Mobility' of another sort meant that thousands of Germans who were arrested east of the Oder–Neisse line were taken to Special Camps in the Soviet zone. Significant numbers of internees were thus not residents of the zone where they were interned, especially in the US zone. In Darmstadt in July 1946, only 54% of the ca. 18,000 internees were residents of the American zone.[124] The proportion of US-zone residents among all US-zone internees over time was probably higher than this snapshot suggests, as locals were more likely to have been released than non-zonal residents.

Details like these complicate attempts to calculate different rates of internment in the various zones. Niethammer claims that one in every 142 residents of the US zone was interned, closely followed by the Soviet zone with one in every 144 residents, and with the French and British zones well behind with one in every 263 and 284 residents, respectively.[125] In fact, based on the more likely total zonal internee figures already estimated, the number of internees in each zone relative to its total population was more probably closer to the following: one in 101 in the US zone, one in 133 in the Soviet zone, one in between 223 and 246 in the British zone, and one in 274 in the French. Yet simply dividing the zonal populations by the number of internees is problematic, because such calculations assume that the broader populations or the internees were immobile, when the opposite was the case. Indeed, if only 54% of US-zone internees were locals as was the case in Darmstadt in July 1946 (a problematic assumption as noted above), (only) one in every 187 US-zone residents was interned.[126] The figures for the other zones would also have to be adjusted. Such statistics are thus highly problematic. Nevertheless, it is clear that one's chances of being interned were significantly higher in the American and Soviet than in the British and French zones.

Before concluding this chapter, another glance at the situation in Austria is useful. It was similar in most respects, notwithstanding the different Soviet approach discussed in Chapter 2. In Austria, too, as already mentioned, many compromised people fled Vienna and the Soviet zone, while the Americans initially occupied Tyrol and made significant arrests – between 2,000 and 3,000 – before handing the

---

[124] Wember, *Umerziehung im Lager*, 242; Jan Lipinsky, 'Mobilität zwischen den Lagern', in von Plato (ed.), *Studien und Berichte*, 225, 236: Heinl: 'Das schlimme Lager', 34.

[125] Niethammer, 'Alliierte Internierungslager (1998)', 100.

[126] Author's calculations, based on likely zonal total internee figures cited earlier, and zonal population figures from Kleßmann, *Die doppelte Staatsgründung*, 67. Note, as did Niethammer, these figures include Berlin in the Soviet-zone population.

territory over to the French.[127] Both of these factors contributed to the relatively high American arrest and internee numbers and to the fact that in spring 1947, 39% of a large sample of Austrian internees in Camp Marcus W. Orr were not residents of the US zone. Meanwhile, about 7% of all sampled internees at this point were foreigners (including Germans), a lower proportion than it had been due to earlier repatriations. Women comprised 3%, a tiny number of whom were interned with infant children or were or became pregnant during their internment. Here, too, the largest age cohort of internees were those in their forties (34%), followed in descending order by those in their thirties, fifties, twenties, and those sixty or over (29%, 18%, 15%, and 4%, respectively). The middle classes were over-represented, especially doctors, lawyers, teachers, and artists (who together comprised 11%), members of the police and other security agencies (8%), and public servants (11%), but such professions were still outnumbered by those who named agriculture and forestry (12%), technical vocations (14%), and business and trade (40%) as their occupations. Here, too, local officials and leaders of the NSDAP and its various organs massively outnumbered nationally prominent figures. Numerous senior figures at regional level (deputy Gau Leaders, heads of Gau departments, former lord mayors of Linz) were interned in the camp, but Gau Leaders such as Scheel or August Eigruber were detained in prisons.[128]

In British-occupied Austria, the situation was similar. The largest British camp, 373 Camp Wolfsberg in Carinthia, held the Carinthian Gau Leader Friedrich Rainer for a brief period before he was transferred as a witness to the IMT and then extradited to Yugoslavia in 1947 where he was sentenced to death and executed. In October 1946, almost 3% of the 3,323 Wolfsberg internees were women, down from 4% a few months earlier. At this point, before significant repatriations, 24% were foreigners: 71% of them were German, 11% Yugoslavs, and the remainder a smattering of other nationalities or stateless people. In April 1947, 41% were in their forties, followed by those in their thirties (26%), in their fifties (22%), those aged up to thirty (8%), and those over sixty

---

[127] Stiefel, *Entnazifizierung in Österreich*, 33; Andreas Maislinger, '"Zurück zur Normalität": Zur Entnazifizierung in Tirol', in Meissl et al. (eds.), *Verdrängte Schuld*, 342; Wilfried Beimrohr, 'Entnazifizierung in Tirol', in Schuster and Weber (eds.), *Entnazifizierung im regionalen Vergleich*, 99–100.

[128] Dohle and Eigelsberger, *Camp Marcus W. Orr*, 97–105, 179, 44. The sample is based on the camp vocational card index encompassing 4,897 cards of internees largely from April and May 1947. The camp held more than 7,200 internees at the beginning of April and 5,758 at the end of May. Ibid., 97–8, 93.

(3%). A year earlier, male internees' self-professed occupations included the following: 7% unskilled workers; 8% each police, public servants, and active soldiers; 14% professionals (teachers, lawyers, doctors, architects, academics, apothecaries, dentists, veterinarians); 14% agricultural or forestry employees; and the remaining 42% in various branches of industry, trade, and business.[129]

In the French zone, the Americans made some prominent arrests early on including the immediate family and entourage of German Labour Front chief Robert Ley and Reich Minister for Foreign Affairs Joachim von Ribbentrop (both of whom were indicted by the IMT as major war criminals) and some high-ranking SS and Hitler Youth leaders. Almost 10% of internees in the French camp at Brederis in Voralberg in spring 1946 were women, likely an unrepresentatively high number, as more men were in other smaller camps for labour deployment. The figure sank to 1% by November, when Brederis was the last remaining camp in the state.[130]

In all zones in Germany (and Austria), some people were interned who should not have been, even according to Allied arrest policies, and every occupying power – even the Soviets – took some steps to release them or at least to assign them a more 'correct' status. As shown in Chapter 2, however, only the western powers began as early as 1945 to make concerted efforts to assess whether the detention of those who had been *correctly* interned should continue. As a result, most low-ranking people who were now considered harmless were released in the western zones in 1946 or 1947, whereas in the Soviet zone they generally remained detained – if they survived – until mid-1948. This procedural failing was doubly unjust because tens of thousands of the lowest-ranking Soviet-zone internees would likely never have been interned in the western zones in the first place. To be sure, one should not overlook the fact that some ordinary members and lowest-ranking functionaries of the NSDAP and its affiliate organizations were interned in the western zones and that ca. 3,000 were still held in French camps in mid-1947. This sizable number contradicts frequent suggestions that only high-ranking Nazis were ever interned in the western zones or remained so after mid-1946.[131] In the American and British zones, in contrast, the Local Group Leaders were the lowest-ranked NSDAP functionaries who were interned to any considerable extent from 1946 onward. There were thus discernible differences in the seniority of interned Nazi functionaries

---

[129] Kastner, '373 Camp Wolfsberg', 74, 68, 79–83. Percentages calculated by the author.
[130] Eisterer, *Französische Besatzungspolitik*, 186, 202, 216.
[131] See, for instance, Möhler, *Entnazifizierung in Rheinland-Pfalz und im Saarland*, 403.

among the western zones at some points and more sizable and enduring differences between the western zones, on the one hand, and the Soviet zone, on the other. A clear pyramidic structure existed everywhere, but it was more bottom-heavy in the French and especially the Soviet zones.

There were additional differences that combined to reduce the relative level of Nazi incrimination among Soviet-zone internees, even if such differences were not as great as is often suggested. The substantial, if often exaggerated, numbers of adolescents and young adults – whether they were accused of 'Werewolf' activity or of otherwise acting against the occupying power or were held on account of their involvement in Nazi youth organizations – had no sizable equivalent in the western zones. The significant, if often exaggerated number of members of postwar political parties interned in the Soviet zone also had no western counterpart (and neither did the even larger numbers prosecuted by SMTs). In contrast, SS members, who accounted for a sizable portion and at certain points more than half of the internees in the western and especially the American and British zones, were detained to a considerable extent not in the Special Camps but in Soviet POW camps.[132] This does not mean, however, that representatives of the Nazi terror apparatus were not among Soviet-zone internees (or SMT convicts). Nor should the crucial role of even the lowliest party and other functionaries – in supporting the Nazi dictatorship, exerting control over the rest of the population, and persecuting the regime's opponents, victims, and non-conformists – be overlooked. Indeed, one should avoid overshooting the mark as numerous historians do in trying to counter the idea (largely a straw man) that Soviet-zone internees were Nazis and war criminals. While perhaps legally innocent, most had held more or less influential political and professional positions in the 'Third Reich'. Even the role of the lowliest Nazi apparatchiks set them apart from other Germans who held no rank in, or were not even members of, the party or its affiliated organizations. Their level of responsibility was generally greater than merely being, 'as Germans', 'morally co-responsible' for the Nazi regime and the crimes it committed.[133] If the level of Nazi incrimination of internees in the various zones thus differed less starkly and was higher than is often suggested, Chapter 4 shows that, after an initial period of reasonably similar treatment, the conditions under which internees were detained varied dramatically.

---

[132] In 1949, Soviet authorities were still assessing the fate of more than 400,000 German POWs in their hands, including 13,000 members of the SS, 4,500 of the SA, and 1,700 of the Gestapo and SD. Schneppen, 'Das Nürnberger Urteil', 55–6.

[133] Greiner, *Suppressed Terror*, 7.

4 Internment Camps

'The Main Task of the Camp Is the Complete Isolation'
of the Detainees

Apart from the questions of who internees were and how quickly they were processed and released, the other key question is how they were treated during their detention. This chapter demonstrates the far worse situation of Soviet-zone internees, including in the opportunities they were afforded for reeducation, retraining, recreation, and religious activity. The fact that significantly fewer internees worked during their confinement in the Soviet zone also meant that they were more exposed to the soul-destroying monotony of life in detention than their western counterparts. Most importantly, they also fared much worse in the extent to which they were isolated from the outside world, properly fed, housed in adequate accommodation, and given appropriate medical care. All of this contributed to their mass death, which constitutes the most dramatic and shocking difference between the western and Soviet zones in the history of Allied internment. The Soviets' failure to keep their internees alive was inhumane and amounted to answering one injustice with another.

Despite such vital dissimilarities, western treatment should not be idealized, nor should second-order differences among the western zones, between individual camps in each zone, and across time be overlooked. For instance, although the NKVD brutalized and tortured countless arrestees before interning them, the evidence suggests that Allied personnel inflicted more direct physical violence in western than in Soviet camps. As Geoffrey P. R. Wallace argues in relation to the treatment of POWs in the twentieth century, 'democracies appear no more immune from the desire to abuse prisoners' than authoritarian regimes; indeed, with Germany's total defeat and the liberation of Allied prisoners in Axis hands, incentives to treat German captives well (or not to abuse them) – whether in the hope of reciprocity or for fear of reprisal – disappeared.[1]

---

[1] Wallace, *Life and Death*, 4, 115–20. Cf. S. P. MacKenzie, 'The Treatment of Prisoners of War in World War II', *Journal of Modern History* 66, no. 3 (1994), 489–503; Moore, 'Prisoners of War'.

It is thus hardly surprising that at least in 1945 and early 1946 internees' treatment in all zones was rough; rations, accommodation, and other conditions were inadequate; and internees were isolated to an extent that contradicted both international norms and idealized scholarly depictions. Yet over time, the western powers took steps to improve internees' treatment, if more for instrumental reasons and in response to diverse criticisms than due to innate normative commitments. Conditions also eventually improved in the Soviet camps, but from a lower starting point, never to the same extent, and only much later, indeed too late for tens of thousands of inmates who did not survive. Black and white depictions of generous western occupiers and brutal Soviets are thus more appropriate in relation to the Allies' treatment of their internees than to other aspects of internment, even if here, too, there were some shades of grey.

In addition to exploring internees' treatment, this chapter examines other questions about the camps. It shows that the number of camps – like the number of internees – was higher than often recognized. It indicates too that Allied reuse of Nazi-era facilities was more widespread than is frequently assumed, especially in the western zones, but that the attention often paid to the reuse of Nazi concentration camps is excessive, especially in relation to the Soviet zone. Facilities with other Nazi pasts – including former POW camps, prisons, military barracks, and forced-labour camps – were more commonly utilized than former concentration camps. Drawing conclusions about the character of Allied camps merely from their pre-1945 pedigrees is therefore unreliable. Finally, the chapter highlights the camps' functional complexity, identifying multiple connections with purposes other than civilian internment and groups of inmates other than civilian internees. Such connections varied from zone to zone and changed over time, as did responsibility for the camps' administration. As is increasingly recognized of camps in other contexts, internment camps in occupied Germany (and Austria) were dynamic institutions that defy simple characterization and generalization.[2]

The Number and Location of Internment Camps

The Allies needed extensive accommodation for the large numbers of arrestees (as well as for millions of POWs, DPs, refugees and expellees, bombed-out residents, and their own personnel), and they found a range of pragmatic solutions amid the turmoil of the initial occupation. Early on, detainees were held in local prisons or bunkers or under guard in

---

[2] See, for example, Nikolaus Wachsmann, *KL: A History of the Nazi Concentration Camps* (New York: Farrar, Straus and Giroux, 2015).

open spaces outside towns, in short, in any available accommodation, as was also the case with the internment of collaborators in liberated Belgium and the Netherlands, for example.[3] Many were thrown together with POWs. For instance, the French camp at Balingen initially held POWs and civilian internees before becoming the main civilian internment camp for the state of Württemberg-Hohenzollern, and the British held both POWs and internees at Westertimke.[4] Some civilians were held in the Americans' infamous 'Prisoner of War Temporary Enclosures', better known as 'Rhine meadow camps', but their numbers were small compared with the masses of POWs and they were relatively quickly separated from the latter.[5] In addition to such early joint accommodation, as mentioned previously, many members of groups like the Waffen-SS were initially treated as surrendered military personnel and only later – in late 1945, 1946, and even 1947 – became civilian internees. Indeed, the frequent emphasis on the apparently deviant Soviet treatment of SS members overlooks the fact that the western powers also at least initially treated many as POWs, and, as shown in Chapter 1, the Allies had agreed on their prerogative to be able to do so. All the Allies categorized detainees or altered their status in ways that contradicted the spirit and often the letter of the 1929 Geneva Convention, inter alia by converting those accorded POW status to civilian internees instead of maintaining their POW status until their final release.[6] For example, in June 1946 the American POW camp at Nuremberg-Langwasser was converted to a civilian internment camp and most of its inmates to civilian internees; similarly, in 1947 several hundred POWs remained in situ when the American POW Enclosure No. 10 at Heilbronn was transformed into a civilian internment camp.[7] The British also

---

[3] Horn, *Internierungs- und Arbeitslager*, 45, 146; Ilse Rathjen-Couscherung, *Eckernförde unter britischer Besatzung: Eine schleswig-holsteinische Stadt 1945–1955* (Eckernförde: Heimatgemeinschaft Eckernförde, 2008), 118, 124; Möhler, *Entnazifizierung in Rheinland-Pfalz und im Saarland*, 371; Kastner, '373 Camp Wolfsberg', 68. Cf. Grevers and Van Haecke, 'Administrative Internment', 289–91.

[4] Steinhart, *Balingen*, 255; Ehresmann, 'Die frühe Nachkriegsnutzung', 22.

[5] Wember, *Umerziehung im Lager*, 45; Strauß, *Kriegsgefangenschaft und Internierung*, 150–4. On the Rhine meadow camps, see Keith Lowe, *Savage Continent: Europe in the Aftermath of World War II* (London: Viking, 2012), 111–24; Rüdiger Overmans, '"Ein untergeordneter Eintrag im Leidensbuch der jüngeren Geschichte"? Die Rheinwiesenlager 1945', in Hans-Erich Volkmann (ed.), *Ende des Dritten Reiches – Ende des Zweiten Weltkrieges: Eine perspektivische Rückschau* (Munich: Piper, 1995), 259–91.

[6] Strauß, *Kriegsgefangenschaft und Internierung*, 425; Wiggers, 'The United States', 91–104; Smith, 'Die deutschen Kriegsgefangenen'; Resmini, 'Lager der Besatzungsmächte', 609; Schoebener, 'Dokumentation einer Kontroverse', 142–3.

[7] Schick, 'Internierungslager', 310; Horn, *Internierungs- und Arbeitslager*, 21–2; Strauß, *Kriegsgefangenschaft und Internierung*, 388. See also Klose, 'Internierungs- und Arbeitslager Regensburg', 14–15.

transferred significant numbers of military personnel to civilian status, including Wehrmacht officers interned at Adelheide (as discussed in Chapter 2), prompting objections from the ICRC.[8]

In 1945–6 the Allies quickly developed a complex system of camps and related facilities specifically for civilian internees. Its extent is often underestimated, as the related facilities are ignored and attention focuses on the main camps and often only the larger and longer-lasting ones. Each occupying power had a number of associated prisons and interrogation centres, which were not only used for internees. Particularly in the pre- and early post-surrender phases, such facilities moved frequently and were rather makeshift. The Americans had five main interrogation centres, including in their Bremen enclave on the North Sea and in the US sector of Berlin, while the French used prisons including one at Neustadt/Haardt.[9] The British initially had three 'Civil Interrogation Camps' and from August 1945 a 'Combined Services Detailed Interrogation Centre' at Bad Nenndorf near Hanover, which attracted notoriety and was the focus of a court-martial when reports of inmates' mistreatment emerged in 1947.[10] In the Soviet zone, the NKVD ran numerous 'Inner Prisons', popularly known as 'GPU cellars', referring to the many urban basements used by the NKVD, which was still widely associated with its predecessor, the Soviet State Political Directorate (GPU). Here, many arrestees spent weeks in horrendous conditions before being interned or tried by SMTs.[11] The related facilities also included the British 'Civilian Internment Settlement' at Adelheide discussed in Chapter 2 and dedicated internee hospitals established by the western powers.[12]

---

[8] See, for example, André Monod, ICRC Vlotho, to C. Pilloud, ICRC Geneva, Re: Transfert de PG dans des camps d'IC, 15 Dec. 1946, ACICR, B G 44 02-056.04.

[9] Meyer, *Entnazifizierung von Frauen*, 79–81; Camps d'internés civils, politiques et administratifs, 6 Oct. 1945, 8, ACICR, B G 44 02-058.01.

[10] Wember, *Umerziehung im Lager*, 54–5, 87, 96–101; Utz Anhalt and Steffen Holz, *Das verbotene Dorf: Das Verhörzentrum der britischen Besatzungsmacht in Bad Nenndorf 1945 bis 1947* (Hanover: Offizin, 2011).

[11] Peter Erler, *GPU-Keller: Arrestlokale und Untersuchungsgefängnisse sowjetischer Geheimdienste in Berlin 1945–1949: Eine Dokumentation* (Berlin: Bund der Stalinistisch Verfolgten, 2005); Greiner, *Suppressed Terror*, 115–37.

[12] Wember, *Umerziehung im Lager*, 44, 56–7, 62–3, 66; Meyer, *Entnazifizierung von Frauen*, 69; Borgstedt, *Entnazifizierung in Karlsruhe*, 69–80. A wider circle of related facilities would include the Ministerial Collecting Center established by the Americans in Kassel-Fürstenhagen, where German ministerial reords were collected and key ministerial personnel were held and interrogated, and from which some went on to influential positions in postwar German public life. See Lester K. Born, 'The Ministerial Collecting Center Near Kassel, Germany', *The American Archivist* 50, no. 3 (1950), 237–58; Daniel E. Rogers, 'Restoring a German Career, 1945–1950: The Ambiguity of Being Hans Globke', *German Studies Review* 31, no. 2 (2008), 306; Astrid M. Eckert, *The*

The number of actual camps is often underestimated but can also be overestimated by focusing on the total over time rather than at any particular moment. Confusion can arise too from particular facilities' changing functions and designations, the use of multiple names, or the reapplication of camp numbers. Significant underestimations are most common for the American zone: von Plato claims that there were eight camps in the US zone and Wolfgang Benz that there were eleven.[13] But Meyer finds there were thirty-seven, which includes some of only brief duration but not others that the Americans had established early on in regions that belonged to the British and French zones. Across the US zone (including Bremen and Berlin) twenty-six camps operated for at least six months, as indicated in Table 4.1. This figure encompasses both the Americans' own camps and those administered by German authorities under American supervision from late 1946, without double-counting those among the former that converted into the latter. The former were called 'Civilian Internment Enclosures' (CIEs) and, except in Bavaria, were numbered according to the US Army that established them (thus CIE No. 74 for the Seventh Army's fourth camp and CIE No. 95 for the Ninth Army's fifth camp). The German-run camps (on which more shortly) were generally called 'Internment and Labour Camps'.[14] The British termed their regular camps 'Civilian Internment Camps' and numbered them one to nine. Ten sites were used in total, all but one for at least six months.[15] Although some authors refer to a smaller number, the French used twelve main *camps d'internement* (sometimes called *camps de concentration*), a figure that excludes some smaller camps in existence for only a brief period, such as one in Koblenz-Metternich.[16] As in the American case, the number of Soviet camps

Struggle for the Files: The Western Allies and the Return of German Archives after the Second World War (Cambridge: Cambridge University Press, 2012), 53–4; Irina Stange, 'Das Bundesministerium des Innern und seine leitenden Beamten', in Frank Bösch and Andreas Wirsching (eds), *Hüter der Ordnung: Die Innenministerien in Bonn und Ost-Berlin nach dem Nationalsozialismus* (Göttingen: Wallstein, 2018), 64, 66.

[13] Von Plato, 'Sowjetische Speziallager', 95; Benz, *Zwischen Hitler und Adenauer*, 119.

[14] Meyer, *Entnazifizierung von Frauen*, 69. Calculations based on ibid., 265–71. Meyer does not include Recklinghausen or Paderborn-Staumühle, which the Americans used briefly before turning them over to the British, or Trier, which was handed to the French. See Hüser, '*Unschuldig' in britischer Lagerhaft?*, 30–2; Emil Zenz, *Die Stadt Trier im 20. Jahrhundert: 1. Hälfte 1900–1950* (Trier: Spee-Verlag, 1981), 420.

[15] Wember, *Umerziehung im Lager*, 55–82, 369–72.

[16] Möhler, 'Internierung im Rahmen der Entnazifizierungspolitik', 62; Camps d'internés civils, politiques et administratifs, 6 Oct. 1945, ACICR, B G 44 02-058.01; Peter Fäßler, 'Lahr unter französischer Besatzung 1945–1952', in Gabriele Bohnert and Dieter Geuenich (eds), *Geschichte der Stadt Lahr*, vol. 3: *Im 20. Jahrhundert* (Lahr: Kaufmann, 1993), 199; Peter Fässler, Reinhard Grohnert, Joachim Haug, Heiko Haumann, and Edgar Wolfrum, 'Hauptstadt ohne Brot: Freiburg im Land Baden (1945–1952)', in

Table 4.1 *Number of internment camps*

	Total over time	No. in operation ≥6 mths	Nov. 1945	Apr. 1946	Jan. 1947	Jan. 1948	Dec. 1948	Dec. 1949
American	40	26	21	20	14	11	4	0
British	10	9	9	10	6	5	1	0
French	13	12	11	10	8	7	3	1
Soviet	12	10	9	9	8	6	3	3
Total	75	57	50	49	36	29	11	4

Note: The American- and British-zone figures of zero for December 1949 exclude those facilities that held only prisoners serving sentences imposed by *Spruchkammern* or *Spruchgerichte*: the labour camps Ludwigsburg No. 77, Bremen-Riespot, and Darmstadt (which closed that month) in the American zone, and the Esterwegen prison in the British zone. Figures based on Meyer, *Entnazifizierung von Frauen*, 69–107, with the addition of the three further camps handed to the British and French; Wember, *Umerziehung im Lager*, 50–82, 369–72; Möhler, 'Internierung im Rahmen der Entnazifizierungspolitik', 62; Möhler, *Entnazifizierung in Rheinland-Pfalz und im Saarland*, 358–93; Grohnert, *Entnazifizierung in Baden*, 162–71; Henke, *Politische Säuberung*, 41; von Plato, 'Zur Geschichte des sowjetischen Speziallagersystems', 28–43; and the various essays on individual camps in von Plato (ed.), *Studien und Berichte*.

depends not just on when, but on where one looks. In early May 1945, the NKVD was operating at least twenty-eight camps and prisons, mainly on territory east of the Oder–Neisse rivers that would soon be transferred from Germany to Poland, including Landsberg/Warta, which has been discussed in previous chapters. They and the two earliest camps within the borders of the Soviet zone in Germany, Fürstenwalde and Weesow, soon closed or were converted to other purposes, but ten new *Spezla-gerja*, or 'Special Camps', were established in the Soviet zone, all of which operated for more than six months.[17] Map 4.1 indicates the location of the camps across occupied Germany.

In Austria, in contrast, the French had the most camps, which were often quite small. In total, they used seventeen sites of incarceration in 1945–6, which included some regular prisons; the Brederis camp, the largest in the state of Voralberg, held only ca. 500 internees in spring 1946. In contrast, after an early period of multisite improvisation, the British ran just three camps: Weissenstein, Wetzelsdorf, and Wolfsberg, which was the largest with ca. 4,000 internees. Similarly, after brief use of multiple sites, the Americans ran two large camps: Hallein for SS members and Marcus W. Orr, which held more than 7,000 internees for most of 1946 and through to spring 1947 and was the only camp remaining after Hallein closed in January 1947.[18]

For obvious pragmatic reasons, the Allies frequently used existing facilities, which by definition had a Nazi past of some sort. It is well known that the Soviets used the former concentration-camp sites of Buchenwald and Sachsenhausen. American and British reuse of Dachau and Neuengamme is also reasonably well known, even if numerous historians fail to mention it while making much of the Soviet examples.[19] It is less well known that the British additionally used the site of the Esterwegen concentration camp, that the Soviet camp at Jamlitz was on the site of Lieberose, a sub-camp of the Sachsenhausen concentration camp, and that the French camp at Lochau near Bregenz in Austria was a former sub-camp of the Dachau concentration camp.

Heiko Haumann and Hans Schadek (eds.), *Geschichte der Stadt Freiburg im Breisgau*, vol. 3: *Von der badischen Herrschaft bis zur Gegenwart* (Stuttgart: Theiss Verlag, 2001), 383. Cf. Biddiscombe, *Denazification of Germany*, 161; Steinhart, *Balingen*, 255.

[17] Von Plato, 'Zur Geschichte des sowjetischen Speziallagersystems', 24, 28–9, 32; Greiner, *Suppressed Terror*, 2–3. Merten incorrectly claims that none of the initial 28 camps was within the Soviet occupation zone. Merten, *Gulag in East Germany*, 114.

[18] Eisterer, *Französische Besatzungspolitik*, 202, 204; Kastner, '373 Camp Wolfsberg', 68–9; Dohle and Eigelsberger, *Camp Marcus W. Orr*, 19–21, 93–4.

[19] E.g., Kitchen, *History of Modern Germany*, 317; Dallas, *1945*, 591; Taylor *Exorcising Hitler*, 323; Anne Applebaum, *Iron Curtain: The Crushing of Eastern Europe, 1944–1956* (New York: Doubleday, 2012), 106–7. Cf. Marcuse, 'Afterlife of the Camps', 186.

Map 4.1 Location of internment camps.

Note: Some short-lived camps are not indicated, and of the early Soviet camps east of the Oder–Neisse line, only Landsberg/Warthe (Gorzów) is shown. Of related facilities such as internee hospitals and interrogation centres, only Bad Nenndorf and Adelheide in the British zone and Waldheim in East Germany are shown.

Redrawn by Cox Cartographic Ltd with permission of Stiftung Gedenkstätten Buchenwald und Mittelbau-Dora from Ritscher et al. (eds), *Das sowjetische Speziallager Nr. 2,* and with additional data from Wember, *Umerziehung im Lager;* Meyer, *Entnazifizierung von Frauen;* Möhler, 'Internierung im Rahmen der Entnazifizierungspolitik'.

Thus three Soviet camps were on the sites of former concentration camps, more than in other zones but not enough to justify suggestions that all or most Soviet camps were former concentration camps (although two of the three that remained in use after October 1948 were former concentration camps).[20] Conversely, Volker Dotterweich's generalization that 'The recently emptied concentration camps started to be filled again' is accurate for the territory of occupied Germany only if one excludes the hundreds of sub-camps, while several of the main camps that were redeployed were not used for civilian internment.[21] Some, such as Bergen-Belsen (but also Dachau, Esterwegen, and Neuengamme for certain periods), were used to accommodate DPs or German refugees and expellees. The Americans used Flossenbürg as a POW camp, mainly for Waffen-SS personnel, until April 1946 when it too became a DP camp. In 1945 the Soviets used Ravensbrück as a repatriation camp for Soviet former POWs, forced labourers, and concentration-camp inmates. On the other hand, some concentration camps the Nazis had established in occupied Europe became postwar internment camps, including Natzweiler-Struthof in France, where German prisoners and French collaborators were held, and Westerbork and Herzogenbusch/ Vught in the Netherlands, where Dutch Nazis were interned.[22]

The significance attached to the reuse of concentration camp sites varies considerably. Especially in the Soviet case, some authors imply that reutilization entailed functional equivalence. For instance, Rudolf Morsey speaks of the 'still-existing concentration camps Buchenwald and Sachsenhausen'.[23] Others merely identify topographical continuity and stress pragmatism as the key factor that explains reutilization.[24] In line with her positive depiction of American internment, Meyer asserts (without evidence) that the Americans' decision *not* to use former

---

[20] E.g., Vollnhals (ed.), *Entnazifizierung: Politische Säuberung*, 54; Kitchen, *History of Modern Germany*, 317.

[21] Dotterweich, 'Die "Entnazifizierung"', 141.

[22] Marcuse, 'Afterlife of the Camps', 189–90; Grevers and Van Haecke, 'Administrative Internment', 286, 291. Marcuse incorrectly states that Flossenbürg was a civilian internment camp. Cf. KZ-Gedenkstätte Flossenbürg, *Was bleibt: Nachwirkungen des Konzentrationslagers Flossenbürg: Katalog zur Dauerausstellung* (Flossenbürg: KZ-Gedenkstätte Flossenbürg, 2011), 60.

[23] Rudolf Morsey, *Die Bundesrepublik Deutschland: Entstehung und Entwicklung bis 1969* (Munich: R. Oldenbourg, 1987), 14.

[24] Horn, *Internierungs- und Arbeitslager*, 146; Jan Lipinsky, 'Sowjetische Speziallager in Deutschland, 1945–1950: Ein Beispiel für alliierte Internierungspraxis oder sowjetisches GULag-System', in Brigitte Kaff (ed.), *'Gefährliche politische Gegner': Widerstand und Verfolgung in der sowjetischen Zone/DDR* (Düsseldorf: Droste, 1995), 32; Müller, 'Sowjetische Speziallager', 25 (but he refers to Bergen-Belsen instead of Neuengamme).

concentration camps (apart from Dachau) was an indication of their desire to treat their internees humanely. Yet in the United States in 1944 various proponents of extensive internment saw the prospect of incarcerating Nazis in concentration camps as both a likely pragmatic necessity and a form of symbolic justice. For instance, Herbert Marcuse suggested that 'detained Nazis could be kept in the concentration camps wherever the prisons are filled', while Henry Stimson told Henry Morgenthau that 'we should take all the members of the SS troops and put them in the same concentration camps where the Germans have had these poor Jewish people'.[25]

The use of sites with problematic Nazi pasts went beyond concentration camps, a point generally noted only in some specialist studies.[26] In fact, the reuse of former POW camps was more common, at least in the western zones. The Soviets used two former POW camps (Neubrandenburg-Fünfeichen and Mühlberg), the French also used a number (including Balingen, Binsenthal, and Trier, while other sites had also briefly served this purpose), the British used six (Eselheide, Fallingbostel, Hemer, Recklinghausen, Sandbostel, and Westertimke), and the Americans a comparable number (including Hammelburg, Ludwigsburg-Aldingen, Moosburg, Nuremberg-Langwasser, and Ziegenhain). Some had been sites of mass suffering and death, especially those that had held large numbers of Soviet POWs (such as Stalag IV B at Mühlberg and Stalag 326 VI K at Stukenbrock/Senne, which became Eselheide), or those that received concentration-camp evacuees in the war's final weeks (like Stalag X B at Sandbostel).[27] Other internment camps, especially in the American zone, utilized former military barracks (including Darmstadt, Garmisch-Partenkirchen, and several camps in and around Ludwigsburg) or training grounds (Schwarzenborn). Equivalents elsewhere were Paderborn-Staumühle in the British and Landau in the French zones, while the Soviets used former barracks at Landsberg/Warta and, briefly, the Seydlitz barracks in Torgau. Additionally, the Soviets used former civilian and military prisons at Bautzen and Torgau-Fort Zinna, while the Americans used the Asperg prison near

[25] Meyer, *Entnazifizierung von Frauen*, 111; Marcuse, 'Dissolution of the Nazi Party and Its Affiliated Organizations', 22 Jul. 1944, in Neumann et al., *Secret Reports*, 257; Beschloss, *The Conquerors*, 96. Cf. Marcuse, 'Afterlife of the Camps', 186.

[26] Horn, *Internierungs- und Arbeitslager*, 45; Wember, *Umerziehung im Lager*, 50; Lipinsky, 'Sowjetische Speziallager', 709.

[27] Michaela Hänke-Portscheller, 'Senne und Mühlberg – Sperrige Erinnerungsorte als didaktische Herausforderung: NS-Kriegsgefangenenlager in der doppelten deutschen Geschichtskultur', in Christoph Kleßmann and Peter Lautzas (eds), *Teilung und Integration: Die doppelte deutsche Nachkriegsgeschichte als wissenschaftliches und didaktisches Problem* (Bonn: Bundeszentrale für politische Bildung, 2005), 152–76.

Ludwigsburg. The German-administered camp at Augsburg-Göggingen in the American zone was on the site of a former forced-labour camp, as was Theley in the French zone, which had also served briefly as a Wehrmacht depot and POW camp. The French used former camps of the Reich Labour Service (*Reichsarbeitsdienst*) at Wörth and Lahr-Dinglingen, and another at Bühl-Altschweier, which had also served briefly both as a convalescent camp for the Wehrmacht and a POW camp. In Saarbrücken, the French used a square near the river Saar, the so-called Liberation Field (*Befreiungsfeld*), where the Nazis had held rallies, and in Regensburg the American POW camp that later became an internment camp was created on a field previously used as a parade ground. Camps with less encumbered pasts included Neumünster-Gadeland in a former leather factory in the British zone and Berlin-Hohenschönhausen and Ketschendorf in the Soviet zone, which were established on the sites of a kitchen complex of the National Socialist People's Welfare organization (*Nationalsozialistische Volkswohlfahrt*) and a workers' accommodation complex, respectively.[28] This diversity suggests that it is problematic to infer anything about the character of Allied internment camps simply from the history of the sites used.

The sites used in Austria were similarly diverse. In addition to the former Dachau sub-camp at Lochau, the French used, among others, a former German Labour Service and Hitler Youth military training camp at Brederis, and a former forced labour camp at Schwaz, which they named 'Oradour' in memory of the French village that the Waffen-SS had totally destroyed in 1944. The Americans used a former Wehrmacht depot for the Marcus W. Orr camp in Salzburg. The British used a former First World War civilian internment camp and Second World War POW camp (Stalag XVIII A) at Wolfsberg but also created two new camps at Weissenstein and Wetzelsdorf.[29] The Allies thus sought and

---

[28] Wember, *Umerziehung im Lager*, 50, 55–82; Greiner, *Suppressed Terror*, 2–3; Kirsten, *Das sowjetische Speziallager Nr. 4*, 20–1; Müller, 'Internierungslager in und um Ludwigsburg', 174–5; Strauß, 'Zwischen Apathie und Selbstrechtfertigung', 291–2; Heinl, 'Das schlimme Lager', 24; Alfred Hausmann, 'Lager Göggingen, 1942–1954' (unpub. paper, 2010), available at: slidex.tips/download/lager-ggggingen (accessed 6 Feb. 2019); Möhler, *Entnazifizierung in Rheinland-Pfalz und im Saarland*, 371–2, 384; Steinhart, *Balingen*, 255; Rainer Möhler, 'Lager Theley', in Rainer Hudemann et al. (eds.), *Stätten grenzüberschreitender Erinnerung – Spuren der Vernetzung des Saar-Lor-Lux-Raumes im 19. und 20. Jahrhundert* (Saarbrücken: Uni Saarland, 2002), available at: www.memotransfront.uni-saarland.de/theley.shtml (accessed 6 Feb. 2019); Fäßler, 'Lahr unter französischer Besatzung', 199; Irmgard Stamm, 'Lagerleben in Altschweier', *Bühler Heimatgeschichte* 5 (1991), 92–3; Klose, 'Internierungs- und Arbeitslager Regensburg', 10.

[29] Eisterer, *Französische Besatzungspolitik*, 200–1; Dohle and Eigelsberger, *Camp Marcus W. Orr*, 12–13; Kastner, '373 Camp Wolfsberg', 64–5, 68.

used any type of available accommodation and created their own only where necessary.

Functions of and Responsibility for the Camps

A tiny number of camps were physically located in prisons, but in time several functioned increasingly as prisons, holding convicts serving a sentence rather than, or as well as, internees awaiting processing. Such additional uses, beyond internment, complicate the picture of these camps. In the Soviet zone, prisoners convicted by SMTs began arriving in significant numbers in Special Camp No. 10 at Torgau from June 1946, in Sachsenhausen from September, and in Bautzen from November, although smaller numbers had been held in Bautzen since November 1945.[30] SMT convicts comprised ca. 15% of the total number of Special Camp inmates over time, but because only internees were released and they also suffered a higher death rate, the proportion of convicted prisoners rose to 49% by October 1948 and 55% by early 1950. Internees and SMT convicts were held in separate zones in Sachsenhausen and Bautzen. After the large releases of internees in summer 1948 and the closure of several camps, internees were predominantly held in Buchenwald. Male SMT convicts with sentences over fifteen years were concentrated in Bautzen and those with shorter sentences and female convicts in Sachsenhausen. The latter two 'camps' had thus largely become prisons, but internees still comprised 15–20% of their inmates in late 1949. In contrast, Buchenwald remained exclusively an internment camp to the end.[31]

In the western zones the situation was slightly more complicated but also somewhat more transparent because official nomenclature better reflected functional differences, at least in the American and British zones. Three groups need to be distinguished, and were more or less strictly separated, from the bulk of internees there. First, Germans convicted by the western powers' military tribunals were held not in internment camps as many SMT convicts were, but in Allied military prisons, such as those at Landsberg/Lech, Werl, and Wittlich. Second, individual war-crimes suspects were generally (but not completely) separated from automatic arrestees. Some were taken into pre-trial custody in military

---

[30] Jeske and Morré, 'Inhaftierung von Tribunalverurteilten', 654.

[31] Von Plato, 'Zur Geschichte des sowjetischen Speziallagersystems', 29, 43; 'Schreiben des Leiters GULag an den stellv. Innenminister Serov zu den Verhältnissen in den Speziallagern bei der Übernahme durch die GULag', 16 Nov. 1948, in Possekel (ed.), *Sowjetische Dokumente*, 336; Kersebom and Niethammer, '"Kompromat" 1949', 515.

prisons. Others were placed in separate zones within internment camps or concentrated in particular camps. In the British zone, camp no. 9 at Esterwegen held a high proportion of suspected war criminals; in July 1946 it was redesignated 'No. 101 Prison Camp'. Additionally, from June 1947, a 'War Crimes Holding Centre' was established in Hamburg-Fischbek, whence extraditions took place.[32] In the American zone, 'War Crimes Central Suspect and Witness Enclosures' were established at CIE No. 78 at Stuttgart-Zuffenhausen and CIE No. 29 at Dachau; from July 1946 the former was dissolved and only Dachau continued to serve this purpose, among others.[33] Third, Germans serving prison sentences imposed by British-zone *Spruchgerichte* for membership of criminal organizations were held at Esterwegen, which in July 1947 became a German-run prison.[34] Meanwhile, in the American zone Germans sentenced to labour camp by *Spruchkammern* were held in what from late 1946 became 'Internment and Labour Camps' under German administration. Not unlike Sachsenhausen and Bautzen, such camps thus held convicts (albeit of different type) as well as internees, and the former eventually outnumbered the latter. Across the camps in Württemberg-Baden, labour-camp inmates outnumbered internees from September 1948 onward.[35] Once the last internees had been processed, the remaining camps were redesignated 'Labour Camps'.[36]

Such changes over time, as well as differences in the inmate populations, make it difficult to generalize accurately and simply about the function and character both of Allied internment camps generally and of individual camps. For instance, in the American zone Nuremberg-Langwasser almost exclusively held SS and Waffen-SS members, whereas NSDAP officials dominated at Garmisch-Partenkirchen. Neustadt in Hesse was particularly unusual, being dedicated in 1947 to accommodating former senior Wehrmacht officers who were cooperating with the Americans on writing the history of the Second World War.

---

[32] Wember, *Umerziehung im Lager*, 29–30, 81–2, 87–8. On Landsberg/Lech, Werl, and Wittlich, see Gerald Reitlinger, 'Werl, Wittlich, and Landsberg: Postscript to the War Trials', *The Jewish Quarterly* 1, no. 3 (1953), 9–17.

[33] Horn, *Internierungs- und Arbeitslager*, 27–9; Meyer, *Entnazifizierung von Frauen*, 76; Hammermann, 'Internierungslager Dachau'; Möhler, *Entnazifizierung in Rheinland-Pfalz und im Saarland*, 377–8.

[34] Wember, *Umerziehung im Lager*, 82.

[35] Ministerialdirektor Koransky, Monatsbericht für September 1948, 20 Oct. 1948, 5, Hauptstaatsarchiv Stuttgart (HStAS), EA 11/102, no. 53.

[36] Some were designated Labour and Detention Camps (*Arbeits- und Festhaltelager*), the latter term referring to the detention of internees whose verdict was not yet legally binding when there was a danger of flight or suppression of evidence. Horn, *Internierungs- und Arbeitslager*, 89–94, 137; Heinl, 'Das schlimme Lager', 92.

Camp 76 at Asperg was used among other things to intern 'obnoxious' Germans repatriated from overseas.[37] Dachau was especially complex, with different compounds serving as POW camp, war-crimes enclosure, and internment camp under American administration and as a German-run internment and labour camp. Neuengamme similarly held diverse groups, including POWs, internees, war-crimes suspects, and Germans who had been expelled from overseas territories. Sachsenhausen for a time had a POW officers' sub-camp as well as the separate zones for internees and SMT convicts. Torgau-Fort Zinna held POWs and intern-ees in its first incarnation as Special Camp No. 8, which moved to the nearby Seydlitz barracks, and then mainly Soviet SMT convicts awaiting deportation in its second incarnation as Special Camp No. 10, which is best described as a transit prison. Indeed, a significant function of the Special Camps was the filtration of Soviet citizens back to the USSR. This was especially the case after the closure of other dedicated filtration camps, but there was some earlier overlap too. From February 1945, the camp at Landsberg/Warta was used primarily to collect 'mobilized' Germans from east of the Oder–Neisse line for deportation to the Soviet Union, before becoming, in an overlapping transition in summer 1945, a Special Camp for civilian internees from further west, while also holding German POWs and Soviet citizens prior to transportation to the USSR.[38]

French camps, in contrast, were somewhat more straightforward. Some were initially exceptional for also housing regular civilian remand prisoners and convicted felons, due to overcrowding in normal prisons. Yet camps in the French zone did not become penal institutions to any meaningful extent as some in the other zones did. The French-zone *Spruchkammern* imposed so few custodial sentences – and in most cases the sentences were regarded as already having been served in internment – that there was virtually no need for penal facilities. For

---

[37] Horn, *Internierungs- und Arbeitslager*, 148; Messenger, 'Beyond War Crimes', 476; Esther-Julia Howell, *Von den Besiegten lernen? Die kriegsgeschichtliche Kooperation der U.S. Armee und der ehemaligen Wehrmachtselite 1945–1961* (Berlin: De Gruyter, 2016), 91, 107, 115.

[38] Hammermann, 'Internierungslager Dachau'; Lindner, 'Das ehemalige KZ Neuengamme'; Greiner, *Suppressed Terror*, 145–9; Brigitte Oleschinski and Bert Pampel, *'Feindliche Elemente sind in Gewahrsam zu halten': Die sowjetischen Speziallager Nr. 8 und Nr. 10 in Torgau 1945–1948* (Leipzig: Gustav Kiepenheuer, 2002), 35–44; Jeske, 'Kritische Bemerkungen', 472; Kirsten, *Das sowjetische Speziallager Nr. 4*, 21–7. On the screening and filtration camps for Soviet citizens, see Peter Ruggenthaler, 'Der lange Arm Moskaus: Zur Problematik der Zwangsrepatriierungen ehemaliger sowjetischer Zwangsarbeiter und Kriegsgefangener in die UdSSR', in Siegfried Mattl, Gerhard Bolz, Stefan Karner, and Helmut Konrad (eds.), *Krieg, Erinnerung, Geschichtswissenschaft* (Vienna: Böhlau Verlag, 2009), 229–46.

instance, of 424 cases before *Spruchkammern* in the Saarland from 1948 (that were generally the most serious) only twenty-one people were classified as Offenders after appeal (and none as Major Offenders); all of them had previously been interned, and further detention was ordered in only four cases. It is thus unsurprising that in September 1948 there were only eleven internees in Theley, the last camp in the state: nine were still awaiting their verdicts and just two were serving a sentence. In August 1949, twenty-seven internees were released from the Trier camp and placed under house arrest, while of the remaining seventeen detainees fourteen were war-crimes suspects.[39]

If the British alone maintained a sharp distinction between penal facilities for convicts and internment camps for others, only the Americans and to some extent the French ever passed responsibility for their camps – and thus for internees – into German hands. As mentioned in Chapter 2, from autumn 1946 the administration of numerous American camps, which had been the responsibility of the US army, was successively transferred to German regional governments. However, the Americans held on to war-crimes suspects and witnesses and dangerous security suspects; retained oversight of the German-administered camps, including over matters such as ration levels; and reserved the authority to approve internees' release. In Austria, in contrast, although Austrian authorities provided guards for the Americans' Marcus W. Orr camp from late 1946, they never took over responsibility for running the camp.[40] Reflecting the policy of decentralization and considerable autonomy in the various states in the French zone, a variety of approaches emerged there: camps were transferred to German authority in September 1947 in Württemberg-Hohenzollern and in May 1948 in the Saarland but remained in French hands until the end in Baden and Rhineland-Palatinate (and in Austria).[41] In contrast, although some in British military government were keen to follow the American example, others opposed such a move, including Robertson, who became Military Governor in late 1947. As a result, even when responsibility for denazification eventually shifted to the German state governments in

---

[39] Möhler, 'Internierung im Rahmen der Entnazifizierungspolitik', 62; Grohnert, *Entnazifizierung in Baden*, 169; Möhler, *Entnazifizierung in Rheinland-Pfalz und im Saarland*, 322, 376; Le Gouverneur Hettier de Boislambert, Délégué Général pour le Gouvernement Militaire de l'Etat Rhéno-Palatin to Carl Sachsse, 1 Sep. 1949, Archiv der Evangelischen Kirche im Rheinland, Düsseldorf (AEKR), 1 OB 017, 11-24-03.

[40] Horn, *Internierungs- und Arbeitslager*, 74–102; Meyer, *Entnazifizierung von Frauen*, 109; Dohle and Eigelsberger, *Camp Marcus W. Orr*, 49–50.

[41] Möhler, 'Internierungslager in der französischen Besatzungszone', 53.

October 1947, the camps remained in British hands.[42] In both the French and British zones, however, German authorities were required to perform various supporting roles, such as provisioning the camps and, later, providing guards. For instance, the Rhineland-Palatinate government provided police to guard the Diez camp from January 1947.[43]

Responsibility for British and Soviet camps nevertheless changed at certain points in revealing ways. The British army was responsible for the civilian internment camps until April 1946, when the military government's Legal Division, Penal Branch, took over.[44] In the Soviet case, Beria's Order No. 00315 of April 1945 had created a 'Department for Special Camps of the NKVD in Germany' within the NKVD. It was independent of the NKVD's Main Administration of Corrective Labour Camps and Labour Settlements (GULAG) and Main Administration for POW and Internee Affairs (GUPVI). The department reported to the NKVD chief in the Soviet zone, Colonel-General Ivan Serov, who was simultaneously deputy head of the SMAD. In August 1948, however, the department was subordinated to the GULAG, perhaps reflecting that by this point almost half of the inmates were SMT convicts.[45] Thus in both the British and the Soviet zones non-convicted internees were eventually held in camps administered by penal bodies.

Isolation and Contact with the Exterior

Isolating internees was perhaps internment's paramount purpose, and all of the occupying powers took rigorous steps to enforce it, at least some of the time. Camps were strictly off-limits to non-authorized personnel, and fences, barbed wire, and watchtowers were installed where necessary to secure their perimeters. Guards were authorized to shoot internees attempting to escape or approaching external fences, and some were shot

---

[42] 'British Military Government Ordinance No. 110: Transfer to the Länder Governments of Responsibility for Denazification', 1 Oct. 1947, in Ruhm von Oppen (ed.), *Documents on Germany*, 249; Wember, *Umerziehung im Lager*, 123–7.

[43] Resmini, 'Lager der Besatzungsmächte', 615–16; Möhler, 'Internierung im Rahmen der Entnazifizierungspolitik', 62; Fässler et al., 'Hauptstadt ohne Brot', 383–4.

[44] Wember, *Umerziehung im Lager*, 32, 115. In Austria, the British Troops Austria were responsible for the internment camps. Kastner, '373 Camp Wolfsberg', 60.

[45] Von Plato, 'Zur Geschichte des sowjetischen Speziallagersystems', 29, 41; Possekel, 'Sowjetische Lagerpolitik', 58–60, 74–5, 89. On the GULAG, see Oleg Vitalevich Khlevniuk, *The History of the Gulag: From Collectivization to the Great Terror* (New Haven, CT: Yale University Press, 2004). On the GUPVI, see Stefan Karner, *Im Archipel GUPVI: Kriegsgefangenschaft und Internierung in der Sowjetunion 1941–1956* (Vienna: R. Oldenbourg, 1995).

dead in the American, British, and Soviet zones. In Austria, Austrian guards opened fire on internees attempting to flee Marcus W. Orr in March 1947.[46] Drastic measures were also taken to deter people from approaching the camps from the outside. At Altenstadt bei Schongau in the American zone, the wife of an internee was shot as she approached the camp fence from the street outside. The British arrested women entering a prohibited zone around Neuengamme, and in December 1946 the Americans arrested a woman for speaking to an inmate at Dachau.[47] Yet there are also reports from both the American and Soviet zones that in 1945 some internees were allowed to return home to collect musical instruments, and in summer and early autumn 1945 some relatives were able to bring packages of food and clothing to the Soviet camp at Bautzen and could occasionally speak with internees. Such practices were the exception, however, and did not last more than a few months at most.[48] Nevertheless, hopes for contact or for any information about detainees persisted. In December 1945, the US military government detachment in the city of Dachau reported that it was receiving a 'continuous flood' of mail 'seeking information on relatives interned in the camp', while internees' families formed a 'transient civilian population that comes and goes to the city'.[49]

Over time significant differences emerged, especially between the approaches of Soviet and the western powers and to a lesser extent among the latter. The Americans were the first officially to relax the policy of total isolation, although they did not introduce all concessions in 1945 as some authors suggest.[50] From August 1945 American-zone internees could receive mail, if their families knew where they were held, which was often not the case. From December 1945 internees were

---

[46] Wember, *Umerziehung im Lager*, 52; Meyer, *Entnazifizierung von Frauen*, 125, 139; Hüser, *'Unschuldig' in britischer Lagerhaft?*, 43–4; Ritscher, *Spezlager Nr. 2 Buchenwald*, 147; Dohle and Eigelsberger, *Camp Marcus W. Orr*, 65.

[47] Horn, *Internierungs- und Arbeitslager*, 175–6; Meyer, *Entnazifizierung von Frauen*, 139; Hüser, *'Unschuldig' in britischer Lagerhaft?*, 43–4; Lindner, 'Das ehemalige KZ Neuengamme', 80; Det E-367, Weekly Intelligence Report, 7 Dec. 1946, Bayerisches Hauptstaatsarchiv, Munich (BHStA), OMGUS CO, 442/7.

[48] Meyer, *Entnazifizierung von Frauen*, 137; Peter Erler, 'Das Speziallager Nr. 3 in Hohenschönhausen Mai 1945–Oktober 1946', in von Plato (ed.), *Studien und Berichte*, 327; Gerhard Sälter, 'Heimliche Briefe: Kassiber aus sowjetischen Speziallagern (1945–1950)', in Cornelia Liebold, Jörg Morré, and Gerhard Sälter (eds.), *Kassiber aus Bautzen: Heimliche Briefe von Gefangenen aus dem sowjetischen Speziallager 1945–1950* (Dresden: Stiftung Sächsische Gedenkstätten zur Erinnerung, 2004), 84. Cf. Stamm, 'Lagerleben in Altschweier', 95.

[49] D. I. Glossbrenner, Operations Report on Mil. Gov. Detachment No. I 367, 17 Dec. 1945, 2, BHStA, OMGUS CO, 475/7.

[50] E.g., Lipinsky, 'Sowjetische Speziallager in Deutschland', 32; Merten, *Gulag in East Germany*, 41.

permitted to write POW cards and from January 1946 they could send weekly, censored letters with no word limit. The volume of resulting mail is indicated by statistics from Marcus W. Orr in Austria, where internees could send and receive mail from November 1945. That month alone, 30,000 cards were sent out of the camp, a figure that rose to over 83,000 by March 1947. From January 1946 more than 40,000 letters arrived each month, reaching a peak of more than 93,000 in January 1947. In Regensburg, in January 1948 when the camp held approximately 3,400 internees, almost 12,000 letters were received and almost 11,000 sent out, and thousands of packages went in and out, as internees sent their possessions home before being released. Only in exceptional circumstances did the Americans permit visits to, and leave from, their camps, but under German administration from the end of 1946 monthly or bimonthly visits and leave in cases of an immediate relative's serious illness or death became the norm for internees (although labour-camp convicts did not get leave). At Easter 1948, more than 3,000 internees (ca. 16%) received three weeks' leave to visit their families. In Regensburg, there were almost 119,000 visits between October 1946 and July 1947.[51] In Austria, a first one-off large-scale visit for relatives was organized at Marcus W. Orr between Christmas 1946 and New Year's Day 1947, more regular visits took place from April 1947, and similar leave arrangements to those in Germany were introduced in early 1947. In Germany, internees also had almost unhindered access to defence lawyers for their denazification proceedings, while interned lawyers also cooperated with the defence counsel appointed at the IMT at Nuremberg.[52]

---

[51] Horn, *Internierungs- und Arbeitslager*, 220–7; Meyer, *Entnazifizierung von Frauen*, 139–40; Hammermann, 'Internierungslager Dachau', 67–8; Dohle and Eigelsberger, *Camp Marcus W. Orr*, 180–1; Oberster Kläger im Hessischen Ministerium für politische Befreiung to Kirchenleitung der Evangelischen Kirche in Hessen und Nassau, 4 Jan. 1949, Zentralarchiv der Evangelischen Kirche in Hessen und Nassau, Darmstadt (ZAEKHN), 155, no. 783; Pater Roth, Monatsbericht über die katholische Seelsorge im Lager Dachau, 1 May 1947, Archiv des Erzbistums München und Freising, Munich (AEM), Nachlass (NL) Faulhaber, no. 6187; Ordinariat des Erzbistums München und Freising to Seelsorgeklerus der Erzdiözese München, 15 Mar. 1948, AEM, NL Faulhaber, no. 8533/2; Der Lagerältester, Internierungs- und Arbeitslager Dachau, to Bishop Hans Meiser, 24 Mar. 1948, Landeskirchliches Archiv der Evangelisch-Lutherischen Kirche in Bayern, Nuremberg (LAELKB), Landeskirchenamt, no. 167; 'Ein "gelungenes" Experiment?', *Niedersächsische Volksstimme*, 14 Apr. 48; Klose, 'Internierungs- und Arbeitslager Regensburg', 52. Cf. Heinl, '"Das schlimme Lager"', 51–2. In contrast, Merten claims that US-zone internees could take leave and could receive visitors already from the end of 1945. Merten, *Gulag in East Germany*, 42.

[52] Dohle and Eigelsberger, *Camp Marcus W. Orr*, 55–6, 59; Klose, 'Internierungs- und Arbeitslager Regensburg', 51; Horn, *Internierungs- und Arbeitslager*, 126–7; Hubert

The British were slower and less generous in allowing contact with the exterior, but claims that their camps were isolated as strictly as the Soviets' are incorrect.[53] From January 1946 British-zone internees were permitted to exchange twenty-five-word cards with relatives. This increased to weekly 250-word, censored letters at the end of 1946. From the second half of 1947 trimonthly visits were allowed, and after experiments in Sandbostel and Fallingbostel, leave was permitted in cases of death or serious illness of immediate relatives.[54]

The French were somewhat inconsistent. The ICRC reported in October 1945 that leave of two hours was regularly permitted in some camps and that internees in most camps could receive packages. However, the latter privilege was sometimes banned for extended periods for disciplinary breaches, and written correspondence was still not permitted in March 1946. Relatives only rarely received permission to visit. In April 1948, numerous internees were granted leave to attend their children's confirmation (as also happened in the other western zones), and at Christmas 1948, Military Governor Kœnig granted five days' leave to 15% of French-zone internees.[55] In Austria, the French were more accommodating: visits, packages, brief furlough were all permitted quite early, security was relatively lax, and Austrian authorities were reasonably well informed about the numbers of internees in individual camps and prisons.[56] The same applied in the German states where French camps were transferred to German administration.[57]

In stark contrast, the Soviets maintained the almost total isolation of their internees until the end. Indeed, according to Serov's 'Provisional Order about the Special Camps of the NKVD on the Occupied Territory of Germany' of July 1945, 'The main task of the camp is the complete

---

Seliger, *Politische Anwälte: Die Verteidiger der Nürnberger Prozesse* (Baden-Baden: Nomos, 2016), 158, 203.

[53] Dolan, 'Isolating Nazism', 15.

[54] Wember,   *Umerziehung   im   Lager*,   136–40;   Ehresmann,   'Die   frühe Nachkriegsnutzung', 29.

[55] Camps d'internés civils, politiques et administratifs, 6 Oct. 1945, ACICR, B G 44 02-058.01; Carl Sachsse to Leitung der Evangelischen Kirche der Rheinprovinz, 27 Apr. 1948, AEKR, 1 OB 017, 11-24-03; Kœnig to Archbishop Bornewasser, 22 Dec. 1948, in Brommer (ed.), *Quellen zur Geschichte von Rheinland-Pfalz*, 734–5; Fäßler, 'Lahr unter französischer Besatzung', 200; Möhler, *Entnazifizierung in Rheinland-Pfalz und im Saarland*, 369, 384.

[56] Eisterer,   *Französische   Besatzungspolitik*,   201;   Wolfgang   Weber   (ed.), *Nationalsozialismus – Demokratischer Wiederaufbau: Lage- und Stimmungsberichte aus den Voralberger Gemeinden des Bezirks Feldkirch im Jahre 1945* (Regensburg: Roderer Verlag, 2001), 142, 146, 149, 151–2.

[57] Harmut Berghoff and Cornelia Rauh, *The Respectable Career of Fritz K.: The Making and Remaking of a Provincial Nazi Leader*, trans. Casey Butterfield (New York: Berghahn Books, 2015), 204.

isolation of the contingent within the camp and the prevention of escapes.'[58] This description could be applied to all four powers' camps at least initially. Yet, as discussed shortly, the western powers also paid increasing, if belated and limited, attention to employing internees productively and reorienting them towards post-Nazi futures, without ever forgetting isolation entirely. The Soviets, in contrast, remained fixated on isolation until the end. In May 1947 the Deputy Head of Civilian Affairs of the Soviet Military Administration in Thuringia, General Ivan Sazonovič Kolesničenko, justified the continuing refusal to allow internees to write to their relatives – and to grant the churches access to the camps – by saying that doing so would hinder the detection of crimes; he claimed that, whereas the western powers had interned mere party members, only criminals were interned in the Soviet zone (which provides another example of the competitive comparisons discussed in Chapter 2). From July 1949 SMT convicts were allowed to write cards, but internees were never permitted to send or receive mail, and neither group could take leave or receive visits. With regard to communication, Soviet-zone internees were by far the worst off and even worse off than German POWs in the USSR.[59]

Indeed, the Special Camps and their inmates remained shrouded in secrecy. No official information about internees' whereabouts or death was given. Repeated Soviet promises to provide such information were never fulfilled and the Tracing Service for Missing Germans in the Soviet occupation zone expressly did not process 'tracing requests for people arrested after May 1945 for political reasons'.[60] As a result, while illicit messages were smuggled in and out (opportunities for which diminished significantly from 1946), many families remained ignorant of arrestees' fate at least until the large-scale releases in summer 1948 and early 1950. At those points, many discharged internees ignored instructions not to speak about the camps and contacted their fellow inmates' relatives with news of detainees' whereabouts or death. For instance, a former internee informed the Archbishop of Cologne, Cardinal Josef Frings, that his

---

[58] Quoted according to the translation published as 'Provisional Order about the Special Camps of the NKVD on the Occupied Territory of Germany', 27 Jul. 1945, in Morsch and Reich (eds.), *Sowjetisches Speziallager in Sachsenhausen*, 313.

[59] Bishop Moritz Mitzenheim, Besprechung mit General Kolesnitschenko, 18 Mar. 1947, Landeskirchenarchiv Eisenach (LKAE), A 930-4: 32; Possekel, 'Sowjetische Lagerpolitik', 90. See Andrej Kosteneckij, 'Deutsche Kriegsgefangene in der Sowjetunion: Heimatkontakte und Rückkehr', in Müller, Nikischkin, and Wagenlehner (eds.), *Tragödie der Gefangenschaft*, 55–8.

[60] Ritscher, *Spezlager Nr. 2 Buchenwald*, 86; Suchdienst für vermisste Deutsche in der SBZ, Protokoll der Karteiführerbesprechung, 17 Feb. 1948, 3, Bundesarchiv Berlin (BAB), DO 105/213.

brother Heinrich had died in Mühlberg.[61] Released internees also reported that certain newspapers were now distributed in the camps, so in the second half of 1948 families sent greetings to internees via the *National-Zeitung*, before it stopped accepting them when the practice came to the authorities' attention.[62] Virtually no non-detained Germans ever gained access to the Soviet camps. On the few occasions when church leaders were admitted to conduct religious services – in Bautzen and Torgau at Christmas 1947, in Buchenwald and Sachsenhausen only in December 1949 – they were not able to speak freely with the inmates.[63]

If the Soviet camps thus remained opaque and ex-territorialized, the western camps became relatively transparent and, especially in the American zone, part of postwar German society. If relatives did not know where detainees were held, they could find out from 1946 via central offices in Hamburg and Frankfurt/Main.[64] Next of kin were officially informed of an internee's death (normally via a German secular or ecclesiastical intermediary) and were generally supposed to be given the opportunity to take possession of the body. There was still no uniform procedure for this in the American zone in early 1946, and procedures were not always implemented properly. In an exceptional case, for which the British apologized, a woman was informed only in February 1946 of her interned husband's death the previous May.[65] The western powers, again the Americans generally more quickly and uniformly than the British and French, also granted the major Christian churches access to the camps. Before Christmas 1945, the Protestant Bishop of

---

[61] Sälter, 'Heimliche Briefe', 90; Josef Kardinal Frings, *Für die Menschen bestellt: Erinnerungen des Alterzbischofs von Köln Josef Kardinal Frings* (Cologne: J. P. Bachem, 1973), 53. See also Edda Ahrberg and Torsten Haarseim, 'Das Ende des Zweiten Weltkrieges in Gardelegen', in Edda Ahrberg, Daniel Bohse, Torsten Haarseim, and Jürgen Richter, *Ausgeliefert: Haft und Verfolgung im Kreis Gardelegen zwischen 1945 und 1961* (Halle: Mitteldeutscher Verlag, 2014), 87, 93.

[62] Ritscher, *Spezlager Nr. 2 Buchenwald*, 87.

[63] Bishop Dibelius to Tulpanov, 5 Mar. 1948, Evangelisches Landeskirchliches Archiv in Berlin (ELAB), NL Otto Dibelius, 603/13; Landesbischof der Ev.-Luth. Landeskirche Sachsens, Kanzlei, to Krummacher, 2 May 1949, Evangelisches Zentralarchiv, Berlin (EZA), 4/736: 60; 'Bericht von Landesbischof M. Mitzenheim über seinen Besuch in Buchenwald', 26 Jan. 1950, in Ritscher et al. (eds.), *Das sowjetische Speziallager Nr. 2*, 95.

[64] Wember, *Umerziehung im Lager*, 138.

[65] Besprechung über Lagerseelsorge in Ludwigsburg, 14 Jan. 1946, LKAS, A 126, no. 2272: 151; correspondence of camp pastor Helmut Adamek with relatives and local pastors regarding deaths in the American camps Schwarzenborn and Ziegenhain, ZAEKHN, 6, nos. 17 and 24; Commander, Military Government Hansestadt Hamburg, to Burgomaster Hamburg, Subj. Internees – Deaths, 20 Mar. 1946, and Commander, Military Government Hansestadt Hamburg, to Burgomaster, Subj. Civilian Internees – Deaths, 12 Feb. 1946, StAH, 131-1 II, no. 607: 19 and 547.

Württemberg and Chair of the Council of the Evangelical Church in Germany (EKD), Theophil Wurm, visited every American camp in and around Ludwigsburg, and the Catholic Archbishop of Munich and Freising, Cardinal Michael von Faulhaber, opened a camp chapel in the SS compound at Dachau.[66] External camp priests were admitted and appointed to most western camps, an exception being the American war-crimes enclosure at Stuttgart-Zuffenhausen. In some cases, such as Neuengamme, this happened as early as summer 1945, but in several others not until spring 1946. The priests were important conduits of information and illicit messages between internees and their families, especially before correspondence was permitted but also thereafter. From 1946 church welfare organizations also accessed the camps to provide material support and even organized legal advice for internees.[67]

Church access was only one element of the western-zone camps' greater transparency and integration into German society. From the beginning, the western powers engaged more openly than the Soviets with secular German authorities at local and regional level on a range of questions relating to internment. For instance, they accepted and some-times acted on petitions for release from regional governments.[68] In later years, German state authorities and other organizations were charged with 'reeducating' or retraining internees (on which more shortly), so public figures including local politicians or academics visited the camps to give talks, while civilian theatre groups and music ensembles also performed before internees.[69] Journalists visited the camps more fre-quently in the American than the British zone, where there was a prefer-ence for allowing local mayors rather than local media into the camps. In general, the Americans' transfer of responsibility for camp administration

---

[66] Evangelischer Oberkirchenrat Stuttgart, re: Seelsorge an den Zivilgefangenen, 18 Dec. 1945, LKAS, A 126, no. 2272: 89; Pater Roth, Monatsbericht für Dezember 1945, 2 Jan. 1946, AEM, GV-REG Akz. 28/10, no. 0744/1.

[67] Oberkirchenrat Stuttgart to pastor Fries, Wiesbaden, 1 Apr. 1946, LKAS, A 126, no. 2273: 138; Andrew H. Beattie, 'Die alliierte Internierung im besetzten Deutschland und die deutsche Gesellschaft: Vergleich der amerikanischen und der sowjetischen Zone', Zeitschrift für Geschichtswissenschaft 62, no. 3 (2014), 244, 254; Andrew H. Beattie, '"Lobby for the Nazi Elite"? The Protestant Churches and Civilian Internment in the British Zone of Occupied Germany, 1945–1948', German History 35, no. 1 (2017), 43–70; Wember, Umerziehung im Lager, 139; Möhler, 'Internierungslager in der französischen Besatzungszone', 58; Möhler, Entnazifizierung in Rheinland-Pfalz und im Saarland, 368, 372; Grohnert, Entnazifizierung in Baden, 168.

[68] See, for example, correspondence between the mayor of Hamburg and British military government, including Rudolf Petersen to 609 Det. MG, 31 Aug. 1945, and Col. R. C. Allhusen to Petersen, 29 Sep. 1945, StAH, 131-1 II, no. 607: 3–4, 5–6, and further correspondence in the same file.

[69] Horn, Internierungs- und Arbeitslager, 199; Wember, Umerziehung im Lager, 170–1, 173; Ehresmann, 'Die frühe Nachkriegsnutzung', 26.

to the German state governments increased German involvement and interest in the camps. Indeed, the nascent German 'public' there assumed a control function that was performed in the British case largely by the British public, including members of parliament, ecclesiastical leaders, and the press.[70] Either way, not only did various Germans have some access to western camps, but internees were also able to leave the camps in certain circumstances, beyond individual furlough. For instance, internee choirs sometimes performed at services in nearby churches.[71]

One should not exaggerate the Americans' transparency, however, as their repeated refusal to grant the Red Cross access to camps in their zone demonstrates. In early 1946, an ICRC delegate in Frankfurt/Main was given permission to visit the camps of the US 3rd and 7th armies, but this was rescinded in June. Headquarters of US Forces, European Theater, granted ICRC delegations the right to inspect American POW camps but expressly disallowed access to civilian internment camps in Germany. Although some senior figures in the American military government were sympathetic, the top leadership – including Clay, who became Military Governor in early 1947 – repeatedly rebuffed the ICRC's entreaties in late 1946 and 1947. The Americans argued that the camps would soon be – and later that they had been – transferred to German authority and that, as they operated under German law (the Liberation Law), they were a domestic matter of no concern to the ICRC. A further argument was that, as Clay put it, there was 'too much need for relief for non-Nazi Germans to bring attention to relief for assistance of Nazis'. Although Schoebener claims (without evidence) that the Americans relented shortly after receiving an ICRC memorandum in February 1947, evidence from the ICRC archives indicates the opposite. The Americans' only concession, in May 1947, was to grant access to the internment camps they themselves administered. As the ICRC noted, this was almost meaningless as by this time virtually no camps remained in American hands, although inspections ensued in Dachau, parts of which were still under US control.[72] After Clay affirmed

---

[70] Wember, *Umerziehung im Lager*, 142–3, 218–20; Beattie, 'Die alliierte Internierung', 249–53.

[71] Horn, *Internierungs- und Arbeitslager*, 200; Lindner, 'Das ehemalige KZ Neuengamme', 86; Klose, 'Internierungs- und Arbeitslager Regensburg', 47.

[72] Most of the correspondence on this is in ICRC Special Delegation Berlin, Memorandum Concerning Visits of Civilian Internment Enclosures Located in the US Zone of Germany by Delegates of the International Committee of the Red Cross, 4 Jun. 1947, ACICR, B G 44 02-054.04. For the Clay quotation and Schoebener's incorrect claim, see Schoebener, 'Dokumentation einer Kontroverse', 144, 146. Cf. Dolan, 'Isolating Nazism', 159–61, 169–70, 211–13, 254.

his 'definite no' to accessing German-administered camps in June, the ICRC appealed in October to the American Red Cross to intervene with relevant authorities in the United States, to no avail. There, too, the view prevailed that 'German detention camps' had nothing to do with the 1929 Geneva Convention or the ICRC. After receiving this news in April 1948, the ICRC effectively gave up.[73]

For their part, the German state governments were keen for independent inspections of the camps they now administered as well as for possible material aid that Red Cross involvement might bring. They wanted to avoid the public relations fallout of denying the Red Cross access, as had happened with Nazi concentration camps. Inspections of some individual German-administered camps did occur in 1946–7 because the state governments granted permission without the knowledge of the Office of Military Government, United States (OMGUS), which forbad them from doing so once it found out.[74] The American position was rather paradoxical: on the one hand, saying the camps were a German matter (which overlooked the continuation of automatic arrest and further American involvement) and, on the other, insisting on their own right to veto access. Yet their approach was at least consistent: in Austria, where the camps remained under direct US control, the ICRC was allowed to inspect American civilian internment camps in the second half of 1946.[75]

The Americans' refusal in Germany put them at odds with the British and French and on par with the Soviets. By October 1945, ICRC delegations had already visited five camps and one prison in the French zone (having been denied access only to the war-criminals prison in Germersheim), and they continued to inspect French camps in the following years. In June 1946 British military government granted the Red Cross full access to any camp at any time, and by July ICRC delegates had visited several British camps. In contrast, the ICRC was never allowed to inspect the Soviet camps.[76]

---

[73] Meyer to ICRC Central Agency for POWs, 26 Jun. 1947, ACICR, B G 44 02-054.06; Gallopin to Gower, 17 Oct. 1947 and 4 May 1948; Gower to Gallopin, 2 Apr. 1948, ACICR, B G 44 02-055.
[74] See ICRC Special Delegation Berlin, Memorandum Concerning Visits of Civilian Internment Enclosures, 4 Jun. 1947, ACICR, B G 44 02-054.04. Cf. Schoebener, 'Dokumentation einer Kontroverse'; Dolan, 'Isolating Nazism', 159–61, 169–70, 211–13.
[75] Dohle and Eigelsberger, *Camp Marcus W. Orr*, 39.
[76] Möhler, *Entnazifizierung in Rheinland-Pfalz und im Saarland*, 372, 383–4; Legal Division, Penal Branch, Civilian Internment Camp Instruction No. 10, 26 Jun. 1946, TNA, FO 1050/1522; Charles Steffen, Délégué du CICR, Vlotho, to Division des Prisonniers, internés et civils, 17 Jul. 1946, ACICR, B G 44 02-056.04; for the Soviet zone, see the

Internees' Families

As reference has been made to the issue of contact between internees and their families, it is worth considering families' situations further before proceeding with the discussion of internees' own treatment. The differing western and Soviet approaches to communication were an important but not the only variable affecting how families were impacted by their loved ones' detention. The almost complete lack of contact with, and information about, Soviet-zone internees was a major source of anguish for their families. In August 1948, the father of an internee arrested as a forty-year old in 1945 and believed to be in Mühlberg reported to the Bishop of the Evangelical-Lutheran Church of Saxony, Hugo Hahn, that worrying about their son had turned his wife into a 'skeleton'; the family's agony continued when they received reports that their son had died but could not get official confirmation.[77] In contrast, familial anguish was reduced in the western zones by correspondence, visits, and furlough, and by the fact that it generally became clear by early or mid-1946 that western-zone internees were not being badly treated. Yet such advantages were unevenly distributed. Families living in the regional vicinity of the camps where their loved ones were detained, or at least in the same occupation zone, were in a much better position to visit and correspond than those living further away or in a different zone, who were generally unable to visit, certainly unable to be visited by the internee, and less able to correspond or send packages.[78]

There were further reasons for some families being more severely affected than others. Internees' age and life-stage altered the impact. Those with young children and/or with aged or infirm parents or spouses were arguably more severely missed – or missed for more reasons – than those without such dependents. Socioeconomic factors also affected internment's impact on families. Interned farmers' or bakers' families, for instance, could try, with difficulty, to continue the family business, whereas salaried employees' families were left without income. Families' housing situations also varied considerably. Many had no real home, given the huge numbers of people who had either fled or been expelled

---

file 'Camps et prisons de la zone soviétique – Correspondence générale' (1946–51), ACICR, B G 44 02-057.03.

[77] A. W. to Hahn, 5 Aug. 1948, Landeskirchenarchiv Dresden (LKAD), 3, no. 42: 76, and subsequent letters in the following weeks: 83–4.

[78] See Vergessen hinter Stacheldraht: Zur Lage und Rechtsnot der in der britischen Zone beheimateten Internierten im Internierungslager Moosburg/Oberbayen, n.d. [ca. April 1947] and further correspondence on the issue, Niedersächsisches Landesarchiv Hanover (NLAH), Nds. 170, no. 855.

from Central and Eastern Europe or whose homes had been destroyed in the war, especially by Allied bombing, while others were evicted by Allied or German authorities.[79]

Indeed, some internees and their relatives believed that internees' families were specifically targeted for eviction and other punitive measures, but this was not generally the case. In August 1945 internees in the Bad Aibling camp in the US zone complained to Cardinal Faulhaber that their 'families are in boundless misery, their accounts are blocked, their apartments are taken'.[80] In March 1946, the wife of a civil servant interned in the British zone bemoaned to the head of the Westphalian evangelical church, Karl Koch, that internees' accounts were blocked and houses confiscated and that no one offered the families help: 'on the contrary, one doesn't forget to harass them in every possible way, to throw them out of their apartments and other such things'.[81] Yet there was no systematic eviction of internees' families. The situation in Lübbecke, where the woman who wrote to Koch lived, was unusually bad because the British control commission was quartered there, necessitating a high degree of requisitioning for British personnel, and practical considerations were generally foremost in requisitioners' minds, not whether an occupant or owner had been interned. Similarly, in July internees in the British camp at Neumünster-Gadeland who identified themselves as 'former National Socialists from Hamburg' wrote to the Mayor of Hamburg, Rudolf Petersen, objecting to the apparent fate of their wives and children, who they claimed were being 'harassed' unnecessarily by being turned out of their homes: 'The mere fact that their husbands and fathers are in British captivity prompts the Housing Office to proceed most inconsiderately.'[82] Even if there was some

---

[79] For a range of 'hardship cases' reflecting diverse and often tragic familial situations as collected and depicted by Protestant camp pastors in Württemburg in early 1947, see LKAS, A 126, no. 2276: 54–65, 76–7. On the housing situation and requisitioning, see Francis Graham-Dixon, *The Allied Occupation of Germany: The Refugee Crisis, Denazification, and the Path to Reconstruction* (London: I. B. Tauris, 2013), 153–9; Margarete Myers Feinstein, 'All under One Roof: Persecutees, DPs, Expellees and the Housing Shortage in Occupied Germany', *Holocaust and Genocide Studies* 32, no. 1 (2018), 29–48.

[80] Seventeen signatories from the Gefangenenlager Bad Aibling to Cardinal Faulhaber, 16 Aug. 1945, AEM, NL Faulhaber, no. 8595.

[81] M. S. to Leitung der Evgl. Kiche für Westfalen, Koch, 18 Mar. 1946, Landeskirchliches Archiv Bielefeld (LKAB), 0.0 neu A, no. 3233. See Bettina Blum, '"My Home, Your Castle": British Requisitioning of German Homes in Westphalia', in Camilo Erlichman and Christopher Knowles (eds.), *Transforming Occupation in the Western Zones of Germany: Politics, Everyday Life, and Social Interactions, 1945–55* (London: Bloomsbury, 2018), 115–32.

[82] Die Internierten Hamburgs im I. Civilian Internment Camp Neumünster to Bürgermeister Petersen, 1 Jul. 1946, StAH, 131-1 II, no. 607: 21–2.

hostility from the new authorities, these evictions were more likely the result of widespread requisitioning for a large planned (but ultimately abandoned) enclave for British occupation personnel that affected significant sections of the population and by no means targeted just the families of internees.[83] Certainly, in many places German authorities seized housing stock and household goods from compromised households and redistributed them to politically unincriminated, often bombed-out citizens; but internees' families were not targeted for such measures because the former were interned; rather, both internment and requisitions were due to purported Nazi activism.[84] Apart from early American and British restrictions on bank accounts, internees' families *as such* did not systematically suffer further punitive measures. Instead they shared in the diverse and widespread tribulations facing the German population in these difficult years, which the absence of, and worry about, their interned loved ones only exacerbated. Indeed, whatever advantages certain families enjoyed vis-à-vis others, they all faced practical, emotional, and other difficulties arising simply from the separation and absence inherent in internment, which took its toll even where conditions were best. By the winter of 1947–8, the Protestant churches in the western zones were concerned that many internees' families were 'at the end of their material resources and their spiritual strength' and needed 'concerted assistance', and the churches sought to help where they could.[85]

Work

Although securing a reparatory labour force had been a key consideration in wartime policy discussions, work was not as central a feature of internment as one might expect. To be sure, to the extent that it did not forget about them, Moscow viewed its detainees as a potential labour source even after the cessation of mass deportations in April 1945. When SMAD and the MVD suggested releasing a large number of internees in late 1946, the Soviet government responded by ordering the deportation to the USSR of 27,500 inmates in exchange for POWs in the Soviet Union who were no longer capable of work. Yet only ca. 4,500 physically

---

[83] Knowles, *Winning the Peace*, 114–15.

[84] Stanciu's study suggests that the households of Berlin city councilors and NSDAP District Leaders were affected by confiscation by east and west Berlin authorities. Stanciu, *'Alte Kämpfer'*, 403–5, 407.

[85] Bishop Schöffel to Pfarrämter der ev.-luth. Landeskirche Hamburg, 9 Jan. 1948, Landeskirchliches Archiv Kiel (LKAK), 32.01, no. 1566. See Beattie, '"Lobby for the Nazi Elite"?', 61.

fit inmates could be found in the Special Camps.[86] In total, between 5% and 10% of the German inmates were deported.[87] More extensive deportations were thus prevented by the appalling conditions in the camps, but also because many internees were in poor health to begin with. Of those arrested by 15 April 1945 under Order No. 0016, only half were fit for physical work. In August 1947, 57% of surviving internees were older than forty-five and 50% were regarded as sick.[88]

In the internment camps in occupied Germany (and Austria) work was often seen as a privilege as it helped to reduce monotony and boredom and entailed higher rations. This was particularly the case – and especially crucial – in the Soviet camps, where only approximately 10% of inmates held some camp function or belonged to a work detail.[89] The Allies' desire to isolate internees and prevent escapes meant that labour deployment outside the camps was limited, especially in the Soviet and British zones. As a result, work there was largely restricted to meeting the camps' own operational needs. In all zones, some internees performed work for outside contractors: in the British case, some made toys for the Young Men's Christian Association (YMCA); in Hohenschönhausen, there was a dedicated work camp where inmates with mechanical skills repaired vehicles for the NKVD/MVD.[90] Only in the American and French zones were external work commandos used to any considerable extent. French-zone internees were employed earliest and most extensively beyond the camps' confines. In autumn 1945, most internees in all but one camp inspected by the ICRC were working externally, mainly in

[86] Possekel, 'Sowjetische Lagerpolitik', 73.
[87] Greiner claims only 5% were deported, but this ignores those transferred to POW status, many of whom were deported. Greiner, *Suppressed Terror*, 40; von Plato, 'Zur Geschichte des sowjetischen Speziallagersystems', 44.
[88] 'Schreiben des Volkskommissars für Inneres Berija an Stalin', 17 Apr. 1945, and 'Bericht des Leiters der SMAD-Verwaltung für Inneres "Über den Zustand der Speziallager und Gefängnisse des MVD in Deutschland"', 15 Aug. 1947, both in Possekel (ed.), *Sowjetische Dokumente*, 176, 305. Cf. Natalja Jeske, 'Versorgung, Krankheit, Tod in den Speziallagern', in von Plato (ed.), *Studien und Berichte*, 193–5.
[89] Horn, *Internierungs- und Arbeitslager*, 147, 209. Until summer 1948 SMT convicts were confined to their barracks and were thus effectively banned from working. Their absence in Buchenwald may explain why between 10% and 20% of inmates there had some form of occupation, although in Mühlberg the proportion was only ca. 10%. Greiner, *Suppressed Terror*, 151–2, 187–8; Ritscher, 'Speziallager Nr. 2 Buchenwald', 309; Kilian, 'Speziallager Nr. 1 Mühlberg', 284; von Plato, 'Zur Geschichte des sowjetischen Speziallagersystems', 36.
[90] Wember, *Umerziehung im Lager*, 133–6; Hüser, *'Unschuldig' in britischer Lagerhaft?*, 68–9; Haritonow, 'Zur Geschichte des Speziallagers in Bautzen', 342–4; Peter Erler, 'Krankheit und Sterben in sowjetischer Lagerhaft: Die Toten von Berlin-Hohenschönhausen', in Stiftung Gedenkstätte Berlin-Hohenschönhausen (ed.), *Totenbuch*, 88–90, 103–5.

rubble-clearing work and road construction. In summer 1946 most internees in the Saarland were engaged in clearing work, and French military government had already regulated the distribution of their pay. In September 1948, 47% of internees nominally held at the Diez camp in Rhineland-Palatinate were not actually living there as they were employed in external work details. In Austria, too, the French made considerable use of smaller external labour deployments in a range of industries.[91] In the US zone in Germany, Horn suggests, only between 30% and 50% of internees were members of internal or external work details in 1946 and 1947. From early 1947 onward, under German administration, they were employed in substantial numbers by private firms, again mainly in rubble-clearing and construction work. But inadequate quantity and quality of guards frequently limited and interrupted their deployment. The German denazification ministries were particularly keen for internees to work and introduced an obligation, if not a compulsion, to do so, both for internees and especially for labour-camp convicts. In February 1948 the Bavarian State Office for Labour Camps, which ran the internment and labour camps, claimed that all fit internees were deployed externally, while unfit internees were engaged internally.[92] In Hesse at least, by this point, a portion of the pay the denazification ministry received for internees' work was transferred to their families or kept in an account for those without families.[93] In all zones, outside work provided opportunities for illicit contact with relatives and others, such that the limitation of external work details in the British and Soviet zones contributed to internees' greater isolation there relative to the American and French zones. Internees nevertheless exploited rare

---

[91] Camps d'internés civils, politiques et administratifs, 6 Oct. 1945, ACICR, B G 44 02-058.01; Möhler, *Entnazifizierung in Rheinland-Pfalz und im Saarland*, 41 (n. 49), 372; Resmini, 'Lager der Besatzungsmächte', 616. Cf. Fässler et al., 'Hauptstadt ohne Brot', 383–4; Eisterer, *Französische Besatzungspolitik*, 193, 201–2.

[92] Horn, *Internierungs- und Arbeitslager*, 209–17; Protokoll über die Besprechung der Abteilungsleiter, 2 Feb. 1948, BHStA, MSo, no. 0009; Hesse, *Konstruktionen der Unschuld*, 214; Müller, 'Internierungslager in und um Ludwigsburg', 185–7. Cf. Sauer, *Demokratischer Neubeginn*, 168. On the use of internees in rubble-clearing work, which was relatively limited compared with other groups, see Treber, *Mythos Trümmerfrauen*, 92–5. On the postwar politics of voluntary, conscription, and forced labour, see Caitlin E. Murdock, 'A Gulag in the Erzgebirge? Forced Labor, Political Legitimacy, and Eastern German Uranium Mining in the Early Cold War, 1946–1949', *Central European History* 47, no. 4 (2014), 791–821.

[93] See Wilhelm Pressel, Hilfswerk der evangelischen Landeskirche Württemberg, to Befreiungsministerium Stuttgart, 9 Apr. 1948, LKAS, A 126, no. 2285: 200; Protokoll über die 32. Sitzung des Entnazifizierungsausschuss beim Länderrat der amerikanischen Zone, 20 Jul. 1948, 6, BHStA, MSo, 0034; and the file Lohnregelung Internierter, HStAS, EA 6/003, no. 2305. Cf. Horn, *Internierungs- und Arbeitslager*, 214; Meyer, *Entnazifizierung von Frauen*, 141.

opportunities such as those provided in winter by wood-chopping expeditions for the British camp at Eselheide.[94]

Reeducation and Recreation

It is often assumed that the Allies should have tried, or did try, to 'reeducate' and democratize internees, but the extent to which they attempted to do so is contested. Horn asserts, 'When you hear the word "internment camp", you think about the re-education of the former "activists" of the Third Reich'; she argues, however, that very little was actually done in this regard in Bavaria.[95] This is another plank in her highly critical depiction of US internment. In contrast, Meyer supports her overwhelmingly positive account by arguing that more was done in Bavaria and even more in the other US-zone states than Horn recognizes. Meyer also interprets the Americans' humane treatment of internees as a form of democratization. Whether adequate rations really qualify as evidence of an 'intention to democratization', as Meyer claims, is debatable, but introducing a degree of democratic self-governance surely counts.[96] Wember similarly interprets British concern to treat internees with respect and, later, to grant them a degree of autonomy and self-governance as a form of democratic reorientation, but he argues that more direct forms of reeducation were contemplated only very late.[97]

The lack of earlier and more concerted efforts is partly attributable to limited resources, but it primarily reflected the Allies' shared belief that internees – regarded as active, committed Nazis – were impossible to reeducate. This view was exemplified by the January 1945 memorandum by British Secretary of State for Foreign Affairs Anthony Eden, quoted in Chapter 2. The same views held sway in relation to Austria. According to the head of intelligence in British military government there in March 1946:

> The Nazis we arrest or dismiss are temporarily lost to society and we must accept that. We are only concerned with making sure that they have no influence in the new Austria. It would be a mistake to assume that they could by and large be converted and it would be inviting trouble to give such persons employment or expect them to become loyal.[98]

---

[94] Siedenhans and Eimer, 'Internierungslager Eselheide', 75; Möhler, 'Internierungslager in der französischen Besatzungszone', 58.

[95] Horn, *Internierungs- und Arbeitslager*, 16. Cf. Niethammer, *Mitläuferfabrik*, 458; Lenzer, *Frauen im Speziallager Buchenwald*, 152–3.

[96] Meyer, *Entnazifizierung von Frauen*, 19, 248.   [97] Wember, *Umerziehung im Lager*, 20.

[98] H. B. Hitchens (Intelligence Organisation), Note for Director Internal Affairs Division, 12 Mar. 1946, cited by Beer, 'Die britische Entnazifizierung', 419. See also 406.

As suggested by the complete absence of reeducation among the numerous goals associated with internment that were discussed in Chapter 1, the aim was not to reeducate, reorientate, or denazify the internees themselves but to denazify German society and allow for its reeducation and reorientation precisely by removing and isolating internees.

As a result, especially in the Soviet zone but also in the western zones in the early months and even years, many internees were condemned to idleness. As Harold Marcuse puts it, they suffered less from 'mistreatment, overwork and intentional physical abuse' than from 'inactivity and neglect'.[99] Such neglect was most severe in the Soviet camps, where it extended to spiritual and cultural matters and where there was no attempt at reeducation or democratization. Indeed, there was barely any effort to inform internees about current affairs, until Soviet-licensed newspapers were distributed from late 1947, as already mentioned. Moreover, all religious activity was forbidden until Christmas 1947. Writing, singing, and possessing books were prohibited, and transgressions were often punished severely. Playing chess was permitted, as were occasional theatrical and musical performances, often by interned professional actors, directors, and musicians, but they were usually for the benefit of Soviet personnel, not fellow inmates. Otherwise, Soviet-zone internees were condemned to idleness and boredom, which many sought to escape through illicit reading, discussion circles, and handicrafts, to the extent that space, hunger, cold, illness, and a lack of materials allowed.[100]

In the western camps there was somewhat less neglect and no enforced idleness. Indeed, British military government believed internees should not be idle. Early on, films showing the results of Nazi concentration-camp atrocities were screened in some British and American camps (as late as May 1946 at Marcus W. Orr), and proceedings of the IMT, or at least its judgement, were broadcast via camp radio.[101] Yet few further attempts at historical or political reeducation ensued until 1947. Even

---

[99] Marcuse, 'Afterlife of the Camps', 191.
[100] 'Provisional Order about the Special Camps of the NKVD', 27 Jul. 1945, in Morsch and Reich (eds.), *Sowjetisches Speziallager in Sachsenhausen*, 316–17; Ritscher, *Spezlager Nr. 2 Buchenwald*, 95–6; Greiner, *Suppressed Terror*, 197; von Plato, 'Zur Geschichte des sowjetischen Speziallagersystems', 36; Kilian, 'Speziallager Nr. 1 Mühlberg', 284; Ritscher, 'Speziallager Nr. 2 Buchenwald', 309–11; Erler, 'Speziallager Nr. 3 in Hohenschönhausen', 327; Lutz Prieß, 'Das Speziallager des NKVD Nr. 6 Jamlitz', in von Plato (ed.), *Studien und Berichte*, 371–2.
[101] Wember, *Umerziehung im Lager*, 134, 167–77; Siedenhans and Eimer, 'Internierungslager Eselheide', 74–5; Horn, *Internierungs- und Arbeitslager*, 201–2, 204–5; Meyer, *Entnazifizierung von Frauen*, 142; Weckel, *Beschämende Bilder*, 20; Dohle and Eigelsberger, *Camp Marcus W. Orr*, 230.

then, efforts varied considerably among British camps and American-zone states. Although the British generally sought to avoid controversial political discussions, both at Neuengamme and in the German-administered camps in the US zone, especially in Hesse and Württemberg-Baden, external speakers gave talks on topical issues.[102] Until then, and in the French zone throughout, internees were left either to their own devices or to the churches. The western powers permitted and to some extent promoted an extensive range of internee-run, rather apolitical cultural, educational, and recreational pursuits, including internee theatres, choirs, orchestras, talks, discussion circles, libraries, and sport. From 1947 they encouraged more or less formalized courses on all manner of practical, vocational, and scientific topics with a view to internees' eventual reintegration into German social and economic life.[103] The offerings were so extensive and, due to the presence of numerous interned academics and other experts, of such quality that there was talk of veritable 'camp universities'. It is generally agreed that much cultural activity was entertaining rather than educational, that educational activities were oriented largely towards vocational or general education rather than historical-political reflection and learning, and that internment did not promote much insight into individual guilt and responsibility for Nazism.[104]

Explicit discussion of the Nazi past was limited, but there were other forms of what is probably better described as democratic reorientation than 'reeducation'. They included the creation of internee-run camp newspapers to promote the open exchange of information, ideas, and opinions and the introduction of limited self-governance and democratic elections for leadership positions in internee self-administrations. These measures were far from universal and did not always achieve the desired results, for instance, when internees elected former NSDAP District or Gau Leaders as their representatives. Such developments gave rise to fears that the camps were 'colleges of National Socialism' that if anything renazified rather than denazified internees, concerns that were also heard

---

[102] Meyer, *Entnazifizierung von Frauen*, 180–95; Horn, *Internierungs- und Arbeitslager*, 193–5; Schuster, *Entnazifizierung in Hessen*, 250–8; Wember, *Umerziehung im Lager*, 172–7.
[103] Wember, *Umerziehung im Lager*, 201–15; Ehresmann, 'Die frühe Nachkriegsnutzung', 29; Horn, *Internierungs- und Arbeitslager*, 192–204; Müller, 'Internierungslager in und um Ludwigsburg', 180; Meyer, *Entnazifizierung von Frauen*, 136–9.
[104] Meyer, *Entnazifizierung von Frauen*, 137; Horn, *Internierungs- und Arbeitslager*, 204; Heinl, '"Das schlimme Lager"', 72–3; Wember, *Umerziehung im Lager*, 72; Strauß, 'Zwischen Apathie und Selbstrechtfertigung', 307–9; Fulbrook, *Reckonings*, 210. In contrast, Merten creates the impression that western-zone internees were reeducated. Merten, *Gulag in East Germany*, 30, 34.

in Austria.[105] The western camps were thus sites of extensive religious and cultural activity, vocational and general learning, and to a lesser extent political discussion and reorientation, but not systematic reeducation.

Conditions

Conditions were extremely poor in camps everywhere at the beginning, but the degree to, and speed with, which they improved differed considerably across and within the various zones. Most accounts stress the 'primitive', 'extremely harsh', and even 'catastrophic' initial conditions, but that the western powers took effective steps to ameliorate the situation.[106] In general, conditions improved in most American and French camps in late 1945 or early 1946, in British camps in early to mid-1946, and in Soviet camps in 1948, although improvements were not linear, due to transfers of internees as well as supply and seasonal problems. Even after these points, heating, sanitary facilities, and other conditions, including internees' clothing, remained unsatisfactory in some western camps and systematically inadequate in the Soviet zone.[107] The western Allies and the German authorities in the US zone were concerned to avoid comparisons with Nazi concentration camps and succeeded in creating conditions that made such comparisons or equations baseless (even if this did not prevent such comparisons being drawn).[108] According to Benz, 'Certainly, the conditions of detention in the most miserable internment camp were still a thousand times better than they had been in National Socialist forced-labour camps, to say nothing of the concentration camps.'[109] Such a view has some merit, although there

[105] Karl-Georg Egel, 'Besuch bei internierten Nationalsozialisten', *Nordwestdeutsche Hefte* 2, no. 2 (1947), 38–9; Ehresmann, 'Die frühe Nachkriegsnutzung', 28–9; Wember, *Umerziehung im Lager*, 195; Beßmann, '"Der sozusagen für Euch alle im KZ sitzt"', 44, 50; Müller, 'Internierungslager in und um Ludwigsburg', 178; Horn *Internierungs- und Arbeitslager*, 164–70, 205, 239; Heinl, '"Das schlimme Lager"', 54–6; Eisterer, *Französische Besatzungspolitik*, 211. On camp newspapers, see Angelika Steinmaus-Pollak, 'Der "Lagerspiegel", Zeitung der Insassen des Internierungs- und Arbeitslagers Regensburg', *Verhandlungen des Historischen Vereins für Oberpfalz und Regensburg* 144 (2004), esp. 94–5.

[106] Wember, *Umerziehung im Lager*, 55, 59, 69, 80, 109–10; Horn, *Internierungs- und Arbeitslager*, 53, 218–19; Eckert, 'Entnazifizierung', 249.

[107] Möhler, 'Internierung im Rahmen der Entnazifizierungspolitik', 63; Wember, *Umerziehung im Lager*, 109, 132–3, 74; Strauß, 'Zwischen Apathie und Selbstrechtfertigung', 301–2; Horn, *Internierungs- und Arbeitslager*, 146, 184–6.

[108] Strauß, *Kriegsgefangenschaft und Internierung*, 396; Strauß, 'Zwischen Apathie und Selbstrechtfertigung', 313; Meyer, *Entnazifizierung von Frauen*, 110, 124–5, 174–5; Beattie, 'Die alliierte Internierung', 250, 254, 255.

[109] Benz, *Zwischen Hitler und Adenauer*, 120.

were considerable variations among Nazi camps, especially over time. More problematically, however, Benz's generalization does not do justice to the severe differences that emerged between the western and the Soviet camps. As Greiner argues, the variation between the US-zone and Soviet camps in particular 'could not have been more pronounced'.[110]

The nature of internees' accommodation varied markedly not just between the zones but also within them. Perhaps the greatest intra-zonal variance was found in the American zone. In Württemberg-Baden most internment camps had stone barracks; in Bavaria most had wooden barracks; but in the largest camp in the zone, at Darmstadt in Hesse, the vast majority of internees lived in tents until summer 1947, which was particularly problematic in winter. A report by Red Cross delegates who inspected the camp (without OMGUS permission) in February 1947 found the state of internees' clothing to be 'wretched' and the sanitary facilities 'most primitive', but it was most concerned about the tents.[111] In the British zone, poorly insulated steel Nissen huts frequently supplemented barracks.[112] In the French zone, several camps including Idar-Oberstein (also known as Algenrodt) and Binsenthal had wooden barracks, but Landau had stone barracks.[113] Most Soviet camps had wooden or stone barracks, but in the Bautzen and Torgau-Fort Zinna prison camps inmates were held in stone cells (supplemented by wooden barracks). Overcrowding was endemic, particularly in the Soviet zone. In Ketschendorf, up to 10,000 internees were crammed into what had been built as accommodation for 500 people, with most sleeping on the bare floor until the first half of 1946.[114] Whatever form it took, the accommodation was generally poorly heated, if at all, and most internees, especially those arrested in summer clothes in 1945, were ill-equipped to withstand winter. They were generally provided with one blanket in the British and French zones, three in the American zone, but none in the Soviet zone in some camps until 1947, and the winter of 1946–7 was one of the coldest on record. At Christmas 1946, temperatures of between

---

[110] Greiner, *Suppressed Terror*, 350.
[111] Horn, *Internierungs- und Arbeitslager*, 146–7; Heinl, '"Das schlimme Lager"', 43; Strauß, *Kriegsgefangenschaft und Internierung*, 392; Civilian Internee Camp, Darmstadt: Visited on February 6 and 13, 1947, by M.M. J. A. Rickli and R. H. Frank, 2–3, ACICR, B G 044 02-55. Cf. Schoebener, 'Dokumentation einer Kontroverse', 147–8.
[112] Hüser, *'Unschuldig' in britischer Lagerhaft?*, 38–9.
[113] Camps d'internés civils, politiques et administratifs, 6 Oct. 1945, ACICR, B G 44 02-058.01
[114] Knabe, *Tag der Befreiung?*, 305; Weigelt, 'Sterben und Tod', 161.

$-2°C$ and $-6°C$ were recorded in barracks at the Regensburg camp in the American zone.[115]

The most important factor, however, was food, and here radical differences developed between the western and the Soviet zones. While internees across the country went hungry and lost weight in summer and autumn 1945, the western Allies took steps to prevent severe malnutrition and starvation. As already mentioned, American-zone internees could receive food parcels early on if their relatives knew where to send them and could afford to do so. At Marcus W. Orr in Austria, internees could receive packages from October 1945, and more than 25,000 arrived every month through to May 1947. Internee doctors regarded them as key to the camp's good, stable nutritional situation. Internees in US-zone camps also benefitted from the Americans' insistence from January 1946 onward that internees receive higher rations than the civilian population (the logic being that they were less able to supplement their rations through other means, including the black market). As a result, in the American zone the nutritional situation was better inside the camps than outside by 1946 at the latest.[116]

In autumn 1945, French-zone internees were supposed to receive roughly the same rations as the civilian population (which the ICRC interpreted as indicating that the French did not consider them as falling under the 1929 Geneva Convention that would have guaranteed them higher POW rations). In the view of the Red Cross, however, the local German officials responsible for provisioning the camps did not display sufficient good will to meet internees' needs, and the rations for working internees were inadequate. The ICRC inspectors claimed that in Landau the rations were just sufficient to stop a man from dying; they feared that internees would eventually resemble the inmates of Nazi concentration camps if current conditions and processing times continued; and they recommended an intervention with the French government. The French closed the Idar-Oberstein camp in early 1946 after an ICRC inspection in December 1945 had found that 14% of internees had nutritional

---

[115] Wember, *Umerziehung im Lager*, 109; Edgar Mais, 'Internierungslager Algenrodt', *Heimatkalender Landkreis Birkenfeld* 30 (1985), 183; Fricke, *Politik und Justiz*, 81; Alexander Häusser and Gordian Maugg, *Hungerwinter: Deutschlands humanitäre Katastrophe 1946/47* (Berlin: List Verlag, 2011); Klose, 'Internierungs- und Arbeitslager Regensburg', 33.

[116] Horn, *Internierungs- und Arbeitslager*, 15, 53, 99, 217–20; Meyer, *Entnazifizierung von Frauen*, 112–20; Strauß, *Kriegsgefangenschaft und Internierung*, 392–8; Dohle and Eigelsberger, *Camp Marcus W. Orr*, 249–50.

oedema and 4% had scurvy; there had been five deaths there from starvation between 19 August and 12 September.[117]

In the British zone, internees were eventually allowed to receive food parcels, especially after a case of starvation in Paderborn-Staumühle in December 1945. When inspections in the spring of 1946 identified further cases of starvation and revealed that internees weighed on average four kilograms – and in Sandbostel nine kilograms – less than the lean civilian population, British military government sought further ways to improve their food intake without officially increasing their rations above those of the civilian population. Camp gardens were developed, and workers' and infirmary rations were distributed to non-working and non-hospitalized internees. As a result, whereas British-zone internees suffered more from hunger than the civilian population in the first post-war winter, the reverse was the case from 1947. Conditions in British camps in Austria were better than in Germany, reflecting the better overall food situation there.[118]

Soviet-zone internees initially were supposed to receive POW-level rations, but following a small reduction in September 1945 their rations were reduced almost by half in November 1946 when the Soviet army succeeded in passing responsibility for provisioning the camps to the SMAD. Slight increases followed in early 1947 and for sick internees again in early 1948. In practice, however, for a range of reasons the ration norms were never fulfilled, food was of poor nutritional quality, and supplements from outside were never allowed. Severe malnutrition combined with exposure to the elements and poor hygiene to cause rampant dystrophy, dysentery, tuberculosis, and typhus, resulting in mass death.[119] If recent research suggests that the reality of hunger in postwar Germany was less severe than widespread German fears about it suggested, malnourishment and cases of starvation in western camps and mass starvation in the Soviet camps indicate that German fears were not merely based on hysterical self-indulgence.[120]

---

[117] Camps d'internés civils, politiques et administratifs, 6 Oct. 1945, 2–4, ACICR, B G 44 02-058.01; Möhler, 'Internierungslager in der französischen Besatzungszone', 58; Möhler, *Entnazifizierung in Rheinland-Pfalz und im Saarland*, 384. Fäßler claims (without evidence) that internees in Lahr-Dinglingen received only 75% of regular civilian-population rations, although those engaged in work received more. Fäßler, 'Lahr unter französischer Besatzung', 199.

[118] Hüser, *'Unschuldig' in britischer Lagerhaft?*, 39–43, 48–9; Wember, *Umerziehung im Lager*, 59, 69, 109–16, 130; Kastner, '373 Camp Wolfsberg', 93.

[119] Greiner, *Suppressed Terror*, 38–9, 182–7; Jeske, 'Versorgung, Krankheit, Tod', 196–223.

[120] See Weinreb, '"For the Hungry Have No Past"'; Jessica Erdelmann, *'Persilscheine' aus der Druckerpresse? Die Hamburger Medienberichterstattung über die Entnazifizierung und*

Medical facilities and treatment also differed starkly between the western and the Soviet camps. The latter were inadequately equipped to cope with tuberculosis and other epidemics, whereas supplies of medical instruments and medicines were better, if variable and often inadequate, in the western zones. There, sick internees who could not be treated adequately in camp infirmaries were generally transferred either to dedicated internee or to regular civilian hospitals, while incurably and terminally ill internees were often released. Such practices were not replicated in the Soviet zone, where the camp infirmaries were in no position to deal with the massive numbers of sick and dying inmates.[121]

Violence and Discipline

As Niethammer argues, 'physical violence and terror played no comparable role' in any Allied internment camps compared with the Nazi concentration camps. Yet this does not mean that the internment experience was devoid of violence. Most physical violence, however, occurred between arrest and arrival in an internment camp. Reports of arrests by all occupying powers indicate that physical beating was widespread, if far from universal. Many arrests following obligatory registrations or during raids by occupation authorities occurred non-violently, if suddenly and unexpectedly. Arrests during the final months of the war and the months immediately thereafter were most likely to be accompanied by violence. However, with the developing Cold War and increased political repression in the Soviet zone, 1947–8 saw increasing instances of arrest-by-kidnapping by Soviet authorities, especially from West Berlin; the targets were more likely to be prosecuted by SMTs for alleged postwar offences than to be interned; similar practices occurred in Soviet-occupied Austria, including Vienna, which like Berlin was under four-power control.[122]

Internierung in der britischen Besatzungszone (Munich: Dölling und Galitz Verlag, 2016), 116, 126.

[121] Wember, *Umerziehung im Lager*, 111–12, 131; Horn, *Internierungs- und Arbeitslager*, 188, 102–6; Strauß, 'Zwischen Apathie und Selbstrechtfertigung', 305–6; Camps d'internés civils, politiques et administratifs, 6 Oct. 1945, 6–7, ACICR, B G 44 02-058.01; Jeske, 'Versorgung, Krankheit, Tod'. For an account of an SS doctor interned in the British zone, see Erich Möllenhoff, *Arzt hinter Stacheldraht: Bericht eines in Westdeutschland internierten deutschen Arztes* (Lindhorst: Askania, 1984).

[122] Niethammer, 'Alliierte Internierungslager (1998)', 112 (quotation), 107–9; Wember, *Umerziehung im Lager*, 38–43, 46; Meyer, *Entnazifizierung von Frauen*, 50–7; Horn, *Internierungs- und Arbeitslager*, 34–45; Müller, 'Internierungslager in und um Ludwigsburg', 172; Fricke, *Politik und Justiz*, 14–15, 29–30, 62–4; Greiner, *Suppressed Terror*, 99–103; Ralph W. Brown III, 'A Cold War Army of Occupation? The Role of USFA in Quadripartite Occupied Vienna 1945–1948', in Ableitinger et al.

Although many of those arrested came more or less directly into an internment camp, others spent days, weeks, and even months in interrogation centres or prisons prior to being transferred to a camp.[123] It was generally in this pre-internment detention that they were most systematically interrogated and most violently treated, especially in the 'GPU cellars', but there are also reports of physical abuse and more rarely of torture in western custody. An inspection of several camps by the ICRC in October 1945 found that one detainee in French custody had been severely beaten.[124] A degree of violence also sometimes accompanied transfers from such locations to internment camps and between the latter in all zones, but again the long marches on foot that many internees in the Soviet zone were forced to undertake were surely worse than their western equivalents.[125] However, with their arrival in the Special Camps, direct physical violence from Soviet personnel largely ceased for Soviet-zone internees. Indeed, after the horrific experiences in the interrogation centres from which so many had come, arriving in an internment camp could seem like arriving in 'paradise'; certainly, most reports do not refer to physical violence at this point.[126] This stands in marked contrast with reports from some western camps, where violent and degrading treatment of new arrivals seems in some cases at least for certain periods – especially from May to July 1945 but even as late as April 1946 – to have constituted a welcome ritual imposed on newly arrived internees.[127]

In some American and British camps this initial violence persisted after arrival, at least through the summer of 1945 and, more

---

(eds.), *Österreich unter alliierter Besatzung*, 359–60; Mulley, 'Befreiung und Besatzung', 375, 392; Karner, 'Zur Politik der sowjetischen Besatzungs- und Gewahrsamsmacht', 414–30.

[123] Wember, *Umerziehung im Lager*, 45, 54–5; Horn, *Internierungs- und Arbeitslager*, 45; Meyer, *Entnazifizierung von Frauen*, 72–3, 79–81.

[124] Fricke, *Politik und Justiz*, 65–8; Greiner, *Suppressed Terror*, 115–17, 124–33; Erler, *GPU-Keller*; Wember, *Umerziehung im Lager*, 87, 96–101; Anhalt and Holz, *Das verbotene Dorf*; Zimmermann, *Staub soll er fressen*, 8–9; *Alliierte Kriegsverbrechen und Verbrechen gegen die Menschlichkeit: Zusammengestellt und bezeugt im Jahre 1946 von Internierten des Lagers 91 Darmstadt* (Kiel: Arndt, 2001 [1st ed. 1953]), 104–15; Camps d'internés civils, politiques et administratifs, 6 Oct. 1945, 3, ACICR, B G 44 02-058.01; Pädagogisches Zentrum des Landes Rheinland-Pfalz, 'Menschen in Lagern an der Nahe und im Hunsrück', *PZ-Informationen*, no. 8: *Geschichte* (1986).

[125] Wember, *Umerziehung im Lager*, 96; Greiner, *Suppressed Terror*, 141–2; Lipinsky, 'Mobilität zwischen den Lagern'; Jeske, 'Versorgung, Krankheit, Tod', 194.

[126] Greiner, *Suppressed Terror*, 116.

[127] See Müller, 'Internierungslager in und um Ludwigsburg', 177–8; 'Entwurf für eine Denkschrift über Vorgänge im Interniertenlager 74', Sep. 1946, HStAS, NL Gottlob Kamm, Q1/16, no. 5; Vogel, *M-AA 509*, 35–7, 39; Wember, *Umerziehung im Lager*, 92–3; Hüser, *'Unschuldig' in britischer Lagerhaft?*, 44–5; Möllenhoff, *Arzt hinter Stacheldraht*, 15–19.

intermittently, beyond that. One contributing factor here was that internees were actually interrogated after arriving in western camps, whereas
internees entering the Soviet camps merely had their details registered
(and any remaining valuables removed), after which the NKVD largely
lost interest in them.[128] Another factor was the early American and
British use at particular camps of guards of other nationalities who
behaved brutally and even lethally, including Belgians at Neuengamme,
Poles at Dachau, and Dutch at Paderborn-Staumühle before the Americans transferred it to the British.[129] Yet American and British personnel
were also brutal in the early stages too, the former seemingly more so
than the latter. There are isolated reports of specific British acts of
violence, including of the commandant of Staumühle hitting a prostrate
internee for refusing to obey an order in December 1945, and some
indications that mistreatment was more widespread.[130] A submission
by internees from November 1946 claimed that 478 internees at Neuengamme had been physically mistreated and that 1,979 had been robbed,
but there are neither reports nor evidence of physical abuse at
Sandbostel.[131] Certainly, both at the time and subsequently, internees
complained vociferously about a wide spectrum of American mistreatment in 1945. It should be noted, however, that American military
authorities also most systematically investigated reports of such behav-
iour with a view to preventing it. Yet a degree of semi-official imprimatur
seems to have accompanied a day of widespread physical abuse in
Marcus W. Orr in March 1946 when new American personnel were
deployed in response to the discovery of an escape tunnel.[132]

---

[128] Wember, *Umerziehung im Lager*, 96; Greiner, *Suppressed Terror*, 143–4; Niethammer, 'Alliierte Internierungslager (1998)', 109–10; Ritscher, *Spezlager Nr. 2 Buchenwald*, 143.

[129] Horn, *Internierungs- und Arbeitslager*, 175; Hüser, '*Unschuldig' in britischer Lagerhaft?*, 31–2; Wember, *Umerziehung im Lager*, 93.

[130] Hüser, '*Unschuldig' in britischer Lagerhaft?*, 42; Wember, *Umerziehung im Lager*, 94–5; Kastner, '373 Camp Wolfsberg', 73.

[131] Hauptlagerführer, No. 6 CIC Neuengamme, to Major Bateman, 19 Nov. 1946, appendix, StAH, Zeitgeschichtliche Sammlung, 731-6 VIII, no. 4. According to a collection of testimony from internees in Neuengamme (prepared for the defence case at the IMT), ca. 30% of inmates of one section of the camp claimed to have been mistreated in some way. Lager I, Erhebungen über Mißhandlungen und Plünderungen, 9 Jul. 1946, StAH, 731-6 VIII, no. 4. Ehresmann, 'Die frühe Nachkriegsnutzung', 26.

[132] See reports from Camp 74 in Ludwigsburg in HStAS, NL Kamm Q1/16, no. 5; Vogel, *M-AA 509*, 36; von Salomon, *Fragebogen*, 544–55, 558–63, 571–2, 585, 606, 613; Horn, *Internierungs- und Arbeitslager*, 161–3, 165, 173–5; Meyer, *Entnazifizierung von Frauen*, 122–5; Wember, *Umerziehung im Lager*, 92–6; Dohle and Eigelsberger, *Camp Marcus W. Orr*, 61–3. Books published by radical right-wing publishers stress and exaggerate violence and torture, e.g., Franz W. Seidler, *Deutsche Opfer: Alliierte Täter*

In contrast, Soviet guards and other camp officials appear to have largely refrained from systematic or arbitrary acts of physical violence or other abuses. As Niethammer argues, 'It is striking in the writings of former internees that they regularly report acts of violence during their arrest and interrogation but hardly any acts of violence from the Soviet camp personnel.' Indeed, the latter's treatment of German inmates appears overwhelmingly 'distant and correct, at times coarse, at times unexpectedly helpful'.[133] Attempts to escape or to establish contact with the outside world and other breaches of camp rules were punished severely, generally through detention in camp prisons, often with reduced rations. This could have fatal consequences, given the already low rations and poor health of internees. Violent punishments were less common.[134] Physical violence was insignificant as a cause of death, although 756 German SMT convicts were executed in the Soviet zone, generally in NKVD prisons, rather than in the camps, with the exceptions of Bautzen and Torgau-Fort Zinna.[135]

In all zones, physical violence was often inflicted by fellow inmates, especially by prisoner-functionaries in the Soviet camps. Every occupying power used internees to manage much of the camps' internal administration and these prisoner-functionaries sometimes used violence to assert their authority and maintain their privileges, especially in the Soviet zone. In Sachsenhausen, prisoner-functionaries of Soviet and Polish nationality apparently maintained 'rule by the stick', that is, a regime of beatings, through to September 1945. After their departure, a predominantly German elite of prisoner-functionaries enjoyed almost unchecked authority over their fellow inmates. Their power rested not least on physical violence, and some were particularly brutal. Greiner speaks of 'mafia-like' characteristics; disagreements and complaints about corruption or mistreatment prompted brutal reprisals, with some victims beaten to death. All of this was tolerated, even desired, by the

---

1945 (Selent: Pour le Mérite, 2013), 287–9. The overall picture here resembles the situation in the Netherlands, where reports of mistreatment prompted investigations that revealed extensive abuse in certain Dutch camps for collaborators, but overwhelmingly correct treatment in others. Grevers and Van Haecke, 'Administrative Internment', 292.

[133] Niethammer, 'Alliierte Internierungslager (1998)', 109.

[134] Ritscher, Spezlager Nr. 2 Buchenwald, 143–5; Greiner, Suppressed Terror, 172–8.

[135] Niethammer, 'Alliierte Internierungslager (1998)', 107–8; Greiner, Suppressed Terror, 157–8. Seventy-three people (including internees as well as SMT convicts) were executed in Bautzen by December 1946, and a number at Torgau-Fort Zinna during its later phase as Special Camp No. 10. Jörg Morré, Totenbuch Speziallager Bautzen 1945–1956 (Bautzen: Stiftung Sächsische Gedenkstätten, 2004), 7; Jeske and Morré, 'Inhaftierung von Tribunalverurteilten', 626, 620; Oleschinski and Pampel, 'Feindliche Elemente sind in Gewahrsam zu halten', 44.

Soviet authorities. The relative lack of violence from Soviet personnel thus does not mean there was no violence in the camps under their control.[136] In the western zones, where death did not become a permanent companion and prospect as it did in the Soviet camps and where prisoner-functionaries were often elected by internees, the former did not (need to) resort to violence against fellow inmates in order to maintain their positions and privileges to the same extent. Meanwhile, offences against camp rules were punished by withdrawal of privileges such as correspondence or visits that did not exist in the Soviet camps.[137]

Ordinary internees were not just passive objects of violence. They sometimes violently resisted their captors and superiors. At Sachsenhausen, internees killed a particularly brutal prisoner-functionary. In the American zone, they occasionally violently resisted attempts by American authorities to remove prisoner-functionaries from their positions or physically attacked German guards who insisted on inspecting packages brought by visitors. Internees also violently punished breaches of informal rules. An internee in an American camp was beaten for eating another internee's spilt food. In the climate of mass starvation in the Soviet camps, theft of food was punished severely; there are reports of offenders being beaten, even to death, and of one being thrown out of a barrack window, upon which camp guards shot him dead.[138] Yet food was not the only cause of inter-internee violence. In Marcus W. Orr, internees twice beat a fellow internee who spoke about democracy in camp radio broadcasts.[139]

Death

The appalling death rate in the Soviet camps undoubtedly constituted their most significant difference from their western counterparts. According to Soviet figures, 42,889 of the 122,671 Germans in the Special Camps died, excluding the 756 who were executed. This represents a death rate of 35%. Although some estimates are as high as 65,000 and even 130,000, the figure of 44,000 is now widely viewed as an approximate minimum of German deaths. This represents 29% of the

---

[136] Greiner, *Suppressed Terror*, 157, 166, 164–5, 176–7.

[137] Wember, *Umerziehung im Lager*, 52–4; Meyer, *Entnazifizierung von Frauen*, 132–6, 163–73; Strauß, *Kriegsgefangenschaft und Internierung*, 382–4. For the disciplinary registers of German-administered camps in Württemberg-Baden in the US zone, see StAL, EL 904, file nos. 9, 28, 42, 65, 134.

[138] Greiner, *Suppressed Terror*, 157, 186–7; Meyer, *Entnazifizierung von Frauen*, 162–5; Horn, *Internierungs- und Arbeitslager*, 219.

[139] Dohle and Eigelsberger, *Camp Marcus W. Orr*, 197.

estimated total of 154,000 German inmates. The numbers varied considerably among the camps, with around 350 dying in each of the two camps in Torgau, ca. 12,000 in Sachsenhausen, and between ca. 3,000 and 7,000 elsewhere.[140] The overall death rate peaked in winter 1946–7, but in individual camps it peaked earlier, in Ketschendorf in early 1946 and in Hohenschönhausen in summer 1945. The death rate was highest in camps such as Ketschendorf and Jamlitz that closed in spring 1947 near the high point of mass death, reaching 33% in the latter. As already mentioned, the vast majority died of hunger-related diseases. In contrast, violent deaths and suicide were proportionally insignificant, the latter accounting for just three of 3,869 identified causes of death (of 4,722 total deaths) in Ketschendorf.[141]

There is a range of views about whether the mass death in the Soviet camps was deliberate. Many former internees assumed that an 'intention to exterminate' them (*Vernichtungsabsicht*) must have been behind the massive death toll in general and the reductions of rations in late 1945 and late 1946 in particular. Yet archival research has found no evidence for such an intention. As a result, most historians are more cautious in their assessments. To be sure, fiercely anti-communist authors such as Knabe speak of the Soviets' 'approving acquiescence' to mass death (*billigend in Kauf genommen*). They argue that the lack of outright intent at best changes the situation from a case of murder to one of negligent homicide, and insist that for the victims it made no difference whether they were killed intentionally or not.[142] Greiner speaks

[140] Greiner, *Suppressed Terror*, 1–3; von Plato, 'Zur Geschichte des sowjetischen Speziallagersystems', 53–5; Jeske, 'Versorgung, Krankheit, Tod', 192–3; Oleschinski and Pampel, *'Feindliche Elemente sind in Gewahrsam zu halten'*, 31, 44. Note, as proportionally fewer Soviet inmates died, the overall death rate for the camps, based on the official figures, was 28% (43,821 of 157,837). Merten claims, 'The German Government now estimates that more than 95,000 people died in the Soviet camps or in transport to them.' Yet the 1992 source he cites actually states, 'The German Government estimated that 65,000 people died in these Soviet-run camps or in transportation to them.' Compare Merten, *Gulag in East Germany*, 2 (and xvi), and Stephen Kinzer, 'Germans Find Mass Graves at an Ex-Soviet Camp', *New York Times*, 24 Sep. 1992. See also Merten, *Gulag in East Germany*, 185, where he misleadingly suggests that his high death figures were 'mostly calculated after the collapse of the GDR', but, as with his figures for the number of internees, his sources are all much older. Cf. n. 30 in Chapter 3 above.

[141] Weigelt, 'Sterben und Tod', 158, 189, 169; Erler, 'Krankheit und Sterben', 105. Yet in his foreword to Merten's book, Erik J. Schmaltz suggests that 'torture and executions ... [led] to mortality rates in the special camps that were much higher than those in the western sectors'. Erik J. Schmaltz, 'Foreword: Stalinism Exported Abroad', in Merten, *Gulag in East Germany*, xviii.

[142] Knabe, *Tag der Befreiung?*, 319–20. Karl Wilhelm Fricke '"Konzentrationslager, Internierungslager, Speziallager": Zur öffentlichen Wahrnehmung der NKWD/

more moderately of the 'unspeakably cynical indifference' to internees' fate (as opposed to the 'coldblooded calculation' of the Nazis' extermination camps in occupied Poland and Belorussia), although the English version of her book takes a somewhat more agnostic position than the German version and many other authors, arguing that 'Soviet officials *most likely* did not intend to kill those interned in the special camps'.[143] Other historians highlight evidence that suggests there was no such intention, including the increase of rations in early 1947 and other, albeit largely futile, efforts of Soviet occupation authorities to address the disastrous situation in the camps. They explain the 1946 reduction of rations with institutional conflicts – von Plato speaks of a 'kafkaesque bureaucratic confusion over responsibilities' – and point out that the reductions applied not only to the camps but to the Soviet zone more broadly and that the USSR faced a serious food crisis in 1946 and indeed more generally in the postwar years. They rightly insist, however, that the lack of evidence for exterminatory intent in no way diminishes either the horror of Soviet indifference to the human suffering and mass death in the camps or the responsibility of the Soviet leadership in Moscow and Berlin for not doing more to stop it.[144] As Lipinsky insists, behind every statistic were an individual fate and an often agonizing death.[145]

Although it has not been systematically investigated, the death rate in the western camps was likely at or below that of the general population. In the British zone, it can be roughly estimated that a minimum of 519 internees died.[146] This represents less than 0.6% of the ca. 91,000

MWD-Lager in Deutschland', in Haustein et al. (eds.), *Instrumentalisierung, Verdrängung, Aufarbeitung*, 61.

[143] Greiner, *Suppressed Terror*, 356, 1 (emphasis added). The original German version is less agnostic, stating that 'no intention to kill is to be imputed to the USSR' (*der UdSSR keine Tötungsabsicht zu unterstellen ist*). Greiner, *Verdrängter Terror*, 9. According to Merten, 'The *explicit* goal of the Soviet special camps in eastern Germany was not labor or murder but isolation', which leaves open the possibility that murder, or death, was an unstated goal. Merten, *Gulag in East Germany*, 167 (emphasis added).

[144] Mironenko et al., 'Vorwort der Herausgeber', 15; von Plato, 'Zur Geschichte des sowjetischen Speziallagersystems', 55 (quotation); Ritscher, *Spezlager Nr. 2 Buchenwald*, 82–3; Possekel, 'Sowjetische Lagerpolitik', 72–5; Ritscher, 'Die wissenschaftliche Aufarbeitung', 179–80; Müller, 'Sowjetische Speziallager', 22, 26, 30.

[145] Lipinsky, 'Sowjetische Speziallager in Deutschland', 42.

[146] The estimate is based on: (1) the author's calculations using death rates for June 1945–May 1946 (from Control Commission for Germany, British Element, QUPEE 76, Re: Death Rate in Civilian Internment Camps for the Year Ended 31 May 1946, n.d. [27 Jun. 1946], TNA, FO 1050/747, 109A) multiplied by Wember's figures for total camp populations (giving a subtotal of 390); (2) Wember's (incomplete) figures for the second half of 1946 (subtotal 31); and (3) Wember's figure of 98 deaths across all camps between December 1946 and June 1948. Wember, *Umerziehung im Lager*, 369–70, 377–9, 151. The total thus does not include any deaths before June 1945, in

internees. Ninety-six died in Neuengamme and 158 in Paderborn-Stau-mühle, which had the worst nutrition problems.[147] Starvation occurred but was a relatively minor cause of death. Between January and March 1946 two internees starved in Sandbostel, three in Westertimke, and four (of at least twenty-eight total deaths over the same period) in Paderborn-Staumühle, but none in the other camps. There are no known cases of starvation in Neuengamme and only one in Neumünster-Gadeland (where an internee exchanged his rations for cigarettes).[148] There were some violent deaths, for instance, when Belgian guards at Neuengamme shot some detainees early on. Suicide was not uncommon among those facing criminal prosecution or extradition, and it increased proportion-ally in 1947 after nutrition improved.[149] Among those who preferred suicide to prosecution and likely extradition was the infamous command-ant of the Sachsenhausen concentration camp, Hans Loritz, who hanged himself in his first night in the war criminals' section of the Neumünster-Gadeland camp in January 1946. He had just been rearrested after the discovery of his real identity, having previously been released from the same camp as an ordinary member of the SS under a false identity. As mentioned in Chapter 3, another was Otto Georg Thierack, former president of the People's Court of Justice and Reich Minister for Justice, who committed suicide in Eselheide to escape prosecution at the trial of jurists by an American military tribunal at Nuremberg.[150]

It is harder to find figures for the American zone, but the death rate there was even lower than in the British zone. Numbers of deaths for particular camps and hospitals include forty-three in Ziegenhain, forty-nine in CIE No. 75 in Kornwestheim (presumably six suicides);

June or October 1946, or after June 1948. Figures are missing for one, four, and one camps in July, August, and September 1946, respectively.

[147] Wember, *Umerziehung im Lager*, 73; Hüser, *'Unschuldig' in britischer Lagerhaft?*, 45, 35.

[148] Public Health Branch to HQ I.A. & C. Division, 27 May 1945, TNA, FO 1050/747, 69A; Wember, *Umerziehung im Lager*, 59, 69, 80, 73, 56. According to Wember, nine cases of starvation are documented, but this ignores the first case in Paderborn from December 1945, as well as two further cases there in April 1946. Heiner Wember, 'Umerziehung im Lager? Britische Internierungspolitik und -praxis', in Knigge-Tesche et al. (eds.), *Internierungspraxis*, 33.

[149] Wember, *Umerziehung im Lager*, 70, 77–8, 373; Siedenhans and Eimer, 'Internierungslager Eselheide', 79.

[150] Dirk Riedel, *Ordnungshüter und Massenmörder im Dienst der 'Volksgemeinschaft': Der KZ-Kommandant Hans Loritz* (Berlin: Metropol, 2010), 332–8; Siedenhans, 'Internierungslager "Eselheide"', 143. On the trial and those, like Thierack, who escaped justice, see Priemel, *Betrayal*, 264–72; Christiane Wilke, 'Fall 3: Juristen vor Gericht, Recht auf dem Prüfstand und das Erbe der "Zivilisation"', in Kim C. Priemel and Alexa Stiller (eds.), *NMT: Die Nürnberger Militärtribunale zwischen Geschichte, Gerechtigkeit und Rechtschöpfung* (Hamburg: Hamburger Edition, 2013), 288–319, esp. 293–4.

sixty-one in Darmstadt, and 105 in the internee hospital in Karlsruhe.[151]
There are no confirmed cases of starvation in American-zone camps,
although the death of an internee in Moosburg from eating poisonous
mushrooms was hunger-related, and a former internee raised the uncor-
roborated claim that four internees had starved there.[152] There were
some suicides in 1945, but they generally decreased thereafter. Four
internees had committed suicide in CIE No. 74 in Ludwigsburg-Oßweil
by early November 1945. In June 1947 a former member of the Gestapo
committed suicide in Camp No. 76 in Asperg before his *Spruchkammer*
hearing.[153] In Marcus W. Orr, the suicide rate increased over time and
comprised over 60% of the forty-six total deaths. Other causes of death in
American-zone camps reflected the age and poor health of internees on
their arrival. Cancer and heart disease were the most common causes in
Darmstadt under American administration and Regensburg under
German administration, while heart disease and failure were most
common in Camp No. 75 at Kornwestheim.[154] As in the British zone,
the death rate would have been higher had terminally ill internees not
been released, but even including their number would not begin to
bridge the gap between the low death rate in the western and the horrific-
ally high mortality in the Soviet camps.

The western and Soviet approaches to the dead and their relatives were
also vastly different. As mentioned, the western powers informed the
relatives and if the family did not take possession of the bodies, the latter

---

[151] Evangelischer Lagerpfarrer, Camp 95, Liste der Verstorbenen des Lagers Ziegenhain,
n.d., ZAEKHN, 5, no. 7; Strauß, 'Zwischen Apathie und Selbstrechtfertigung', 306;
Sterbe-Liste, HHStA, 522, no. 264: 2–3; Nachweis über Verstorbene im
Interniertenkrankenhaus 2 Karlsruhe, StAL, EL 904, no. 1. Note that this covered
the period October 1945 to August 1947 and not the hospital's entire existence.
According to Strauß, there is no evidence of deaths from illness in Heilbronn, and he
makes no mention of any deaths. Strauß, *Kriegsgefangenschaft und Internierung*, 399.
Müller indicates the existence of 140 graves of those who died in the camps in and
around Ludwigsburg. Müller, 'Internierungslager in und um Ludwigsburg', 191.

[152] Horn, *Internierungs- und Arbeitslager*, 218; Meyer, *Entnazifizierung von Frauen*, 110. The
internee claimed additionally that there had been five suicides in 1945, that six were
shot in 1945–6, and that fifty-one had died by June 1947 in the camp hospital or after
being released as incurable. L. H., Tegernsee, to Cardinal Faulhaber, 11 Jul. 1948,
AEM, NL Faulhaber, no. 8533/2. Cf. Zeitler, 'Lageralltag', 383.

[153] Lagerarzt to Commander, Camp 74, 8 Nov. 1945, StAL, EL 904, no. 43;
Lagervorsteher, Camp 76 Asperg, to Minister für politische Befreiung, Abteilung
Interniertenlager, Ludwigsburg, 20 Jun. 1947, StAL, EL 904, no. 78. Cf. Horn,
Internierungs- und Arbeitslager, 234–5; Niethammer, 'Was wissen wir?', 53; Borgstedt,
Entnazifizierung in Karlsruhe, 73.

[154] Dohle and Eigelsberger, *Camp Marcus W. Orr*, 312; Heinl, '"Das schlimme Lager"', 50;
Klose, 'Internierungs- und Arbeitslager Regensburg', 39; Strauß, 'Zwischen Apathie
und Selbstrechtfertigung', 306. See also Lagerarzt to Commander, Camp 74, 8
Nov. 1945, StAL, EL 904, no. 43.

were buried in local cemeteries. In contrast, the Soviets buried internees in unmarked mass graves (after the rising death rate made it difficult to continue with the initial individual burials) and kept the locations and the deaths secret.[155] This practice reflected divergent Soviet approaches to death and burial more broadly and the different scale of the phenomenon the Soviet authorities were dealing with.[156] It also linked the Soviet camps' total isolation and secretiveness and their appalling conditions and mortality. It highlights the inhumanity of internees' treatment in the Soviet zone and the starkest contrast with the western powers' treatment of their internees.

---

[155] See Morsch and Reich (eds.), *Sowjetisches Speziallager in Sachsenhausen*, 376–9; Susanne Hattig, Silke Klewin, Cornelia Liebold, and Jörg Morré, *Geschichte des Speziallagers Bautzen, 1945–1956: Katalog zur Ausstellung der Gedenkstätte Bautzen*, ed. Stiftung Sächsische Gedenkstätten (Dresden: Michael Sandstein, 2004), 111–13; Weigelt, 'Sterben und Tod', 178–86; Lenzer, *Frauen im Speziallager Buchenwald*, 96.

[156] Seth Bernstein, 'Burying the Alliance: Interment, Repatriation and the Politics of the Sacred in Occupied Germany', *Journal of Contemporary History* 52, no. 3 (2017), 710–30.

Conclusion

This book has argued that internment warrants more and closer attention than it has often received and that the history of Germany's (and Austria's) occupation and postwar transition is incomplete and indeed distorted if internment is left out of the story. Yet the book has also shown that, as only one aspect of a multifaceted Allied approach to the personnel of Nazi Germany, internment cannot be understood in isolation. It was a measure in its own right but was related in various ways to the occupying powers' policies on the prosecution of Nazi crimes and on denazification, narrowly understood. Instead of overlooking important differences or insisting on strict categorical distinctions, it is more useful to see internment, denazification (narrowly understood), and prosecutions as discrete but connected elements of the attempted eradication of Nazism and, importantly, of militarism, as many former military and paramilitary personnel were targeted. Indeed, internment was intimately connected to questions concerning demilitarization, POWs, and reparations.[1] Recognizing the connections and tensions among these various elements of the Allied program is equally important as identifying what distinguished them from one another. It is just as misleading to collapse (western) internment into the prosecution of Nazi crimes as to condemn (Soviet) internment for insufficient integration with denazification. The various policies and measures did not always work in harmony. For instance, German and Austrian judicial authorities often found it difficult to locate or access suspects interned by the occupying forces.[2] Internment could thus hinder as well as help the cause of justice.

The existence of distinct but intersecting measures confirms that not all Germans were treated the same. Internment was a key part of what US Secretary of War Henry Stimson called a 'firm but discriminating

---

[1] Cf. Vollnhals, 'Internierung, Entnazifizierung und Strafverfolgung', 223; Niethammer, 'Was wissen wir?', 44; Niethammer, 'Alliierte Internierungslager (1998)', 112–14.

[2] Raim, *Nazi Crimes against Jews*, 307.

treatment' of Germany.[3] As Wember suggests, whereas trials targeted specific criminals and denazification (narrowly understood) encompassed anyone in or seeking a responsible postwar position (and in the US zone the entire adult population), internment targeted

the intermediate level of Nazi functionaries, that is, those who could not be proven to have [or who may not have] committed an individual criminal offense, but who through their position and actions fundamentally contributed to keeping the Nazi state alive and the war machinery at work until the total defeat, and without whose collaboration the terror apparatus would have collapsed.[4]

Of course, the extent to which internees actually met Wember's characterization varied, and some people were targeted by more than one of these measures (and indeed by others such as being detained as POWs). Yet none of the measures was predicated on undifferentiated accusations of national collective guilt. To be sure, not least through the IMT and the Americans' successor trials at Nuremberg, the Allies sought to show where Germany as a whole had gone wrong, as Kim Priemel has recently demonstrated. However, as Olick notes, the IMT expressly 'rejected collective guilt, but condemned entire organizations'.[5] This was not the contradiction it might appear, because the distinction is crucial: both the Nuremberg trials and internment indicate that the Allies generally eschewed concrete accusations against a singular, undifferentiated German nation but did regard multiple smaller, if still sizable collectives as incriminated and/or as responsible for particular aspects of the country's waywardness.[6] Significantly, however, such incrimination was not assumed a priori to be proven, at least by the western powers. Against Soviet wishes, the IMT acquitted both individual defendants and indicted organizations and also insisted that members of the convicted organizations still had to be tried individually. Similarly, many internees in the western zones (whether members of the indicted organizations or not) were given opportunities to argue that further sanctions were unwarranted. In both contexts, the Soviets were much less concerned with due process and regarded virtually everyone they arrested as effectively guilty,

---

[3] Stimson quoted in Olick, *In the House of the Hangman*, 81.
[4] Wember, *Umerziehung im Lager*, 19, 8 (quotation).
[5] Priemel, *Betrayal*, 3–6; Olick, *In the House of the Hangman*, 113.
[6] Some authors ignore the distinction between the putative collective condemnation of all Germans and that of particular organizations. See Biddiscombe, *Denazification of Germany*, 28, 29. For an example of an account that would benefit from this distinction but, in its absence, focuses on the dichotomy of singular collective guilt versus complete individuation, see Adams, *From Crusade to Hazard*, 14.

but, again, not qua Germans, but by virtue of their positions or alleged roles.

Despite such differences, the book has shown that western and Soviet internment had much in common. Previous accounts' double standards and blind spots have reflected and reproduced overwhelmingly negative assessments of Soviet and more positive and even uncritical assessments of western internment. Yet western internment was less unproblematic and Soviet internment less deviant from the supposedly 'good' western model than is often assumed. The differences were both qualitative and quantitative, but not categorical. For instance, western internment may have been brief relative to its Soviet counterpart, but the former still lasted longer than is often recognized, indeed much too long from internees' (and others') perspectives. In both cases, it was indefinite but not perpetual. Above all, internment in all zones was fundamentally political, preventative, and extrajudicial, and not merely retrospective and pre-judicial as is often assumed to have been the case in the western zones. The occupying powers were not just concerned with prosecuting individual and 'organizational' criminals but also wanted to exact extra-judicial punishment, protect themselves (and their German collaborators), and fashion a new Germany in their own image. Detaining and isolating key segments of Nazi Germany's personnel was a pragmatic, logical step towards these multiple shared goals. However divergent the occupying powers' ideologies and the political systems they sought to install in their spheres of influence in Germany, they all saw activists, functionaries, and leaders of the Nazi state and movement at various levels as potential opponents to be neutralized and obstacles to be removed.

Acknowledging such commonalities does not obscure the fact that internment served the Soviet zone's Stalinization. Indeed, it reveals the two slightly different ways in which this occurred. In every zone the removal of Nazis, including through internment, was an essential pre-requisite for the creation of new regimes, which inevitably reflected the occupiers' own ideological and geopolitical preferences. Internment thus ultimately facilitated democratization in the western zones and Stalinization in the Soviet zone, because on both sides it cleared the way for the installation of new elites who were more amenable to the occupiers' agenda. The eradication of Nazism and the installation of Stalinism were thus not a contradiction, let alone alternatives, but two sides of the same coin. *Additionally*, the internment (and, even more so, the prosecution by SMTs) of other, non-Nazi critics and opponents of the nascent communist-dominated regime served Stalinization even more directly (and had little to do with eradicating Nazism). Internment thus aided Stalinization in two distinct ways, but the former cannot be reduced to the latter because it also helped eradicate Nazism.[7] To be sure, the two aspects of Stalinization were intimately related: seeming to confirm widespread fear and loathing of the 'Bolsheviks', the sweeping arrests, lack of transparency, secretiveness, and lethal treatment of internees and other arrestees, whether Nazis or not, prompted (further) criticism of, and opposition to, the Soviet occupiers and their German communist allies, who then cracked down all the more severely on their critics and opponents.[8] This vicious cycle helps explain the greater extent and longer duration of internment in the Soviet than the western zones as well as the increasing use of SMTs for political repression. The Soviet occupation created and manufactured opposition and dealt with it in Stalinist tradition, albeit with much anti-Nazi rhetoric. In contrast, the western occupiers did not encounter as much hostility to begin with; were more attuned to German, international, and their own domestic or internal criticism of their more moderate and transparent, but still illiberal measures; and sought deescalation by granting concessions, improving conditions, and winding down their internment programs, albeit not as quickly as is often assumed.

Recognizing not just the nature but the extent and duration of internment across the occupation zones helps explain the seemingly remarkable smoothness of Germany's transition after the Second World War that baffled many contemporaries and continues to fascinate historians. The impact of catastrophic military defeat and destruction, the concomitant preoccupation with physical survival, and the associated widespread ideological disillusionment with National Socialism, not least as its remaining adherents increasingly turned their apocalyptic violence towards various segments of the German population, were important, as were revelations of the full extent of Nazi crimes.[9] Yet the assertion not just of the Allies' military supremacy but also of their political resolve to occupy and control the country for the foreseeable future was also crucial. If the orgy of violence that was inflicted on 'defeatists' and 'deserters' as the war's end drew near was an attempted demonstration by those who remained committed that their time was not yet up, so the mass incarceration of Nazis was an unequivocal Allied demonstration that their time had indeed passed and a new era had begun.[10] Internment

---

[7] Cf. Boldorf, 'Brüche oder Kontinuitäten?'.

[8] Gary Bruce, *Resistance with the People: Repression and Resistance in Eastern Germany, 1945–1955* (Lanham, MD: Rowman & Littlefield, 2003), 42, 48–9, 70–8.

[9] See Bessel, *Germany 1945*; Keller, *Volksgemeinschaft am Ende*; Kershaw, *The End*; Jarausch, *After Hitler*, 3–6, 13–15.

[10] See Keller, *Volksgemeinschaft am Ende*, 434.

was thus not least a statement of power that underlined Allied supremacy and determination to enforce fundamental change.

In addition to this symbolic significance, internment had crucial practical impacts that help explain the apparent absence of 'Nazis' that so puzzled the occupiers and many returning émigrés. To be sure, some former supporters of National Socialism genuinely disavowed the creed and many now claimed, with more dissembling and denial, never to have really supported the regime.[11] But the fact that tens of thousands of core party, paramilitary, and military personnel were interned for upward of two years contributed significantly to the lack of Nazis to be found at large in Germany. It also helps explain the absence of meaningful challenges both to the Allies and to emergent German local and regional political movements and institutions during the occupation period. That there were no serious equivalents to the *Freikorps* (Free Corps, nationalist paramilitary units) that emerged after the First World War was surely not least due to the fact that so many senior, middling, and more junior party leaders and officials and paramilitary officers were behind barbed wire.[12] In general, the fact that the Allies interned more than 400,000 people without trial indicates that coercion was a bigger part of the story and that denazification, broadly understood, was more severe than is commonly believed, especially in the western zones. In light of the true extent and duration of internment, it is no longer acceptable to overlook or gloss over the incarceration of significant numbers of various groups of Nazi personnel including local and functional elites, as otherwise excellent accounts still do, thus creating a false impression of a toothless or non-existent purge.[13]

---

[11] See, for example, Padover, *Experiment in Germany*, 62; Echternkamp, *Bundesrepublik Deutschland*, 65; Konrad H. Jarausch, *Broken Lives: How Ordinary Germans Experienced the Twentieth Century* (Princeton, NJ: Princeton University Press, 2018), 266–7.

[12] Perry Biddiscomb's discussion of the relative lack of *Freikorps* after the end of the Second World War focuses on military veterans. It overlooks the extensive internment of party and other non-military figures who, as Biddiscomb himself stresses, had been instrumental in the half-hearted and largely inconsequential *Freikorps* revival during 1944 and early 1945 and who might have been crucial to any subsequent renaissance. Perry Biddiscombe, 'The End of the Freebooter Tradition: The Forgotten *Freikorps* Movement of 1944/45', *Central European History* 32, no. 1 (1999), 79–83, 63–7, 75–6.

[13] For examples of works that mention internment at most in passing and do not see it as worthy of exploration, see Hoser, 'Entnazifizierung in der Stadt Dachau', 197, 227; Christina Ullrich, *'Ich fühl mich nicht als Mörder!' Die Integration von NS-Tätern in die Nachkriegsgesellschaft* (Darmstadt: Wissenschaftliche Buchgesellschaft, 2011); Dams and Stolle, *The Gestapo*, 163; Siemens, *Stormtroopers*, 231, 319 (n. 11). In contrast, others pay their internment some attention, e.g., Eckart Conze, Norbert Frei, Peter Hayes, and Moshe Zimmermann, *Das Amt und die Vergangenheit: Deutsche Diplomaten im Dritten Reich und in der Bundesrepublik* (Munich: Pantheon, 2012 [1st ed. 2010]), 324–42; Stanciu, *'Alte Kämpfer'*, 336–72.

Above all, internment contributed to a clearing of the decks that allowed a new German political class to take over in the immediate postwar months and years. Perhaps somewhat exaggeratedly, Dieter Pohl argues that Soviet arrests (that admittedly went well beyond internment in the Soviet zone) constituted 'the most severe intervention in the political and social order in Brandenburg after 1945'.[14] A comparable claim for the western zones seems even less justified, not least because internment there was somewhat briefer, much less lethal, and, at least in the British and French zones, considerably less sweeping than in Soviet zone. Yet across Germany and in the western zones of Austria, Allied internment helped exclude from public life a significant portion of the former Nazi elites at various levels for a crucial transitional period. As Klaus-Dietmar Henke argues, 'seen politically this giant exclusionary action by the victors' right was a highly effective flanking measure for the Allied efforts at democratization in the unsettled first two, three postwar years, in which not only damaging ideologies and compromised institutions but precisely also undesirable people were to be kept under quarantine'.[15] As already indicated, the meaning and nature of 'democratization' differed under the various occupying powers, while 'damaging ideologies' and 'undesirable people' were defined much more broadly and loosely in the Soviet zone; there, too, the quarantine lasted not two or three years but between three and almost five. Again, though, these are quantitative and qualitative, not functional or categorical differences.

For all its short-term severity – which had considerable longer-term significance – internment was temporary and precisely its temporariness helps to clarify the paradox of new beginning *and* continuity in postwar Germany. Like denazification more broadly, internment facilitated a new beginning but also allowed for continuity, albeit a partial and broken continuity.[16] The detention of compromised personnel – like other measures – was only ever intended to be temporary, and thus internees' eventual release was no betrayal or abandonment of denazification but was integral thereto and inevitable. The vast majority of former Nazis, including those who were interned (and who survived), were eventually reintegrated into German society. Many returned to their former professions, especially those whose expertise remained in, or quickly returned to, high demand. For example, of forty-eight members of the Hamburg

---

[14] Pohl, *Justiz in Brandenburg*, 95.
[15] Henke, 'Trennung vom Nationalsozialismus', 33. Cf. Möhler, *Entnazifizierung in Rheinland-Pfalz und im Saarland*, 409; Twerase, 'Die amerikanische Säuberungspolitik', 391.
[16] Cf. Niethammer, *Mitläuferfabrik*, 22.

judiciary who were interned, twenty would return to its employ, with several remaining into the 1960s and some into the early 1970s. While it is tempting to focus on this remarkable continuity, one should not overlook the significant number that did not return.[17] As Paul Hoser notes in relation to the American zone:

Of all internees, the active, leading National Socialists spent the longest time in the camp (up to three years). After that, despite partial downgrading [of denazification sanctions] by the appeal panels, they often remained socially déclassé and isolated, needed more time than the average of the rest of the population to raise their low standard of living, and very frequently had permanently played out their influential role.

The 'often-draconian punishment' of internment was thus not entirely negated by the relatively 'generous clemency' that followed.[18] And one should not diminish the interruption and the significant sanction that internment constituted even for those who did return.

On the other hand, there is some evidence that internment itself fostered the renewal of networks of former Nazis and their successful manoeuvring into new positions in the emerging Cold War constellation. For instance, several former members of the Abwehr and the Gestapo established or reestablished contact in American internment camps and went on to become key players in the Gehlen Organization, the American-sponsored German intelligence service that would form the nucleus of the later West German Bundesnachrichtendienst (Federal Intelligence Service) and which, among other things, carried out a lengthy campaign of observation and harassment of supposedly subversive communists and other leftists in the late 1940s and 1950s.[19]

---

[17] Hubert Rottleuthner, *Karrieren und Kontinuitäten deutscher Justizjuristen vor und nach 1945* (Berlin: Berliner Wissenschafts-Verlag, 2010), 268, 271–3. See also Anton F. Guhl, 'Entlassung, Entnazifizierung, Rehabilitierung? Die Philosophische Fakultät der Hamburger Universität zwischen Bruch und Kontinuität nach 1945', in Myriam Richter and Mirko Nottscheid (eds.), *100 Jahre Germanistik in Hamburg: Traditionen und Perspektiven* (Berlin: Dietrich Reimer Verlag, 2011), 261–80.

[18] Hoser, 'Entnazifizierung in Bayern', 505. Cf. Stanciu, *'Alte Kämpfer'*, 410–12.

[19] Gerhard Sälter, *Phantome des Kalten Krieges: Die Organisation Gehlen und die Wiederbelebung des Gestapo-Feindbildes 'Rote Kapelle'* (Berlin: Ch. Links Verlag, 2016), 59, 66, 73, 74, 289, 376. See also Boghardt, 'Dirty Work?', 401, 404, 410; Michael Wala, 'The Value of Knowledge: Western Intelligence Agencies and Former Members of the SS, Gestapo and Wehrmacht during the Early Cold War', and Dominik Rigoll, 'From Denazification to Renazification? West German Government Officials after 1945', both in Erlichman and Knowles (eds.), *Transforming Occupation*, 271–82, 251–70; Dominik Rigoll, 'Das Gründungspersonal der Bonner Bundesbehörden: Über Karriere- und Rekrutierungsmuster nach 1945', in Frank Bösch and Martin Sabrow (eds.), *ZeitRäume: Potsdamer Almanach des Zentrums für Zeithistorische Forschung 2016* (Göttingen: Wallstein, 2016), 55–73.

Similarly, key figures in the formation of the neo-Nazi Socialist Reich Party, which was banned in West Germany in 1952, had gotten to know one another in internment.[20]

If such internees appeared to emerge from western internment unscathed and with their confidence and elements of their worldview largely intact, albeit now in the service of western anti-communism rather than Nazi anti-bolshevism, this was not necessarily representative. Many internees were profoundly shaken by the experience of being targeted, as were their families. As is increasingly recognized of denazification more broadly, internment's subjective impact – as opposed to the perhaps gentler longer-term physical, material, or professional impact – was significant. As Hoser again puts it, 'The arrest and transfer to the internment camps was a direct shock, as no one knew what fate awaited him' (or her).[21] Both Allied and numerous German observers feared the worst from the camps. Like denazification, internment was regarded by many critics as excessive and misguided and as a danger to democracy. Some claimed in alarmist and rather inaccurate fashion that the western camps were becoming seedbeds of support for communism. More commonly, critics feared the camps were rekindling rather than eradicating Nazism.[22] For instance, a Senior British Political Officer in Styria feared of the Wolfsberg camp:

Although the inmates are supposed to be only the really bad Nazis, this is not so. It is not difficult to imagine what is happening to these intelligent and fit people – kept warm – well fed – nothing to do except talk and plan for the day they come out (the day we go!) – all disgruntled whether bad Nazis or not so bad – thrown into each other's company – nothing constructive.[23]

However, despite a shared sense of suffering the perceived injustice of internment, a united camp society failed to emerge. Various groups of internees blamed each other for Germany's defeat, for Nazism's betrayal or perversion, and, above all, for their current situation.[24]

---

[20] Kurt P. Tauber, *Beyond Eagle and Swastika: German Nationalism since 1945*, vol. 1 (Middletown, CT: Wesleyan University Press, 1967), 692.

[21] Hoser, 'Entnazifizierung in Bayern', 505. Cf. Ulrich Herbert, *Geschichte Deutschlands im 20. Jahrhundert* (Munich: C. H. Beck, 2014), 566–9; Hoser, 'Entnazifizierung in der Stadt Dachau', 197; Rauh-Kühne, 'Life Rewarded the Latecomers', 72; Koch, 'Karlsruhe', 185; Conze et al., *Das Amt*, 343; Jarausch, *Broken Lives*, 182.

[22] See Beattie, 'Verdiente Strafe des harten Kerns?', 71–3; Erdelmann, *'Persilscheine' aus der Druckerpresse?*, 114, 119–20.

[23] K. C. Boyd, Memorandum 'Denazification' to Chief of Staff, ACA(BE), 2 Mar. 1946, cited in Beer, 'Die britische Entnazifizierung', 422. See also Erdelmann, *'Persilscheine' aus der Druckerpresse?*, 90–1.

[24] See Conze et al., *Das Amt*, 333; Beattie, 'Verdiente Strafe des harten Kerns?', 68, 72.

Reflecting not least their varying degrees and sources of support for, and levels of involvement in, National Socialism, internees reacted in diverse ways and drew multiple lessons from the experience. A minority subsequently expressed gratitude for the opportunities (for reflection, retraining, or refamiliarization with Christianity) that internment afforded. Kiesinger, for instance, spoke of having things 'that otherwise are almost always lacking: time and leisure to talk, listen, think through, and discuss'. His postwar democratic political career, which arguably began with his democratic missionary work overseeing a 'camp university' and running a study group for youthful internees in the Ludwigsburg-Oßweil camp and which took him to the pinnacle of West German politics, was clearly exceptional.[25] Others harboured profound resentment over their incarceration long afterward, although again its political valence varied. Some became bitter, vocal opponents of their interning power. Von Salomon became staunchly and outspokenly anti-American, advocated German neutrality, and even displayed some sympathy for the GDR.[26] Others sought a new political home on the extreme-right fringe, and not a few participated in a range of internee organizations that emerged in West Germany in the 1950s, seeking rehabilitation, compensation, and camaraderie. The majority did not return to political activity but increasingly realized that 'our time' had passed.[27]

If many former western internees struggled for orientation and felt out of step with the postwar *Zeitgeist*, they were generally better off than former Soviet internees, above all because many of the latter suffered lasting physical and psychological damage from their appalling treatment and experiences, but also because they were even older on their release due to their longer incarceration and had not had the same opportunities for retraining and integration into postwar German life as their western counterparts.[28] To be sure, there were parallels with former western internees for those former Soviet internees who ended up in West Germany. Some joined victims' organizations and a few wrote about

[25] Gassert, *Kiesinger*, 166–75 (quotation 170). Cf. Wember, *Umerziehung im Lager*, 229–34.
[26] Fröhlich, *Soldat ohne Befehl*, 344–9, 360–71.
[27] See correspondence of former NSDAP Gau Speaker and Gau Main Office Leader of Württemberg-Hohenzollern Karl Hornickel. Quotation in Hornickel to Eugen Steinhilber, 29 Nov. 1974, HStAS, Q 1/27, no. 3; Karl-Heinz Grotjahn, 'Gegen "Folterparagraph und Teufelsgesetz": Die IdEG, Interessengemeinschaft der Entnazifizierungsgeschädigten e.V. Hannover', *Hannoversche Geschichtsblätter* 57–58 (New Series) (2003/4), 151–203; Lenzer, *Frauen im Speziallager Buchenwald*, 160–4. Cf. Stanciu, *'Alte Kämpfer'*, 363–9.
[28] Kwiatkowski, *Nach Buchenwald*, 46–58; Lenzer, *Frauen im Speziallager Buchenwald*, 178–90; Stanciu, *'Alter Kämpfer'*, 348–9, 358–9.

their experiences, attacking the Soviets just as von Salomon attacked the Americans. Indeed, in the anti-communist climate of West Germany from the Berlin Blockade through to the construction of the Berlin Wall, former inmates of the Soviet camps were 'welcome eyewitnesses' of communist injustice (whereas the 'abuses' of the western powers were a more awkward proposition). Yet they felt increasingly unwanted during the later era of détente.[29] The heaviest burden was undoubtedly borne by those survivors of the Soviet camps who remained in East Germany. To be sure, most eventually integrated successfully there too, some even joining the SED. Indeed, former interned adolescents who stayed in the GDR appear to have achieved higher levels of educational qualifications both than those who headed to West Germany and than the average of their wider East German age cohorts. Yet many former internees believed they were under particular surveillance and that they and their families were discriminated in various ways. Above all, many feared repercussions, including imprisonment, if they discussed their experiences even within their immediate family. They thus suffered a 'burden of silence' that only ended in 1990 with the collapse of the East German dictatorship and the discovery of mass graves from the Soviet camps.[30] Against this background, it is unsurprising that the ensuing public and scholarly discussion of the topic was intense and that former internees have been heavily invested in the course of public and scholarly debate about the experiences they were unable to openly discuss for four decades.[31]

A key issue – whether for former internees, historians, or public memory – has been the question of the camps' overall characterization. Unsurprisingly, there is no consensus and most controversy surrounds the Soviet camps. The complexity of internment's aims, functions, and

---

[29] Von Plato, 'Sowjetische Speziallager', 97 (quotation); Andrew H. Beattie, '"Sowjetische KZs auf deutschem Boden": Die sowjetischen Speziallager und der bundesdeutsche Antikommunismus', *Jahrbuch für historische Kommunismusforschung* (2011), 123–33; Greiner, *Suppressed Terror*, 252–81; Boll, *Sprechen als Last und Befreiung*, 217–334.

[30] Ursula Fischer, *Von der Last des Schweigens* (Berlin: Dietz Verlag, 1997); Kwiatkowski, *Nach Buchenwald*, 78, 84–5, 88–94; Boll, *Sprechen als Last und Befreiung*, 341–6; Eva Ochs, *'Heute kann ich das ja sagen': Lagererfahrungen von Insassen sowjetischer Speziallager in der SBZ/DDR* (Cologne: Böhlau, 2006), 230–79. Female former internees from Buchenwald interviewed by Lenzer seem not to have integrated or advanced professionally and educationally as well as the mainly male youth cohort studied by Kwiatkowski. See Lenzer, *Frauen im Speziallager Buchenwald*, 165–9.

[31] See Petra Haustein, *Geschichte im Dissens: Die Auseinandersetzungen um die Gedenkstätte Sachsenhausen nach dem Ende der DDR* (Leipzig: Leipziger Universitätsverlag, 2006); Beattie, *Playing Politics with History*, 213–19; Beattie, '"Sowjetische KZs auf deutschem Boden"', 133–6; Anna Saunders, *Memorializing the GDR: Monuments and Memory after 1989* (New York: Berghahn Books, 2018), 110–58.

execution and the diversity and mutability of its targets as well as of the camp sites and detention conditions would seem to defy simple or simplistic characterizations. Yet the latter nevertheless abound in the existing literature. In this concluding section, I explore and critique previous approaches and suggest a way forward.

A range of terms has been used to describe the Soviet camps. Given their massive death rate, it is perhaps unsurprising that they have been called 'death camps' (*Todeslager*).[32] However, this begs the question of whether death was the purpose or merely an appalling by-product: Were they camps of, or for, death? It is also problematic that 'death camp' is a common synonym for the Nazi extermination camps Auschwitz, Chełmno, Bełżec, Majdanek, Sobibór, and Treblinka in occupied Poland and Belorussia. Irrespective of their views on the term 'death camp', most authors rightly insist that the Soviet-zone camps were not sites of organized mass murder, so they cannot be called 'extermination camps' (*Vernichtungslager*).[33]

Numerous authors characterize the Soviet camps as 'outposts of the GULAG'.[34] This designation is particularly compelling for the period from 1948 to 1950, when the Department for Special Camps was subordinated to the GULAG. More generally, it captures several features of their history: arbitrariness, political repression, and indifference to mass suffering and death; the NKVD background, affiliation, and mentality of many Soviet personnel; and the desire for labour. Yet it fails to explain why subordination to the GULAG came so late and it glosses over differences, such as the almost total enclosure and seclusion of the Special Camps, in contrast to the often porous border between GULAG 'camps' and the local (if often remote and therefore isolated) outside world, the lack of any rhetoric directed at the inmates about their 'reeducation', and the absence of a steady stream of 'redeemed' prisoners being released.[35] It also overlooks connections to, and parallels with, the GUPVI system for POWs and civilian deportees. Indeed, Greiner suggests that 'one might consider the special camps a hybrid form combining the two Soviet models'.[36] However, both designations – whether as

---

[32] Preissinger, *From Sachsenhausen to Buchenwald*; Merten, *Gulag in East Germany*, 168.

[33] Eckert, 'Entnazifizierung', 248; Lipinsky, 'Sowjetische Speziallager in Deutschland', 35; Müller, 'Sowjetische Speziallager', 22; Greiner, *Suppressed Terror*, 356; Applebaum, *Iron Curtain*, 107–8.

[34] For instance: Knabe, *Tag der Befreiung?*, 217; Lipinsky, 'Sowjetische Speziallager in Deutschland', 40; Fricke, '"Konzentrationslager, Internierungslager, Speziallager"', 58–9; Merten, *Gulag in East Germany*. Cf. Ritscher, 'Die wissenschaftliche Aufarbeitung', 183–5, 192.

[35] Stone, *Concentration Camps*, 64, 67–9, 75, 77; Applebaum, *Iron Curtain*, 107–8.

[36] Greiner, *Suppressed Terror*, 352–5, 357 (quotation).

GULAG outpost or GULAG-GUPVI hybrid – ignore the initial connections and similarities with western internment camps, fail to capture the Soviet camps' denazificatory context and function, and minimize crucial differences that persisted after 1948, above all the lack of forced labour in the 'Special Camps'. That absence means that it is utterly inappropriate to call the latter 'forced labour camps' as some uninformed authors have.[37]

The choice ultimately boils down to one between 'internment' and 'concentration camp', terms for which there are no consensual definitions or understandings. Many historians treat them as separate categories, but the distinctions between them are not self-evident. On some dictionary definitions, concentration camps appear to be a subset of internment camps, whereas some scholars treat internment camps as a subset of broadly defined concentration camps.[38] Either way, the connotations of the latter term are more pejorative than the former, not least because it is still primarily associated with Nazi camps.[39] Largely for this reason, historians almost unanimously reject calling the western camps 'concentration camps' and insist they were 'internment camps'.[40]

In contrast, numerous authors call the Soviet camps 'concentration camps'.[41] While delivered strongly, their arguments are often dubious.

---

[37] Fitzgibbon, *Denazification*, 101; McKale, *Nazis after Hitler*, 90.

[38] For instance, the *Oxford English Dictionary* defines an internment camp as 'a camp in which prisoners of war, enemy aliens, political prisoners, etc., are detained without trial', and a concentration camp as 'a camp in which large numbers of people, esp. political prisoners or members of persecuted minorities, are deliberately imprisoned in a relatively small area with inadequate facilities, sometimes to provide forced labour or to await mass execution'. See 'Internment Camp, n.' and 'Concentration Camp, n.', in *Oxford English Dictionary Online* (Oxford University Press, June 2018), available at: www.oed.com/view/Entry/403843?redirectedFrom=concentration+camp and www.oed.com/view/Entry/98094?redirectedFrom=internment+camp (accessed 6 Feb. 2019). According to Pitzer, 'A concentration camp exists wherever a government holds groups of civilians outside the normal legal process', whereas in internment camps, 'people are detained for a fixed or indefinite priod of time, usually in the wake of a crisis'. Pitzer, *One Long Night*, 5–6. See also Kotek and Rigoulot, *Jahrhundert der Lager*, 17–21; Stone, *Concentration Camps*, 4.

[39] Cf. Nikolaus Wachsmann, 'The Nazi Concentration Camps in International Context: Comparisons and Connections', in Jan Rüger and Nikolaus Wachsmann (eds.), *Rewriting German History: New Perspectives on Modern Germany* (London: Palgrave Macmillan, 2015), 307.

[40] This is true even of critical authors. See Horn, *Internierungs- und Arbeitslager*, 15; Fäßler, 'Lahr unter französischer Besatzung', 199; Fässler et al., 'Hauptstadt ohne Brot', 383. For partial exceptions, see Peterson, *American Occupation*, 145; Schwinge, 'Rückblick auf die Zeit der amerikanischen Besetzung', 323–4.

[41] In addition to those cited later, see Eckert, 'Entnazifizierung', 248; Fricke, '"Konzentrationslager, Internierungslager, Speziallager"', 49–54; Knabe, *Tag der Befreiung?*, 357; Olschewski, *'Freunde' im Feindesland*, 168 (n. 545); Merten, *Gulag in East Germany*, 119, 132.

One highlights topographical continuity. Knabe asks whether 'Buchenwald stopped being a concentration camp because it was administered no longer by the SS but by the Soviet secret police'.[42] Yet one could also ask whether Dachau, Esterwegen, and Neuengamme ceased being concentration camps just because the Americans and British administered them. Moreover, such arguments do not cope with POW camps or other sites that were later used for internment, or with Nazi concentration camps that became POW, DP, or refugee camps. Indeed, if it is increasingly understood that concentration camps have had diverse physical forms and do not all look like Dachau, it also needs to be recognized that looking like Dachau does not necessarily mean a camp is a concentration camp; put another way, even a camp that 'is' Buchenwald is not necessarily 'Buchenwald'.[43] Another argument focuses on the Soviet camps' appalling conditions, but similarities in this regard do not entail categorical similarity. Otherwise, badly resourced POW or refugee camps might also be deemed concentration camps.[44] Additionally, although Greiner concedes that comparing the Soviet-zone camps with pre-war Nazi concentration camps 'reveals more differences than commonalities', she insists that 'these differences seem less significant from the perspective of many individual detainees'. Yet many western-zone internees also felt they were being held in concentration camps, and the subjective perceptions of those affected should not be decisive.[45] The purpose, function, and targets of encampment are surely more important. Some arguments focus on this. For instance, Neubert argues that Soviet-zone detainees were mainly arrested for standing in the Soviets' way and concludes that 'The camps were therefore above all concentration camps that served the communists' consolidation of power. The reckoning with National Socialism was ultimately no longer the main motive for maintaining the camps.'[46] Yet consolidating power and removing people who stood in the occupiers' way was one of the main purposes of Allied internment from the beginning and was not confined to the Soviets.

On the other hand, many historians reject calling the Soviet camps 'concentration camps', viewing this as an unacceptable equation with

---

[42] Hubertus Knabe, 'Die sowjetischen Lager in Deutschland – Deutungen und Fehldeutungen: Vortrag zur Veranstaltung der Konrad-Adenauer-Stiftung "Zukunft braucht Erinnerung – System und Wirklichkeit der Speziallager in der SBZ/DDR 1945–1950"' (Aug. 2006), 5, available at: www.kas.de/upload/dokumente/2006/potsdam0806_Knabe.pdf (accessed 6 Feb. 2019).

[43] See Stone, *Concentration Camps*, 7, 11; Wachsmann, 'Nazi Concentration Camps', 309.

[44] Cf. Kotek and Rigoulot, *Jahrhundert der Lager*, 19.

[45] Greiner, *Suppressed Terror*, 356–7; Beattie, 'Die alliierte Internierung', 255–6; Streim, 'Germans in the *Lager*', 36, 38.

[46] Neubert, 'Politische Verbrechen', 863–4.

their Nazi predecessors. Some insist that the differences between Buchenwald before and after 1945, for instance, were so great that to use the same term for both is misleading. Niethammer argues that Allied civilian internment camps, including the Soviets', had more in common with Allied POW camps than with Nazi concentration camps.[47] The term's association with Nazi brutality and murderousness makes applying it to the Soviet camps problematic. In particular, distinctions between the extermination camps in the occupied East and 'mere' concentration camps within the borders of the German Reich or even between 'mere' political, social, and racial persecution in the 1930s and the murderous and genocidal slave-labour of the war years are often overlooked.[48] Against this background, the implications of applying the term to postwar detention camps with significant Nazi populations must be borne in mind. It may not necessarily constitute equationism, set one off against another, or downplay crucial differences, but all too often it does.[49]

If this moniker is morally, politically, and historically loaded, what of the alternative? While some historians call the Soviet camps 'internment camps', others are reluctant to do so, arguing that the term minimizes significant differences from the western camps such as more arbitrary practices, inferior conditions, and the massive death rate.[50] In addition to these aspects and her unwarranted dismissal of any denazificatory function or origins, Greiner proposes three further reasons against calling the

---

[47] Niethammer, 'Alliierte Internierungslager (1998)', 112–15. See Annette Leo, 'Konzentrationslager Sachsenhausen und Speziallager Nr. 7', in Günter Heydemann and Heinrich Oberreuter (eds.), *Diktaturen in Deutschland – Vergleichsaspekte: Strukturen, Institutionen und Verhaltensweisen* (Bonn: Bundeszentrale für politische Bildung, 2003), 249–82; Ritscher, *Spezlager Nr. 2 Buchenwald*, 33–4.

[48] The *Collins Dictionary* defines a 'concentration camp', in British English, as 'a guarded prison camp in which nonmilitary prisoners are held, esp one of those in Nazi Germany in which millions were exterminated'. 'Concentration Camp', *Collins Free Online Dictionary*, available at: www.collinsdictionary.com/dictionary/english/concentration-camp (accessed 6 Feb. 2019). For a discussion of how Auschwitz tends to dominate understandings of Nazi concentration camps and detract from their diversity, see Wachsmann, *KL*, 10–16.

[49] Cf. Ritscher, 'Die wissenschaftliche Aufarbeitung', 183; Beattie, *Playing Politics with History*, 217–19; Beattie, 'Ein neuer Historikerstreit?', 28–31.

[50] See Wember, *Umerziehung im Lager*, 88–91; Horn, *Internierungs- und Arbeitslager*, 15; Strauß, *Kriegsgefangenschaft und Internierung*, 423–8. For instance, Lipinsky argues that the Soviet camps 'were not "internment camps"', as the duration of detention and everyday life differed from western practice to such an extent that this term would seem belittling [*verharmlosend*]'. Lipinsky, 'Sowjetische Speziallager in Deutschland', 35. Cf. von Plato, 'Zur Geschichte des sowjetischen Speziallagersystems', 46; Ritscher, *Spezlager Nr. 2 Buchenwald*, 34–6.

Soviet camps 'internment camps', which warrant some discussion. First, she points to the incarceration of SMT convicts. She dates this to May 1946 (ignoring the tiny numbers prior to that date) and argues, 'From this time on, special camps can no longer be seen as temporary sites of internment; they had been transformed into permanent installations for long-term detainees.'[51] This argument applies, if at all, only to a minority of camps (Bautzen, Sachsenhausen, and Torgau no. 10) and not to the remainder, and it overlooks that non-convicted internees still comprised a majority of the total camp population in October 1948 and 45% in December 1949. Moreover, it is illogical to suggest that the camps were *never* internment camps because of later functions they acquired. A glance at the American-zone camps is instructive here. No one would suggest that they ceased being internment camps when they began to accommodate prisoners the *Spruchkammern* had sentenced to labour camp or when such convicts began to outnumber internees, let alone that the camps *never* constituted internment camps because they (or some of them) became labour camps. They ceased being internment camps when they no longer held any internees.

Second, Greiner points to the Soviet camps' longevity. She asserts, 'Internment is a sweeping, large-scale measure applied in war or other crisis situations and thus for a limited time period.' The Soviet authorities, however, 'transformed what is normally a state of emergency into the new norm until long after the GDR came into being'.[52] In fact, the last Soviet camps closed within four to six months of the GDR's foundation on 7 October 1949. Soviet internment certainly lasted longer than western internment but not by as much as is often assumed. Germans remained interned without trial in all zones in 1949. To be sure, in that year their number did not exceed three figures in the western zones whereas it exceeded 13,000 in the Soviet zone. Yet the last French camp closed only in December 1949, 'long after' the FRG's foundation in May and just a couple of months before the last Soviet camps. Moreover, numerous Soviet camps closed in the years 1946–8 and thus operated no longer than many western camps. Clearly, temporariness and longevity are relative and imprecise criteria. The Soviet camps did not become permanent institutions and there is no evidence that they were ever intended to. Moreover, western internment arguably also lasted longer than necessary and certainly after any war-related need for pacification had expired or any 'crisis situation' or 'state of emergency' had passed. Indeed, as shown throughout this book, internment in occupied

[51] Greiner, *Suppressed Terror*, 351.   [52] Ibid., 350.

Germany was always about more than securing immediate physical control of occupied territory.

Third, as already quoted in the Introduction, Greiner suggests that western policy reflected the western powers' determination to 'counter state-sanctioned injustice with the democratic rule of law – an intention that the Soviet occupying power did not honour'.[53] This assessment undoubtedly applies to general western and Soviet policy towards Germany but not to western internment. The western powers were concerned, after an initial period of harsh treatment and privation, for their internees' physical and psychological welfare and hoped to integrate them into Germany's nascent postwar democracy; they also displayed some concern for due process and eventually gave many internees opportunities to argue their case for release or to defend themselves against various charges. But, as shown in Chapter 2, even internment's supporters in western administrations and military governments regarded it as inconsistent with individual liberties and the rule of law, in fact precisely as a necessary suspension thereof.

Underlying Greiner's and others' reluctance to call the Soviet camps 'internment camps' are not just exaggerated beliefs about the differences between the western and Soviet zones, but also the misplaced presumption that the term entails a positive assessment. Yet the lack of explicitly negative commentary in dictionary definitions does not mean that detention conditions in anything called an internment camp are satisfactory, that internment is justified generally and individually, that it lasts no longer than necessary, or that internees' rights are respected. Instances of 'civilian internment' elsewhere have attracted considerable criticism, if more for denying internees' basic rights and for disproportionateness than for physical mistreatment or neglect.[54] It is thus not only circular but also ignorant to argue that the Soviet camps cannot be called internment camps because that implies too positive an assessment. What is more, there is no reason that 'internment camps' cannot differ in terms of arbitrariness of confinement, detention conditions, and rates of illness and death, without such differences necessarily entailing categorical distinctiveness (an argument that also applies, of course, to 'concentration camps', some of which are worse than others in various respects, while they also change over time). What they all have in common, however, is the mere act of extrajudicial internment, which is inherently a denial of internees' most basic rights. For, as Hannah Arendt posited, such detention 'kill[s] the juridical person in man', by placing the camp

---

[53] Greiner, *Suppressed Terror*, 348.
[54] See the Introduction for references to civilian internment elsewhere.

'outside the normal penal system, and by selecting its inmates outside the normal judicial procedure in which a definite crime entails a predictable penalty'.[55]

If the arguments against calling the Soviet camps 'internment camps' are thus problematic, the term by itself is nevertheless inadequate. First, it does not sufficiently address functional complexity, changes over time, and differences among individual camps. This applies to the western zones too. Distinctions within the zones, even camp-specific designations, are therefore advisable. The French camps were and remained largely internment camps, although some were initially also POW camps. The same applies to the British camps, although Neuengamme served further purposes and Esterwegen became a prison camp for *Spruchgericht* convicts. Numerous internment camps in the American zone also served as POW camps, while some served as war-crimes holding centres and several assumed the additional function of labour camps. In the Soviet zone, meanwhile, some camps served exclusively as internment camps, while others served additionally as POW, prison, and/or filtration camps. Acknowledging this complexity is more productive than persisting with one-dimensional characterizations. Again, the American zone provides an example of a bifold designation that does justice to different functions and categories of inmate. Once the camps started also to accommodate prisoners who had been sentenced to labour by the *Spruchkammern*, they became known as 'internment and labour camps'. In similar vein, the Soviet camps, or at least those that held SMT prisoners, should be termed 'internment and prison camps'.

Second, even if the primary function of most of the Soviet camps, and the sole function of some, was and remained internment, simply dubbing them 'internment camps' does not sufficiently capture crucial dissimilarities from the western camps. This book has consistently highlighted the common ground and shared characteristics of internment across the zones. In every zone, it was an amorphous mixture of prophylactic isolation, collective punishment, detention for potential judicial or

---

[55] Arendt argued, somewhat problematically and without reference to internment camps, that DP and refugee camps among others do this, as opposed to Soviet labor and Nazi concentration camps that also destroyed the 'moral person' and Nazi extermination camps that destroyed the biological person. Hannah Arendt, 'Concentration Camps', *Partisan Review* 15, no. 7 (1948), 749–59 (main text quotation 753). Cf. Robert Jan van Pelt, 'Paradise/Hades, Purgatory, Hell/Gehenna: A Political Typology of the Camps', in Friedman (ed.), *The Routledge History of the Holocaust*, 193. Yet there are different degrees to which the juridical person can be killed or revived. While all internment camps in occupied Germany stood outside the normal legal system, various degrees of judicial, semi-judicial, or administrative recourse were introduced in the western but not the Soviet camps.

semi-judicial prosecution, corralling of potential reparatory labour force, and clearing of the decks for a new start to German public life. In every zone, internment was an extrajudicial measure and was governed by broadly defined security and political considerations. In every zone, it went well beyond targeting Hitler's top henchmen and reached down into the lower echelons of the Nazi hierarchy, while non- and anti-Nazis were also caught up. In every zone, isolation was a key early priority and internees were subjected to rough treatment and inadequate, tough conditions.

Yet the book has also consistently highlighted crucial differences, including some among the western zones. The latter, however, paled in comparison with the differences between the western and the Soviet zones. Soviet arrest categories were more expansive and less precise than their western equivalents. Pre-internment detention conditions and interrogations were much more torturous. Conditions in the camps were and remained completely inadequate and Soviet authorities reacted with appalling indifference to the catastrophically poor health and mass death of their inmates, whereas the western powers took decisive action to reduce and prevent malnutrition. Only the Soviets kept their internees in near total isolation until the end, deported significant numbers as forced labourers, failed to give them any opportunity to argue for their release, and continued to detain even many detainees who were acknowledged to be least dangerous for approximately three years. Only the Soviets made (often exaggerated) use of internment to stamp out youthful criticism and non-conformity and to neutralize non-Nazi opponents and critics of the sociopolitical transformation of their zone. Soviet internment was thus marked by excessive arbitrariness, repression, terror, and lethality that had no equivalent in the western zones but are characteristic of Stalinism. The Soviet camps in occupied Germany are thus best understood as Stalinist internment (and prison) camps, but internment camps nonetheless, comparable with, related to, but also clearly distinguishable from the western powers' internment camps. While they contributed to the Soviet zone's Stalinization, they were above all an attempt to use extrajudicial detention to eradicate Nazism.

Glossary of German Terms

Abwehr	Wehrmacht intelligence and counterintelligence
Bereichsleiter	Area Leader, rank held by NSDAP Deputy District Leaders
Blockleiter	NSDAP Block Leader
Bund Deutscher Mädel	League of German Girls, the NSDAP female youth organization
Gau	Administrative region in Nazi Germany
Gemeinschaftsleiter	Community Leader, rank held by NSDAP Cell Leaders
Kreisleiter	NSDAP District Leader
Lagerspruchkammer(n)	Spruchkammer(n) established at internment camps
Nachlass	Personal papers
Ortsgruppenamtsleiter	Department Leader within NSDAP local groups
Ortsgruppenleiter	NSDAP Local Group Leader
Reichssicherheitshauptamt	Reich Security Main Office
Scharführer	SA and SS rank equivalent to staff sergeant
Schutzstaffel	Protective Squadron, the elite guard of the NSDAP
Sicherheitsdienst	Security Service of the SS
Spruchgericht(e)	Summary court(s) in the British zone that prosecuted members of organizations deemed criminal by the IMT
Spruchkammer(n)	Denazification panel(s) in the American and French zones
SS-Helferinnen	Female auxiliaries in the SS
SS-Kriegshelferinnen	Female auxiliaries in the Waffen-SS

Sturmabteilung	Storm Division, the Nazi stormtroopers
Unterscharführer	SA and SS rank equivalent to sergeant
Waffen-SS	Armed SS
Wehrmacht	Nazi Germany's armed forces
Zellenleiter	NSDAP Cell Leader

Bibliography

Archives Consulted

Archiv des Erzbistums München und Freising, Munich (AEM)
Archiv der Evangelischen Kirche im Rheinland, Düsseldorf (AEKR)
Archives du Comité international de la Croix-Rouge, Geneva (ACICR)
Bayerisches Hauptstaatsarchiv, Munich (BHStA)
Bundesarchiv Berlin (BAB)
Evangelisches Landeskirchliches Archiv in Berlin (ELAB)
Evangelisches Zentralarchiv, Berlin (EZA)
Hauptstaatsarchiv Stuttgart (HStAS)
Hessisches Hauptstaatsarchiv, Wiesbaden (HHStA)
Landeskirchenarchiv Dresden (LKAD)
Landeskirchenarchiv Eisenach (LKAE)
Landeskirchliches Archiv Bielefeld (LKAB)
Landeskirchliches Archiv der Evangelisch-Lutherischen Kirche in Bayern, Nuremberg (LAELKB)
Landeskirchliches Archiv Kiel (LKAK)
Landeskirchliches Archiv Stuttgart (LKAS)
The National Archives of the United Kingdom, London (TNA)
Niedersächsisches Landesarchiv Hanover (NLAH)
Staatsarchiv Hamburg (StAH)
Staatsarchiv Ludwigsburg (StAL)
Zentralarchiv der Evangelischen Kirche in Hessen und Nassau, Darmstadt (ZAEKHN)

Published Documents

Agde, Günter, *Sachsenhausen bei Berlin: Speziallager Nr. 7 1945–1950: Kassiber, Dokumente und Studien* (Berlin: Aufbau Taschenbuch, 1994).
Békés, Csaba, László Borhi, Peter Ruggenthaler, and Ottmar Traşcă (eds.), *Soviet Occupation of Romania, Hungary, and Austria, 1944/45–1948/49* (Budapest: Central European University Press, 2015).
Brommer, Peter (ed.), *Quellen zur Geschichte von Rheinland-Pfalz während der französischen Besatzung, März 1945 bis August 1949* (Mainz: Kommission des Landtages für die Geschichte des Landes Rheinland-Pfalz, 1985).

Bundesgesetzblatt für die Republik Österreich, 1945, available at: www.ris.bka.gv.at/Bgbl-Pdf (accessed 6 Feb. 2019).

Elzer, Herbert (ed.), *Dokumente zur Deutschlandpolitik,* Series I, vol. 5: *Europäische Beratende Kommission 15. Dezember 1943 bis 31. August 1945* (Munich: R. Oldenbourg, 2003).

Foitzik, Jan (ed.), *Sowjetische Kommandanturen und deutsche Verwaltung in der SBZ und frühen DDR: Dokumente* (Berlin: de Gruyter, 2015).

Foitzik, Jan, and Nikita W. Petrow (eds.), *Die sowjetischen Geheimdienste in der SBZ/DDR von 1945 bis 1953* (Berlin: De Gruyter, 2009).

Foreign Relations of the United States: The Conference of Berlin (The Potsdam Conference) 1945, vol. II (Washington, DC: United States Government Printing Office, 1960).

The Conference at Quebec 1944 (Washington, DC: United States Government Printing Office, 1972).

The Conferences at Malta and Yalta 1945 (Washington, DC: United States Government Printing Office, 1955).

Diplomatic Papers 1943, vol. I: *General* (Washington, DC: United States Government Printing Office, 1963).

Diplomatic Papers 1944, vol. I: *General* (Washington, DC: United States Government Printing Office, 1966).

Diplomatic Papers, 1945, vol. III: *European Advisory Commission; Austria; Germany* (Washington, DC: United States Government Printing Office, 1968).

Gelberg, Karl-Ulrich (ed.), *Kriegsende und Neuanfang in Augsburg 1945: Erinnerungen und Berichte* (Munich: R. Oldenbourg, 1996).

Gesetz Nr. 104 zur Befreiung von Nationalsozialismus und Militarismus, 5 Mar. 1946, available at: www.verfassungen.de/bw/wuerttemberg-baden/befreiungsgesetz46.htm (accessed 6 Feb. 2019).

Hessischer Landtag, 1. Wahlperiode, *Stenographische Berichte,* available at: starweb.hessen.de/starweb/LIS/plenarprotokolle.htm (accessed 6 Feb. 2019).

Information Bulletin: Magazine of US Military Government in Germany, 1948–9, available at: digicoll.library.wisc.edu/cgi-bin/History/History-idx?type=browse&scope=History.GerRecon (accessed 6 Feb. 2019).

Jordan, Ulrike (ed.), *Conditions of Surrender: Britons and Germans Witness the End of the War* (London: I. B. Tauris, 1997).

Laufer, Jochen P., and Georgij P. Kynin (eds.), *Die UdSSR und die deutsche Frage 1941–1948: Dokumente aus dem Archiv für Außenpolitik der Russischen Föderation,* vol. 1: *22. Juni 1941 bis 8. Mai 1945* (Berlin: Duncker & Humblot, 2004).

Law for the Liberation from National Socialism and Militarism, 5 Mar. 1946, available at: images.library.wisc.edu/History/EFacs/GerRecon/Denazi/reference/history.denazi.i0013.pdf (accessed 6 Feb. 2019).

Marrus, Michael R., *The Nuremberg War Crimes Trial 1945–46: A Documentary History* (Boston: Bedford Books, 1997).

Military Government Gazette Germany, British Zone of Control, 1947, available at: deposit.d-nb.de/online/vdr/rechtsq.htm (accessed 6 Feb. 2019).

Military Government Gazette Germany, United States Area of Control (Office of Military Government for Germany (U.S.), 1948, available at: deposit.d-nb .de/online/vdr/rechtsq.htm (accessed 6 Feb. 2019).

Milner, L. (ed.), *Political Leaders of the NSDAP* (London: Almark, 1972).

Neumann, Franz, Herbert Marcuse, and Otto Kirchheimer, *Secret Reports on Nazi Germany: The Frankfurt School Contribution to the War Effort*, ed. Raffaele Laudani (Princeton, NJ: Princeton University Press, 2013).

Office of Military Government for Germany (US), *Report of the Military Governor, 1 April 1947–30 April 1948*, no. 34, *Denazification (Cumulative Review)*, available at: digicoll.library.wisc.edu/cgi-bin/History/History-idx?type=div& did=History.Denazi.i0001&isize=M (accessed 6 Feb. 2019).

Office of Military Government, United States, 'Diese Schandtaten: Eure Schuld!' (poster), 1945, available online at: Lebendiges Museum Online, www.hdg.de/lemo/bestand/objekt/plakat-schande-schuld.html. Translation by the website of the UK Imperial War Museum, available at: www.iwm .org.uk/collections/item/object/29110 (both accessed 6 Feb. 2019).

Weekly Information Bulletin, 1945–6, available at: digicoll.library.wisc.edu/cgi-bin/History/History-idx?type=browse&scope=History.GerRecon (accessed 6 Feb. 2019).

Pelly, M. E., and H. H. Yasamee (eds.), *Documents on British Foreign Policy Overseas*, Series I, vol. V: *Germany and Western Europe 11 August–31 December 1945* (London: Her Majesty's Stationery Office, 1990).

Possekel, Ralf (ed.), *Sowjetische Dokumente zur Lagerpolitik* (Berlin: Akademie Verlag, 1998) (vol. 2 of Sergej Mironenko, Lutz Niethammer, and Alexander von Plato (eds.), *Sowjetische Speziallager in Deutschland 1945 bis 1950*).

Ruhm von Oppen, Beate (ed.), *Documents on Germany under Occupation, 1945–1954* (London: Oxford University Press, 1955).

Smith, Bradley F. (ed.), *The American Road to Nuremberg: The Documentary Record 1944–1945* (Stanford, CA: Hoover Institution Press, 1982).

Smith, Jean Edward (ed.), *The Papers of General Lucius D. Clay, Germany 1945–1949*, 2 vols. (Bloomington: Indiana University Press, 1974).

Söllner, Alfons (ed.), *Zur Archäologie der Demokratie in Deutschland*, vol. 1: *Analysen politischer Emigranten im amerikanischen Geheimdienst 1943–1945* (Frankfurt/Main: Europäische Verlagsanstalt, 1982).

Staatsgesetzblatt für die Republik Österreich, available at: www.ris.bka.gv.at/Bgbl-Pdf/ (accessed 6 Feb. 2019).

Supreme Headquarters, Allied Expeditionary Forces (SHAEF), Office of the Chief of Staff, *Handbook for Military Government in Germany Prior to Defeat or Surrender*, December 1944, available at: cgsc.cdmhost.com/cdm/ ref/collection/p4013coll9/id/11 (accessed 6 Feb. 2019).

Trial of the Major War Criminals before the International Military Tribunal, Nuremberg, 14 November 1945–1 October 1946, vol. I: *Official Documents* (Nuremberg: International Military Tribunal Nuremberg, 1947).

Verordnungsblatt für die Britische Zone, 1947, available at: deposit.d-nb.de/online/ vdr/rechtsq.htm (accessed 6 Feb. 2019).

Vollnhals, Clemens (ed.), *Entnazifizierung: Politische Säuberung und Rehabilitierung in den vier Besatzungszonen 1945–1949* (Munich: Deutscher Taschenbuch Verlag, 1991).

(ed.), *Entnazifizierung und Selbstreinigung im Urteil der evangelischen Kirche: Dokumente und Reflexionen 1945–1949* (Munich: Chr. Kaiser, 1989).

Weber, Wolfgang (ed.), *Nationalsozialismus – Demokratischer Wiederaufbau: Lage- und Stimmungsberichte aus den Voralberger Gemeinden des Bezirks Feldkirch im Jahre 1945* (Regensburg: Roderer Verlag, 2001).

Secondary Sources

Ableitinger, Alfred, Siegfried Beer, and Eduard G. Staudinger (eds.), *Österreich unter alliierter Besatzung 1945–1955* (Vienna: Böhlau, 1998).

Adams, Bianka J., *From Crusade to Hazard: The Denazification of Bremen Germany* (Lanham, MD: Scarecrow Press, 2009).

Agamben, Giorgio, 'The Camp as the *Nomos* of the Modern', in Hent de Vries and Samuel Weber (eds.), *Violence, Identity, and Self-Determination* (Stanford, CA: Stanford University Press, 1997), 106–18.

Ahrberg, Edda, and Torsten Haarseim, 'Das Ende des Zweiten Weltkrieges in Gardelegen', in Edda Ahrberg, Daniel Bohse, Torsten Haarseim, and Jürgen Richter, *Ausgeliefert: Haft und Verfolgung im Kreis Gardelegen zwischen 1945 und 1961* (Halle: Mitteldeutscher Verlag, 2014), 37–101.

Ahrens, Ralf, 'Von der "Säuberung" zum Generalpardon: Die Entnazifizierung der westdeutschen Wirtschaft', in *Jahrbuch für Wirtschaftsgeschichte 2010/2: Europäische Wirtschaftseliten nach dem Zweiten Weltkrieg*, ed. Marcel Boldorf (Berlin: Akademie Verlag, 2010), 25–45.

Alliierte Kriegsverbrechen und Verbrechen gegen die Menschlichkeit: Zusammengestellt und bezeugt im Jahre 1946 von Internierten des Lagers 91 Darmstadt (Kiel: Arndt, 2001 [1st ed. 1953]).

Anhalt, Utz, and Steffen Holz, *Das verbotene Dorf: Das Verhörzentrum der britischen Besatzungsmacht in Bad Nenndorf 1945 bis 1947* (Hanover: Offizin, 2011).

Antons, Jan-Hinnerk, 'Displaced Persons in Postwar Germany: Parallel Societies in a Hostile Environment', *Journal of Contemporary History* 49, no. 1 (2014), 92–114.

Applebaum, Anne, *Iron Curtain: The Crushing of Eastern Europe, 1944–1956* (New York: Doubleday, 2012).

Arendt, Hannah, 'Concentration Camps', *Partisan Review* 15, no. 7 (1948), 743–63.

Bajohr, Frank, 'The "Folk Community" and the Persecution of the Jews: German Society under National Socialist Dictatorship, 1933–1945', *Holocaust and Genocide Studies* 20, no. 2 (2006), 183–206.

Bärwald, Helmut, 'Terror als System', in Günther Scholz (ed.), *Verfolgt – verhaftet – verurteilt: Demokraten im Widerstand gegen die rote Diktatur – Fakten und Beispiele* (Berlin: Westkreuz-Verlag, 1990), 13–34.

Bateman, Aaron, 'The KGB and Its Enduring Legacy', *The Journal of Slavic Military Studies* 29, no. 1 (2016), 23–47.

Beattie, Andrew H., 'Die alliierte Internierung im besetzen Deutschland und die deutsche Gesellschaft: Vergleich der amerikanischen und der sowjetischen Zone', *Zeitschrift für Geschichtswissenschaft* 62, no. 3 (2014), 239–56.

'Ein neuer Historikerstreit? Kommunismus und Nationalsozialismus in der deutschen Erinnerungs- und Geschichtspolitik seit 1990', in Wolfgang Benz (ed.), *Ein Kampf um die Deutungshoheit: Politik, Opferinteressen und historische Forschung – Die Auseinandersetzungen um die Gedenk- und Begegnungsstätte Leistikowstraße Potsdam* (Berlin: Metropol-Verlag, 2013), 16–36.

'"Lobby for the Nazi Elite"? The Protestant Churches and Civilian Internment in the British Zone of Occupied Germany, 1945–1948', *German History* 35, no. 1 (2017), 43–70.

Playing Politics with History: The Bundestag Inquiries into East Germany (New York: Berghahn Books, 2008).

'"Sowjetische KZs auf deutschem Boden": Die sowjetischen Speziallager und der bundesdeutsche Antikommunismus', *Jahrbuch für historische Kommunismusforschung* (2011), 119–37.

'Verdiente Strafe des harten Kerns oder ungerechte Besatzungsmaßnahme? Die SS und die alliierte Internierung im besetzten Deutschland', in Jan Erik Schulte and Michael Wildt (eds.), *Die SS nach 1945: Entschuldungsnarrative, populäre Mythen, europäische Erinnerungsdiskurse* (Göttingen: Vandenhoeck & Ruprecht, 2018), 57–74.

Becker, Annette, 'Captive Civilians', in Jay Winter (ed.), *The Cambridge History of the First World War*, vol. 3: *Civil Society* (Cambridge: Cambridge University Press, 2014), 257–81.

Beer, Siegfried, 'Die britische Entnazifizierung in Österreich 1945–1948', in Walter Schuster and Wolfgang Weber (eds.), *Entnazifizierung im regionalen Vergleich*, 399–430.

Beimrohr, Wilfried, 'Entnazifizierung in Tirol', in Walter Schuster and Wolfgang Weber, *Entnazifizierung im regionalen Vergleich*, 97–116.

Benser, Günter, 'Konzeptionen und Praxis der Abrechnung mit dem deutschen Faschismus', *Zeitschrift für Geschichtswissenschaft* 32, no. 10 (1984), 951–67.

Benz, Wolfgang, *Zwischen Hitler und Adenauer: Studien zur deutschen Nachkriegsgesellschaft* (Frankfurt/Main: Fischer Taschenbuch Verlag, 1991).

Benz, Wolfgang (ed.), *Wie wurde man Parteigenosse? Die NSDAP und ihre Mitglieder* (Frankfurt/Main: Fischer, 2009).

Bernstein, Seth, 'Burying the Alliance: Interment, Repatriation and the Politics of the Sacred in Occupied Germany', *Journal of Contemporary History* 52, no. 3 (2017), 710–30.

Beschloss, Michael, *The Conquerors: Roosevelt, Truman and the Destruction of Hitler's Germany, 1941–1945* (New York: Simon & Schuster, 2002).

Bessel, Richard, *Germany 1945: From War to Peace* (London: Simon & Schuster, 2009).

Beßmann, Alyn, '"Der sozusagen für Euch alle im KZ sitzt": Britische Internierungspraxis im ehemaligen KZ Neuengamme und deutsche Deutungsmuster', in KZ-Gedenkstätte Neuengamme (ed.), *Beiträge zur Geschichte der nationalsozialistischen Verfolgung in Norddeutschland*, vol. 12: *Zwischenräume:*

Displaced Persons, Internierte und Flüchtlinge in ehemaligen Konzentrationslagern (Bremen: Edition Temmen, 2010), 35–54.

Biddiscombe, Perry, *The Denazification of Germany: A History 1945–1950* (Stroud: Tempus, 2007).

'The End of the Freebooter Tradition: The Forgotten *Freikorps* Movement of 1944/45', *Central European History* 32, no. 1 (1999), 53–90.

The Last Nazis: Werewolf Guerrilla Resistance in Europe 1944–1947 (Stroud: Tempus, 2006).

'Operation Selection Board: The Growth and Suppression of the Neo-Nazi "Deutsche Revolution" 1945–47', *Intelligence and National Security* 11, no. 1 (1996), 59–77.

Bienert, Michael C., *Zwischen Opposition und Blockpolitik: Die 'bürgerlichen' Parteien und die SED in den Landtagen von Brandenburg und Thüringen (1946–1952)* (Düsseldorf: Droste Verlag, 2016).

Biess, Frank, *Homecomings: Returning POWs and the Legacies of Defeat in Postwar Germany* (Princeton, NJ: Princeton University Press, 2006).

Birke, Adolf M., 'Geschichtsauffassung und Deutschlandbild im Foreign Office Research Department', in Bernd Jürgen Wendt (ed.), *Das britische Deutschlandbild im Wandel des 19. und 20. Jahrhundert* (Bochum: Studienverlag Brockmeyer, 1984), 171–97.

Bischof, Günter, 'Allied Plans and Policies for the Occupation of Austria, 1938–1955', in Rolf Steininger, Günter Bischof, and Michael Gehler (eds.), *Austria in the Twentieth Century* (New Brunswick, NJ: Transaction, 2002), 162–89.

Bispinck, Henrik, and Katharina Hochmuth (eds.), *Flüchtlingslager im Nachkriegsdeutschland: Migration, Politik, Erinnerung* (Berlin: Ch. Links, 2014).

Bloxham, Donald, 'British War Crimes Trial Policy in Germany, 1945–1957: Implementation and Collapse', *The Journal of British Studies* 42, no. 1 (2003), 91–118.

Blum, Bettina, '"My Home, Your Castle": British Requisitioning of German Homes in Westphalia', in Camilo Erlichman and Christopher Knowles (eds.), *Transforming Occupation*, 115–32.

Boghardt, Thomas, 'Dirty Work? The Use of Nazi Informants by U.S. Army Intelligence in Postwar Europe', *The Journal of Military History* 79, no. 2 (2015), 387–422.

Böhler, Jochen, and Robert Gerwarth (eds.), *The Waffen-SS: A European History* (Oxford: Oxford University Press, 2017).

Boldorf, Marcel, 'Brüche oder Kontinuitäten? Von der Entnazifizierung zur Stalinisierung in der SBZ/DDR (1945–1952)', *Historische Zeitschrift* 289 (2009), 287–323.

Boll, Friedhelm, *Sprechen als Last und Befreiung: Holocaust-Überlebende und politisch Verfolgte zweier Diktaturen* (Bonn: Dietz, 2003).

Borgstedt, Angela, 'Die kompromittierte Gesellschaft: Entnazifizierung und Integration', in Peter Reichel, Harald Schmid, and Peter Steinbach (eds.), *Der Nationalsozialismus – Die zweite Geschichte: Überwindung, Deutung, Erinnerung* (Munich: C. H. Beck, 2009), 85–104.

Entnazifizierung in Karlsruhe 1946 bis 1951: Politische Säuberung im Spannungsfeld von Besatzungspolitik und lokalpolitischem Neuanfang (Konstanz: UVK Verlagsgesellschaft, 2001).

Born, Lester K., 'The Ministerial Collecting Center Near Kassel, Germany', *The American Archivist* 50, no. 3 (1950), 237–58.

Bower, Tom, *Blind Eye to Murder: Britain, America, and the Purging of Nazi Germany – A Pledge Betrayed* (London: André Deutsch, 1981).

Braun, Günter, and Gunter Ehnert, 'Das Speziallager Buchenwald in einem zeitgenössischen Bericht: Ein seltenes Dokument und ein außergewöhnlicher Fall aus der Internierungspraxis des NKWD', *Deutschland Archiv* 28, no. 2 (1995), 163–78.

Browder, George C., *Foundations of the Nazi Police State: The Formation of Sipo and SD* (Lexington: University Press of Kentucky, 2004).

Brown, Ralph W. III, 'A Cold War Army of Occupation? The Role of USFA in Quadripartite Occupied Vienna 1945–1948', in Alfred Ableitinger et al. (eds.), *Österreich unter alliierter Besatzung*, 349–60.

Bruce, Gary, *Resistance with the People: Repression and Resistance in Eastern Germany, 1945–1955* (Lanham, MD: Rowman & Littlefield, 2003).

Buchstab, Günter (ed.), *Verfolgt und entrechtet: Die Ausschaltung Christlicher Demokraten unter sowjetischer Besatzung und SED-Herrschaft 1945–1961: Eine biographische Dokumentation* (Düsseldorf: Droste, 1998).

Buscher, Frank M., *The U.S. War Crimes Trial Program in Germany, 1946–1955* (New York: Greenwood Press, 1989).

Buschfort, Wolfgang, 'Gefoltert und geschlagen', in Günther Scholz (ed.), *Verfolgt – verhaftet – verurteilt: Demokraten im Widerstand gegen die rote Diktatur – Fakten und Beispiele* (Berlin: Westkreuz-Verlag, 1990), 59–66.

Carruthers, Susan L., *The Good Occupation: American Soldiers and the Hazards of Peace* (Cambridge, MA: Harvard University Press, 2016).

Casey, Steven, *Cautious Crusade: Franklin D. Roosevelt, American Public Opinion, and the War against Nazi Germany* (New York: Oxford University Press, 2001).

Christgau, John, *Enemies: World War II Alien Internment* (Lincoln: University of Nebraska Press, 2009 [1st ed. 1985]).

Cohen, David, 'Transitional Justice in Divided Germany after 1945', in John Elster (ed.), *Retribution and Reparation in the Transition to Democracy* (Cambridge: Cambridge University Press, 2006), 59–88.

Cohen, Gerhard Daniel, *In War's Wake: Europe's Displaced Persons in the Postwar Order* (Oxford: Oxford University Press, 2012).

'Concentration Camp', in *Collins Free Online Dictionary*, available at: www.collinsdictionary.com/dictionary/english/concentration-camp (accessed 6 Feb. 2019).

'Concentration Camp, n.', in *Oxford English Dictionary Online* (Oxford University Press, June 2018), available at: www.oed.com/view/Entry/403843?redirectedFrom=concentration+camp (accessed 6 Feb. 2019).

Conze, Eckart, Norbert Frei, Peter Hayes, and Moshe Zimmermann, *Das Amt und die Vergangenheit: Deutsche Diplomaten im Dritten Reich und in der Bundesrepublik* (Munich: Pantheon, 2012 [1st ed. 2010]).

Cornelius, Kai, *Vom spurlosen Verschwindenlassen zur Benachrichtigungspflicht bei Festnahmen* (Berlin: Berliner Wissenschafts-Verlag, 2006).

Dallas, Gregor, *1945: The War That Never Ended* (New Haven, CT: Yale University Press, 2005).

Dams, Carsten, and Michael Stolle, *The Gestapo: Power and Terror in the Third Reich*, trans. Charlotte Ryland (Oxford: Oxford University Press, 2014).

Dohle, Oskar, and Peter Eigelsberger, *Camp Marcus W. Orr: 'Glasenbach' als Internierungslager nach 1945* (Linz and Salzburg: Oberösterreichisches Landesarchiv and Salzburger Landesarchiv, 2011).

Dolan, Kristen J., 'Isolating Nazism: Civilian Internment in American Occupied Germany, 1944–1950' (unpublished PhD thesis, University of North Carolina, Chapel Hill, 2013).

Dotterweich, Volker, '"Arrest" und "Removal": Die amerikanische Besatzungsdirektive JCS 1067 und die Entnazifizierungskonzeption der Westmächte', in Walther L. Bernecker and Volker Dotterweich (eds.), *Deutschland in den internationalen Beziehungen des 19. und 20. Jahrhunderts: Festschrift für Josef Becker zum 65. Geburtstag* (Munich: Vögel, 1996), 287–316.

'Die "Entnazifizierung"', in Josef Becker, Theo Stammen, and Peter Waldmann (eds.), *Vorgeschichte der Bundesrepublik Deutschland* (Munich: Fink, 1979), 123–61.

Douglas, R. M., *Orderly and Humane: The Expulsions of the Germans after the Second World War* (New Haven, CT: Yale University Press, 2012).

Dove, Richard (ed.), *'Totally Un-English'? Britain's Internment of 'Enemy Aliens' in Two World Wars* (Amsterdam: Rodopi, 2005).

Echternkamp, Jörg, *Die Bundesrepublik Deutschland 1945/1949–1969* (Paderborn: Ferdinand Schöningh, 2013).

Eckert, Astrid M., *The Struggle for the Files: The Western Allies and the Return of German Archives after the Second World War* (Cambridge: Cambridge University Press, 2012).

Eckert, Rainer, 'Entnazifizierung', in Rainer Eppelmann, Horst Möller, Günter Nooke, and Dorothee Wilms (eds.), *Lexikon des DDR-Sozialismus: Das Staats- und Gesellschaftssystem der Deutschen Demokratischen Republik* (Paderborn: Ferdinand Schöningh, 1997), 247–51.

Edele, Mark, *Stalin's Defectors: How Red Army Soldiers Became Hitler's Collaborators, 1941–1945* (Oxford: Oxford University Press, 2017).

Egel, Karl-Georg, 'Besuch bei internierten Nationalsozialisten', *Nordwestdeutsche Hefte* 2, no. 2 (1947), 38–9.

Ehresmann, Andreas, 'Die frühe Nachkriegsnutzung des Kriegsgefangenen- und KZ-Auffanglagers Sandbostel unter besonderer Betrachtung des britischen No. 2 Civil Internment Camp Sandbostel', in KZ-Gedenkstätte Neuengamme (ed.), *Beiträge zur Geschichte der nationalsozialistischen Verfolgung in Norddeutschland*, vol. 12: *Zwischenräume: Displaced Persons, Internierte und Flüchtlinge in ehemaligen Konzentrationslagern* (Bremen: Edition Temmen, 2010), 22–34.

Eisterer, Klaus, *Französische Besatzungspolitik: Tirol und Voralberg 1945/46* (Innsbruck: Haymon Verlag, 1991).

Erdelmann, Jessica, *'Persilscheine' aus der Druckerpresse? Die Hamburger Medien-berichterstattung über die Entnazifizierung und Internierung in der britischen Besatzungszone* (Munich: Dölling und Galitz Verlag, 2016).

Erler, Peter, 'Bettina Greiner, Verdrängter Terror: Geschichte und Wahrneh-mung sowjetischer Speziallager in Deutschland', *Sehepunkte* 10, nos. 7–8 (2010), available at: www.sehepunkte.de/2010/07/18023.html (accessed 6 Feb. 2019).

GPU-Keller: Arrestlokale und Untersuchungsgefängnisse sowjetischer Geheimdienste in Berlin 1945–1949: Eine Dokumentation (Berlin: Bund der Stalinistisch Verfolgten, 2005).

'Krankheit und Sterben in sowjetischer Lagerhaft: Die Toten von Berlin-Hohenschönhausen 1945–1949', in Stiftung Gedenkstätte Berlin-Hohenschön-hausen (ed.), *Totenbuch: Sowjetisches Speziallager Nr. 3 und Haftarbeitslager Berlin-Hohenschönhausen 1945–1949* (Berlin: Jaron Verlag, 2014), 83–117.

Erler, Peter, 'Das Speziallager Nr 3. Hohenschönhausen Mai 1945–Oktober 1946', in Alexander von Plato (ed.), *Studien und Berichte*, 318–30.

Erlichman, Camilo, and Christopher Knowles (eds.), *Transforming Occupation in the Western Zones of Germany: Politics, Everyday Life, and Social Interactions, 1945–55* (London: Bloomsbury, 2018).

Fait, Barbara, 'Die Kreisleiter der NSDAP – nach 1945', in Martin Broszat, Klaus-Dietmar Henke, and Hans Woller (eds.), *Von Stalingrad zur Währungsunion: Zur Sozialgeschichte des Umbruchs in Deutschland* (Munich: R. Oldenbourg, 1988), 213–99.

Fäßler, Peter, 'Lahr unter französischer Besatzung 1945–1952', in Gabriele Bohnert and Dieter Geuenich (eds.), *Geschichte der Stadt Lahr*, vol. 3: *Im 20. Jahrhundert* (Lahr: Kaufmann, 1993), 180–206.

Fässler, Peter, Reinhard Grohnert, Joachim Haug, Heiko Haumann, and Edgar Wolfrum, 'Hauptstadt ohne Brot: Freiburg im Land Baden (1945–1952)', in Heiko Haumann and Hans Schadek (eds.), *Geschichte der Stadt Freiburg im Breisgau*, vol. 3: *Von der badischen Herrschaft bis zur Gegenwart* (Stuttgart: Theiss Verlag, 2001), 371–427.

Feinstein, Margarete Myers, 'All under One Roof: Persecutees, DPs, Expellees and the Housing Shortage in Occupied Germany', *Holocaust and Genocide Studies* 32, no. 1 (2018), 29–48.

Finn, Gerhard, 'Die Speziallager der sowjetischen Besatzungsmacht 1945 bis 1950', in Deutscher Bundestag (ed.), *Materialien der Enquete-Kommission 'Aufarbeitung von Geschichte und Folgen der SED-Diktatur in Deutschland'*, vol. IV (Frankfurt/Main: Suhrkamp, 1995), 337–98.

Fippel, Günter, *Antifaschisten in 'antifaschistischer' Gewalt: Mittel- und ostdeutsche Schicksale in den Auseinandersetzungen zwischen Demokratie und Diktatur (1945 bis 1961)* (Guben: Verlag Andreas Peter, 2003).

Demokratische Gegner und Willküropfer von Besatzungsmacht und SED in Sachsenhausen (1946 bis 1950): Das sowjetische Speziallager Sachsenhausen – Teil des Stalinschen Lagerimperiums (Leipzig: Leipziger Universitätsverlag, 2008).

Fischer, Ursula, *Von der Last des Schweigens* (Berlin: Dietz Verlag, 1997).

FitzGibbon, Constantine, *Denazification* (London: Michael Joseph, 1969).

Foitzik, Jan, *Sowjetische Militäradministration in Deutschland (SMAD) 1945–1949* (Berlin: Akademie Verlag, 1999).

Foitzik, Jan, and Nikita W. Petrow, 'Der Apparat des NKWD-MGB der UdSSR in Deutschland: Politische Repression und Herausbildung deutscher Staatssicherheitsorgane in der SBZ/DDR 1945–1953', in Jan Foitzik and Nikita W. Petrow (eds.), *Die sowjetischen Geheimdienste in der SBZ/DDR von 1945 bis 1953* (Berlin: De Gruyter, 2009), 13–65.

Fredericksen, Oliver J., *The American Military Occupation of Germany 1945–1953* (Darmstadt: Historical Division, US Army Europe, 1953).

Frei, Norbert, 'Nach der Tat: Die Ahnung deutscher Kriegs- und NS-Verbrechen in Europa–eine Bilanz', in Norbert Frei (ed.), *Transnationale Vergangenheitspolitik*, 7–36.

    (ed.), *Transnationale Vergangenheitspolitik: Der Umgang mit deutschen Kriegsverbrechern in Europa nach dem Zweiten Weltkrieg* (Göttingen: Wallstein, 2006).

Vergangenheitspolitik: Die Anfänge der Bundesrepublik und die NS-Vergangenheit (Munich: Deutscher Taschenbuch Verlag, 1999 [1st ed. 1996]).

'Von deutscher Erfindungskraft, Oder: Die Kollektivschuldthese in der Nachkriegszeit', in Norbert Frei, *1945 und wir: Das Dritte Reich im Bewußtsein der Deutschen* (Munich: C. H. Beck, 2005), 145–55.

Fricke, Karl Wilhelm, '"Konzentrationslager, Internierungslager, Speziallager": Zur öffentlichen Wahrnehmung der NKWD/MWD-Lager in Deutschland', in Petra Haustein et al. (eds.), *Instrumentalisierung, Verdrängung, Aufarbeitung*, 44–62.

Politik und Justiz in der DDR: Zur Geschichte der politischen Verfolgung 1945–1968: Bericht und Dokumentation (Cologne: Verlag Wissenschaft und Politik, 1979).

Friedmann, Wolfgang, *The Allied Military Government of Germany* (London: Stevens & Sons, 1947).

Frings, Josef Kardinal, *Für die Menschen bestellt: Erinnerungen des Alterzbischofs von Köln Josef Kardinal Frings* (Cologne: J. P. Bachem, 1973).

Fröhlich, Gregor, *Soldat ohne Befehl: Ernst von Salomon und der Soldatische Nationalismus* (Paderborn: Ferdinand Schöningh, 2018).

Fry, Helen, *Denazification: Britain's Enemy Aliens, Nazi War Criminals and the Reconstruction of Post-war Europe* (Stroud: History Press, 2010).

Fülberth, Georg, *Geschichte der Bundesrepublik Deutschland* (Cologne: PapyRossa, 2015).

Fulbrook, Mary, *Reckonings: Legacies of Nazi Persecution and the Quest for Justice* (Oxford: Oxford University Press, 2018).

Fürstenau, Justus, *Entnazifizierung: Ein Kapitel deutscher Nachkriegsgeschichte* (Neuwied: Luchterhand, 1969).

Gassert, Philipp, *Kurt Georg Kiesinger 1904–1988: Kanzler zwischen den Zeiten* (Munich: Deutsche Verlags-Anstalt, 2006).

Gebhardt, Miriam, *Als die Soldaten kamen: Die Vergewaltigung deutscher Frauen am Ende des Zweiten Weltkriegs* (Munich: Deutsche Verlags-Anstalt, 2015).

Gedenkstätte Berlin-Hohenschönhausen (ed.), *Speziallager – Internierungslager: Internierungspolitik im besetzten Nachkriegsdeutschland* (Berlin: Gedenkstätte Berlin-Hohenschönhausen, 1996).

Geyer, Michael, and Sheila Fitzpatrick (eds.), *Beyond Totalitarianism: Stalinism and Nazism Compared* (Cambridge: Cambridge University Press, 2009).

Gierth, Grit, and Bettina Westfeld, 'Zur Tätigkeit sowjetischer Militärtribunale in Sachsen', in Andreas Hilger et al. (eds.), *Sowjetische Militärtribunale*, vol. 2, 539–70.

Gieseke, Jens, *Die Stasi 1945–1990* (Munich: Pantheon, 2011).

Gimbel, John, *A German Community under American Occupation: Marburg, 1945–52* (Stanford, CA: Stanford University Press, 1961).

Ginsburgs, George, *Moscow's Road to Nuremberg: The Soviet Background to the Trial* (The Hague: Nijhoff, 1996).

Glees, Anthony, 'War Crimes: The Security and Intelligence Dimension', *Intelligence and National Security* 7, no. 3 (1992), 242–67.

Goeschel, Christian, 'Suicide at the End of the Third Reich', *Journal of Contemporary History* 41, no. 1 (2006), 153–73.

Graham-Dixon, Francis, *The Allied Occupation of Germany: The Refugee Crisis, Denazification, and the Path to Reconstruction* (London: I. B. Tauris, 2013).

Graml, Hermann, 'Strukturen und Motive alliierter Besatzungspolitik in Deutschland', in Wolfgang Benz (ed.), *Deutschland unter alliierter Besatzung 1945–1949/55: Ein Handbuch* (Berlin: Akademie Verlag, 1999), 21–32.

Greiner, Bettina, *Suppressed Terror: History and Perception of Soviet Special Camps in Germany* (Lanham, MD: Lexington Books, 2014).

  Verdrängter Terror: Geschichte und Wahrnehmung sowjetischer Speziallager in Deutschland (Hamburg: Hamburger Edition, 2010).

Greiner, Bettina, and Alan Kramer (eds.), *Welt der Lager: Zur 'Erfolgsgeschichte' einer Institution* (Hamburg: Hamburger Edition, 2013).

Grevers, Helen, and Lawrence Van Haecke, 'The Use of Administrative Internment after WWII: The Different Policies of the Belgian and Dutch Governments', in Margo de Koster, Hervé Leuwer, Dirk Luyten, and Xavier Rousseaux (eds.), *Justice in Wartime and Revolutions: Europe, 1795–1950* (Brussels: Algemeen Rijksarchief, 2012), 277–94.

Griffith, William E., 'Denazification in the United States Zone of Germany', *Annals of the American Academy of Political and Social Science*, 267 (Jan. 1950), 68–76.

Grohnert, Reinhard, *Die Entnazifizierung in Baden 1945–1949: Konzeptionen und Praxis der 'Epuration' am Beispiel eines Landes der französischen Besatzungszone* (Stuttgart: W. Kohlhammer, 1991).

Grossmann, Atina, 'Grams, Calories, and Food: Languages of Victimization, Entitlement, and Human Rights in Occupied Germany, 1945–1949', *Central European History* 44, no. 1 (2011), 118–48.

Grotjahn, Karl-Heinz, 'Gegen "Folterparagraph und Teufelsgesetz": Die IdEG, Interessengemeinschaft der Entnazifizierungsgeschädigten e.V. Hannover' *Hannoversche Geschichtsblätter* 57–58 (New Series) (2003/4), 151–203.

Guhl, Anton F., 'Entlassung, Entnazifizierung, Rehabilitierung? Die Philosophische Fakultät der Hamburger Universität zwischen Bruch und Kontinuität nach 1945', in Myriam Richter and Mirko Nottscheid (eds.), *100 Jahre Germanistik in Hamburg: Traditionen und Perspektiven* (Berlin: Dietrich Reimer Verlag, 2011), 261–80.

Haar, Ingo, 'Zur Sozialstruktur und Mitgliederentwicklung der NSDAP', in Wolfgang Benz (ed.), *Wie wurde man Parteigenosse?*, 60–73.

Hammermann, Gabriele, 'Das Internierungslager Dachau 1945–1948', *Dachauer Hefte* 19 (2003), 48–70.

'Verhaftungen und Haftanstalten der sowjetischen Geheimdienstorgane am Beispiel Thüringens', in Alexander von Plato (ed.), *Studien und Berichte*, 158–71.

Hammond, Paul Y., 'Directives for the Occupation of Germany: The Washington Controversy', in Harold Stein (ed.), *American Civil-Military Decisions: A Book of Case Studies* (Birmingham: University of Alabama Press, 1963), 311–464.

Hanisch, Ernst, 'Braune Flecken im Goldenen Westen: Die Entnazifizierung in Salzburg', in Sebastian Meissl et al. (eds.), *Verdrängte Schuld*, 321–36.

Hänke-Portscheller, Michaela, 'Senne und Mühlberg – Sperrige Erinnerungsorte als didaktische Herausforderung: NS-Kriegsgefangenenlager in der doppelten deutschen Geschichtskultur', in Christoph Kleßmann and Peter Lautzas (eds.), *Teilung und Integration: Die doppelte deutsche Nachkriegsgeschichte als wissenschaftliches und didaktisches Problem* (Bonn: Bundeszentrale für politische Bildung, 2005), 152–76.

Haritonow, Alexandr, 'Zur Geschichte des Speziallagers Nr. 4 (3) in Bautzen', in Alexander von Plato (ed.), *Studien und Berichte*, 331–52.

Hattig, Susanne, Silke Klewin, Cornelia Liebold, and Jörg Morré, *Geschichte des Speziallagers Bautzen, 1945–1956: Katalog zur Ausstellung der Gedenkstätte Bautzen*, ed. Stiftung Sächsische Gedenkstätten (Dresden: Michael Sandstein, 2004).

Hausmann, Alfred, 'Lager Göggingen, 1942–1954' (unpublished paper, 2010), available at: slidex.tips/download/lager-ggggingen (accessed 6 Feb. 2019).

Häusser, Alexander, and Gordian Maugg, *Hungerwinter: Deutschlands humanitäre Katastrophe 1946/47* (Berlin: List Verlag, 2011).

Haustein, Petra, *Geschichte im Dissens: Die Auseinandersetzungen um die Gedenkstätte Sachsenhausen nach dem Ende der DDR* (Leipzig: Leipziger Universitätsverlag, 2006).

Haustein, Petra, Annette Kaminsky, Volkhard Knigge, and Bodo Ritscher (eds.), *Instrumentalisierung, Verdrängung, Aufarbeitung: Die sowjetischen Speziallager in der gesellschaftlichen Wahrnehmung, 1945 bis heute* (Göttingen: Wallstein, 2006).

Heinl, Falko, '"Das schlimme Lager, in dem man gut leben konnte": Das Internierungslager in Darmstadt von 1946 bis 1949' (unpublished MA thesis, Technische Universität Darmstadt, 2005).

Heitzer, Enrico, 'Speziallagerforschung und Gedenkstättenarbeit seit 1990', in Detlef Brunner and Elke Scherstjanoi (eds.), *Moskaus Spuren in Ostdeutschland 1945 bis 1949: Aktenerschließung und Forschungspläne* (Berlin: De Gruyter Oldenbourg, 2015), 109–19.

Henke, Klaus-Dietmar, *Politische Säuberung unter französischer Besatzung: Die Entnazifizierung in Württemberg-Hohenzollern* (Stuttgart: Deutsche Verlags-Anstalt, 1981).

'Die Trennung vom Nationalsozialismus: Selbstzerstörung, politische Säuberung, "Entnazifizierung", Strafverfolgung', in Klaus-Dietmar Henke and Hans Woller (eds.), *Politische Säuberung in Europa: Die Abrechnung mit*

Faschismus und Kollaboration nach dem Zweiten Weltkrieg (Munich: Deutscher Taschenbuch Verlag, 1991), 20–83.

Herbert, Ulrich, *Geschichte Deutschlands im 20. Jahrhundert* (Munich: C. H. Beck, 2014).

Hesse, Hans, *Konstruktionen der Unschuld: Die Entnazifizierung am Beispiel von Bremen und Bremerhaven 1945–1953* (Bremen: Selbstverlag des Staatsarchivs Bremen, 2005).

Hilger, Andreas, and Nikita Petrov, '"Erledigung der Schmutzarbeit"? Die sowjetischen Justiz- und Sicherheitsapparate in Deutschland', in Andreas Hilger et al. (eds.), *Sowjetische Militärtribunale*, vol. 2, 59–152.

Hilger, Andreas, and Mike Schmeitzner, 'Einleitung: Deutschlandpolitik und Strafjustiz: Zur Tätigkeit sowjetischer Militärtribunale in Deutschland 1945–1955', in Andreas Hilger et al. (eds.), *Sowjetische Militärtribunale*, vol. 2, 7–33.

Hilger, Andreas, Mike Schmeitzner, and Ute Schmidt (eds.), *Sowjetische Militärtribunale*, vol. 2: *Die Verurteilung deutscher Zivilisten 1945–1955* (Cologne: Böhlau, 2003).

Hirsch, Francine, 'The Soviets at Nuremberg: International Law, Propaganda, and the Making of the Postwar Order', *The American Historical Review* 113, no. 3 (2008), 701–30.

Hoffmann, Stefan-Ludwig, 'Besiegte, Besatzer, Beobachter: Das Kriegsende im Tagebuch', in Daniel Fulda, Dagmar Herzog, Stefan-Ludwig Hoffmann, and Till van Rahden (eds.), *Demokratie im Schatten der Gewalt: Geschichten des Privaten im deutschen Nachkrieg* (Göttingen: Wallstein, 2010), 25–55.

'Germany Is No More: Defeat, Occupation, and the Postwar Order', in Helmut Walser Smith (ed.), *The Oxford Handbook of Modern German History* (Oxford: Oxford University Press, 2011), 593–694.

Hofmann, Rosmarie, and Bodo Ritscher, 'Auswahlbiografie zur Geschichte der sowjetischen Speziallager in der SBZ/DDR', in Petra Haustein et al. (eds.), *Instrumentalisierung, Verdrängung, Aufarbeitung*, 271–97.

Holborn, Hajo, *American Military Government: Its Organization and Policies* (Buffalo, NY: William S. Hein, 1975 [1st ed. 1947]).

Holian, Anna, 'The Ambivalent Exception: American Occupation Policy in Postwar Germany and the Formation of Jewish Refugee Spaces', *Journal of Refugee Studies* 25, no. 3 (2012), 452–73.

Between National Socialism and Soviet Communism: Displaced Persons in Postwar Germany (Ann Arbor: University of Michigan Press, 2011).

Horn, Christa, *Die Internierungs- und Arbeitslager in Bayern 1945–1952* (Frankfurt/Main: Peter Lang, 1992).

Hoser, Paul, 'Die Entnazifizierung in Bayern', in Walter Schuster and Wolfgang Weber (eds.), *Entnazifizierung im regionalen Vergleich*, 473–510.

'Entnazifizierung in der Stadt Dachau', in Norbert Göttler (ed.), *Nach der 'Stunde Null': Stadt und Landkreis Dachau 1945 bis 1949* (Munich: Herbert Utz Verlag, 2008), 194–242.

Howell, Esther-Julia, *Von den Besiegten lernen? Die kriegsgeschichtliche Kooperation der U.S. Armee und der ehemaligen Wehrmachtselite 1945–1961* (Berlin: De Gruyter, 2016).

Huber, Florian, *Kind, versprich mir, dass du dich erschießt: Der Untergang der kleinen Leute 1945* (Berlin: Berlin Verlag, 2015).

Hüser, Karl, *'Unschuldig' in britischer Lagerhaft? Das Internierungslager No. 5 Staumühle 1945–1948* (Cologne: SH-Verlag, 1999).

'Internment Camp, n.', in *Oxford Englisch Dictionary Online* (Oxford University Press, June 2018), available at: www.oed.com/view/Entry/98094?redirected From=internment+camp (accessed 6 Feb. 2019).

Jarausch, Konrad H., *After Hitler: Recivilizing Germans, 1945–1995* (New York: Oxford University Press, 2006).

Broken Lives: How Ordinary Germans Experienced the Twentieth Century (Princeton, NJ: Princeton University Press, 2018).

Jeske, Natalja, 'Kritische Bemerkungen zu den sowjetischen Speziallagerstatistiken', in Alexander von Plato (ed.), *Studien und Berichte*, 457–80.

'Versorgung, Krankheit, Tod in den Speziallagern', in Alexander von Plato (ed.), *Studien und Berichte*, 189–223.

Jeske, Natalja, and Jörg Morré, 'Die Inhaftierung von Tribunalverurteilten in der SBZ', in Andreas Hilger et al. (eds.), *Sowjetische Militärtribunale*, vol. 2, 609–61.

Jones, Heather, 'Prisoners of War', in Jay Winter (ed.), *The Cambridge History of the First World War*, vol. 2: *The State* (Cambridge: Cambridge University Press, 2014), 266–90.

Jones, Jill, 'Eradicating Nazism from the British Zone of Germany: Early Policy and Practice', *German History* 8, no. 2 (1990), 145–62.

Judt, Tony, *Postwar: A History of Europe since 1945* (London: Pimlico, 2005).

Jürgensen, Kurt, 'Towards Occupation: First Encounters in North Germany', in Ulrike Jordan (ed.), *Conditions of Surrender*, 53–66.

Kansteiner, Wulf, 'Losing the War, Winning the Memory Battle: The Legacy of Nazism, World War II, and the Holocaust in the Federal Republic of Germany', in Richard Ned Lebow, Wulf Kansteiner, and Claudio Fogu (eds.), *The Politics of Memory in Postwar Europe* (Durham, NC: Duke University Press, 2006), 102–46.

Karner, Stefan, *Im Archipel GUPVI: Kriegsgefangenschaft und Internierung in der Sowjetunion 1941–1956* (Vienna: R. Oldenbourg, 1995).

'Zur Politik der sowjetischen Besatzungs- und Gewahrsamsmacht: Das Fallbeispiel Margarethe Ottilinger', in Alfred Ableitinger et al. (eds.), *Österreich unter alliierter Besatzung*, 401–30.

Kastner, Florentine, 'Britische Besatzungslager in Österreich nach dem Zweiten Weltkrieg', *Acta Universitatis Carolinae Studia Territorialia*, nos. 3–4 (2011), 59–80.

'373 Camp Wolfsberg: Britische Besatzungslager in Österreich von 1945 bis 1948' (unpublished MPhil thesis, Universität Wien, 2011).

Kater, Michael, *Hitler Youth* (Cambridge, MA: Harvard University Press, 2004).

Kehoe, Thomas, 'Control, Disempowerment, Fear, and Fantasy: Violent Criminality during the Early American Occupation of Germany, March–July 1945', *Australian Journal of Politics and History* 62, no. 4 (2016), 561–75.

Kellenbach, Katharina von, *The Mark of Cain: Guilt and Denial in the Post-war Lives of Nazi Perpetrators* (Oxford: Oxford University Press, 2013).

Keller, Sven, *Volksgemeinschaft am Ende: Gesellschaft und Gewalt 1944/45* (Munich: Oldenbourg Verlag, 2013).

Kenney, Padraic, *Dance in Chains: Political Imprisonment in the Modern World* (New York: Oxford University Press, 2017).

Kersebom, Heinz, and Lutz Niethammer, '"Kompromat" 1949: Eine statistische Annäherung an Internierte, SMT-Verurteilte, antisowjetische Kämpfer und die Sowjetischen Militärtribunale', in Alexander von Plato (ed.), *Studien und Berichte*, 510–32.

Kershaw, Ian, *The End: Hitler's Germany, 1944–1950* (London: Allen Lane, 2011).

Khlevniuk, Oleg Vitalevich, *The History of the Gulag: From Collectivization to the Great Terror* (New Haven, CT: Yale University Press, 2004).

Kilian, Achim, 'Das Speziallager Nr. 1 Mühlberg 1945–1948', in Alexander von Plato (ed.), *Studien und Berichte*, 279–90.

Kirsten, Holm, *Das sowjetische Speziallager Nr. 4 Landsberg/Warthe* (Göttingen: Wallstein, 2005).

Kitchen, Martin, *A History of Modern Germany 1800–2000* (Oxford: Blackwell, 2005).

Kleßmann, Christoph, *Die doppelte Staatsgründung: Deutsche Geschichte 1945–1955* (Göttingen: Vandenhoeck & Ruprecht, 1982).

Klose, Albrecht, 'Das Internierungs- und Arbeitslager Regensburg 1945–1948', *Verhandlungen des Historischen Vereins für Oberpfalz und Regensburg* 144 (2004), 7–84.

Knight, Robert, 'Denazification and Integration in the Austrian Province of Carinthia', *The Journal of Modern History* 79, no. 3 (2007), 572–612.

Koch, Manfred, 'Karlsruhe – Landeshauptstadt oder Aschenbrödel?', in Karl Moersch and Reinhold Weber (eds.), *Die Zeit nach dem Krieg: Städte im Wiederaufbau* (Stuttgart: W. Kohlhammer, 2008), 180–203.

Kochavi, Arieh J., *Prelude to Nuremberg: Allied War Crimes Policy and the Question of Punishment* (Chapel Hill: University of North Carolina Press, 1998).

Königseder, Angelika, 'Das Ende der NSDAP: Die Entnazifizierung', in Wolfgang Benz (ed.), *Wie wurde man Parteigenosse?*, 151–66.

Kotek, Joël, and Pierre Rigoulot, *Das Jahrhundert der Lager: Gefangenschaft, Zwangsarbeit, Vernichtung* (Berlin: Propyläen, 2000).

Kowalczuk, Ilko-Sascha, and Stefan Wolle, *Roter Stern über Deutschland: Sowjetische Truppen in der DDR* (Berlin: Ch. Links, 2010).

Kowalski, Hans-Günter, 'Die "European Advisory Commission" als Instrument alliierter Deutschlandplanung 1943–1945', *Vierteljahreshefte für Zeitgeschichte* 19 (1971), 261–93.

Knabe, Hubertus, 'Einführung', in Stiftung Gedenkstätte Berlin-Hohenschönhausen (ed.), *Totenbuch: Sowjetisches Speziallager Nr. 3 und Haftarbeitslager Berlin-Hohenschönhausen 1945–1949* (Berlin: Jaron Verlag, 2014), 7–13.

'Die sowjetischen Lager in Deutschland – Deutungen und Fehldeutungen: Vortrag zur Veranstaltung der Konrad-Adenauer-Stiftung "Zukunft braucht Erinnerung – System und Wirklichkeit der Speziallager in der SBZ/DDR 1945–1950"' (August 2006), available at: www.kas.de/upload/dokumente/2006/potsdam0806_Knabe.pdf (accessed 6 Feb. 2019).

Tag der Befreiung? Das Kriegsende in Ostdeutschland (Berlin: Propyläen, 2005).

Knigge-Tesche, Renate, Peter Reif-Spirek, and Bodo Ritscher (eds.), *Internierungspraxis in Ost- und Westdeutschland nach 1945* (Erfurt: Gedenkstätte Buchenwald, 1993).

'Vorwort der Herausgeber', in Renate Knigge-Tesche et al. (eds.), *Internierungspraxis in Ost- und Westdeutschland*, 7–8.

Knowles, Christopher, *Winning the Peace: The British in Occupied Germany, 1945–1948* (London: Bloomsbury, 2017).

Kosteneckij, Andrej, 'Deutsche Kriegsgefangene in der Sowjetunion: Heimatkontakte und Rückkehr', in Klaus-Dieter Müller, Konstantin Nikischkin, and Günther Wagenlehner (eds.), *Die Tragödie der Gefangenschaft in Deutschland und der Sowjetunion 1941–1956* (Cologne: Böhlau, 1998), 53–65.

Kuretsidis-Haider, Claudia, 'Volksgerichtsbarkeit und Entnazifizierung in Österreich', in Walter Schuster and Wolfgang Weber (eds.), *Entnazifizierung im regionalen Vergleich*, 563–601.

Kwiatkowski, Tina, *Nach Buchenwald: Die Beeinflussung Jugendlicher durch ihre Internierung im Speziallager Nr. 2 Buchenwald* (Munich: Rainer Hampp Verlag, 2002).

KZ-Gedenkstätte Flossenbürg, *Was bleibt: Nachwirkungen des Konzentrationslagers Flossenbürg: Katalog zur Dauerausstellung* (Flossenbürg: KZ-Gedenkstätte Flossenbürg, 2011).

Lange, Irmgard, *Entnazifizierung in Nordrhein-Westfalen: Richtlinien, Anweisungen, Organisation* (Siegburg: Republica Verlag, 1976).

Latotzky, Alexander, *Kindheit hinter Stacheldraht: Mütter mit Kindern in sowjetischen Speziallagern und DDR-Haft* (Leipzig: Forum Verlag, 2004).

Leo, Annette, 'Konzentrationslager Sachsenhausen und Speziallager Nr. 7', in Günter Heydemann and Heinrich Oberreuter (eds.), *Diktaturen in Deutschland – Vergleichsaspekte: Strukturen, Institutionen und Verhaltensweisen* (Bonn: Bundeszentrale für politische Bildung, 2003), 249–82.

Lewis, Mark, *The Birth of the New Justice: The Internationalization of Crime and Punishment, 1919–1950* (Oxford: Oxford University Press, 2014).

Lindner, Jörn, 'Das ehemalige KZ Neuengamme als Internierungslager 1945–1948', in Geerd Dahms (ed.), *Die Stunde Null: Nachkriegsjahre in Bergedorf und Umgebung* (Hamburg: Kultur- & Geschichtskontor, 2005), 68–89.

Lipinsky, Jan, 'Mobilität zwischen den Lagern', in Alexander von Plato (ed.), *Studien und Berichte*, 224–40.

'Sowjetische Speziallager', in Rainer Eppelmann, Horst Möller, Günter Nooke, and Dorothee Wilms (eds.), *Lexikon des DDR-Sozialismus: Das Staats- und Gesellschaftssystem der Deutschen Demokratischen Republik* (Paderborn: Ferdinand Schöningh, 1997), 708–11.

'Sowjetische Speziallager in Deutschland 1945–1950: Ein Beispiel für alliierte Internierungspraxis oder sowjetisches GULag-System', in Brigitte Kaff (ed.), *'Gefährliche politische Gegner': Widerstand und Verfolgung in der sowjetischen Zone/DDR* (Düsseldorf: Droste, 1995), 27–43.

Lobeck, Lenore, 'Zum Beispiel Schwarzenberg: Verhaftungen im Landkries Schwarzenberg im Zeitraum 1945–1950', *Zeitschrift des Forschungsverbundes SED-Staat* 34 (2013), 35–51.

Long, Bronson, *No Easy Occupation: French Control of the German Saar, 1944–1957* (Rochester: Camden House, 2015).

Lowe, Keith, *Savage Continent: Europe in the Aftermath of World War II* (London: Viking, 2012).

Lyth, Peter J., 'Traitor or Patriot? Andrey Vlasov and the Russian Liberation Movement 1942–45', *Journal of Strategic Studies* 12, no. 2 (1989), 230–8.

MacKenzie, S. P., 'The Treatment of Prisoners of War in World War II', *Journal of Modern History* 66, no. 3 (1994), 487–520.

Mais, Edgar, 'Internierungslager Algenrodt', *Heimatkalender Landkreis Birkenfeld* 30 (1985), 179–85.

Maislinger, Andreas, '"Zurück zur Normalität": Zur Entnazifizierung in Tirol', in Sebastian Meissl et al. (eds.), *Verdrängte Schuld*, 337–48.

Marcuse, Harold, 'The Afterlife of the Camps', in Jane Caplan and Nikolaus Wachsmann (eds.), *Concentration Camps in Nazi Germany: The New Histories* (New York: Routledge, 2010), 186–211.

McCreedy, Kenneth O., 'Planning the Peace: Operation Eclipse and the Occupation of Germany', *The Journal of Military History* 65, no. 3 (2001), 713–39.

McKale, Donald M., *Nazis after Hitler: How Perpetrators of the Holocaust Cheated Justice and Truth* (Lanham, MD: Rowman & Littlefield, 2012).

Meinicke, Wolfgang, 'Die Entnazifizierung in der sowjetischen Besatzungszone 1945 bis 1948', *Zeitschrift für Geschichtswissenschaft* 32, no. 10 (1984), 968–79.

Meissl, Sebastian, Klaus-Dieter Mulley, and Oliver Rathkolb (eds.), *Verdrängte Schuld, verfehlte Sühne: Entnazifizierung in Österreich 1945–1955* (Munich: R. Oldenbourg Verlag, 1986).

Merten, Ulrich, *The Gulag in East Germany: Soviet Special Camps, 1945–1950* (Amherst: Teneo Press, 2018).

Messenger, David A., 'Beyond War Crimes: Denazification, "Obnoxious" Germans and US Policy in Franco's Spain after the Second World War', *Contemporary European History* 20, no. 4 (2011), 455–78.

Meyer, Dennis, 'Entnazifizierung', in Torben Fischer and Matthias N. Lorenz (eds.), *Lexikon der 'Vergangenheitsbewältigung' in Deutschland: Debatten- und Diskursgeschichte des Nationalsozialismus nach 1945* (Bielefeld: transcript, 2007), 18–19.

Meyer, Kathrin, *Entnazifizierung von Frauen: Die Internierungslager der US-Zone Deutschlands 1945–1952* (Berlin: Metropol, 2004).

'Die Internierung von NS-Funktionären in der US-Zone Deutschlands', *Dachauer Hefte* 19 (2003), 24–47.

Meyer-Seitz, Christian, *Die Verfolgung von NS-Straftaten in der sowjetischen Besatzungszone* (Berlin: Berlin Verlag, 1998).

Miller, Michael D., and Andreas Schulz, *Gauleiter: The Regional Leaders of the Nazi Party and their Deputies, 1925–1945* (San Jose, CA: R. James Bender, 2012).

Mironenko, Sergej, Lutz Niethammer, and Alexander von Plato (eds.), in collaboration with Volkhard Knigge and Günter Morsch, *Sowjetische Speziallager in Deutschland 1945 bis 1950*, 2 vols. (Berlin: Akademie Verlag, 1998): vol. 1: Alexander von Plato (ed.), *Studien und Berichte*; vol. 2: Ralf Possekel (ed.), *Sowjetische Dokumente zur Lagerpolitik*.

Mironenko, Sergej, Lutz Niethammer, Alexander von Plato, Volkhard Knigge, and Günter Morsch, 'Vorwort der Herausgeber', in Alexander von Plato (ed.), *Studien und Berichte*, 11–18.

Möhler, Rainer, *Entnazifizierung in Rheinland-Pfalz und im Saarland unter französischer Besatzung von 1945 bis 1952* (Mainz: v. Hase & Koehler, 1992).

'Die Internierungslager in der französischen Besatzungszone', in Gedenkstätte Berlin-Hohenschönhausen (ed.), *Speziallager – Internierungslager*, 50–60.

'Internierung im Rahmen der Entnazifizierungspolitik in der französischen Besatzungszone', in Renate Knigge-Tesche et al. (eds.), *Internierungspraxis in Ost- und Westdeutschland*, 58–68.

'Lager Theley', in Rainer Hudemann et al. (eds.), *Stätten grenzüberschreitender Erinnerung – Spuren der Vernetzung des Saar-Lor-Lux-Raumes im 19. und 20. Jahrhundert* (Saarbrücken: Uni Saarland, 2002), available at: www.memotransfront.uni-saarland.de/theley.shtml (accessed 6 Feb. 2019).

Moisel, Claudia, 'Résistance und Repressalien: Die Kriegsverbrecherprozesse in der französischen Zone und in Frankreich', in Norbert Frei (ed.), *Transnationale Vergangenheitspolitik*, 247–82.

Möllenhoff, Erich, *Arzt hinter Stacheldraht: Bericht eines in Westdeutschland internierten deutschen Arztes* (Lindhorst: Askania, 1984).

Moore, Bob, 'Prisoners of War', in John Ferris and Evan Mawdsley (eds.), *The Cambridge History of the Second World War*, vol. 1: *Fighting the War* (Cambridge: Cambridge University Press, 2015), 664–89.

Morré, Jörg, 'Speziallager als Mittel sowjetischer Repression', *Horch und Guck: Zeitschrift der Gedenkstätte Museum in der 'Runden Ecke' Leipzig* 24, no. 1 (2015), 64–8.

Totenbuch Speziallager Bautzen 1945–1956 (Bautzen: Stiftung Sächsische Gedenkstätten, 2004).

Morsch, Günter, and Ines Reich (eds.), *Sowjetisches Speziallager Nr. 7/Nr. 1 in Sachsenhausen (1945–1950): Katalog der Ausstellung in der Gedenkstätte und Museum Sachsenhausen* (Berlin: Metropol, 2005).

Morsey, Rudolf, *Die Bundesrepublik Deutschland: Entstehung und Entwicklung bis 1969* (Munich: R. Oldenbourg, 1987).

Mosely, Philip E., 'Dismemberment of Germany: The Allied Negotiations from Yalta to Potsdam', *Foreign Affairs* 28, no. 3 (1950), 487–98.

Mueller, Wolfgang, *Die sowjetische Besatzung in Österreich 1945–1955 und ihre politische Mission* (Vienna: Böhlau, 2005).

Mühe, Kathrin, 'Frauen in den sowjetischen Speziallagern', *Deutschland Archiv* 37, no. 4 (2004), 629–39.

Mühlenberg, Jutta, *Das SS-Helferinnenkorps: Ausbildung, Einsatz und Entnazifizierung der weiblichen Angehörigen der Waffen-SS* (Hamburg: Hamburger Edition, 2011).

Müller, Klaus-Dieter, 'Sowjetische Speziallager in Deutschland und ihre Rolle in der deutsch-sowjetischen Geschichte: Einführende Überlegungen', in Günter Fippel, *Demokratische Gegner und Willküropfer von Besatzungsmacht und SED in Sachsenhausen (1946 bis 1950): Das sowjetische Speziallager Sachsenhausen – Teil des Stalinschen Lagerimperiums* (Leipzig: Leipziger Universitätsverlag, 2008), 9–37.

'Verbrechensahndung und Besatzungspolitik: Zur Rolle und Bedeutung der Todesurteile durch Sowjetische Militärtribunale', in Andreas Weigelt et al. (eds.), *Todesurteile sowjetischer Militärtribunale gegen Deutsche*, 15–62.

Müller, Rolf-Dieter, *Hitler's Wehrmacht, 1935–1945*, trans. Janet W. Ancker (Lexington: University Press of Kentucky, 2016).

Müller, Ulrich, 'Die Internierungslager in und um Ludwigsburg 1945–1949', *Ludwigsburger Geschichtsblätter* 45 (1991), 171–95.

Mulley, Klaus-Dieter, 'Befreiung und Besatzung: Aspekte sowjetischer Besatzung in Niederösterreich 1945–1948', in Alfred Ableitinger et al. (eds.), *Österreich unter alliierter Besatzung*, 361–400.

'Zur Administration der Entnazifizierung in Niederösterreich', in Walter Schuster and Wolfgang Weber (eds.), *Entnazifizierung im regionalen Vergleich*, 267–302.

Murdock, Caitlin E., 'A Gulag in the Erzgebirge? Forced Labor, Political Legitimacy, and Eastern German Uranium Mining in the Early Cold War, 1946–1949', *Central European History* 47, no. 4 (2014), 791–821.

Naimark, Norman M., *The Russians in Germany: A History of the Soviet Zone of Occupation, 1945–1949* (Cambridge, MA: Harvard University Press, 1995).

Neiberg, Michael, *Potsdam: The End of World War II* (New York: Basic Books, 2015).

Neubert, Erhard, 'Politische Verbrechen in der DDR', in Stéphane Courtois, Nicolas Werth, Jean-Louis Panné, Andrzej Paczkowski, Karel Bartosek, and Jean-Louis Margolin, *Das Schwarzbuch des Kommunismus: Unterdrückung, Verbrechen und Terror*, trans. Irmela Arnsperger et al. (Munich: Piper, 1998), 829–84.

Neumann, Klaus, *In the Interest of National Security: Civilian Internment in Australia during World War II* (Canberra: National Archives of Australia, 2006).

Neumann, Vera, 'Häftlingsstruktur im Speziallager Buchenwald: Quellenbestand und Wertung', in Alexander von Plato (ed.), *Studien und Berichte*, 481–96.

Niethammer, Lutz, 'Alliierte Internierungslager in Deutschland nach 1945: Vergleich und offene Fragen', in Christian Jansen, Lutz Niethammer, and Bernd Weisbrod (eds.), *Von der Aufgabe der Freiheit: Politische Verantwortung und bürgerliche Gesellschaft im 19. und 20. Jahrhundert, Festschrift für Hans Mommsen zum 5. November 1995* (Berlin: Oldenbourg Akademieverlag, 1995), 469–92.

'Alliierte Internierungslager in Deutschland nach 1945: Ein Vergleich und offene Fragen', in Alexander von Plato (ed.), *Studien und Berichte*, 97–116.

Die Mitläuferfabrik: Die Entnazifizierung am Beispiel Bayerns (Berlin: J. W. H. Dietz, 1982 [1st ed. 1972]).

'Was wissen wir über die Internierungs- und Arbeitslager in der US-Zone?' in Renate Knigge-Tesche et al. (eds.), *Internierungspraxis in Ost- und Westdeutschland*, 43–57.

Noblemann, Eli E., 'Quadripartite Military Government Organization and Operations in Germany', *The American Journal of International Law* 41, no. 3 (1947), 650–5.

Nolzen, Armin, 'Funktionäre in einer faschistischen Partei: Die Kreisleiter der NSDAP, 1932/33 bis 1944/45', in Till Kössler and Helke Stadtland (eds.),

Vom Funktionieren der Funktionäre: Politische Interessenvertretung und gesellschaftliche Integration in Deutschland nach 1933 (Essen: Klartext, 2004), 37–75.

'The NSDAP, the War, and German Society', in Ralf Blank, Jörg Echternkamp, and Karola Fings et al. (eds.), *Germany and the Second World War*, vol. IX: *German Wartime Society 1939–1945: Politicization, Disintegration, and the Struggle for Survival* (Oxford: Oxford University Press, 2008), 111–206.

Oberreuter, Heinrich, and Jürgen Weber (eds.), *Freundliche Feinde? Die Alliierten und die Demokratiegründung in Deutschland* (Munich: Olzog, 1996).

Ochs, Eva, *'Heute kann ich das ja sagen': Lagererfahrungen von Insassen sowjetischer Speziallager in der SBZ/DDR* (Cologne: Böhlau, 2006).

Oleschinski, Brigitte, and Bert Pampel, *'Feindliche Elemente sind in Gewahrsam zu halten': Die sowjetischen Speziallager Nr. 8 und Nr. 10 in Torgau 1945–1948* (Leipzig: Gustav Kiepenheuer, 2002).

Olick, Jeffrey K., *In the House of the Hangman: The Agonies of German Defeat, 1943–1949* (Chicago: University of Chicago Press, 2005).

Olschewski, Berit, *'Freunde' im Feindesland: Rote Armee und deutsche Nachkriegsgesellschaft im ehemaligen Großherzogtum Mecklenburg-Strelitz 1945–1953* (Berlin: Berliner Wissenschafts-Verlag, 2009).

Orlow, Dietrich, *The Nazi Party, 1919–1945: A Complete History* (New York: Enigma Books, 2008).

Otto, Wilfriede, 'Die Waldheimer Prozesse', in Alexander von Plato (ed.), *Studien und Berichte*, 533–53.

Overmans, Rüdiger, '"Ein untergeordneter Eintrag im Leidensbuch der jüngeren Geschichte"? Die Rheinwiesenlager 1945', in Hans-Erich Volkmann (ed.), *Ende des Dritten Reiches – Ende des Zweiten Weltkrieges: Eine perspektivische Rückschau* (Munich: Piper, 1995), 259–91.

Pädagogisches Zentrum des Landes Rheinland-Pfalz, 'Menschen in Lagern an der Nahe und im Hunsrück', *PZ-Informationen*, no. 8: *Geschichte* (1986).

Padover, Saul K., *Experiment in Germany: The Story of an American Intelligence Officer* (New York: Duell, Sloan and Pearce, 1946).

Panayi, Panikos, *Prisoners of Britain: German Civilian and Combatant Internees during the First World War* (Manchester: Manchester University Press, 2012).

Patt, Avinoam J., and Michael Berkowitz (eds.), *'We Are Here': New Approaches to Jewish Displaced Persons in Postwar Germany* (Detroit, MI: Wayne State University Press, 2010).

Pelt, Robert Jan van, 'Paradise/Hades, Purgatory, Hell/Gehenna: A Political Typology of the Camps', in Jonathan C. Friedman (ed.), *The Routledge History of the Holocaust* (Abingdon: Routledge, 2011), 191–202.

Peterson, Edward N., *The American Occupation of Germany: Retreat to Victory* (Detroit, MI: Wayne State University Press, 1977).

Petrov, Nikita, 'Die Apparate des NKVD/MVD und des MGB in Deutschland (1945–1953): Eine historische Skizze', in Alexander von Plato (ed.), *Studien und Berichte*, 143–57.

Pichler, Roland, 'Volksgerichtsbarkeit und Entnazifizierung unter besonderer Berücksichtigung der Verfahren gegen Frauen vor dem Volksgericht Wien' (unpublished Dr. iur. thesis, University of Vienna, 2016), available at: othes.univie.ac.at/41841/1/2016-03-30_0101619.pdf (accessed 6 Feb. 2019).

Pieper, Volker, and Siedenhans, Michael, with collaboration from Olaf Eimer, *Die Vergessenen von Stukenbrock: Die Geschichte des Lagers in Stukenbrock-Senne von 1941 bis zur Gegenwart* (Bielefeld: Verlag für Regionalgeschichte, 1988).

Pitzer, Andrea, *One Long Night: A Global History of Concentration Camps* (New York: Little, Brown, 2017).

Plato, Alexander von, 'Internierungen in Ost und West nach 1945: Elemente des Vergleichs der Opferhierarchien und Opferkonkurrenzen', in Petra Haustein et al. (eds.), *Instrumentalisierung, Verdrängung, Aufarbeitung*, 100–13.

'Sowjetische Speziallager', in Martin Sabrow (ed.), *Erinnerungsorte der DDR* (Munich: C. H. Beck, 2009), 90–7.

(ed.), *Studien und Berichte* (Berlin: Akademie Verlag, 1998) (vol. 1 of Sergej Mironenko, Lutz Niethammer, and Alexander von Plato (eds.), *Sowjetische Speziallager in Deutschland 1945 bis 1950*).

'Zur Geschichte des sowjetischen Speziallagersystems in Deutschland: Einführung', in Alexander von Plato (ed.), *Studien und Berichte*, 19–75.

Plischke, Elmer, 'Denazification in Germany: A Policy Analysis', in Robert Wolfe (ed.), *Americans as Proconsuls: United States Military Government in Germany and Japan, 1944–52* (Carbondale: Southern Illinois University Press, 1984), 198–225.

'Denazifying the Reich', *The Review of Politics* 9, no. 2 (1947), 153–72.

Pohl, Dieter, *Justiz in Brandenburg 1945–1955: Gleichschaltung und Anpassung* (Munich: Oldenbourg, 2001).

Pomorski, Stanislaw, 'Conspiracy and Criminal Organization', in George Ginsburgs and V. N. Kudriavtsev (eds.), *The Nuremberg Trial and International Law* (Dordrecht: Martinus Nijhoff, 1990), 213–48.

Possekel, Ralf, 'Sowjetische Lagerpolitik in Deutschland', in Ralf Possekel (ed.), *Sowjetische Dokumente zur Lagerpolitik*, 15–110.

'Strukturelle Grausamkeit: Die sowjetische Internierungspolitik in Deutschland als Produkt sowjetischer Herrschaftspraktiken 1945 bis 1950', in Klaus-Dieter Müller, Konstantin Nikischkin, and Günther Wagenlehner (eds.), *Die Tragödie der Gefangenschaft in Deutschland und der Sowjetunion 1941–1956* (Cologne: Böhlau, 1998), 225–53.

Preissinger, Adrian, *From Sachsenhausen to Buchenwald: Death Camps of the Soviets, 1945–1950*, trans. Heather Clary-Smith (Ocean City, MD: Landpost Press, 1994).

Priemel, Kim Christian, *The Betrayal: The Nuremberg Trials and German Divergence* (Oxford: Oxford University Press, 2016).

Priemel, Kim C., and Alexa Stiller (eds.), *Reassessing the Nuremberg Military Tribunals: Transitional Justice, Trial Narratives, and Historiography* (New York: Berghahn Books, 2012).

Prieß, Lutz, 'Deutsche Kriegsgefangene als Häftlinge in den Speziallagern des NKVD in der SBZ', in Alexander von Plato (ed.), *Studien und Berichte*, 250–63.

'Das Speziallager des NKVD Nr. 6 Jamlitz', in Alexander von Plato (ed.), *Studien und Berichte*, 364–74.

Pritchard, Gareth, *Niemandsland: A History of Unoccupied Germany, 1944–1945* (Cambridge: Cambridge University Press, 2012).

Prusin, Alexander V., 'A Community of Violence: The SiPo/SD and Its Role in the Nazi Terror System in Generalbezirk Kiew', *Holocaust and Genocide Studies* 21, no. 1 (2007), 1–30.

Rademacher, Michael, *Die Kreisleiter der NSDAP im Gau Weser-Ems* (Marburg: Tectum Verlag, 2005).

Raim, Edith, *Nazi Crimes against Jews and German Post-war Justice: The West German Judicial System during Allied Occupation, 1945–1949* (Berlin: Walter de Gruyter, 2015).

Rathjen-Couscherung, Ilse, *Eckernförde unter britischer Besatzung: Eine Schleswig-holsteinische Stadt 1945–1955* (Eckernförde: Heimatgemeinschaft Eckernförde, 2008).

Rathkolb, Oliver, 'Historische Fragmente und die "unendliche Geschichte" von den sowjetischen Absichten in Österreich 1945', in Alfred Ableitinger et al. (eds.), *Österreich unter alliierter Besatzung*, 137–58.

Rauh-Kühne, Cornelia, 'Die Entnazifizierung und die deutsche Gesellschaft,' *Archiv für Sozialgeschichte* 35 (1995), 35–70.

'Life Rewarded the Latecomers: Denazification during the Cold War', in Detlef Junker (ed.), *The United States and Germany in the Era of the Cold War, 1945–1990: A Handbook*, vol. 1: *1945–1968* (Cambridge: Cambridge University Press, 2004), 65–72.

Reibel, Carl-Wilhelm, *Das Fundament der Diktatur: Die NSDAP-Ortsgruppen 1932–1945* (Paderborn: Ferdinand Schöningh, 2002).

Reichelt, Olaf, *'Wir müssen doch in die Zukunft sehen …': Die Entnazifizierung in der Stadt Oldenburg unter britischer Besatzungshoheit 1945–1947* (Oldenburg: Isensee Verlag, 1998).

Reitlinger, Gerald, 'Werl, Wittlich, and Landsberg: Postscript to the War Trials', *The Jewish Quarterly* 1, no. 3 (1953), 9–17.

Resmini, Bertram, 'Lager der Besatzungsmächte in Rheinland-Pfalz: Kriegsgefangene, Internierte und Verschleppte im Rheinland nach dem Zweiten Weltkrieg', *Jahrbuch für westdeutsche Landesgeschichte* 19 (1993), 601–21.

Richter, Hedwig, *Die DDR* (Paderborn: Ferdinand Schöningh, 2009).

Riedel, Dirk, *Ordnungshüter und Massenmörder im Dienst der 'Volksgemeinschaft': Der KZ-Kommandant Hans Loritz* (Berlin: Metropol, 2010).

Rieke, Dieter, *Geliebtes Leben: Erlebtes und Ertragenes zwischen den Mahlsteinen jüngster deutscher Geschichte* (Berlin: Berlin Verlag, 1999).

Rigoll, Dominik, 'From Denazification to Renazification? West German Government Officials after 1945', in Camilo Erlichman and Christopher Knowles (eds.), *Transforming Occupation*, 251–70.

'Das Gründungspersonal der Bonner Bundesbehörden: Über Karriere- und Rekrutierungsmuster nach 1945', in Frank Bösch and Martin Sabrow (eds.), *ZeitRäume: Potsdamer Almanach des Zentrums für Zeithistorische Forschung 2016* (Göttingen: Wallstein, 2016), 55–73.

Staatsschutz in Westdeutschland: Von der Entnazifizierung zur Extremistenabwehr (Göttingen: Wallstein, 2013).

Ritscher, Bodo, *Spezlager Nr. 2 Buchenwald* (Weimar: Gedenkstätte Buchenwald, 1995).

'Speziallager Nr. 2 Buchenwald', in Alexander von Plato (ed.), *Studien und Berichte*, 291–317.

'Die wissenschaftliche Aufarbeitung der Geschichte der sowjetischen Speziallager in der SBZ/DDR seit Beginn der 1990er Jahre – Zwischenbilanz und Ausblick', in Petra Haustein et al. (eds.), *Instrumentalisierung, Verdrängung, Aufarbeitung*, 170–92.

Rosmarie Hofmann, Gabriele Hammermann, Wolfgang Röll, and Christian Schölzel (eds.), *Die sowjetischen Speziallager in Deutschland 1945–1950: Eine Bibliographie, Mit einem Anhang: Literatur zum historisch-sozialen Umfeld der Speziallager* (Göttingen: Wallstein, 1996).

Rikola-Gunnar Lüttgenau, Gabriele Hammermann, Wolfang Röll, and Christian Schölzel (eds.), *Das sowjetische Speziallager Nr. 2 1945–1950: Katalog zur ständigen historischen Ausstellung* (Göttingen: Wallstein Verlag, 1999).

Rock, David, and Stefan Wolff (eds.), *Coming Home to Germany? The Integration of Ethnic Germans from Central and Eastern Europe in the Federal Republic* (New York: Berghahn Books, 2002).

Rogers, Daniel E., 'Restoring a German Career, 1945–1950: The Ambiguity of Being Hans Globke', *German Studies Review* 31, no. 2 (2008), 303–24.

Römer, Sebastian, *Mitglieder verbrecherischer Organisationen nach 1945: Die Ahndung des Organisationsverbrechens in der britischen Zone durch die Spruchgerichte* (Frankfurt/Main: Peter Lang, 1995).

Ross, Corey, *The East German Dictatorship: Problems and Perspectives in the Interpretation of the GDR* (London: Bloomsbury, 2002).

Ruggenthaler, Peter, 'Der lange Arm Moskaus: Zur Problematik der Zwangsrepatriierungen ehemaliger sowjetischer Zwangsarbeiter und Kriegsgefangener in die UdSSR', in Siegfried Mattl, Gerhard Bolz, Stefan Karner, and Helmut Konrad (eds.), *Krieg, Erinnerung, Geschichtswissenschaft* (Vienna: Böhlau Verlag, 2009), 229–46.

Rupieper, Hermann-J., 'Amerikanische Besatzungspolitik', in Wolfgang Benz (ed.), *Deutschland unter alliierter Besatzung 1945–1949/55: Ein Handbuch* (Berlin: Akademie Verlag, 1999), 33–47.

Salomon, Ernst von, *Der Fragebogen* (Reinbek bei Hamburg: Rowohlt, 2011 [1st ed. 1951]).

Sälter, Gerhard, 'Heimliche Briefe: Kassiber aus sowjetischen Speziallagern (1945–1950)', in Cornelia Liebold, Jörg Morre, and Gerhard Sälter (eds.), *Kassiber aus Bautzen: Heimliche Briefe von Gefangenen aus dem sowjetischen Speziallager 1945–1950* (Dresden: Stiftung Sächsische Gedenkstätten zur Erinnerung, 2004), 83–104.

Phantome des Kalten Krieges: Die Organisation Gehlen und die Wiederbelebung des Gestapo-Feindbildes 'Rote Kapelle' (Berlin: Ch. Links Verlag, 2016).

Sauer, Paul, *Demokratischer Neubeginn in Not und Elend: Das Land Württemberg-Baden von 1945 bis 1952* (Ulm: Vaas, 1989).

Saunders, Anna, *Memorializing the GDR: Monuments and Memory after 1989* (New York: Berghahn Books, 2018).

Scheliha, Wolfram von, 'Ein Bärendienst an den Stalinismus-Opfern', *Horch und Guck: Zeitschrift der Gedenkstätte Museum in der 'Runden Ecke' Leipzig*, no. 3 (2009), 72–3.

'Speziallager-Opfer in den Fallen der Geschichte', *Deutschland Archiv* 43, no. 6 (2010), 1124–6.

Scherbakova, Irina, 'Sowjetische Staatsangehörige und sonstige Ausländer in den Speziallagern', in Alexander von Plato (ed.), *Studien und Berichte*, 241–9.

Schick, Christa, 'Die Internierungslager', in Martin Broszat, Klaus-Dietmar Henke, and Hans Woller (eds.), *Von Stalingrad zur Währungsunion: Zur Sozialgeschichte des Umbruchs in Deutschland* (Munich: R. Oldenbourg, 1988), 301–25.

Schießl, Sascha, *'Das Tor zur Freiheit': Kriegsfolgen, Erinnerungspolitik und humanitärer Anspruch im Lager Friedland (1945–1970)* (Göttingen: Wallstein, 2016).

Schmaltz, Erik J., 'Foreword: Stalinism Exported Abroad', in Ulrich Merten, *The Gulag in East Germany*, xv–xxii.

Schmeitzner, Mike, 'Genossen vor Gericht: Die sowjetische Strafverfolgung von Mitgliedern der SED und ihrer Vorläuferparteien 1945–1954', in Andreas Hilger et al. (eds.), *Sowjetische Militärtribunale*, vol. 2, 265–344.

'Konsequente Abrechnung? NS-Eliten im Visier sowjetischer Gerichte 1945–1947', in Andreas Weigelt et al. (eds.), *Todesurteile sowjetischer Militärtribunale gegen Deutsche*, 63–102.

Schmidt, Ute, '"Vollständige Isolierung erforderlich ...": SMT-Verurteilungen im Kontext der Gleichschaltung der Blockparteien CDU und LDP 1946–1953', in Andreas Hilger et al. (eds.), *Sowjetische Militärtribunale*, vol. 2, 345–94.

Schmiechen-Ackermann, Detlef, 'Der "Blockwart": Die unteren Parteifunktionäre im nationalsozialistischen Terror- und Überwachungsapparat', *Vierteljahreshefte für Zeitgeschichte* 48, no. 4 (2000), 575–602.

Schneppen, Heinz, 'Das Nürnberger Urteil über die "verbrecherische Organisationen" und seine Folgen', *Zeitschrift für Geschichtswissenschaft* 63, no. 1 (2015), 28–67.

Schoebener, Burkhard, 'Dokumentation einer Kontroverse: Die Bemühungen des Internationalen Roten Kreuzes 1946/47 um den völkerrechtlichen Schutz deutscher Zivilinternierter in der US-Zone', *Die Friedenswarte: Journal of International Peace and Organization* 68 (1990), 140–51.

Schöne, Jens, *Die DDR: Eine Geschichte des 'Arbeiter- und Bauernstaates'* (Berlin: Berlin Story Verlag, 2014).

Schrag, Steven David, 'ASHCAN: Nazis, Generals and Bureaucrats as Guests at the Palace Hotel, Mondorf les Bains, Luxembourg, May–August 1945' (unpublished PhD thesis, University of Toledo, 2015).

Schroeder, Klaus, *Die DDR: Geschichte und Strukturen* (Stuttgart: Reclam, 2011).

Schulte, Jan-Erik, Peter Liebe, and Bernd Wegner (eds.), *Die Waffen-SS: Neue Forschungen* (Paderborn: Ferdinand Schöningh, 2014).

Schuster, Armin, *Die Entnazifizierung in Hessen 1945–1954: Vergangenheitspolitik in der Nachkriegszeit* (Wiesbaden: Historische Kommission für Nassau, 1999).

Schuster, Walter, 'Politische Restauration und Entnazifizierungspolitik in Oberösterreich', in Walter Schuster and Wolfgang Weber (eds.), *Entnazifizierung im regionalen Vergleich*, 157–215.

Schuster, Walter, and Wolfgang Weber (eds.), *Entnazifizierung im regionalen Vergleich* (Linz: Archiv der Stadt Linz, 2004).

Schwarze, Gisela, *Eine Region im demokratischen Aufbau: Der Regierungsbezirk Münster 1945/46* (Düsseldorf: Patmos Verlag, 1984).

Schwelling, Birgit, *Heimkehr – Erinnerung – Integration: Der Verband der Heimkehrer, die ehemaligen Kriegsgefangenen und die westdeutsche Nachkriegsgesellschaft* (Paderborn: Ferdinand Schöningh, 2010).

Schwinge, Erich, 'Rückblick auf die Zeit der amerikanischen Besetzung: Morgenthau-Plan und die Mißachtung des Völkerrechts', in Bernard Willms (ed.), *Handbuch zur deutschen Nation: Geistiger Bestand und politische Lage* (Tübingen: Hohenrain-Verlag, 1986), vol. 1, 305–32.

Seegers, Lu, *'Vati blieb im Krieg': Vaterlosigkeit als generationelle Erfahrung im 20. Jahrhundert – Deutschland und Polen* (Göttingen: Wallstein, 2013).

Seidel, J. Jürgen, *'Neubeginn' in der Kirche? Die evangelischen Landes- und Provinzialkirchen in der SBZ/DDR im gesellschaftspolitischen Kontext der Nachkriegszeit (1945–1953)* (Göttingen: Vandenhoeck & Ruprecht, 1989).

Seidler, Franz W., *Deutsche Opfer: Alliierte Täter 1945* (Selent: Pour le Mérite, 2013).

Seliger, Hubert, *Politische Anwälte: Die Verteidiger der Nürnberger Prozesse* (Baden-Baden: Nomos, 2016).

Service, Hugo, *Germans to Poles: Communism, Nazism and Ethnic Cleansing after the Second World War* (Cambridge: Cambridge University Press, 2013).

Siedenhans, Michael, 'Das Internierungslager "Eselheide" in Stukenbrock-Senne', *Heimat-Jahrbuch Kreis Gütersloh* (1986), 140–4.

Siedenhans, Michael, and Olaf Eimer, 'Das Internierungslager Eselheide und das Sozialwerk Stukenbrock', in Volker Pieper and Michael Siedenhans, *Die Vergessenen von Stukenbrock*, 72–101.

Siemens, Daniel, *Stormtroopers: A New History of Hitler's Brownshirts* (New Haven, CT: Yale University Press, 2017).

Skrentny, Werner, 'Was aus Hamburgs Nazis wurde', in Maike Bruhns et al. (eds.), *'Hier war doch alles nicht so schlimm': Wie die Nazis in Hamburg den Alltag eroberten* (Hamburg: VSA-Verlag, 1984), 138–44.

Slaveski, Filip, *The Soviet Occupation of Germany: Hunger, Mass Violence, and the Struggle for Peace, 1945–1947* (Cambridge: Cambridge University Press, 2013).

Smith, Arthur L., Jr., 'Die deutschen Kriegsgefangenen und Frankreich', *Vierteljahreshefte für Zeitgeschichte* 32, no. 1 (1984), 103–21.

Smith, Bradley F., *The Road to Nuremberg* (London: André Deutsch, 1981).

Stamm, Irmgard, 'Lagerleben in Altschweier', *Bühler Heimatgeschichte* 5 (1991), 92–106.

Stanciu, Anja, *'Alte Kämpfer' der NSDAP: Eine Berliner Funktionselite 1926–1949* (Cologne: Böhlau, 2018).

Stange, Irina, 'Das Bundesministerium des Innern und seine leitenden Beamten', in Frank Bösch and Andreas Wirsching (eds.), *Hüter der Ordnung: Die Innenministerien in Bonn und Ost-Berlin nach dem Nationalsozialismus* (Göttingen: Wallstein, 2018), 55–121.

Stegemann, Wolf, 'Waren NS-Funktionäre keine Nazis? Die Entnazifizierung in Dorten – Fallbeispiele Ortsgruppenleiter', in Wolf Stegemann (ed.), *Dorsten nach der Stunde Null – Die Jahre danach, 1945 bis 1950* (Dorsten: Dorstener Forschungsgruppe, 1986), 138–45.

Steinbach, Peter, *Nationalsozialistische Gewaltverbrechen: Die Diskussion in der deutschen Öffentlichkeit nach 1945* (Berlin: Colloquium Verlag, 1981).

Steinhart, Margarete, *Balingen 1918–1948: Kleinstadt im Wandel* (Balingen: Stadtverwaltung Balingen, 1991).

Steinmaus-Pollak, Angelika, 'Der "Lagerspiegel", Zeitung der Insassen des Internierungs- und Arbeitslagers Regensburg', *Verhandlungen des Historischen Vereins für Oberpfalz und Regensburg* 144 (2004), 85–142.

Stelzl-Marx, Barbara, 'Entnazifizierung in Österreich: Die Rolle der sowjetischen Besatzungsmacht', in Walter Schuster and Wolfgang Weber (eds.), *Entnazifizierung im regionalen Vergleich*, 431–54.

Steuwer, Janosch, and Hanne Leßau, '"Wer ist ein Nazi? Woran erkennt man ihn?" Zur Unterscheidung von Nationalsozialisten und anderen Deutschen', *Mittelweg 36* 23, no. 1 (2014), 30–51.

Stibbe, Matthew, 'Civilian Internment and Civilian Internees in Europe, 1914–1920', in Matthew Stibbe (ed.), *Captivity, Forced Labour and Forced Migration in Europe during the First World War* (London: Routledge, 2009), 49–81.

'Ein globales Phänomen: Zivilinternierung im Ersten Weltkrieg in transnationaler und internationaler Dimension', in Christoph Jahr and Jens Thiel (eds.), *Lager vor Auschwitz: Gewalt und Integration im 20. Jahrhundert* (Berlin: Metropol, 2013), 158–76.

Stiefel, Dieter, *Entnazifizierung in Österreich* (Vienna: Europaverlag, 1981).

'Nazifizierung plus Entnazifizierung = Null? Bemerkungen zur besonderen Problematik der Entnazifizierung in Österrreich', in Sebastian Meissl et al. (eds.), *Verdrängte Schuld*, 28–36.

'Der Prozeß der Entnazifizierung in Österreich', in Klaus-Dietmar Henke and Hans Woller (eds.), *Politische Säuberung in Europa: Die Abrechnung mit Faschismus und Kollaboration nach dem Zweiten Weltkrieg* (Munich: Deutscher Taschenbuch Verlag, 1991), 108–47.

Stone, Dan, *Concentration Camps: A Short History* (Oxford: Oxford University Press, 2017).

Strauß, Christof, *Kriegsgefangenschaft und Internierung: Die Lager in Heilbronn-Böckingen 1945–1947* (Heilbronn: Stadtarchiv Heilbronn, 1998).

'Zwischen Apathie und Selbstrechtfertigung: Die Internierung NS-belasteter Personen in Württemberg-Baden', in Paul Hoser (ed.), *Kriegsende und Neubeginn: Die Besatzungszeit im schwäbisch-alemannischen Raum* (Constance: UVK, 2003), 287–313.

Streim, Gregor, 'Germans in the *Lager*: Reports and Narratives about Imprisonment in Post-war Allied Internment Camps', in Helmut Schmitz (ed.),

A Nation of Victims? Representations of German Wartime Suffering from 1945 to the Present (Amsterdam: Rodopi, 2007), 31–49.

Szanajda, Andrew, *The Allies and the German Problem, 1941–1949: From Cooperation to Alternative Settlement* (Basingstoke: Palgrave, 2015).

Taylor, Frederick, *Exorcising Hitler: The Occupation and Denazification of Germany* (London: Bloomsbury, 2011).

Thacker, Toby, *The End of the Third Reich: Defeat, Denazification and Nuremberg, January 1944–November 1946* (Stroud: Tempus, 2006).

Théofilakis, Fabien, *Les prisonniers de guerre allemands, France, 1944–1949: Une captivité de guerre en temps de paix* (Paris: Fayard, 2014).

Treber, Leonie, *Mythos Trümmerfrauen: Von der Trümmerbeseitigung in der Kriegs- und Nachkriegszeit und der Entstehung eines deutschen Erinnerungsortes* (Essen: Klartext Verlag, 2014).

Turner, Ian D., 'Denazification in the British Zone', in Ian D. Turner (ed.), *Reconstruction in Post-war Germany: British Occupation Policy and the Western Zones* (Oxford: Berg, 1989), 239–67.

Tweraser, Kurt, 'Die amerikanische Säuberungspolitik in Österreich', in Walter Schuster and Wolfgang Weber (eds.), *Entnazifizierung im regionalen Vergleich*, 363–97.

'Von der Militärdiktatur 1945 zur milden Bevormundung des "Bargaining-Systems" der fünfziger Jahre: Verhaltensmuster und Interaktionen von Amerikanern und Österreichern auf der Military-Government-Ebene', in Alfred Ableitinger et al. (eds.), *Österreich unter alliierter Besatzung*, 301–48.

Twomey, Christina, *Australia's Forgotten Prisoners: Civilians Interned by the Japanese in World War II* (Melbourne: Cambridge University Press, 2007).

Ullrich, Christina, '*Ich fühl mich nicht als Mörder!' Die Integration von NS-Tätern in die Nachkriegsgesellschaft* (Darmstadt: Wissenschaftliche Buchgesellschaft, 2011).

Utley, Freda, *The High Cost of Vengeance* (Chicago: Henry Regnery, 1949).

Vance, Jonathan F. (ed.), *Encyclopedia of Prisoners of War and Internment*, 2nd ed. (Millerton, NY: Grey House Publishing, 2006).

Vogel, Karl, *M-AA 509: Elf Monate Kommandant eines Internierungslagers* (Memmingen: Self-published, 1951).

Vogt, Timothy R., *Denazification in Soviet-Occupied Germany: Brandenburg, 1945–1948* (Cambridge, MA: Harvard University Press, 2000).

Vollnhals, Clemens, *Evangelische Kirche und Entnazifizierung 1945–1949: Die Last der nationalsozialistischen Vergangenheit* (Munich: Oldenbourg, 1989).

'Internierung, Entnazifizierung und Strafverfolgung von NS-Verbrechen in der sowjetischen Besatzungszone', in Andreas Hilger, Mike Schmeitzner, and Clemens Vollnhals (eds.), *Sowjetisierung oder Neutralität: Optionen sowjetischer Besatzungspolitik in Deutschland und Österreich 1945–1955* (Göttingen: Vandenhoeck & Ruprecht, 2006), 223–47.

Vorstand der Sozialdemokratischen Partei Deutschlands (ed.), *Der Freiheit verpflichtet: Gedenkbuch der deutschen Sozialdemokratie im 20. Jahrhundert* (Marburg: Schüren, 2000).

Wachsmann, Nikolaus, *KL: A History of the Nazi Concentration Camps* (New York: Farrar, Straus and Giroux, 2015).

'The Nazi Concentration Camps in International Context: Comparisons and Connections', in Jan Rüger and Nikolaus Wachsmann (eds.), *Rewriting German History: New Perspectives on Modern Germany* (London: Palgrave Macmillan, 2015), 306–25.

Wadl, Wilhelm, 'Entnazifizierung in Kärnten', in Walter Schuster and Wolfgang Weber (eds.), *Entnazifizierung im regionalen Vergleich*, 251–66.

Wahl, Alfred, *La seconde histoire du Nazisme dans l'Allemagne fédérale depuis 1945* (Paris: Armand Collin, 2006).

Waibel, Dieter, *Von der wohlwollenden Despotie zur Herrschaft des Rechts: Entwicklungsstufen der amerikanischen Besatzung Deutschlands 1944–1949* (Tübingen: J. C. B. Mohr, 1996).

Wala, Michael, 'The Value of Knowledge: Western Intelligence Agencies and Former Members of the SS, Gestapo and Wehrmacht during the Early Cold War', in Camilo Erlichman and Christopher Knowles (eds.), *Transforming Occupation*, 271–82.

Wallace, Geoffrey P. R., *Life and Death in Captivity: The Abuse of Prisoners during War* (Ithaca, NY: Cornell University Press, 2015).

Wambach, Julia, 'Vichy in Baden-Baden: The Personnel of the French Occupation in Germany after 1945', *Contemporary European History* (published online 20 Dec. 2018), 1–23, doi.org/10.1017/S0960777318000462 (accessed 6 Feb. 2019).

Weale, Adrian, *The SS: A New History* (London: Little Brown, 2010).

Weber, Hermann, *Die DDR 1945–1990*, 3rd revised and expanded ed. (Munich: R. Oldenbourg, 2000).

Geschichte der DDR, updated and expanded ed. (Munich: Deutscher Taschenbuch Verlag, 1999).

Weber, Jürgen, *Germany 1945–1990: A Parallel History*, trans. Nicholas T. Parsons (Budapest: Central European University Press, 2004).

Weckel, Ulrike, *Beschämende Bilder: Deutsche Reaktionen auf alliierte Dokumentarfilme über befreite Konzentrationslager* (Stuttgart: Franz Steiner Verlag, 2012).

Wegehaupt, Phillip, 'Funktionäre und Funktionseliten der NSDAP: Vom Blockleiter zum Gauleiter', in Wolfgang Benz (ed.), *Wie wurde man Parteigenosse?*, 39–59.

Wegner, Bernd, *The Waffen-SS: Organization, Ideology, and Function* (Oxford: Blackwell, 1990).

Wehler, Hans-Ulrich, *Deutsche Gesellschaftsgeschichte*, vol. 4: *Vom Beginn des Ersten Weltkriegs bis zur Gründung der beiden deutschen Staaten 1914–1949* (Munich: C. H. Beck, 2003).

Weigelt, Andreas, 'Sterben und Tod im Speziallager Ketschendorf', in Andreas Weigelt, *Totenbuch: Sowjetisches Speziallager Nr. 5 Ketschendorf 1945–1947*, ed. Initiativgruppe Internierungslager Ketschendorf/Speziallager Nr. 5 e.V. (Berlin: Wichern-Verlag, 2014), 151–241.

Weigelt, Andreas, Klaus-Dieter Müller, Thomas Scharschmidt, and Mike Schmeitzner (eds.), *Todesurteile sowjetischer Militärtribunale gegen Deutsche (1944–1947): Eine historisch-biographische Studie* (Göttingen: Vandenhoeck & Ruprecht, 2015).

Thomas Scharschmidt, and Mike Schmeitzner, 'Vorwort der Herausgeber', in Andreas Weigelt et al. (eds.), *Todesurteile sowjetischer Militärtribunale gegen Deutsche*, 7–10.

Weinreb, Alice, '"For the Hungry Have No Past nor Do They Belong to a Political Party": Debates over German Hunger after World War II', *Central European History* 45, no. 1 (2012), 50–78.

Weitkamp, Sebastian, 'Internierungslager und Spruchgerichtsgefängnis Esterwegen 1945–1951', in Bernd Faulenbach and Andrea Kaltofen (eds.), *Hölle im Moor: Die Emslandslager 1933–1945* (Göttingen: Wallstein, 2017), 249–54.

Welsh, Helga A., *Revolutionärer Wandel auf Befehl? Entnazifizierungs- und Personalpolitik in Thüringen und Sachsen (1945–1948)* (Munich: R. Oldenbourg, 1989).

Wember, Heiner, 'Umerziehung im Lager? Britische Internierungspolitik und -praxis', in Renate Knigge-Tesche et al. (eds.), *Internierungspraxis in Ost- und Westdeutschland*, 30–42.

Umerziehung im Lager: Internierung und Bestrafung von Nationalsozialisten in der britischen Besatzungszone Deutschlands (Essen: Klartext, 1991).

Wienand, Christiane, *Returning Memories: Former Prisoners of War in Divided and Reunited Germany* (Rochester, NY: Camden House, 2015).

Wiggers, Richard D., 'The United States and the Denial of Prisoner of War (POW) Status at the End of the Second World War', *Militärgeschichtliche Zeitschrift* 52, no. 1 (1993), 91–104.

Wildt, Michael, *An Uncompromising Generation: The Nazi Leadership of the Reich Security Main Office*, trans. Tom Lampert (Madison: University of Wisconsin Press, 2010).

(ed.), *Nachrichtendienst, politische Elite und Mordeinheit: Der Sicherheitsdienst des Reichsführers SS* (Hamburg: Hamburger Edition, 2003).

Wilke, Christiane, 'Fall 3: Juristen vor Gericht, Recht auf dem Prüfstand und das Erbe der "Zivilisation"', in Kim C. Priemel and Alexa Stiller (eds.), *NMT: Die Nürnberger Militärtribunale zwischen Geschichte, Gerechtigkeit und Rechtschöpfung* (Hamburg: Hamburger Edition, 2013), 288–319.

Woller, Hans, *Gesellschaft und Politik in der amerikanischen Besatzungszone: Die Region Ansbach und Fürth* (Munich: Oldenbourg, 1986).

Die Loritz-Partei: Geschichte, Struktur und Politik der Wirtschaftlichen Aufbau-Vereinigung (WAV) 1945–1955 (Stuttgart: Deutsche Verlags-Anstalt, 1982).

Yelton, David K., *Hitler's Volkssturm: The Nazi Militia and the Fall of Germany, 1944–1945* (Lawrence: University Press of Kansas, 2002).

Zahra, Tara, '"Prisoners of the Postwar": Expellees, Displaced Persons, and Jews in Austria after World War II', *Austrian History Yearbook* 41 (2010), 191–215.

Zeitler, Peter, 'Lageralltag in amerikanischen Internierungscamps (1945–1948): Dargestellt am Schicksal eines oberfränkischen SA-Führers', *Archiv für Geschichte von Oberfranken* 76 (1996), 371–92.

Zenz, Emil, *Die Stadt Trier im 20. Jahrhundert: 1. Hälfte 1900–1950* (Trier: Spee-Verlag, 1981).

Ziegler, Walter, 'Gaue und Gauleiter im Dritten Reich', in Horst Möller, Andreas Wirsching, and Walter Ziegler (eds.), *Nationalsozialismus in der*

Region: Beiträge zur regionalen und lokalen Forschung und zum internationalen Vergleich (Munich: R. Oldenbourg, 1996), 139–58.

Ziemke, Earl F., *The U.S. Army in the Occupation of Germany 1944–1946* (Washington, DC: Center of Military History United States Army, 1975).

Zimmermann, Ekkehard, *Staub soll er fressen: Die Internierungslager in den Westzonen Deutschlands* (Frankfurt/Main: Haag und Herchen, 2008).

Index